The Response of Orthodox Jewry in the United States to the Holocaust;

The Activities of the
Vaad ha-Hatzala Rescue Committee
1939-1945

The Response of Orthodox Jewry in the United States to the Holocaust;

The Activities of the
Vaad ha-Hatzala Rescue Committee
1939-1945

by
Efraim Zuroff

THE MICHAEL SCHARF PUBLICATION TRUST
of the YESHIVA UNIVERSITY PRESS
NEW YORK

KTAV PUBLISHING HOUSE, INC.
HOBOKEN, NEW JERSEY

Copyright © 2000
Yeshiva University Press

Library of Congress Cataloging-in-Publication Data

Zuroff, Efraim.
   The response of Orthodox Jewry in the United States to the Holocaust : the activities
of the Vaad ha-Hatzala Rescue Committee, 1939-1945 / by Efraim Zuroff.
      p. cm.
   Includes bibliographical references.
   ISBN 0-88125-666-8
   1. Vaad Hatzala (New York, N.Y.) 2. World War, 1939-1945--Jews--Rescue. 3.
Holocaust, Jewish (1939-1945) I. Title.

D804.6 Z87 2000
940.53'18--dc21   99-052401

Distributed by
KTAV Publishing House, Inc.
900 Jefferson Street
Hoboken, NJ 07030

Dedicated to all those who tirelessly attempted to save the Jews of Europe from annihilation at the hands of the Nazis and their collaborators.

Table of Contents

Acknowledgements

This study could never have been completed without the support and assistance provided by numerous individuals over the course of more than two decades. The help they supplied took various forms. Some provided copies of, or granted access to, valuable documentation, others shared memories and insights that clarified important episodes, quite a few gave sage advice and constructive criticism. Various individuals provided different forms of technical assistance, such as translations, which proved to be extremely important.

First and foremost, I owe a tremendous debt of thanks to my mentor in Holocaust studies Professor Yehuda Bauer of the Institute of Contemporary Jewry of the Hebrew University of Jerusalem and Yad Vashem, who served as advisor for this research and never lost hope that it would be completed, despite the fact that for many years my efforts to track down and prosecute Nazi war criminals were accorded a higher priority. It was Professor Bauer who inspired me to immerse myself in the study of the *Shoa* and as a result I have devoted my career to recording its events, commemorating its victims and punishing its perpetrators. As the world's leading expert on rescue efforts during the Holocaust, he provided much sage advice and insight regarding this extremely complex subject.

This research could never have been completed without numerous documents which I was able to obtain from private individuals, many of whom personally participated in the events described. First and foremost, I would like to express special thanks to Rabbi Yoseph David Epstein of Brooklyn, who served as personal secretary to Mir rosh yeshiva Rabbi Eliezer Yehuda Finkel and who made available to me his own personal archives, as well as the archives of Rabbi Mayer Ashkenazi, the rabbi of the Russian Jewish community in Shanghai, and an additional collection of documents regarding the efforts to rescue Polish refugee Torah scholars via the Far East. Rabbi Epstein also granted two lengthy interviews and was always willing to provide whatever assistance he could to help me complete this project.

Another person who made available his personal archives and shared his recollections of his participation in rescue activities was Rabbi Aaron Milewsky of Jerusalem, who served as a rabbi in Montevideo, Uruguay, during World War II and played an active role in relief efforts on behalf of the rabbis and yeshiva students stranded in Shanghai. Others who provided important documentation which helped illuminate significant aspects of the activities of the *Vaad ha-Hatzala* were Dr. David Kranzler who sent me a copy of Frank Newman's personal diary; Rabbi Dr. Aharon Rakeffet who made available documents from the archives of Rabbi Eliezer Silver; Rabbi Marvin Tokayer who provided me with a copy of the Jewcom report on the arrival of Jewish refugees in Japan; and Joseph Hellerstein, who served as secretary of the *Agudat ha-Rabbanim* for four decades, and made available important documents related to the activities of that organization. Special thanks are due the Sternbuch families of Zurich (Elias Sternbuch) and London (Rabbi Avraham Sternbuch) who granted me full access to the archives of HIJEFS (Hilfsverein Juedische Fluchtlinge in Shanghai) which functioned as the Swiss branch of the *Vaad ha-Hatzala*. The documents from this collection are of particular importance in describing the rescue efforts launched by the *Vaad* in the years 1944-1945.

Other persons who provided important information in personal interviews or by responding in writing to my queries are: Rabbi Moshe Cohen, Rabbi Asher Czeczyk, Rabbi Zelig Epstein, Rabbi Zev Gotthold, Rabbi Yizhak Grozalsky, Hermann Hollander, Dr. Gershon Kranzler, Hermann Landau, Rabbi Zvi Milner, Rabbi Yaakov Nayman, Frank Newman, Rabbi Mayer Pantel, Rabbi Shimon Romm, Pinchas Schoen, Elijah Stein, Rabbi Mayer Strassfeld, Rabbi Zalman Ury, Rabbi Simcha Wasserman, Rabbi Alex Weisfogel, and Tova Wiernik.

No scholarly work of this scope can be completed without the help of the dedicated staff of the research institutes, libraries and archives which house the documents and other materials which form the basis of this research. I spent many days, and in some cases weeks, in these institutions and owe them a debt of thanks, first and foremost to the Yeshiva University Archives, which houses the records of the *Vaad ha-Hatzala*. I also reviewed the documents in the archives of: *Agudat ha-Rabbanim*, Agudat Yisrael be-Eretz Yisrael, Agudath Israel of America (Rabbi Moshe Kolodny), American Jewish Historical Society, (Dr. Nathan Kaganoff) American Jewish Joint Distribution Committee (Rose Klepfisz, Denise Bernard Gluck, Eric Nooter) Jewish Agency (New York), Beit Lochamei ha-Gettaot, Bar-Ilan University Holocaust Research Institute (Dr. Judy Baumol), Central Zionist Archives, Franklin D. Roosevelt Library, National Archives (Washington D.C.), Heichal Shlomo, Wiener Library, World Agudat Yisrael, Yad Vashem (Dr. Yaakov Lozowick, Dr. Robert Rozett), and YIVO Institute.

It is practically impossible to complete a project of this scope without considerable financial assistance. During the prolonged research process, I was the beneficiary of three grants from the Memorial Foundation for Jewish Culture, a generous scholarship from the National Foundation for Jewish Culture and the Henry d'Avigdor Goldsmid Memorial Fund Award in Holocaust Studies of the Institute of Contemporary Jewry of the Hebrew University.

I was also the recipient of an Egit Grant for Holocaust and Jewish Resistance Literature sponsored by the Jacob and Clara Egit Foundation of Toronto, Canada via the Histadrut Assistance Fund which helped facilitate the publication of this volume.

I also want to express my gratitude to the publishers of this study, to Professor Jeffrey Gurock and the Michael Scharf Publications Trust of Yeshiva University Press for their expert handling of this project. As an alumnus of YUHSM and Yeshiva University and a member of a family which devoted more than 150 years of service to the premier institution of modern Orthodoxy in the United States, I am especially pleased that this research will be published by Yeshiva University.

Also deserving of special thanks is Bernard Scharfstein of KTAV Publishing House who helped realize this project and whose active support and encouragement over the years have enabled me to reach many people all over the world.

In our office in Jerusalem, Talma Hurvitz my loyal and trusted coworker, has done so much to facilitate my efforts in many different areas related to the Holocaust over most of the past decade. I have also benefited enormously from the advice, support and friendship of colleagues and contemporaries who became good friends such as Dr. Seymour Adler, Rabbi Daniel Landes, Prof. Dov Levin, Aryeh Rubin, Yossi Klein Halevi, Shmulik Laster and Rabbi Dr.

Jeffrey Woolf. David and Rachel Levmore and Tommy and Esther Lamm have been close friends and neighbors for many years.

Achronim, achronim chavivim, last but by no means least, I want to thank my wonderful family, whose patience and encouragement were ultimately rewarded, long after most people would have given up on this project. In that regard, I want to especially thank my father Rabbi Dr. Abraham N. Zuroff who helped me in innumerable ways to write this research and never lost hope that it would actually be completed. His devotion to the task went far beyond his parental obligations. My wife Elisheva's grandfather Shmaryahu ha-Cohen Margalit z"l was another relative who made a special effort to help me write this book.

Besides my parents, the person who bore the brunt of the frustration involved in working for more than two decades on the history of the *Vaad ha-Hatzala* was my wife Elisheva who oftentimes had to compete with the rabbinic rescue agency for my attention and energies, a situation which she handled with understanding and identification. I can only hope that our children - Avigayil, Itamar, Elchanan and Ayelet - will appreciate this book and internalize its important lessons.

Foreword

There are still many gaps in the historiography of the Holocaust. One of them is a detailed study of the reactions of Orthodox Jews, both in and outside of Europe, during the catastrophe. A recent book by Eliezer Schweid investigates the *spiritual* responses of some of the great Orthodox thinkers and teachers. But of the desperate rescue attempts by Orthodox Jews outside of Europe, relatively little has been published. Efraim Zuroff follows in the footsteps of David Kranzler and other pioneers in this field, and for the first time tells the full story of the American-based *Vaad ha-Hatzalah*, during the early war years. The Vaad, originally established to help yeshivot and their leaders who found themselves in war-torn Europe, evolved into a full-fledged rescue organization, representing American Orthodox Jewry in general rescue efforts. Of course, even after it broadened its aims, the emphasis still lay on what it saw as the crux of the matter: to preserve Torah scholarship and the sages who represented it, so as to ensure Torah scholarship for the future, and thereby preserving the Jewish traditions and the Jewish people as they understood them.

The immense growth of Jewish traditional scholarship after the war and up to the present necessarily colors such accounts. It is important to explain how it came about that new centers of Orthodox Torah scholarship developed, mainly but not exclusively in Israel and North America, despite the vast tragedy that descended on the Jewish people. Although the success of the *Vaad* is obvious today, it could not properly be gauged in the 1940s; at that time they quite rightly thought only of the tragedy they were witnessing, although of course they were happy about every person or group rescued.

Efraim Zuroff has utilized hitherto unused sources (along with some known ones, of course). His descriptions make fascinating reading; his analysis is thought-provoking and innovative. A panorama unfolds that is new in Holocaust historiography: Orthodox leaders, many of whom were recent arrivals in the United States, with the help of the North American Orthodox establishment, took upon themselves the mundane tasks of collecting funds and finding ways of transmitting them to groups in Europe. A main focus of the story is the rescue of yeshivot and sages that had managed to escape to Lithuania from Poland at the beginning of hostilities. These yeshivot were the main target of rescue operations. The strained and problematic relationships with non-Orthodox American Jews are discussed, as are contacts with non-Jewish, mainly governmental, individuals and agencies. Orthodoxy in the United States at the time was activist and determined; clearly, much of what they tried to do had to fail, because of circumstances beyond the *Vaad*'s control. Zuroff describes both the successes and the failures. This book unlocks another important facet of Jewish responses during the Holocaust, and I hope its story will be included in future teaching about the subject, to Jews and non-Jews alike.

Professor Yehuda Bauer
Jerusalem

Introduction

Historians and researchers have been trying to record and analyze the events of the Holocaust for more than fifty years. As might be expected, the initial focus of their efforts was primarily on the origins of the Final Solution and its implementation throughout Europe. Scholars, therefore, directed most of their attention to Germany where they sought to study the Nazi movement and analyze the activities of its leaders, members and sympathizers in order to attempt to understand how they were able to seize control of an ostensibly cultured country and convince significant portions of the population to participate in the mass murder of European Jewry.

Almost simultaneously, an effort was being made, primarily by Jewish scholars, to examine the responses of the victims. How did the Jews of Europe react to the rise of Nazism and to what extent did the various European Jewish communities attempt to fight against the Nazi movement from its establishment until after the outbreak of World War II?[1]

These questions have preoccupied historians for decades and the efforts to clarify additional chapters and study new dimensions of the historical record continue to this day. Recent research, for example, has provided new information and insights on such issues as the activities and motives of the perpetrators, the extent of active participation in the crimes of the Holocaust,[2] the role played by local (non-German or Austrian) Nazi collaborators in the implementation of the Final Solution,[3] the history of European Jewry on the eve of the Holocaust, and the fate of Jewish communities under Nazi occupation and in Axis satellite states.[4] Additional research is being done regarding Jewish leadership during the Holocaust, the extent and success of its opposition to the Nazis and the dilemmas which Jewish leaders were forced to confront before and during World War II.[5]

Only a quarter of a century after the end of the war, did researchers begin to relate to the external circle of those connected to the events of the Holocaust. These initial studies dealt, for example, with the response of Allied governments to the persecution of European Jewry and the immigration policies adopted during the thirties by the United States[6] and Great Britain.[7] Additional research dealt with the responses of the neutrals[8] and international organizations and agencies such as the International Red Cross,[9] the Catholic Church[10] and other religious bodies.[11] It was at this point, that the initial studies appeared which chronicled the response of the Jews living in Allied countries to the persecution of European Jewry and the extent to which they attempted (let alone succeeded), to assist their beleaguered European coreligionists.[12]

It was only natural that most of the research in the latter category would relate to American Jewry, which at that time was the largest Jewish community in the Free World. Yet despite its preeminent position in the Jewish world and the large number of books and articles which deal with various aspects of its response to the persecution of European Jewry, to this day a comprehensive study of American Jewry during the Holocaust has never been published. The main reason for this surprising state of affairs relates to the structure of the American Jewish community, which lacked a dominant national leadership and was divided into innumerable organizations and movements during the period of World War II. Thus, for example, studies have been written regarding the activities of important organizations such as the Joint Distribution Committee[13] and the American Jewish Committee,[14] as well as of the attempts to unite the community by establishing various umbrella organzations,[15] but we still lack research on significant community bodies such as the American Jewish Congress, the Jewish Labor Committee, The Emergency Committee to Save the Jewish People of Europe, B'nai B'rith and others, without which it would be impossible to present a comprehensive and exhaustive account of the response of American Jewry to the persecution and murder of European Jewry during the Holocaust.

One of the important groups whose activities have not yet been studied in-depth is American Orthodox Jewry. Although this community constituted a minority among American Jews and its leaders did not occupy important positions in national Jewish organizations, Orthodox Jews were extremely active in the relief and rescue efforts launched from the United States and recorded several notable successes in this regard. Through the *Vaad ha-Hatzala* (Rescue Committee) established by the *Agudat ha-Rabbanim* (Union of Orthodox Rabbis of the United States and Canada), the largest association of American Orthodox rabbis, the community initially succeeded in rescuing numerous rabbis and yeshiva students and later was able to save many additional Jews.

Until relatively late in the war, Orthodox groups focused exclusively on rescuing rabbis and yeshiva students, a policy which frequently led to bitter debates within the American Jewish community. Orthodox rescue activists also argued with their non-Orthodox counterparts about various issues related to the violation of American laws, when it became clear that certain U.S. regulations were detrimental to the efforts being made to rescue European Jews.

It is, therefore, particularly illuminating to study and analyze the positions adopted by the American Orthodox community regarding the extremely difficult dilemmas faced by Jewish rescue activists in the Free World, in order to understand how people who adhered to the *halacha* dealt with these questions. The rabbis who headed the Orthodox community adopted a set of rescue priorities which was different from the one which guided the relief and rescue activities of the general American Jewish organizations. The different world views of those who headed American Jewry's rescue agencies also found expression in the attitude toward the United States government, American regulations, American policy vis-a-vis Germany, the nature of relief activities and the importance attributed to unified communal efforts. The debates within the American Jewish community had a negative impact on the relations between certain elements of American Orthodoxy (primarily the ultra-Orthodox), and the rest of the American Jewry, as well as on their relations with other Diaspora communities.

To this day, there is an acerbic debate between the ultra-Orthodox community and the rest of world Jewry regarding the activities of the *Vaad ha-Hatzala* during the Holocaust. The former have bitter claims against the Jewish Establishment in general, and the Zionist movement in particular, which have found expression in numerous polemical publications.[16] Yet to date, not a single objective historical study of the activities of the *Vaad ha-Hatzala* has ever been published.

The primary objective of this book is therefore to present the first comprehensive history of the *Vaad ha-Hatzala*, and examine the extent to which it succeeded in fulfilling its objectives (a subject bitterly debated between ultra-Orthodox spokesmen who magnify and glorify its achievements and others who are skeptical about the role it played in rescue efforts). It will also analyze the *Vaad*'s rescue philosophy and modus operandi and describe how they differed from those of their counterparts at the Joint Distribution Committee and how these differences affected the relative success achieved by each of these relief agencies. It will also seek to assess the attitude of Orthodox leaders to the attempts to unite American Jewry in order to facilitate rescue efforts, a subject which reflects not only on the policies adopted in the Orthodox community, but also on the response of American Jewry as a whole to the Holocaust and its efforts to assist European Jewry. To what extent were Orthodox leaders willing, for example, to make compromises in order to achieve communal unity on relief and rescue issues? Which points did Orthodox leaders consider negotiable in this debate and on which issues were they unwilling to compromise? The answers to these questions offer important insights into the thinking of leading Orthodox and ultra-Orthodox rabbis and help elucidate the bitter debates in the Jewish world regarding rescue efforts during the Holocaust, which continue to this day and adversely affect the relations between the *haredi* community and their non-haredi coreligionists.

This study is for the most part based on primary sources, many of which have never been used by historians. The most important among them is the archives of the *Vaad ha-Hatzala* which is currently housed at the Yeshiva University Archives in New York City. Needless to say, no study of the rabbinic rescue organization could be written without access to its primary documentation. At the same time, it is important to note that prior to their arrival at their current home, the documents were housed in physically unsuitable circumstances for many years, and some of them were destroyed, and others were partially ruined.

Perhaps even more significant is the fact that the *Vaad ha-Hatzala* was initially established as an ad-hoc committee to deal with a specific emergency. None of its founders had any idea at that time that it would eventually become a full-fledged relief and rescue agency which functioned for more than a decade. And, in fact, the paucity of official documentation regarding its initial years clearly reflects this reality. It was only toward the end of the war, that the *Vaad* began to conduct its administrative (not financial) affairs in a more orderly manner, and therefore numerous documents which one would expect to find in such a collection are simply not there (probably because they never existed). Thus, for example, with a few exceptions, there are no minutes of any meetings conducted before 1945, a fact which I believe stems not from the loss of documents, but from the fact that the *Vaad*'s administrative efforts left a lot to be desired. Yet despite the absence of such documents, this collection is an indispensable source for our study of the *Vaad*'s activities, successes, and failures.

Two very important sources which supplement the documentation missing from the *Vaad*'s records are the archives of the Joint Distribution Committee, which is housed at the organization's New York headquarters, and those of the Council of Jewish Federations and Welfare Funds, which I perused at the American Jewish Historical Society on the campus of Brandeis University. These two organizations were in constant, and often contentious, contact with the leaders of the *Vaad* and its representatives throughout the United States during the entire period of World War II. The documents in these archives provide numerous details regarding the *modus operandi* of the *Vaad*, and especially its fundraising efforts. They also help clarify the *Vaad*'s successes and failures in this critical field of activity and the differences between its tactics and those of their more veteran rivals. These documents enable a detailed presentation and analysis of the debate among various American Jewish relief agencies regarding the extent to which they should adhere to U.S. regulations in those cases in which such laws hampered rescue efforts.

Extremely valuable material is also found in the archives of Orthodox rabbis and rabbinical associations in the United States, Israel and other countries. The documents in the archives of the Central Relief Committee, the Orthodox component of the JDC (presently housed at Yeshiva University), shed much light on the history of the leading *yeshivot* in Poland and Lithuania and their extensive ties with American Orthodox Jewry during the period from World War I until the Nazi invasion of the Soviet Union. The Jerusalem archives of Agudat Yisrael be-Eretz Yisrael also contains important documentation on the relations between these Torah institutions and Orthodox communities elsewhere, as well as on the plight of the *yeshivot* which escaped from Eastern Poland to Lithuania following the outbreak of World War II and the desperate efforts of their *roshei yeshiva* (and those of the local Lithuanian *yeshivot*) to arrange for their emigration to safe havens. There is considerable documentation on the latter subject in the archives of Rabbi Yitzchak ha-Levi Herzog who served as Ashkenazic Chief Rabbi of Palestine prior to and during World War II. He also maintained close contacts with the leading rabbis and *roshei yeshiva* in Eastern Europe, many of whom appealed to him for assistance in obtaining *aliyah* certificates for themselves and their students.

Numerous similar appeals were directed privately to the leaders of the *Vaad ha-Hatzala* and can be found in the archives of Rabbi Eliezer Silver, who headed the rabbinic rescue organization, and Rabbi Yisrael ha-Levi Rosenberg, one of its prominent leaders. These repositories also yielded considerable documentation which illuminated various aspects of the history of the *Vaad*, particularly regarding the relations between the rabbis who were active on behalf of the *Vaad* as well as between the rabbinic rescue agency and the various organizations whose members participated in its activities. Material regarding the latter subject can also be found in the archives of American Agudat Yisrael, which contains important documentation concerning the efforts of Orthodox leaders to establish a unified communal framework to facilitate relief and rescue activities.

Much valuable material is also found in other personal archives and private collections. One of the most important of these is the archives of Dr. Samuel Schmidt, who was sent from the United States by the *Vaad ha-Hatzala* as an emissary to the Polish rabbis and yeshiva students who had escaped to Lithuania and later traveled on its behalf to South America. Both trips were part of the *Vaad*'s efforts to facilitate the emigration from Europe of refugee Torah scholars. Another extremely important collection is the private archives of Rabbi Yoseph David Epstein, who served as the private secretary of Rabbi Eliezer Yehuda Finkel, the *rosh yeshiva* of the Mir Yeshiva. He escaped from Poland together with the yeshiva and traveled with them to the Far East, where he remained for the duration of the war. Rabbi Epstein preserved numerous important documents, as well as the archives of Rabbi Mayer Ashkenazi, the spiritual leader of the Shanghai Ashkenazic community. The latter led the efforts to obtain Shanghai entry permits for the refugee Torah scholars, some of whom were saved with these documents.

Two additional private collections of unique importance are the archives of Frank Newman and Rabbi Aaron Milewsky. The former, a young New York businessman, was sent by the *Vaad ha-Hatzala* to the Far East in order to help facilitate the emigration of refugee rabbis and yeshiva students. His diary and accompanying documents reveal important details regarding these efforts. Rabbi Milewsky, who was the leading Orthodox rabbi in Montevideo, Uruguay served as the contact person between *Vaad ha-Hatzala* in New York and the refugee Torah scholars stranded in Shanghai during the period in which American regulations barred communications between the United States and Japanese-occupied China.

I also found important documents in the archives of Dr. Zerach Warhaftig, who was a leader of the Polish refugees, initially in Lithuania and later in the Far East, and of Dr. Yitzchak (Ignacy) Schwarzbart who represented the Zionists in the Polish parliament-in-exile in London, and attempted to assist the Polish refugees stranded in Shanghai and Central Asia. Both collections are housed in the Yad Vashem Archives. Other archives with important documentation related to the history of the *Vaad ha-Hatzala* are: YIVO, which holds the archives of the American Jewish Committee, which includes valuable material regarding the efforts to establish an umbrella organization for American Jewry in the wake of the news of the implementation of the Final Solution in Europe, as well as a valuable collection on Shanghai; the Central Zionist Archives which houses numerous documents regarding the plight of the Polish Jews who escaped to Lithuania following the outbreak of World War II; the National Archives of Canada and the archives of the Canadian Jewish Congress both of which contain extensive documentation on the *Vaad's* efforts to obtain entry to Canada for refugee rabbis and yeshiva students; the papers of the Emergency Committee to Save the Jewish People of Europe which contain material on the rabbis' protest march in Washington in 1943 and this rescue organization's ties with the *Vaad ha-Hatzala*; as well as the U.S. National Archives, Wiener Library, Bar-Ilan University's Holocaust Research Institute, Beit Lochamei ha-Gettaot, World Agudat Yisrael, and the Rabbinical Council of America.

Given the extensive geographic scope and semi-clandestine nature of the *Vaad's* relief and rescue operations, it was practically inevitable that there would be serious lacunae in the existing documentation regarding various aspects of the *Vaad's* activities. I therefore sought to supplement the available archival materials with interviews. Unfortunately, by the time this project was launched in late 1973, all the major participants in the creation and history of the *Vaad ha-Hatzala* had already passed away. Nonetheless, I was able to interview quite a few individuals with first-hand knowledge of the rabbinic rescue organization, and/or the historical events and personages which played an important role in its activities. Among those persons were, for example, rabbis and yeshiva students rescued by the *Vaad ha-Hatzala*, as well as individuals who assisted the rabbinic rescue agency in its efforts. Of particular interest were the interviews with Rabbi Yoseph David Epstein and Rabbi Aaron Milewsky, both of whom played active roles in the rescue of numerous refugee Torah scholars. Yet while these interviews provided much valuable information in determining historical veracity, priority was accorded to original documentation from the war years.

This study was originally planned as a comprehensive history of the *Vaad ha-Hatzala* from its establishment in November 1939 until the end of World War II. In the course of the research it became clear, however, that there was far too much documentation to include in one volume. The paucity of historical research on American Orthodoxy during World War II in general, and on the *Vaad ha-Hatzala* in particular, and the bitter debates in the Jewish world regarding the *Vaad*'s achievements or lack thereof, made it particularly important to present an in-depth chronicle of the history of the rabbinic rescue agency and a detailed comparison and analysis of its relations with the other American Jewish overseas relief agencies, particularly the Joint Distribution Committee.

I therefore decided to divide this study into two parts, the first of which covers the period from the *Vaad*'s establishment as an organization for the rescue of Torah scholars until the rabbinic rescue agency decided to change its official policy and start trying to save all Jews. This decision, which took place in early January 1944, marked the transformation of the *Vaad* from a relatively small rescue organization with a limited and highly particularistic objective to a full-fledged relief agency which ultimately conducted negotiations with SS leader Heinrich Himmler for the rescue of all surviving Jews living under Nazi occupation. Given the plethora of documentation and sources regarding this latter period and its historical importance, I believe that it deserves to be dealt with in a comprehensive fashion in a full-length study which hopefully will be written in the near future. This volume includes an Afterword on the *Vaad*'s activities during the years 1944-1945, but it is only the proverbial tip of the iceberg for a period which is of unique interest not only to scholars and students of the Holocaust, but also for those interested in American Orthodoxy, religious Jewry and the internal rifts in the Jewish world.

Despite the fact that this volume does not present the entire history of the *Vaad ha-Hatzala* (which continued to operate for several years after World War II), there is much to be learned from the rabbinic rescue agency's activities during the years 1939-1944. The response of the American Orthodox rabbis to the plight of the Polish refugee rabbis and yeshiva students in Lithuania, and later in the Far East and Central Asia raised fundamental questions regarding such critical issues as rescue priority during the Holocaust, the value and price of achieving communal unity, and the extent to which existing laws should be adhered to in cases in which they hamper or prevent the rescue ·of Jewish lives. The *Vaad*'s activities delineated an Orthodox position on these issues and underscored the significant differences between the rabbis who headed the rabbinical rescue agency and other Jewish leaders. The debates between the different relief and rescue organizations and their successes and failures provide much material for consideration, analysis and reflection. Even more important, they force us to ask difficult questions regarding the present and future of the Jewish people throughout the world. And that, after all, is ultimately one of the most significant reasons we seek to study our history.

Notes

1. For surveys on the historiography of the Holocaust see Yisrael Gutman and Gideon Greif (editors), *The Historiography of the Holocaust Period*, Jerusalem, 1988.
2. Daniel Jonah Goldhagen, *Hitler's Willing Executioners; Ordinary Germans and the Holocaust*, New York, 1996.
3. There is no comprehensive study on the phenomenon of collaboration with the Nazis during the Holocaust, but simultaneously with the increased efforts to prosecute Eastern European Nazi collaborators who escaped to Western democracies after World War II (but unconnected to this phenomenon) a growing number of studies on this important subject have been published over the course of the past few years. See for example on the subject of Lithuania Emanuel Zingeris (editor), *Atminties Dienos; Days of Memory*, Vilnius, 1995.
4. See, for example, the *Pinkas Ha-Kehillot* series published by Yad Vashem which summarizes - in encyclopedic form - the history of the Jewish communities affect-

ed by the Holocaust. To date, volumes have been published on communities in Poland, Germany, Rumania, Lithuania, Latvia and Estonia, Greece, Libya and Tunisia.

5. See, for example, Yisrael Gutman and Cynthia J. Haft (editors), *Patterns of Jewish Leadership In Nazi Europe 1933-1945*, Jerusalem, 1979; Yehuda Bauer, *Jews for Sale? Nazi-Jewish Negotiations 1933-1945*, New Haven and London, 1994.

6. David S. Wyman, *Paper Walls; America and the Refugee Crisis 1938-1941*, Amherst, 1968; idem., *The Abandonment of the Jews; America and the Holocaust*, New York, 1984; Henry L. Feingold, *Politics of Rescue; the Roosevelt Administration and the Holocaust 1938-1945*, New Brunswick, 1970.

7. Bernard Wasserstein, *Britain and the Jews of Europe, 1939-1945*, London, 1979.

8. See, for example, Jacques Picard, *Die Schweiz und die Juden 1933-1945*, Zurich, 1994.

9. See, for example, Arieh Ben-Tov, *Facing the Holocaust in Budapest; The International Committee of the Red Cross and the Jews in Hungary 1943-1945*, Geneva, 1988.

10. See, for example, John F. Morley, *Vatican Diplomacy and the Jews During the Holocaust 1939-1943*, New York, 1980.

11. Franklin L. Littel and Hubert G. Locke (editors), *The German Church Struggle and the Holocaust*, Detroit, 1974.

12. See, for example, Yisrael Gutman and Efraim Zuroff (editors), *Rescue Efforts During the Holocaust*, Jerusalem, 1977.

13. Yehuda Bauer, *My Brothers' Keeper; A History of the American Jewish Joint Distribution Committee 1929-1939*, Philadelphia, 1974; idem., *American Jewry and the Holocaust; The American Jewish Joint Distribution Committee 1939-1945*, Jerusalem and Detroit, 1981.

14. Naomi W. Cohen, *Not Free to Desist; The American Jewish Committee 1906-1966*, Philadelphia, 1972.

15. See, for example, Edward Pinsky, "Cooperation Among American Jewish Organizations and Their Efforts to Rescue European Jewry During the Holocaust 1939-1945," doctoral dissertation submitted to New York University, 1980.

16. Meir Sompolinsky, "Jewish Institutions in the World and the Yishuv as Reflected in the Holocaust Historiography of the Ultra-Orthodox," in Gutman and Greif, *The Historiography of the Holocaust Period*, pp. 609-630.

Chapter 1

Historic Ties

World War I marked the emergence of American Jewry as the major force in Jewish relief work in Europe. Whereas before the war the burden of supporting needy Jews and Jewish institutions had been borne primarily by European Jews,[1] after the outbreak of World War I those individuals and institutions that had previously played an active role in Jewish philanthropy were unable to respond adequately to the plight of the war-stricken Jewish communities in Eastern Europe and the Middle East. The scope of the damage and destruction wrought in the Jewish communities of the Russian, Austro-Hungarian, and, to a lesser extent, Ottoman empires was enormous, and the need for immediate assistance was urgent. In the course of the war, hundreds of thousands of Jews had been forced to flee from their homes, hundreds of Jewish villages had been severely damaged, and tens of thousands of Jewish homes had been destroyed. The existence of the Jewish community of Palestine was seriously endangered by starvation and persecution by the Turkish authorities.[2] Organized East European Jewish life was in a state of chaos and thus the burden of assistance fell upon the American Jewish community.

The need for extraordinary measures to confront the emergency situation was obvious to those in the United States involved in Jewish relief work. In October 1914 the American Jewish Committee issued a call to representatives of other American Jewish organizations to join in establishing a fundraising mechanism to deal with the emergency, declaring:

The stupendous conflict which is now raging on the European continent is a calamity, the extent of which transcends imagination. While all mankind is directly or indirectly involved in the consequences, the burden of suffering and of destitution rests with special weight upon our brethren in Eastern Europe. The embattled armies are spreading havoc and desolation within the Jewish Pale of Settlement in Russia and the Jews of Galicia and East Prussia dwell in the very heart of the war zone. Hundreds of thousands of Jews are in the contending armies. Fully one-half of all the Jews of the world live in the regions where active hostilities are in progress. The Jews of Palestine, who have largely depended on Europe for assistance, have been literally cut off from their sources of supply, while the Jews of Germany, Belgium, France and England are struggling with burdens of their own. In this exigency it is evident that the Jews of America must once again come to the rescue. They must assume the duty of giving relief commensurate with the existing needs. They must be prepared to make sacrifices and to proceed systematically in collecting and distributing a fund which will, so far as possible, alleviate this extraordinary distress. There is probably no parallel in history to the present status of the Jews.[3]

At the outbreak of World War I, however, there was no permanent organization for American Jewish overseas relief.[4] The first group to attempt to organize large-scale fundraising to transmit aid to Jews in distress in Europe were the Orthodox. On October 4, 1914, the Central Committee for the Relief of Jews Suffering Through the War was established upon the initiative of Orthodox rabbis, prominent laymen, and the Union of Orthodox Congregations, headed by Leon Kamaiky (president), Harry Fischel (treasurer), and other prominent Orthodox personages. The Central Relief Committee, as it came to be called, represented the overwhelmingly Eastern European immigrant community which expressed its affiliational loyalties in Orthodox frameworks.[5]

Shortly thereafter the American Jewish Committee issued a call to other Jewish organizations to join together in establishing a representative committee which would centralize fundraising and coordinate distribution in order to deal most effectively with what was obviously an "extraordinary emergency."[6] The result of this initiative was the formation on October 25, 1914, of the American Jewish Relief Committee headed by Louis Marshall (president) and Felix Warburg (treasurer), both members of the American Jewish Committee and stalwarts of the German Jewish aristocracy[7] whose members occupied most of the leadership positions in the American Jewish community.

Efforts to fully merge the two committees were not entirely successful, as the Orthodox group believed that it could best fulfill its function by maintaining its separate identity. Nonetheless, the Central Relief Committee was eager to cooperate with its non-Orthodox counterparts, and thus a centralized organizational framework for relief work was created on November 27, 1914, with the establishment of the Joint Distribution Committee of the American Friends of War Sufferers, which was to distribute the funds raised separately by the two committees. (The official name of the organization was the American Jewish Joint Distribution Committee. It was frequently referred to as "the Joint" or "JDC"). Slightly more than a year later, on November 29, 1915, the People's Relief Committee, which had been established in August 1915 and represented Jewish socialist and labor organizations, joined the JDC, thereby unifying the overseas relief efforts of the American Jewish community.[8]

By the end of 1915 the Joint Distribution Committee had raised approximately $1.5 million and had transmitted considerable aid to Jews in distress both in Eastern Europe and in Palestine. The assistance took various forms: foodstuffs, medicine, and funds—all of which were badly needed by the beleaguered Jewish communities in the war zone. By the end of 1918 the JDC had collected over $16.5 million (of which close to $15 million was sent abroad);[9] an achievement which made it the major relief organization in the Jewish world.

In addition, American Jews, on an individual basis, sent millions of dollars to relatives and friends in distress in the countries at war. (In fact, the remittances and food parcels sent privately amounted to a far larger sum than the relief transmitted by the JDC and other agencies.)[10] These much-needed goods and dollars, sent through both organized and private channels, did much to alleviate the plight of East European Jewry (and of the Palestinian Jewish community) during World War I and the tumultuous period immediately afterwards. Thus American Jewry became the leading provider of relief for Jews in distress, primarily in Eastern Europe but elsewhere as well.[11] In the words of noted Zionist leader Max Nordau, the American Jews "have little or no help from European Jewry. As they have to bear practically the whole burden alone, they are under no obligation of taking counsel with anybody else, and may act with entire independence."[12]

Orthodox Jews in the United States played a significant role in the overseas relief efforts of the American Jewish community during World War I and the interwar period. As was noted above, they were the first group to attempt to organize a centralized fundraising framework to deal with the emergency, and later they joined with other elements in the community to create the Joint Distribution Committee. Initially, there had been criticism among American Jewish community leaders regarding the establishment of the Central Relief Committee, which was viewed as a particularistic— exclusively Orthodox—organization. From the outset, however, its founders claimed that it had been established to fill a specific purpose for which it was uniquely qualified: to reach "the Orthodox elements, the rabbis, the synagogue people, the religious and spiritual leaders of traditional Judaism" or, in the words of Rabbi Bernard Drachman, a prominent Orthodox rabbi, "the elements and organizations not accessible to the American Jewish Committee."[13] This stance was a continuation of the policy pursued by Orthodox leaders prior to World War I, when they had favored the creation of their own institutions for social work. It also was an expression of the desire of Orthodox elements to prove that they could care for their own and gain the recognition of the Reform leadership in communal affairs.[14]

The fundraising record of the Central Relief Committee seems to validate the thinking of its founders. From its establishment in the fall of 1914 until 1922, it was active in 2,366 locations and raised approximately $10 million. It concentrated its efforts primarily in the synagogues and among the masses of poor and middle-class Jews of East European origin.[15] Moreover, Orthodox fundraising for overseas relief was not confined to the Central Relief Committee. In 1915, Orthodox rabbis founded *Ezrat Torah*, a special fund to assist needy rabbis, yeshiva students, and religious functionaries in Europe and Palestine. During its first five years, *Ezrat Torah* distributed more than $250,000 to needy individuals, and it raised much larger sums during the interwar period.[16] These efforts were a reflection of

American Orthodoxy's ambivalent attitude toward Jewish communal affairs. On the one hand, Orthodox leaders sought to attain a more prominent role in community leadership. At the same time, however, they insisted on establishing separate frameworks to deal with their particularistic needs.

One of the organizations that played a critical role in molding the involvement and response of American Orthodoxy in communal issues, and especially overseas relief efforts, was the *Agudat ha-Rabbanim,* or Union of Orthodox Rabbis of the United States and Canada. Founded in New York City on July 29, 1902,[17] the organization was established primarily to respond to the crisis engendered by the rapid assimilation among Jewish immigrants to the United States. Rabbi Moses Zebulun Margolies, one of the founders, described the situation that necessitated the establishment of the *Agudat ha-Rabbanim* as follows:

> The Kashrus situation was an eyesore and an abomination to the G-d-fearing man and needed attention. Religious education was at its lowest ebb. Sabbath observance was becoming obsolete and no one raised a voice of warning. Irresponsibility in purely rabbinical functions, particularly in marriage and divorce, was threatening the sanctity of the marriage relationship. All this was from time immemorial the particular province of the Rav and if changed conditions have deprived the individual rabbi of his power to stand in the breach, then it devolved upon a united rabbinate to shoulder the burden.[18]

Given the composition of the Orthodox community in the United States, the preponderance of whose members were recent immigrants from Eastern Europe,[19] there was an urgent need for a unified rabbinic association which would supervise the administering of religious service, establish Jewish schools, and protect the traditional Jewish lifestyle and values against the inroads being made by assimilation. *Agudat ha-Rabbanim* sought to unite the American Orthodox rabbinate in order to achieve those goals by organizing more effective action in the areas of Jewish education, *kashrut* supervision, Sabbath observance, personal status, and rabbinic affairs.[20] Almost all the prominent East European Orthodox rabbis in America[21] joined the rabbinic association, which became a major force in the Orthodox community.[22]

During its early years, the *Agudat ha-Rabbanim* dealt primarily with the internal Orthodox communal problems it had been founded to solve: religious observance (particularly in the areas of *kashrut,* Sabbath, and family purity), education, and rabbinic affairs. Thus, for example, one of the more important campaigns it waged was to attempt to ensure that only duly ordained rabbis would perform religious ceremonies. The *Agudat ha-Rabbanim* also sought to bar unqualified supervisors from the kosher meat industry. Efforts were invested to unite the Orthodox rabbinate, establish Jewish day schools, and promote Sabbath observance.[23] The latter campaign took various forms: efforts to institute a five-day work week, attempts to find employment for Sabbath observers, provision of legal aid to approximately 70,000 Sabbath observers arrested for working on Sunday, and the publication of a special monthly, the *Sabbath Journal,* in English, Yiddish, and Hebrew. These activities were all carried out under the auspices of the Sabbath Alliance of America founded by *Agudat ha-Rabbanim* in 1905.[24]

Early in its existence *Agudat ha-Rabbanim* also became active in overseas relief work. Initially the rabbinic association raised money to assist the Jews being affected by the 1903–1905 pogroms in Russia and to aid those coreligionists who immigrated to the United States. In addition, *Agudat ha-Rabbanim* helped find jobs for many Polish and Russian rabbis who fled to America.[25]

When World War I broke out, members of *Agudat ha-Rabbanim* called upon American Jewry—in speeches in synagogues as well as in special declarations—to aid their beleaguered European coreligionists.[26] Moreover, the leaders of the rabbinic association actively participated in the establishment of the Central Relief Committee, which was founded in early October 1914.[27] *Agudat ha-Rabbanim,* which had been among the first to call for the establishment of such a framework, cooperated with representatives of other Orthodox organizations and leading Orthodox public figures in establishing Central Relief, and they wanted it to encompass as wide a public as possible.[28] Thus among the leaders of the Orthodox overseas relief agency may be found not only leading members of the *Agudat ha-Rabbanim* such as Rabbis Hillel Klein, Moses Zebulun Margolies, and Yisrael Halevi Rosenberg, but also Rabbi Meir Berlin of the Mizrachi and Leon Kamaiky, publisher of the Yiddish daily *Morgn Dzurnal,* as well as such prominent Orthodox laymen as Harry Fishel, Morris Engelman, Albert Lucas, and Julius Dukas, all of whom were known for their involvement in Jewish philanthropy and communal affairs.[29]

As the situation of East European Jewry rapidly deteriorated, *Agudat ha-Rabbanim* became increasingly involved in overseas relief work, which became its major field of activity. Extensive efforts were invested to raise funds for the Central Relief Committee. When support for its activities dropped in the summer of 1915, *Agudat ha-Rabbanim* convened a special meeting to deal with the problem. The rabbis issued a declaration on behalf of the relief agency, declared the first day of Selichot a fast day, and called for a special convention to raise funds. At the request of the Central Relief Committee, the rabbinic association sent out 10,000 letters soliciting contributions and issued numerous declarations. The rabbis also proposed that a special 10 cent tax be levied on all High Holy Days synagogue seats in order to raise funds for the Orthodox relief agency.[30]

One of the original purposes for the establishment of the Central Relief Committee had been to assist the rabbis, yeshivot, and religious functionaries in distress in Europe. The plight of these individuals and institutions were, needless to say, of special concern to those who had founded the American Orthodox relief agency. The magnitude of the crisis in Europe, however, made it extremely difficult for existing American Jewish fundraising agencies to meet the needs of this group.[31] Thus while the Central Relief Committee set aside special allocations to aid religious institutions and functionaries, the sums were relatively small in comparison to their needs. The assistance provided by the Central Relief Committee was problematic, moreover, because it was provided in the form of soup kitchens and bread lines, which meant that the recipients were forced to stand on line to receive their portions. *Agudat ha-Rabbanim* realized that such aid was not suitable for rabbis, religious functionaries, and yeshiva students, many of whom considered it beneath their dignity to wait on bread lines and would have preferred to starve rather than seek aid in this form. They therefore sought a means of providing direct assistance to these individuals.[32]

The first call for concrete action was issued by Rabbi Yisrael Halevi Rosenberg, one of the leaders of *Agudat ha-Rabbanim* and a first vice-president of the Central Relief Committee. At the thirteenth annual convention of the *Agudat ha-Rabbanim*, held in the spring of 1915, he called for the establishment of a special fund to support European rabbis and yeshivot. He contended that the rabbis and yeshiva students could not remain solely dependent on the assistance provided by the general relief agencies because they would rather suffer hunger than go to the public soup kitchen. Moreover, if *bnai Torah* were not cared for, they would be terribly embarrassed and would consequently lose their status and influence in their communities.[33]

The actual decision to establish a separate fundraising agency called *Ezrat Torah* "to come to the aid of the yeshivot, *roshei yeshivot,* and their students, rabbis, and religious functionaries in the countries at war"[34] was made in late August 1915, at a meeting called by *Agudat ha-Rabbanim* to find a new source of funds for the Central Relief Committee. The ironic circumstances of the foundation of *Ezrat Torah* were subsequently explained in one of its publications:

> Even though many rabbis participated in the founding and administration of Central Relief and all the rabbis in this country participated in its fundraising activities, and its initial goal was to support yeshivot and holy institutions, the rabbis nonetheless found it necessary to create a special institution entitled *Ezrat Torah* for rabbis and religious functionaries because they are suffering the most in physical and spiritual terms and because they are bashful and consequently could not benefit in the proper manner from the general [fundraising] institutions.[35]

Rabbi Rosenberg was chosen to head the committee that was to administer the new fundraising agency. It began by writing to several distinguished European rabbis in order to obtain specific information on the individuals and institutions in need. Eventually the European rabbis were chosen to represent *Ezrat Torah* and to distribute its funds to the rabbis, students, and yeshivot that were found deserving. Additional funds were sent directly to individual rabbis and scholars who appealed to *Ezrat Torah*, so that the efforts of the existent relief agencies would not be hampered as a result of its establishment and the public would not be confused by the introduction of still another Orthodox agency for overseas relief. Thus public appeals for funds were reduced to a minimum, with only one day a year—the Sabbath preceding the seventh of Adar, the date of the birth and demise of Moses—set aside for such activities.[36]

In 1916 the religious Zionist movement Mizrachi joined *Agudat ha-Rabbanim* in the administration of *Ezrat Torah*. A joint committee composed of 24 members, 12 from each group, was chosen to run the organization. Rabbi Yisrael Rosenberg of *Agudat ha-Rabbanim*, who had been the first to call for the establishment of a separate fundraising agency specifically for rabbis and yeshiva students, was elected chairman, Dr. Hillel Klein was elected treasurer, and Rabbi Ishkolsky, secretary. Among the members of the joint committee were Rabbis Eliezer Silver (Harrisburg, PA), Joseph Konvitz (Elizabeth, NJ) of *Agudat ha-Rabbanim*, Meir Berlin, and Wolf (Zeev) Gold of the Mizrachi.[37]

During World War I, leading European sages frequently turned to *Ezrat Torah* for assistance. For example, at the semiannual convention of *Agudat ha-Rabbanim* in Harrisburg, Pennsylvania, in late 1917, letters asking *Ezrat Torah* to send immediate aid were publicized. Among those who appealed for help were the "Chofetz Chaim" (Rabbi Yisrael Meir ha-Kohen Kagan of Radin); Rabbi Avraham Duber Kahana Shapiro, who was president of the *Agudat ha-Rabbanim* of Lithuania and Chief Rabbi of Kovno; and Rabbi Moshe Mordechai Epstein, who was *rosh yeshiva* of Slabodka Yeshiva. In the wake of these appeals, the leaders of *Ezrat Torah* decided to send all the organization's available funds to the major yeshivot of Mir, Slabodka, Radin, Slutzk, Navardok, Telz, Lomza, and Slonim and to several smaller schools. Over $4,000 was transmitted to these institutions and these funds were extremely helpful in enabling several of the yeshivot to survive the difficult wartime conditions.[38]

During its initial years, *Ezrat Torah* was not particularly successful in fundraising. From its establishment in the fall of 1915 until the end of 1919 it raised only $107,697.[39] In comparison, from the fall of 1914 until February 1919 Central Relief raised $5,544,782 and the American Jewish Relief Committee raised $22,680,281. (People's Relief, which was established in August 1915, had raised $3,622,562 by February 1919.)[40] *Ezrat Torah's* importance, therefore, was primarily twofold: the distribution of relief to rabbis and yeshiva students in a manner that took into account their particular sensitivities, and its efforts to ensure that Orthodox Jews would not be discriminated against in the distribution of aid by the general Jewish relief agencies.[41]

In addition to the sums it raised, *Ezrat Torah* also distributed funds it received from the JDC and Central Relief. During the war years the latter two organizations gave *Ezrat Torah* $155,000 for distribution, enabling the Orthodox relief agency to expand its aid program to include needy rabbis and their families (as opposed to the *roshei yeshiva* and their students, who had initially received priority in the distribution of relief funds).[42]

Agudat ha-Rabbanim considered the establishment of *Ezrat Torah* its crowning achievement in the field of overseas relief during World War I. Unlike the Central Relief Committee, which was created upon the initiative of several Orthodox organizations and public figures, *Ezrat Torah* was founded solely by *Agudat ha-Rabbanim,* and it was the rabbinic association—together with the Mizrachi, which joined in the task a year later—that provided the leadership and main support for the relief organization. The members of *Agudat ha-Rabbanim* bore the major burden of the fundraising activities for *Ezrat Torah,* and *Agudat ha-Rabbanim* and the Mizrachi were actively involved in obtaining the subventions which the Central Relief Committee made available to *Ezrat Torah* for distribution. The special relationship between the rabbinic association and the overseas relief agency it founded was best described in an *Ezrat Torah* publication:

> *Ezrat Torah* is currently considered the favorite child of *Agudat ha-Rabbanim.* She created, raised, and fostered it. It is thanks to *Agudat ha-Rabbanim* which sought at every convention to find the means to strengthen this institution and thanks to the energy of the members of the administration of *Ezrat Torah* that this institution exists to this day.[43]

Agudat ha-Rabbanim's active involvement in overseas relief deserves further scrutiny as it reflects the basic attitude of the Orthodox rabbinic leadership on a critical communal issue, an issue that created considerable controversy in the American Jewish community when it arose again during World War II. The fundraising activities of the *Agudat ha-Rabbanim* indicate a certain ambivalence on the part of the rabbis vis-à-vis broad-based communal efforts. On the one hand, the rabbinic association participated in the establishment of the Central Relief Committee, which, although Orthodox in orientation, was founded to create a unified fundraising framework for the entire Jewish community. On the other hand, the leaders of *Agudat ha-Rabbanim* deemed it necessary to establish a special relief agency to deal specifically with the needs of rabbis, yeshiva students, and religious functionaries. In practice, while continuing actively to support the Central Relief Committee, they established an organization that was somewhat similar and in a certain sense competed for the same charity dollars. Instead of seeking to achieve their particularistic goals within the unified communal framework, the rabbis of *Agudat ha-Rabbanim* created a separate agency to attend to their specific needs, while at the same time supporting the general organizations that dealt with the plight of the "common" Jew.

In order to understand the complexities of the stance adopted by the rabbis, we must examine the relationship between the *Agudat ha-Rabbanim* and the yeshivot of Eastern Europe. While obviously concerned about the plight of all their coreligionists in the war zones, the leaders and members of the rabbinic association were especially worried about the fate of the world-famous Eastern European centers of talmudic learning, the prominent *roshei yeshiva*, their students, and their families. The reasons for their concern were manifold. First, almost every member of *Agudat ha-Rabbanim* had studied in one or more of these yeshivot and was personally acquainted with many of these institutions and *roshei yeshiva*.[44] In fact, membership in *Agudat ha-Rabbanim* was dependent on studies toward the *yadin-yadin* ordination, which at that time were available only in European yeshivot.[45] Thus as "alumni"[46] of the leading Torah academies and as individuals whose entire lives had been molded by the years they had spent studying at these institutions, the leaders of *Agudat ha-Rabbanim* were particularly sensitive to the needs of their former teachers and classmates.[47] For years after they had immigrated to the United States, many of the rabbis maintained close contacts with their former mentors and continued to look to the East European rabbis and yeshivot for guidance and inspiration.[48] As far as the rabbis of *Agudat ha-Rabbanim* were concerned, those institutions and individuals were the wellsprings of authentic Judaism and the heart of Torah-true Jewry.[49]

There were additional factors which reinforced the rabbis' sense of responsibility toward the East European Torah institutions. First and foremost was the deterioration in America of traditional Jewish life, a process that manifested itself in the rapid decline in religious observance and the increased inroads made by assimilation among American Jews.[50] These developments were viewed with a grave sense of alarm by the leadership of *Agudat ha-Rabbanim,* which had been founded to combat these phenomena. They considered the yeshivot the cornerstone of religious education and the hope for the continuity of Orthodoxy.[51] Given the fact that the yeshivot in America had still not reached the stage where they could fulfill the role played by their East European counterparts, the rabbis realized that they had a special obligation to assist these bastions of traditional Orthodoxy (just as they simultaneously sought to foster the establishment and development of similar institutions in the United States).[52]

The relative affluence of American Jewry (in comparison to the financial plight of their East European coreligionists) was another factor which motivated the rabbis to engage in relief work on behalf of European Torah institutions. If American Jews were not as religiously observant as their East European brethren, the least they could do was help support those who were maintaining Judaism's time-honored traditions. Time and again the rabbis stressed that European Jews had been sent by G-d to America to ensure that in time of crisis, aid would be forthcoming for Jews in distress. In the words of a fundraising appeal by *Agudat ha-Rabbanim,* American Jewry (i.e., the European immigrants to America) had been "sent across the ocean to provide sustenance for their brothers in other countries in their time of need."

The rabbis frequently used the expression *le'michya shlacham* (They were sent to provide sustenance),[53] based on Genesis 45:5, in which Joseph consoled his brothers that their selling him into slavery had indeed been preordained by G-d (since it was designed to create a solution for the famine which was to affect the land of Canaan, leaving Jacob and his sons without sufficient food). In the same way, the fundraising activities of the Orthodox rabbis on behalf of the European yeshivot were proof that their immigration to the United States had indeed been preordained, a factor of considerable consolation to the immigrant rabbis in view of the low level of religiosity and Torah learning in the American Jewish community.

The extensive efforts of *Agudat ha-Rabbanim* on behalf of European rabbis and yeshivot during World War I were in essence a microcosm of a wider phenomenon. Just as American Jewry emerged during this period as the major force in overseas Jewish relief work, the Orthodox community in the United States became the major source of financial support for European Torah institutions. From World War I on, European rabbis and especially *roshei yeshiva* increasingly turned to their American Orthodox counterparts for assistance in meeting their financial obligations and undertaking new projects.

The increased dependence on American sources of financial aid was dictated by circumstances in Eastern Europe. The end of World War I did not bring about a significant change in the abysmal state of most of the East European Jewish communities. In the aftermath of the war, approximately one million Polish Jews were homeless and starving, bloody pogroms took place in eastern Galicia and northeastern Poland, and the Jewish communities suffered severely as a result of the various wars which were waged in the wake of the establishment of the new nation-states of Poland and Lithuania, the Communist revolution, and the ensuing upheavals in the Soviet Union. It is estimated that approximately 200,000 Jews were killed or died as a result of persecution in eastern Poland and the Ukraine during the years 1918–1921 and that there were about 275,000 Jewish orphans in Poland and the Ukraine. In addition, the interwar period saw the steady and rapid deterioration of the Jews' financial positions throughout Eastern Europe in the wake of crop failures and the nationalistic economic measures implemented in many of the new nation-states which sought to replace Jews with natives. Thus the Joint Distribution Committee, which originally had viewed itself as a temporary organization created to deal with a particular emergency, slowly evolved into a permanent institution (although the formal decision to organize on a permanent basis was made only in 1929.)[54]

The yeshivot of Eastern Europe were, needless to say, directly affected by all these problems, but they also had to face several additional difficulties, which made them increasingly dependent on aid from the United States. Before World War I, the yeshivot had been supported primarily by local (East European and especially Russian) sources.[55] In the wake of the war and its tumultuous aftermath, these sources could no longer bear the financial burden of supporting the Torah institutions, which had to overcome a myriad of additional problems that jeopardized their existence.

First and foremost was the need for many of the yeshivot to relocate. In the course of World War I several of the larger schools—Mir,[56] Slabodka,[57] and Radin,[58] for example—had either fled or been exiled to the Russian interior, and upon cessation of the hostilities, they sought, to return to their former locations, which were now part of the new Polish republic or the independent republic of Lithuania. Other yeshivot, such as Slutzk[59] and Navardok (Nowogrudok),[60] which found themselves under Communist rule in the Soviet Union as a result of the new borders, decided to move to Poland, where Jewish institutions were afforded religious and educational freedom.

In both cases, extremely large sums were required to transfer these students from the Soviet Union.[61] In addition, upon their return to their former locations, they often found their original buildings destroyed or badly damaged, and funds were needed either to make extensive renovations or to buy new edifices. Those yeshivot that decided to relocate had to do so as well.[62] There were also other immediate problems, such as a shortage of the necessary books, because all the printing plates for the Babylonian Talmud in the major printing presses in Vilna, Warsaw, and Lemberg had been destroyed during the war.[63]

The leaders of *Agudat ha-Rabbanim* invested extensive efforts to provide the maximum assistance to the yeshivot through the Central Relief Committee and *Ezrat Torah*. Thus, for example, *Agudat ha-Rabbanim* put pressure on the JDC to grant Central Relief the right to transmit some of the funds it raised directly to yeshivot. An agreement was eventually reached between the various components of the JDC that both Central Relief and People's Relief would be able independently to distribute up to one-third of the funds they transmitted to the JDC for cultural activities.[64]

In addition, immediately after World War I *Agudat ha-Rabbanim* established a joint committee with Central Relief to supervise religious education in Europe and Palestine. Rabbi Yisrael Rosenberg headed a special delegation sent to Europe on behalf of the Central Relief Committee to examine the state of religious education. On the basis of the report he submitted, the monthly allocations to the various religious educational institutions were determined. By the end of 1923 the Central Relief Committee had transmitted more than $1 million to support Torah education abroad[65] and *Ezrat Torah* had disbursed $518,133 (of which $267,000 had been received from the Central Relief Committee and the JDC).[66]

Despite the extensive efforts of the leaders of Orthodox Jewry in the United States to provide the East European yeshivot with sufficient funds to meet their needs, these institutions suffered from

chronic financial problems throughout the interwar period. Right
after the Communist revolution in Russia, several yeshivot—in particular the Mir Yeshiva, which was close to the Russian border—
absorbed large numbers of students who had escaped from the
Soviet Union in order to engage in intensive Torah study, which was
forbidden under the Communist regime; they thereby incurred considerable financial expenses.[67]

During the 1930s the absorption of dozens of students from
Germany exacerbated the financial plight of various yeshivot,[68] as in
the wake of anti-Jewish measures which resulted in the impoverish-
ment of German Jewry, these students became totally dependent on
the yeshivot for all their needs.[69] Moreover, the interwar period, and
particularly its latter decade, was, marked by an extremely large
increase in the number of students studying at the major Polish
yeshivot.[70] The following table presents data on the number of students studying at most of the major Polish yeshivot during the 5690
(1929–1930)[71] and 5698 (1937–1938)[72] academic years, clearly indicating the sharp increase in the number of young men enrolled in
these institutions.

Institution	Students Enrolled			
	In 5690 (1929-1930)	In 5698 (1937-1938)	Change	% of change
Brisk, "Torat Chesed"	112	207	+95	+84.8%
Baranowitz, "Ohel Torah"	206	267	+61	+29.6%
Baranowitz, "Torat Chesed"	64	221	+157	+245.0%
Bialystok, "Beit Yoseph"	210	317	+107	+50.9%
Grodno, "Sha'ar ha-Torah"	170	209	+39	+22.9%
Kamenetz, "Knesset Beit Israel"	122	326	+204	+167.2%
Kletzk, "Etz Chaim"	149	24	+95	+63.7%
Kobrin	107	48	-59	-55.0%
Lomza	238	224	-14	-5.8%
Mir	350	477	+127	+36.2%
Pinsk, "Beit Yoseph"	160	154	-6	-3.7%
Radin	248	234	-14	-5.6%
Slonim	205	224	+19	+9.2%
	2,341	**3,152**	**+811**	**+28.8%**

Needless to say, the rise in the number of students created additional financial difficulties for the yeshivot, most of which already
had serious problems meeting their budget as a result of the decrease

in relief funds from the United States (due to local economic difficulties and subsequently the Depression) and the rapidly deteriorating political and economic situation of the Jews of Eastern Europe.[73] The solution in such cases was, invariably, to seek additional means of raising money from the more affluent Jewish communities in the West,[74] and especially in the United States.

The activities of the Central Relief Committee and *Ezrat Torah* laid the foundation in the United States for attempts by the yeshivot to engage in independent fundraising. These campaigns usually took two forms. The first was the opening in New York City of an office to raise funds and develop a circle of regular supporters. Thus, for example, by 1928 practically every one of the major Polish and Lithuanian yeshivot had already opened a permanent fundraising office in New York City. These offices maintained close contacts with *Agudat ha-Rabbanim* and the Orthodox overseas relief agencies.[75]

The second means by which the yeshivot sought to raise funds was to send their leading *roshei yeshiva* and/or their representatives to America to participate personally in fundraising activities. The reasoning was that the *roshei yeshiva* could serve as the most effective spokesmen on behalf of their institutions. It was assumed that the fact that these scholars, who were well-known throughout the Orthodox world for their dedication to intensive Torah study, had taken the trouble to travel thousands of miles to America and spend months of their valuable time traveling from community to community to raise funds would have an impact on the potential donors.

One of the first visits to the United States by famous Torah scholars was organized by the Central Relief Committee. A delegation composed of Rabbi Abraham Yitzhak ha-Cohen Kook, Ashkenazi Chief Rabbi of Palestine; Rabbi Avraham Duber Kahana Shapiro, president of the *Agudat ha-Rabbanim* of Lithuania and Chief Rabbi of Kovno; and Rabbi Moshe Mordechai Epstein, *rosh yeshiva* of the Slabodka Yeshiva was brought to the United States in 1924 to launch a campaign to raise $1 million. During the eight months they spent in the United States, the rabbis visited communities throughout the New York City area, as well as in Baltimore, Chicago, Detroit, Philadelphia, and Pittsburgh. They were honored by various dignitaries and were received by President Coolidge in the White House. By the time the rabbis left America in November 1924, the

Central Relief Committee had collected $400,000. Besides the financial success of the mission, it made Orthodox Jewry in the United States more cognizant of its responsibility toward the European yeshivot.[76]

This visit was followed by the visits of numerous European *roshei yeshiva*. Among the noted rabbis who came to the United States during the interwar period were Rabbis Eliezer Yehuda Finkel of Mir, Moshe Mordechai Epstein and Yitzchak Sher of Slabodka, Chaim Mordechai Katz and Eliyahu Bloch of Telz, Yechiel Michael Gordon of Lomza, Aaron Kotler of Kletzk, Shimon Shkopf of Grodno, Boruch Ber Leibowitz and Reuven Grazowsky of Kamenetz, Meir Shapiro of Lublin, and Elchanan Wasserman of Baranowitz.[77] These visits became increasingly frequent as the political and economic situation of European Jewry deteriorated. Thus, what was a relatively rare occurrence in the early 1920s became a common phenomenon by the mid-1930s, by which time the East European yeshivot were increasingly dependent on financial assistance from abroad and especially from the United States.[78] For example, the first delegation from the Mir Yeshiva traveled to America in 1925; within a few years, Rabbi Abraham Kalmanowitz, its president, was going there twice a year on a regular basis.[79]

The visits of the *roshei yeshiva* to America, it should be noted, were usually not confined to fundraising activities. The rabbis frequently gave guest lectures at American yeshivot, attended conventions of *Agudat ha-Rabbanim,* and undoubtedly inspired some American Jewish youth to consider the possibility of studying in their institutions.[80] Thus these visits played an important role in the development of the relations between Orthodox Jewry in the United States and the Torah centers of Eastern Europe. In the course of the interwar period, we see the gradual strengthening of the ties between the two major centers of Orthodox life. While American Jewry sent dollars and young men to the European yeshivot,[81] the latter sent their alumni to man rabbinic posts in the United States, and sent their prominent *roshei yeshiva* to raise funds, recruit students, and, it was hoped, inspire religious commitment.

The rabbis of *Agudat ha-Rabbanim* played a critical role in the development of this relationship. Linked by mutual interest, common ideology, and personal ties to the East European yeshivot and *roshei yeshiva*, they created the institutional frameworks and channels for relief and communication and were the most enthusiastic proponents in America of the traditional East European Orthodox values.[82] Thus it was hardly surprising that when faced with grave crises upon the outbreak of World War II, the leading East European rabbis and *roshei yeshivot* turned to American Jewry, and especially to the leaders of *Agudat ha-Rabbanim*, for assistance.

Notes

1. Zosa Szajkowski, "Private and Organized American Jewish Overseas Relief (1914–1938)," *American Jewish Historical Quarterly*, LVII, no. 1 (September 1967), pp. 52–55.

2. Yehuda Bauer, *My Brother's Keeper; A History of the American Jewish Joint Distribution Committee 1929–1939* (Philadelphia, 1974), p. 6.

3. Herman Bernstein, "The History of American Jewish Relief," p. 69, unpublished manuscript written in 1928, now in the library of the Joint Distribution Committee in New York City. Bernstein was personally involved in the attempts to respond to the crisis. He succinctly termed the events in Europe a "stupendous emergency." "Jewish War Relief," *American Jewish Yearbook*, 5678 (1917–1918) (Philadelphia, 1917), pp. 198–199.

4. Zosa Szajkowski, "Concord and Discord in American Jewish Overseas Relief 1914–1924," *YIVO Annual of Jewish Social Science*, XIV (New York, 1969), p. 100.

5. Ibid., p. 105; Bernstein, "History," p. 67; Bauer, *My Brother's Keeper,* p. 6.

6. The term is Bernstein's. Bernstein, "History," p. 68.

7. Bauer, *My Brother's Keeper,* pp. 6, 22.

8. Ibid., pp. 6–7; Bernstein, "History," pp. 69–71; Szajkowski, "Concord," p. 100.

9. Bauer, *My Brother's Keeper,* pp. 7–8, 305; For partial figures on the funds raised by the JDC's three constituent agencies, see Szajkowski, "Concord," p. 113.

10. Szajkowski, "Private," pp. 62–64.

11. According to available statistics, the funds for Jewish relief work in the territory occupied by Germany came almost exclusively from the United States. Zosa Szajkowski, "Jewish Relief in Eastern Europe 1914–1917," *Leo Baeck Institute Yearbook*, Vol. X (London, 1965), p. 49. Considerable sums were sent to the Palestinian Jewish community as well as to the Jews of Turkey and Greece. Bauer, *My Brother's Keeper*, p. 15.

12. Quoted in Zosa Szajkowski, "Disunity in the Distribution of American Jewish Overseas Relief (1919–1939)," *American Jewish Historical Quarterly*, LVIII, no. 3 (March 1969), p. 487.

13. Szajkowski, "Concord," p. 106.

14. Ibid.

15. Ibid., pp. 114, 131.

16. *Jubilee Book of Esras Torah (1915–1935)* (Brooklyn, NY, n.d.) (hereafter called *Esras Torah Jubilee*), p. 14. For figures on the sums raised by *Ezrat Torah* see (for the years 1915–1935) *Esras Torah Jubilee*, p. 26, and (for the years 1935–1945) Asher Rand, editor. *Eidut L'Yisroel* (New York, n.d.), p. 296. A significant portion of the funds distributed by *Ezrat Torah* during World War I were subventions from the Central Relief Committee and the JDC, but as time went on, most of the funds allocated by *Ezrat Torah* were raised by that organization.

17. *Sefer ha–Yovel Shel Agudas ha–Rabbanim ha–Ortodoxsim di–Artzot ha–Brit ve–Kanada (5662–5687)* (New York, 5688 [1927/1928]), p. 22.

18. Aaron Rothkoff, *Bernard Revel; Builder of American Jewish Orthodoxy* (Philadelphia, 1972), pp. 14–15.

19. For a description of the immigrant Orthodox community in America during this period see Rothkoff, *Bernard Revel*, pp. 3–26; Gilbert Klaperman, *The Story of Yeshiva University* (New York, 1969), pp. 1–16.

20. *Sefer ha–Yovel*, p. 22.

21. Although the *Agudat ha–Rabbanim* sought to unite the ranks of the Orthodox rabbinate, they did not invite their American–born and/or Western European-trained Orthodox colleagues to join their organization. The opposition to rabbis such as Bernard Drachman, Henry Schneeberger, and Henry Pereira Mendes stemmed from the fact that they were viewed as "Americanizers," who advocated various forms of modernization to combat the problems which *Agudat ha–Rabbanim* sought to solve. The leadership of the rabbinic association therefore perceived them as a threat to the traditional form of rabbinic authority which had evolved in Eastern Europe and which they sought to preserve in the United States. For an extensive examination of the issue, see Jeffrey S. Gurock, "Resisters and Accommodators: Varieties of Orthodox Rabbis in America 1886–1983," *American Jewish Archives*, XXXV, no. 2 (November 1983), pp. 111–112. The issues of the attitude of the *Agudat ha–Rabbanim* toward their modern Orthodox colleagues will be discussed in further detail below.

22. Charles S. Liebman, "Orthodoxy in American Jewish Life," *American Jewish Yearbook*, 66, 1965 (Philadelphia, 1966), p. 32; Aaron Rakeffet–Rothkoff, "The East European Immigrant Rabbinate During Its Formative Years," *Gesher*, 5, no. 1 (1976), pp. 149–150.

23. *Sefer ha–Yovel*, pp. 23–34.

24. Moshe Davis, "Jewish Religious Life and Institutions in America," *The Jews, Their History, Culture, and Religion*, ed. Louis Finkelstein (New York, 1944), p. 408.

25. *Sefer ha–Yovel*, p. 34.

26. Ibid., p. 58.

27. Ibid., p. 59; Szajkowski, "Concord," p. 105.

28. *Sefer ha–Yovel*, p. 59.

29. Szajkowski, "Concord," p. 105.

30. Evidence of *Agudat ha–Rabbanim*'s increased involvement in overseas relief may be seen from the fact that a large portion of the sessions of the rabbinic association's thirteenth annual convention, held in Iyar 5657 (spring 1915), were devoted to discussions of fundraising activities for the Central Relief Committee. *Sefer ha–Yovel*, pp. 60–61.

31. Ibid., pp. 58–59; Davis, "Jewish Religious Life," p. 409.

32. *Sefer ha–Yovel*, pp. 63–64.

33. Rand, *Eidut L'Yisroel*, p. 11.

34. *Sefer ha–Yovel*, p. 64.

35. *Esras Torah Jubilee*, p. 14.

36. Ibid.; *Sefer ha–Yovel*, p. 64.

37. Ibid., p. 65.

38. Ibid., p. 66; Davis, "Jewish Religious Life," p. 409.

39. *Esras Torah Jubilee*, p. 26.

40. Szajkowski, "Concord," p. 113.

41. *Sefer ha–Yovel*, p. 70.

42. *Esras Torah Jubilee*, pp. 14, 26.

43. Ibid., p. 14; *Sefer ha–Yovel*, pp. 63, 70.

44. The only notable exception was Rabbi Hillel Klein, who had been ordained at the Hildesheimer seminary in Berlin. Unlike his colleagues, who had all been born in the Russian empire, Klein was born in Hungary. Gurock, "Resisters," p. 121.

45. Liebman, "Orthodoxy," p. 33.

46. The term is used loosely, since there was no such thing as a formal graduation from a traditional Eastern European yeshiva.

47. "The attitude of American Jewry to the European yeshivot is rooted in the depths of its Torah leadership, and these public figures, all of whom had been educated in those yeshivot, were still emotionally tied to European Jewry." Letter from Rabbi Yoseph Epstein, secretary of the *rosh yeshiva* of the Mir Yeshiva, to the author, April 20, 1974.

48. Thus, for example, when *Agudat ha–Rabbanim* was invited to join the Jewish Agency, they decided to consult with European sages prior to responding. *Sefer ha–Yovel*, p. 102. Another area in which questions were addressed to European rabbis was *kashrut*. See Harold P. Gastwirt, *Fraud, Corruption and Holiness; The Controversy Over the Supervision of Jewish Dietary Practice in New York City 1881–1940* (Port Washington, NY: 1974), pp. 142–143. On an individual level, Rabbi Eliezer Silver, for example, maintained a steady correspondence with his former teacher, Rabbi Chaim Ozer Grodzinski of Vilna, whose advice he sought on a wide range of communal issues. See the correspondence between the two rabbis in the Silver Archives, Harrisburg, PA.

49. Rabbi Yaakov Levinson, "*Chovat ha–Hatzala*," *Ha–Pardes*, 14, no. 11 (Shevat 5701/February 1941), 11–12.

50. Aaron Rakeffet–Rothkoff, *The Silver Era in American Jewish Orthodoxy; Rabbi Eliezer Silver and his Generation* (Jerusalem and New York, 1981), pp. 13–30; Rabbi Leo Jung, *The Path of a Pioneer: The Autobiography of Leo Jung* (London and New York, 1980), p. 105; Gastwirt, *Fraud*, p. 7.

51. On the importance of the yeshiva in the Orthodox world see William B. Helmreich, *The World of the Yeshiva: An Intimate Portrait of Orthodox Jewry* (New York and London, 1982), p. 330.

52. For a description of the involvement of *Agudat ha–Rabbanim* in the development of the Rabbi Issac Elchanan Theological Seminary (of Yeshiva University) see Rothkoff, *Bernard Revel*, pp. 142–147; Gurock, "Resisters," pp. 132–134. Both note the efforts of the leaders of *Agudat ha–Rabbanim* to increase their influence on the school's educational policies, which did not always conform to the rabbis' conception of how a yeshiva should be run.

53. *Sefer ha–Yovel*, p. 128. Rabbi Grodzinski used the same term in praising the efforts of American Jewry to assist the yeshivot during World War I. Aaron Sursky, Ed., *Achiezer: Kovetz Igrot, Pirkei Chayim* (Bnei Brak, 5730 [1970]), pp. 133–136.

54. Bauer, *My Brother's Keeper*, pp. 9–32.

55. Shaul Stampfer, "Shalosh Yeshivot Litaeeyot ba–Mei'ya ha–Tsha Esrei," Ph.D. dissertation, Hebrew University of Jerusalem 5741 (1981), pp. 107–110; Yoseph Epstein, "Yeshivat Mir," in Samuel K. Mirsky, Ed., *Mosdot ha–Torah be–Airopa*

be–Binyanam u–ve–Churbanam (New York, 1956), p. 110; Mordechai Gifter, "Yeshivat Telz," in Mirsky, *Mosdot*, pp. 180–182.

56. For a detailed history of the Mir Yeshiva see Epstein, "Yeshivat Mir," pp. 87–132. During World War I the Mir Yeshiva moved to Poltava (Ukraine).

57. During World War I the Czar decreed that no Jews could remain in Kovno and its suburbs because of the fortifications in the area. The Slabodka Yeshiva therefore moved to Minsk and later to Kremenchug. Ephraim Oshry, "Yeshivat 'Knesset Yisrael' be–Slabodka," in Mirsky, *Mosdot*, p. 133.

58. The Radin Yeshiva initially moved to Smilowitz near Minsk and later to Somitch in the Mogilev district. David Zariz, "Yeshivat Radin," in Mirsky, *Mosdot*, p. 191.

59. After Rabbi Isser Zalman Meltzer, the *rosh yeshiva*, was arrested several times by the *Yevsektzsia*, he decided in 1923 to flee to Kletzk, a small village on the Polish side of the border, to which his son–in–law, rabbi Aron Kotler, had moved (together with some of the students) two years previously. Hillel Zeidman, "Yeshiva 'Etz Chaim' de–Kletzk," in Mirsky, *Mosdot*, p. 233.

60. When the Russian authorities began harassing the yeshiva, the administration decided to flee to Poland and establish two yeshivot, one in Bialystok and one in Mezritch. During the latter half of 1922, the students were smuggled across the border by professional smugglers. Y. L. Nekritch, "Yeshivot Navardok," in Mirsky, *Mosdot*, pp. 264–266.

61. The Navardok Yeshiva ("Beit Yoseph") paid professional smugglers 5 to 10 rubles for every student smuggled across the border. A total of 500 students were taken across, so the expense was considerable. Nekritch, "Yeshivot Navardok," p. 265.

62. See, for example, Epstein, "Yeshivat Mir," p. 100; Zariz, "Yeshivat Radin," p. 196.

63. Rothkoff, *Bernard Revel*, pp. 60–61; Davis, "Jewish Religious Life," p. 412; *Sefer ha–Yovel*, p. 85.

64. *Sefer ha–Yovel*, p. 130; Zosa Szajkowski, "Disunity in the Distribution of American Jewish Overseas Relief 1919–1939," *American Jewish Historical Quarterly*, LVIII, no. 4 (June 1969), p. 485.

65. *Sefer ha–Yovel*, p. 130.

66. *Esras Torah Jubilee*, p. 26.

67. Epstein, "Yeshivat Mir," p. 114.

68. Among the yeshivot that had students from Germany were Mir, Telz, Slabodka, Kamenetz, and Baranowitz. See the articles on the individual yeshivot in Mirsky, *Mosdot*, pp. 114, 160, 180, 319, 334.

69. Epstein, "Yeshivat Mir," p. 114; Gifter, "Yeshivat Telz," p. 182.

70. Dr. Mark Wischnitzer, who was the executive secretary of the Haffkine Foundation, which was founded to assist the East European yeshivot, poses two explanations for the increase in yeshiva students. One was that Orthodox circles, which had been on the defensive in the nineteenth century, realized after World War I that they had to combat laxity in religious observance, atheism, and especially Communism, in a more active manner. Another explanation was based on socio-economic factors. Since Jews were not allowed to study in most public and especially vocational schools, and since emigration was practically impossible and the yeshivot cared for all the students' needs, they constituted a viable alternative for those Jewish youth who had a feel for religious Judaism. Mark Wischnitzer, "Der

Banayung phun Yeshivas in Mizrach Airope Noch der Ershter velt–Milchome,"
YIVO Bleter, vol. XXXI–XXXII (1948), p. 34.

71. *Yekapa oyf di Churvos phun Milchomes un Mehumes Pinkas phun Gegent Komitet Yekapa in Vilna 1919–1930* (Vilna, 1931), p. 699.

72. "1938 Digest of Data, Orthodox Higher Educational Institutions Supported by the Joint Distribution Committee Through the Central Relief Committee," Archives of the Central Relief Committee, Yeshiva University, New York City. (Hereafter called ACRC)

73. Bauer, *My Brother's Keeper*, pp. 29–33, 41–42, 305–306.

74. Among the yeshivot that conducted appeals abroad (outside the United States) were: Telz (South Africa), Radin (England), and Kletzk (England). See the articles on the individual yeshivot in Mirsky, *Mosdot*, pp. 182, 210, 234.

75. Among the yeshivot with offices in New York were Mir, Slabodka, Telz, Radin, Lomza, Kamenetz, and Kletzk. The *Sefer ha–Yovel* published in 1928 by *Agudat ha–Rabbanim* includes greetings from the American offices of these yeshivot. Invariably, the greetings praise the rabbinic association and thank it for its efforts on behalf of their yeshiva (with the implied hope that such efforts will continue). *Sefer ha–Yovel*, pp. 186–196.

76. Aaron Rothkoff, "The 1924 Visit of the Rabbinical Delegation to the United States," *Masmid*, 1959, pp. 122–125.

77. For details regarding these visits see the articles on the individual yeshivot in Mirsky, *Mosdot*, pp. 110–112, 154, 182, 219, 234, 301–302, 317–318, 400–401; Rothkoff, *Bernard Revel*, pp. 154–158.

78. The Mir Yeshiva, for example, received all its income during the initial nine months of 1938 from abroad. Seventy–four percent of the funds came from the United States, with two–thirds of that sum transmitted by the yeshiva's New York office. Wischnitzer, "Der Banayung," p. 33.

79. Epstein, "Yeshivat Mir," p. 112.

80. Rothkoff, *Bernard Revel*, pp. 119–125; *Sefer ha–Yovel*, p. 103, Rothkoff, "1924 Visit," pp. 122–125.

81. During the interwar period, students from America began to attend the famous European yeshivot. Approximately 30 Americans studied at Mir, and others studied at Slabodka, Telz, Grodno, Kamenetz, and Baranowitz. An indication of the significant "American presence" at Slabodka was the fact that the American consul in Lithuania attended the cornerstone-laying ceremony for a new building, which took place in 1932. See the articles on the individual yeshivot in Mirsky, *Mosdot*, pp. 107, 160–162; 302, 319, 334.

82. Gurock, "Resisters," pp. 100–187.

Chapter 2

The Establishment of the Emergency Committee for War-Torn Yeshivot

In the wake of the outbreak of World War II on September 1, 1939, and the subsequent Soviet invasion of Eastern Poland on September 17, 1939, the Polish[1] yeshivot were forced to confront a plethora of extremely serious problems which threatened their existence. Whereas before the war these institutions had suffered from chronic financial difficulties but had been allowed to function unhampered, the conquest of Poland by the Germans and the Soviets not only exacerbated their financial plight but, more important, jeopardized their *raison d'être*, the study of Torah, as well as their institutional existence. Almost all the major Polish yeshivot were located in the Kresy region of Eastern Poland, which had been occupied by the Soviets, whose inimical attitude toward Jewish religious and educational institutions was well-known. Several of the *roshei yeshiva* and many students had personally experienced life under the Communist regime during the period immediately following the end of World War I and had chosen to flee to independent Poland. Others were well aware of the systematic persecution of Jewish institutions by the Soviets. Needless to say, the situation of the yeshivot in the German-occupied zone was also terrible.

It was therefore obvious to many of the *roshei yeshiva* and yeshiva students that the days of the yeshivot in Poland were numbered.

23

The Orthodox journalist Shmuel Rotshtein described the mood prevalent in the yeshivot in the Soviet-occupied zone as follows:

> No one doubted that the Soviet regime would place its harsh hand on the source of the spiritual life, the yeshivot, just as it had done in Russia. The *roshei yeshiva* and students would be arrested and exiled—and what was to be the fate of the Torah? It was obvious that they must flee, that the yeshivot must be transferred to secure places.[2]

Yet while the dangers that existed in both the Soviet and Nazi-occupied zone of Poland were fairly obvious, the question of relocation was purely theoretical as long as there was no place readily accessible to which the *roshei yeshiva* could transfer their entire institutions. Thus the news that the city of Vilna (Vilnius) and its environs was to be handed over by the Soviets to the neutral republic of Lithuania[3] had a tremendous impact on the rabbis and yeshiva students in both sectors of occupied Poland, but especially in the Soviet zone, where the overwhelming majority of the major yeshivot were located and which bordered on Lithuania. The agreement between the Lithuanians and the Soviets was concluded on October 10, 1939, the announcement was broadcast on Kaunas radio on October 11,[4] and within a brief period, *behalat nesi'a* (travel frenzy) seized most of the student body of many of the yeshivot in Eastern Poland.[5] Hasty preparations were made for departure, with the students of the Kletzk Yeshiva (October 14)[6] and the Mir Yeshiva (October 15)[7] among the first to leave for Vilna.

Within days, hundreds of others joined the mass exodus to "Jerusalem of Lithuania," as Vilna was often called, where they hoped to be able to continue their studies and maintain their particular lifestyle. There was a sense of urgency about the flight, as initially there was no border to cross and transportation—albeit very congested—was still functioning, so it was at that point relatively easy to reach Vilna, which had still not been formally annexed. The Lithuanians entered Vilna on October 28; only in mid-November was the new border between Lithuania and Soviet-occupied Poland established and civilian traffic between the two areas halted.[8] By that time approximately 1,500–1,600 rabbis and yeshiva students, as well as the families of the *roshei yeshiva* and administrators, had arrived in Vilna as refugees, among them practically the entire student body and faculty of such leading yeshivot as Mir (approximately 300 students in Vilna), Kamenetz (about 200), Radin, Grodno, Bialystok and Slonim. Among the arrivals were such famous *roshei yeshiva* as Rabbis Aron Kotler (Kletzk), Eliezer Yehuda Finkel (Mir), Boruch Ber Leibowitz (Kamenetz), Elchanan Wasserman ("Ohel Torah" of Baranowitz), Avraham Yaphin ("Beit Yoseph" of Bialystok), and Shabtai Yogel (Slonim), as well as leading communal rabbis such as Rabbi Yitzchak Ze'ev Soloveitchik of Brisk.[9]

While the majority and the best known of the arrivals, as well as all the yeshivot which arrived more or less intact, were from Soviet-occupied Poland, mention should be made of the fact that rabbis and yeshiva students also reached Vilna from the German-occupied zone, from whence the journey to Lithuania was more perilous.[10] (Some of the students of the yeshivot in Eastern Poland were originally from communities in the Nazi-occupied zone and were at home when the war broke out, or went home following its outbreak, so they too reached Vilna from the German zone.)[11]

The decision made in the yeshivot to flee to Vilna, was taken independently in each institution; at this point there was no coordination among the various yeshivot. Moreover, even within the yeshivot there appears to have been little coordination. It was the students or groups of students—since they did not decide as one unit—rather than the *roshei yeshiva* who played the primary role in initiating this course of action. According to the testimonies of several of the individuals who fled to Vilna, almost identical developments occurred independently in practically every yeshiva. The news that Vilna was being turned over to Lithuania and that transportation still existed between Eastern Poland and Vilna galvanized the students into action.[12] They, in effect, dragged the rabbis and administrations with them, since factors such as age, outlook, status, and circumstances made the latter groups more conservative and less likely to undertake rapid or radical change. (Almost all the *roshei yeshiva* and administrators, for example, in contrast to their students, were married and had children.[13] Moreover, they had ultimate responsibility for the fate of the institutions, and that consideration was a deterrent against hasty action.)[14]

In addition, despite the obvious reasons for leaving the Soviet zone, there were those who doubted whether moving to Vilna would solve the problem. They were not certain that Lithuania would remain independent for long, an opinion reflected in popular jokes which circulated at the time in Eastern Poland: "Vilna has indeed been handed over to Kovno, but Kovno will soon be taken over by Moscow," or "Vilna does not belong to Lithuania, it's vice versa."[15] Others thought that the announcement regarding the turning over of Vilna to the Lithuanians was merely a Soviet ploy to discover those opposed to the Communist regime in order to deport them to Siberia,[16] and there were those who thought that Hitler would soon be defeated.[17]

Despite these factors and the difficulties in obtaining transportation to Vilna (the trains were extremely overcrowded),[18] most of the students viewed the return of Vilna to Lithuania as a fortuitous opportunity to escape Soviet rule, something that ought to be exploited as quickly as possible before the border was closed. In fact, some yeshiva students considered the matter so urgent that they traveled to Vilna on the Sabbath.[19]

The developments surrounding the decision to flee are significant because under normal circumstances yeshiva students do not play a role in determining yeshiva policy. It is the *roshei yeshiva* who decide crucial questions, and their decisions are binding vis-à-vis the students as well as the faculty. In this case the students came to the *roshei yeshiva* to inform them of their decision to go to Vilna and the "question" they posed was, in essence, rhetorical.[20] In effect, the students dragged their mentors along with them. The *roshei yeshiva* and the administration, whose major goal was to preserve their institutions intact, realized that in order to do so they would have to go to Vilna as well.[21] This decision was of critical importance, since it altered the normal course of events in these institutions and had far-reaching implications vis-à-vis the eventual rescue of a significant portion of the rabbis and yeshiva students.

* * *

The rabbis and yeshiva students who escaped to Vilna arrived in a city terribly overburdened with refugees. Thousands of Polish Jews, including hundreds of members of Zionist youth movements,[22] had likewise fled from occupied Poland to Vilna following the announcement of its impending incorporation into the Baltic republic, and they constituted only a fraction of the estimated 37,000–57,000 foreigners who had taken up residence in Lithuania by November 1939. Owen J. C. Norem, the senior diplomat at the American Legation in Kovno (Kaunas), described the plight of the newcomers and the need for relief as follows:

> People have emerged from the hiding places resembling animals in condition. Disease threatens to become of epidemic proportions and medical aid is necessary.... Lithuania has assumed a tremendous burden of relief with no immediate hope of assistance from any other country than the United States of America.... Long queues are still being formed outside the food supply depots, the stores and also the banks. The producer with goods remains wary and insists on bartering for the time being. It is reminiscent of the postwar era when a pair of boots commanded 40 eggs and 2 pounds of butter, etc.[23]

Thus the situation of the refugees did not look promising. Moreover, practically all the rabbis and yeshiva students who escaped to Vilna arrived penniless[24] and were forced to seek assistance for food, housing, and clothing from local Jewish sources. The address they turned to upon their arrival was that of the local *Vaad ha-Yeshivot,* headed by the venerable sage Rabbi Chaim Ozer Grodzinski, the world-renowned leader of Orthodox Jewry and the leading rabbinic figure in Vilna. It was only natural that the rabbis and students should turn to Rabbi Grodzinski and the *Vaad ha-Yeshivot,* because throughout the interwar period the *Vaad* had played a major role in funding the yeshivot of Eastern Poland and had served as the major agency for the distribution of financial aid from abroad from such organizations as the Central Relief Committee.[25] Rabbi Grodzinski, in particular, was known for his devotion to, and energetic efforts on behalf of, the Torah institutions and was considered to be among the major spiritual and financial patrons of the Polish and Lithuanian yeshivot.[26] In fact, it is highly likely that his presence in Vilna was a factor in the decisions of the rabbis and students to flee there, since they knew they could count on his assistance.[27]

The task of providing for the physical needs of the refugee rabbis and yeshiva students was enormous and became increasingly difficult as more and more refugees arrived in Vilna. Rabbi Grodzinski and his helpers made extensive efforts to feed, house, and clothe the rabbis and students and enable them to resume their studies, but the needs were obviously beyond their limited resources. A visitor to Vilna who was there several days after the city was annexed to Lithuania described the plight of the refugee rabbis and students as follows:

> Their quarters are in small, unheated synagogues. At times there are fifty men sleeping together on hard benches and floors, not having removed their clothes for weeks and months. Nevertheless they study all day with the same enthusiasm as though nothing had happened.
>
> While they learn it seems that they are not at all aware of their troubles, poverty, cold and hunger.... Shrunken, pale and starved they study as always and more.[28]

Thus it was clear to those involved in the effort to provide for the refugee scholars that massive aid would have to come from abroad. Under those circumstances, the most logical address to turn to was those Orthodox circles in the United States who had borne the major burden of supporting Torah education in Eastern Europe throughout the interwar period: the leadership of *Agudat ha-Rabbanim*, the Central Relief Committee, and *Ezrat Torah*. In fact, even before the Russian invasion of Poland (and well before the large influx of refugee rabbis and yeshiva students to Vilna), Rabbi Grodzinski had turned to his former student Rabbi Eliezer Silver of Cincinnati, one of the leading Orthodox rabbis in the United States and a member of the presidium of the *Agudat ha-Rabbanim*,[29] and appealed to him for financial aid for the refugee rabbis and students who had reached Vilna.[30]

As time went by, however, and the number of rabbis and students reaching Vilna increased significantly, the appeals to Orthodox leaders abroad,[31] and especially in America, became more frequent and more urgent. Once the massive influx of refugees began arriving in Vilna, it became increasingly clear that extremely large sums of aid would be required to deal with this emergency. In numerous cables, Rabbi Grodzinski, his co-workers, and other rabbis urgently called upon the leaders of the Orthodox relief agencies to send financial aid. Thus, for example, on November 5, 1939, Rabbi Grodzinski cabled the Central Relief Committee in New York City:

Here com jeshivos Mir Kamenec Kleck Brisk Radun Grodno Baranowicz Wolozin Lomza Pinsk Bialystok Mazevic Slonim Ostrow Ostrug moze [sic] sixteen hundred students many instructions [sic] families many rabbis families live in awful nuhuman [sic]= economic conditions. Help urgent.[32]

The message was clear, the needs were obvious, and it was a well-known fact that those to whom the appeal had been addressed were anxious to be of assistance. The question was whether they would be able to provide the necessary sums.

The rabbinic leadership of American Orthodoxy had closely followed the developments in Eastern Europe after the outbreak of World War II, and even before the initial appeals for aid had come from Europe, they called upon the public to contribute funds to help the beleaguered yeshivot. Thus, as early as September 8, 1939, *Agudat ha-Rabbanim* published two appeals for aid in the Jewish press—one for contributions to alleviate the plight of the Jews in the areas affected by the war, and another for funds to help rescue the yeshivot in those areas.[33] Shortly thereafter, an emergency meeting of the executive committee of the *Agudat ha-Rabbanim* was convened in New York to attempt to take specific measures to help the yeshivot.

Besides the leading members of *Agudat ha-Rabbanim*, those in attendance included the New York representatives of the major Polish yeshivot as well as Rabbi Yechiel Mordechai Gordon, the *rosh yeshiva* of the Lomza Yeshiva, who happened to be on a fundraising mission in the United States when war broke out. No record of discussions at the meeting exists, but apparently the major problem on the agenda was to convince the public that the yeshivot were continuing to function—that they had not been disbanded as a result of the war and that they were in acute need of material aid. The rabbis at the meeting therefore issued the following public appeal:

The latest dispatches from the Sage of our time, Rabbi Hayim Ozer of Vilna, report that the Yeshivot continue to exist. In all the history of the Jewish people our Holy Torah has demonstrated wonderful qualities of endurance, continuing to exist besides all hindrances, despite all harsh decrees. We are convinced that in these trying times too, the bastions of the Torah under the leadership of the Torah hero, the teachers who have shown much self-sacrifice and devotion, will continue to exist in their present locations or be transferred to more secure places. In any case, the rescue of the Yeshivot will demand tremendous material means and considerable financial assistance. It is incumbent upon us to offer speedy aid to the Yeshivot at their first call.[34]

It is not clear what the public response to this appeal was, but as the situation in Poland continued to deteriorate, and in view of the announcement that Vilna was to be handed over by the Russians to the Lithuanians, the leadership of *Agudat ha-Rabbanim* decided to take special steps to assist the major Polish yeshivot. Thus on October 17, 1939, the executive committee met again to discuss the plight of the yeshivot and decided to establish a special organization for the rescue of rabbis and yeshiva students and to launch a national campaign to raise funds for this specialized rescue work. The official announcement, it was decided, would be made at an emergency conference of *Agudat ha-Rabbanim* to be held in New York on November 13–14, 1939, which would also serve as the rabbinic association's semiannual convention.

Hundreds of rabbis attended the emergency meeting in New York.[35] Rabbi Eliezer Silver of Cincinnati played a major role in organizing the convention and he was chosen to deliver the opening address. A leading spokesman for American Orthodoxy and a noted talmudic scholar, Silver had played a prominent role in *Agudat ha-Rabbanim* for many years. In his remarks, he noted that no date had been set for *Agudat ha-Rabbanim*'s semiannual conference but, in view of the plight of European Jewry, it was decided to convene the rabbis as soon as possible so that the rabbinic association could take concrete action to alleviate the situation. In Rabbi Silver's opinion, while the Orthodox rabbis had to help the Joint Distribution Committee expand its relief work overseas, they had a particular obligation to establish a special fund to save the yeshivot, which he referred to as our "columns of support" and which fulfill a special role in the Jewish world.

On a practical level, he suggested sending an emissary to meet with the leading rabbis and *roshei yeshiva* and especially with Rabbi Grodzinski in order to ascertain the specific needs of the yeshivot, and he raised the possibility of establishing a Yeshiva-in-Exile (modeled after the recently founded University-in-Exile). Other speakers at the convention were Rabbi Yisrael ha-Levi Rosenberg, who was a leading figure in *Agudat ha-Rabbanim* (he served as president, chairman of the presidency, or honorary president of the rabbinic association for almost three decades) and was the founder and president of *Ezrat Torah*;[36] Rabbi Joseph Soloveitchik of Boston, a noted talmudic scholar who was later to head the Rabbi Isaac Elchanan Theological Seminary of Yeshiva University and was scion of one of Eastern Europe's most distinguished rabbinic families;[37] and Rabbi Aaron Teitelbaum of the Central Relief Committee.[38]

The rabbis assembled decided to establish a special fund to rescue the yeshivot and, upon Rabbi Rosenberg's suggestion, unanimously elected Rabbi Eliezer Silver to head the new project, which was to be called the "Emergency Committee for War-Torn Yeshivot." Other officers were:

Honorary chairmen:
    Rabbi Yisrael Halevi Rosenberg
    Rabbi Bernard (Dov Ber) Levinthal
Vice-presidents:
New York area:
    Rabbis Rosen, Seltzer and Karlinsky
Outside New York:
    Rabbis Joseph Solovietchik (Boston),
    Natolevich (Louisville),
    Efraim Epstein (Chicago) and
    Professor Nathan Isaacs (Boston)
Executive Committee:
    Rabbi Yechiel Mordechai Gordon
Rabbis:

Dushevitz	Faivelson	Chaim Epstein
Levinson	Teitelbaum	Razin
Zalmanowitz	Charlap	Olschwang
Dachowitz	Scheinkopf	Falkowitz
Bloch	Shraga	Rosenberg

Treasurers:
    Israel Rosenberg and Hirsh Manishewitz
Publicity Committee:
    Rabbis Pardes, Yosher, Levitch, Reichman,
    Kaplan and Altusky.[39]

The convention concluded with the adoption of the following resolutions:

1.   The convention lays stress upon the great and worthy tasks of the Central Relief and Joint Distribution Committee to whom millions of our brethren, sufferers from the World War of 1914 owe their very lives and existence, and for whose aid millions of troubled, tormented and persecuted are waiting. The convention requests of American Jewry that it should fulfill its duty toward its greatest and noblest world philanthropic organization.

2.   In the olden days of the destruction of the Temple, Rabbi Johanan ben Zakkai pleaded for the great Academy of Yavneh and her scholars because he believed that the Torah was the Jewish citadel. In the tragedy that has befallen our people at the present day when complete destruction threatens the very life of the Jewish people, it should be our sacred duty to save our Yavnehs of today—the Holy Yeshivoth—in which the only salvation of Judaism and Jewish life lies. The convention, therefore, resolves to launch a national campaign for the War-Torn Yeshivoth.

3.   The task of the campaign shall be the salvation of the great Yeshivoth which this war has uprooted from their sites, whose faculties and student bodies (approximately 4,000 bearers of the Light of Learning) are today refugees in Vilna, inadequately clad against the rigors of Winter, starving and exhausted. They are to receive immediate attention to reorganize and to assure their continued existence under proper and permanent conditions.

4.   The two months of Tebet and Shebat of this year 5700 (December 13, 1939 to February 9, 1940) are designated for the campaign amongst the Jewry of America.

5.   A two-week period will be proclaimed in Greater New York to be dedicated to the proper execution of the above-mentioned campaign.

6.   A duty shall be imposed upon the Rabbis throughout the land to devote themselves wholeheartedly to the services of the above-mentioned campaign: each to devote not less than two weeks to act as members in the various delegations, visit cities, appeal in synagogues, and visit individual philanthropists.

A list has already been compiled of more than 150 rabbis who have, during the convention, offered freely of their services to the campaign.

7.   It has been decided to send a special delegation to Vilna to consult Rabbi Ch. O. Grodzinski and the Deans of the various Yeshivoth which refuge there and to discuss ways and means for the reconstruction and further maintenance of the Yeshivoth.

8.   The convention wishes to remind everyone of the duty which he must fulfill toward: the great Yeshivoth of Europe which, by grace of G-d, have been able to remain at their sites and whose needs have now been multiplied: towards the seats of Torah here in America and toward the holy places of learning in Eretz Israel which are facing very difficult times.

9.   A duty is imposed upon every rabbi to lecture from the pulpit concerning the tragic status of the Jewish people, to arouse his congregants to penance and to strengthen in every Jew his ties to the law, the Torah and the People of Israel.[40]

On November 15, 1939, the day after the conclusion of the convention, Rabbi Eliezer Silver opened an office of the Emergency Committee for War-Torn Yeshivoth at 673 Broadway, New York City—the same address as the *Agudat ha-Rabbanim*—and thus the rescue committee which eventually became known as the *Vaad ha-Hatzala* (or *Vaad Hatzala*) began operation.[41] During its initial months Orthodox rabbis all over the United States began to raise funds, and the Sabbaths of January 6, 13, and 20, 1940, were designated for special fundraising appeals on behalf of the *Vaad*.[42]

Although the establishment of a separate fund for the rescue of the refugee rabbis and yeshiva students was ostensibly a logical step for *Agudat ha-Rabbanim* to take in view of its special interest in their fate, the decision to found *Vaad ha-Hatzala* and the *Vaad's* initial activities aroused considerable controversy in the Jewish community and were greeted with a certain degree of skepticism even within Orthodox circles. The opposition in the general Jewish community stemmed from the fact that the establishment of the *Vaad* undermined the recently achieved unity in fundraising efforts and was based on priorities that were not universally accepted by the Jewish community. The skepticism among the Orthodox was the result of doubts as to whether the establishment of a new fundraising agency was justified in view of the existence of the Central Relief

Committee and *Ezrat Torah*. These questions and the *Vaad's* respons-es to them deserve further scrutiny, since they afford us important insight into the *Weltanschauung* of the leadership of all Jewish fundraising agencies and allow us to focus on the major issues of contention, which were seriously to hamper relations among vari-ous segments of American Jewry throughout the period of the Holocaust.

After several short-lived attempts to combine into one unified campaign the fundraising efforts of the American Jewish communi-ty's major agencies involved in overseas and domestic relief (Joint Distribution Committee, United Palestine Appeal, and the National Coordinating Committee for Aid to Refugees and Emigrants Coming from Germany [NCCR]), unity was finally achieved on January 10, 1939, with the establishment of the United Jewish Appeal. The impetus for this development were the events of *Kristallnacht* (Night of the Broken Glass), November 9–10, 1938, and Goering's subsequent demand that German Jewry pay an indemni-ty of one billion marks to the Nazi authorities for the damages wrought in that pogrom. The establishment of the United Jewish Appeal assured a unified communal fundraising response and a min-imum of duplication, a positive development in view of the increased needs of Jews in distress the world over, and particularly in war-torn Europe. Thus upon the outbreak of World War II the American Jewish community had a unified fundraising mechanism and a clear-cut division of labor among its major relief agencies. The Joint dealt with overseas relief throughout the Diaspora, the United Palestine Appeal handled aid to the Jewish community in Eretz Yisrael (Palestine), and the National Refugee Service (formerly called the NCCR) cared for the needs of the refugees entering the United States.

This framework proved fairly successful during its initial year of operation, raising more than $16 million, a sum considerably higher than the projected total for the three agencies had they conducted independent campaigns. Thus despite various differences of opinion regarding allocation, the 1939 agreement was renewed, with minor changes. In fact, in November 1939 the Council of Jewish Federations and Welfare Funds, which had played an instrumental role in achieving unity among the three major relief agencies, urged the United Jewish Appeal to expand and incorporate ORT (Organization for Rehabilitation through Training, which specialized in vocational training), HIAS (Hebrew Immigrant Aid Society, which assisted Jews seeking to emigrate to places other than Palestine), and JTA (Jewish Telegraphic Agency), each of which had been conducting independent fundraising campaign.[43]

It is against this background that the establishment of the *Vaad ha-Hatzala* as a separate campaign for overseas relief must be examined. The choice the rabbis faced was the following. They could either abide by the arrangement then in effect, whereby fundraising within the American Jewish community was unified and all overseas relief, including assistance to rabbis and yeshiva students, was handled by the JDC; or they could create a special framework and launch a separate fundraising campaign solely for the needs of the yeshivot and the rabbis. The leadership of the *Agudat ha-Rabbanim*, while cognizant of the problematic aspects of bolting the unified fundraising framework, chose the latter course of action, a choice predicated by several factors operating on various levels.

On an ideological level, the rabbis of *Agudat ha-Rabbanim* were absolutely convinced that the entire future of the Jewish people was dependent on the continuation of the study of Torah—hence the enormous significance they attributed to the survival of the yeshivot, which they viewed as the fortresses of the age-old legacy of Torah scholarship. Thus in his keynote address at the convention, Rabbi Silver explained the need for establishing the *Vaad* by stating that the yeshivot were Judaism's "columns of support,"[44] and in a speech delivered shortly thereafter in Chicago he referred to them as the *"kiyum"* (very existence) of the Jewish people.[45] The great importance attributed by the rabbis to the study of Torah, it should be noted, was rooted in the religious obligation of each Jew to engage in Torah study on a daily basis. The fact that what might appear on the surface to be a purely intellectual pursuit has a strong religious component lends it a special sense of urgency and immediacy[46] and helps explain why the rescue of the rabbis and yeshiva students of Europe's premier Torah institutions was accorded top priority by the leaders of the *Agudat ha-Rabbanim*.

Moreover, their religious outlook made it difficult for the Orthodox rabbis to accept the leadership of the JDC on an issue of such cardinal importance for them. If they had chosen to continue to abide by the arrangement whereby all overseas relief was allocated and administered by the JDC, then the fate of Europe's leading rabbis and yeshiva students would in effect have been decided to a large extent by non-Orthodox Jews who might have a modicum of respect for Jewish tradition but whose *Weltanschauung* and lifestyle were worlds apart from that of the Torah scholars. How could Orthodox rabbis defer on such important questions to Reform Jews whose lifestyle was the antithesis of Orthodox practice and whose goal of full acculturation into American society was in many respects anathema to their core beliefs? And while it was true that the Central Relief Committee was a component of the JDC and that various Orthodox leaders were members of the Joint's Cultural Committee,[47] which extended support to Orthodox educational institutions, the fact remained that the leadership of the Joint Distribution Committee was composed primarily of the German Jewish "aristocrats" whose understanding and appreciation of Torah scholarship were hardly on a level that the East European-born and -bred leadership of *Agudat ha-Rabbanim* could respect.[48] Thus while they understood the importance of the JDC's work, they opted for their own particularistic rescue operation designed to save the yeshivot.

The conceptual framework for this course of action was clearly formulated in the initial two resolutions passed at the *Agudat ha-Rabbanim* convention. They stressed the importance of the Joint's activities and called upon American Jewry to support the philanthropic organization financially, yet at the same time noted American Jewry's "sacred duty" to save the yeshivot which were the "very life of the Jewish people" and announced the establishment of a special campaign for that purpose.[49] Rabbi Silver also stressed this approach in a fundraising appeal in Chicago shortly after the establishment of the *Vaad*. The JDC's activities, he noted, could be classified as "*mamash pikuach nefesh*" (truly a matter of the rescue of lives), but the yeshivot were the *kiyum* of the Jewish people and hence the decision to undertake a separate fundraising campaign.[50]

On a practical level, there were also reasons which in the rabbis' minds justified the establishment of the *Vaad*. It was common belief among the members of *Agudat ha-Rabbanim* that rabbis and yeshiva students would only feel comfortable turning to an organization such as *Vaad ha-Hatzala*, whose operations were especially designed to suit the needs of that population.[51] This was a traditional Orthodox argument and, in fact, was one of the major reasons for the establishment of *Ezrat Torah* in World War I. The rabbis apparently did not want their colleagues, or the yeshiva students, to be forced to turn to general soup kitchens and thereby face the unpleasant prospect of losing their standing in the community.[52] The establishment of a rescue fund whose specific goal was to assist rabbis and yeshiva students would, it was probably assumed, have the opposite effect.

Another factor to take into account is the personal ties between the leadership of the *Agudat ha-Rabbanim* and the rabbis and *roshei yeshiva* in Europe. As was noted above, almost all the members of the American rabbinic association had studied in East European yeshivot, in most cases in those yeshivot that had escaped to Vilna. Many of the American rabbis were personally acquainted with many of the refugee rabbis and *roshei yeshiva,* having studied either under or with them or having met them when the latter had visited the United States,[53] and consequently the degree of involvement and obligation felt by the members of *Agudat ha-Rabbanim* was far greater than if these refugees had been unknown to them. The fact, moreover, that the appeals for help had come from Rabbi Chaim Ozer Grodzinski, whose preeminence in the Orthodox world was unquestioned, added to the motivation to take concrete action.[54] Thus when faced with the decision of entrusting their colleagues' fate to the JDC or founding a separate rescue campaign controlled by the *Agudat ha-Rabbanim*, the American Orthodox rabbis opted for the latter. Thus ideological, practical, and personal factors combined to convince the rabbis to leave the unified community framework and choose financial and operational independence.

On an internal level, within the Orthodox world and the ranks of the *Agudat ha-Rabbanim,* the considerations regarding this decision were different. The choice the rabbis faced was whether to use the existing Orthodox framework, in this case *Ezrat Torah,* or to create a new mechanism. There was no ideological conflict involved, nor was there any dispute regarding practical aspects of the problem and the possible means of solution. What was involved was indeed a practical problem, but not in the same sense as the factors that mitigated against continuing within the framework of the JDC. The question was whether *Ezrat Torah* would be able to undertake what appeared destined to become a large-scale operation. The opinion of most of the rabbis was negative. They viewed *Ezrat Torah* as a small-scale organization which was unsuited for the task at hand because it lacked the necessary funds, means, and manpower to tackle a problem of this magnitude.

In the words of a member of *Agudat ha-Rabbanim* acquainted with the workings of the various Orthodox organizations, *Ezrat Torah* "thought in terms of $5 not $1,000." Therefore the rabbis voted to establish a special relief agency to rescue the yeshivot.[55] It should be noted, however, that there were rabbis who initially questioned the wisdom of such a course of action and were skeptical about the establishment of the emergency committee. For example, Rabbi Yisrael Halevi Rosenberg, who was the founder and president of *Ezrat Torah*, was initially hesitant about taking such a step.[56] On the other hand, it stands to reason that in his case there was a personal element to his opposition. As the primary force behind *Ezrat Torah* for many years, he was probably inclined to view it, despite its limitations, as the most suitable organization to which to entrust the task of rescuing the yeshivot. Thus his ultimate support for the establishment of the *Vaad* and his proposal that Rabbi Silver head it were of considerable significance, since they underlined the united position of the leading figures in American Orthodoxy on this issue.

In that context, an additional element must be considered: the personal factor, specifically the role of Rabbi Eliezer Silver. It was the Cincinnati rabbi who led the campaign to establish the Emergency Committee as a separate agency for the rescue of the yeshivot, and it was he who was chosen by the members of *Agudat ha-Rabbanim* to head the nascent organization. Rabbi Silver was known for his profound Torah scholarship, intensive involvement in Jewish communal affairs, and fiery personality, and thus he appeared to be a suitable choice to head an emergency campaign of this sort. The question remains, however, whether it was necessary to establish a separate framework for the rescue of the yeshivot. Perhaps the same results could have been achieved had Rabbi Silver and those chosen to head the new organization devoted themselves to working on behalf of *Ezrat Torah*.

It may be that Rabbi Silver's zeal in pressing for the establishment of the Emergency Committee was to a certain extent predicated upon his desire to head the special rescue efforts. As a person who rarely if ever shied away from a challenge and was always willing to fight for what he considered to be a just cause, he possibly viewed the circumstances of the rabbis and yeshiva students in Vilna as a unique opportunity to perform a vitally important task for the cause of Orthodox Judaism, even if doing so meant bolting the communal fundraising framework. Silver, moreover, had ambition and may have viewed the crisis as an opportunity to display his leadership and strengthen his position within the community. On a practical level, it might have proven difficult for Rabbi Silver, an avowed individualist who had considerable charisma and was an excellent fundraiser, to subordinate himself to Rabbi Eliyahu Henkin, the executive secretary of *Ezrat Torah*. While the latter was universally respected for his scholarship and piety, he was extremely reticent, a trait hardly condusive to running the type of large-scale campaign envisioned by the leadership of *Agudat ha-Rabbanim*.[57] It should also be noted that Rabbi Yechiel Gordon of the Lomza Yeshiva, the only *rosh yeshiva* from a yeshiva that had escaped to Vilna, was in the United States at the time; his involvement in the preliminary discussions leading to the establishment of the Emergency Committee, and his agreeing to serve in a key position (chairman of the executive committee under Rabbi Silver), lent additional support for this critical step.[58]

One additional factor should be noted in connection with the decision to opt for an independent framework. It is not entirely clear whether those who decided to launch this special campaign had any idea that it would develop into a full-fledged relief organization which would eventually play an active role in general rescue work beyond the rescue of rabbis and yeshiva students, and would compete with the JDC for the charity dollars of American Jewry. It appears that the founders of the *Vaad* had no such intention and that the subsequent developments were more a product of circumstance than of long-range planning. For example, Rabbi Wasserman of *Vaad ha-Hatzala* wrote on December 19, 1939, to Abraham Horowitz of the Central Relief Committee that the Emergency Committee had been organized to deal with a specific emergency and that the campaign launched was "one-time" and designed for the specific purpose of arranging the relocation of the yeshivot, a task that was too great for the "overburdened" resources of the JDC.[59]

Of course there is always the possibility that the heads of the *Vaad* were hiding their true intentions—particularly if they really aspired to establish a rival organization—and that letters of this sort were designed to minimize the opposition of the Joint and of Central Relief; however, it seems clear that the rabbis did not harbor any grandiose plans. The issue foremost in their minds was the task at hand, and they sought to take whatever steps they considered necessary to achieve their goal. They were aware of the negative aspects of the course they had chosen and took, or at least planned to take, measures designed to minimize the damage to the unified community fundraising campaign,[60] but the key issue remained the immediate question of the rescue of the yeshivot. Under those circumstances, all the factors combined to produce the decision of the *Agudat ha-Rabbanim* to establish the Emergency Committee for War-Torn Yeshivot.

Notes

1. These events did not affect the yeshivot in Lithuania, which maintained its neutrality during this period (until it was occupied by the Soviets in June 1940) and was not adversely affected by the outbreak of hostilities.
2. Aaron Sursky, ed., *Achiezer: Kovetz Igrot, Pirkei Chayim* (Bnei Brak, 5730-1970), p. 724.
3. According to the terms of the Soviet–Lithuanian agreement signed on July 12, 1920, Vilna and its environs were supposed to be part of the republic of Lithuania. The Poles, however, captured the area in the course of the Polish–Lithuanian war in 1920 and refused to return it to the Lithuanians, who throughout the interwar period continued to press their claim to their historic capital. Yitzhak Arad, *Vilna ha–Yehudit be–Ma'avak ve–Kilayon* (Jerusalem and Tel-Aviv, 1976), pp. 15–16. In return for Vilna, the Russians demanded and received the right to station 25,000 troops in Lithuania. See Owen J. C. Norem, *Timeless Lithuania* (Chicago, 1943), pp. 160–172.
4. Leonas Sabaliunas, *Lithuanian Crisis: Nationalism to Communism 1939–1940* (Bloomington and London, 1972), p. 153. According to other sources, the announcement was made two days earlier. See Elchanan Herzman, *Mofait ha–Dor* (Jerusalem, 1976), p. 39, and interview by the author with Rabbi Yaakov Nayman, July 26, 1977.
5. See, for example, Yoseph Epstein, "Yeshivat Mir," in Samuel K. Minsky, ed., *Mosdot ha-Torah be-Airopa be-Binyanam u-ve-Churbanam* (New York, 1956), pp. 116–117, which describes the conditions and atmosphere at the Mir Yeshiva following the outbreak of World War II.
6. Hillel Zeidman, "Yeshiva 'Etz Chaim' de Kletzk," in Mirsky, *Mosdot*, p. 238.
7. Epstein, "Yeshivat Mir," p. 117.
8. Yitzhak Arad, "Concentration of Refugees in Vilna on the Eve of the Holocaust," *Yad Vashem Studies*, IX (Jerusalem, 1973) (hereafter called Arad/YVS), pp. 201–206.
9. Cables of Rabbi Chaim Ozer Grodzinski (November 5, 1939) and Rabbi Yoseph Shub (November 6, 1939) to Central Relief Committee, ACRC; letter of Rabbi Eliyahu Bloch to Rabbi Moshe Blau, November 16, 1939, Archives of Merkaz Agudat Yisrael be–Eretz Yisrael (hereafter called AAYEY), file 62; letter of Y. Zacks to Rabbi Moshe Blau, November 17, 1939, AAYEY, file 62.
10. See, for example, the testimonies of Rabbi Abraham Nadelman and Motel Grajer, Archives of the Wiener Library (hereafter called AWL), Box 532, files 27, 32. These testimonies were recorded in Vilna by a special committee of refugee jour-

nalists and writers, mostly from Warsaw, who sought to record and report on the atrocities committed by the Nazis in Poland. See their letter to Moses Beckelman, March 20, 1940, AWL, Box 532.

11. See, for example, the testimonies of Yankel Forrajter and Leizer Gottleib, AWL, Box 532, files 12, 28.

12. Interviews by the author with Rabbi Asher Czeczyk (Radin Yeshiva), July 5, 1977; Rabbi Yaakov Nayman (Baranowitz Kollel), July 26, 1977; Rabbi Zelig Epstein (Mir Yeshiva), July 7, 1977; Rabbi Moshe Cohen (Kletzk Yeshiva), Yad Vashem Archives (hereafter called YVA), 0–3,3856; Herzman, *Mofait ha–Dor*, p. 39; "Be–Yemei Sufa" (the diary of Rabbi Yitzhak Edelstein), *Gal–ed*, 3 (1976), p. 329.

13. This is evident from the lists of rabbis and yeshiva students for whom *Vaad ha–Hatzala* attempted to obtain visas to the United States. These lists are in the archives of the *Vaad*, Yeshiva University (hereafter called AVH), not arranged by file at the time of access, and in the archives of the Central Relief Committee, ACRC, file 492–2.

14. Interview of the author with Rabbi Yoseph David Epstein (secretary of the *rosh yeshiva* of the Mir Yeshiva), November 26, 1984.

15. "Be–Yemei Sufa," p. 329.

16. Herzman, *Mofait ha–Dor*, p. 39.

17. According to Rabbi Yoseph David Epstein, immediately after the war broke out, one of the *gedolim* (renowned Torah sages) had said that on the basis of his interpretation of a specific verse (Rabbi Epstein did not specify the sage or the verse), he believed that Hitler would fall by himself in the near future. Interview of the author with Rabbi Epstein, November 26, 1984.

18. Interview of the author with Rabbi Zalman Ury, November 27, 1978; "Be–Yemei Sufa," p. 330.

19. Ibid.

20. Epstein, "Yeshiva Mir," p. 117; Herzman, *Mofait ha–Dor*, pp. 39–40; "Be–Yemei Sufa," p. 326; Rabbi Zelig Epstein, "Yeshivat Sha'ar ha–Torah be–Grodno," in Mirsky, *Mosdot*, p. 303; interview with Rabbi Moshe Cohen, YVA, 0–3/3856; interview with Rabbi Asher Czeczyk; M. Weisbord, "Bein ha–Meitzarim, *Sefer Zikaron le–Kehillat Lomza* (Tel–Aviv, 1952), pp. 83–84.

21. Interview with Rabbi Yoseph David Epstein, November 26, 1984. There was one exception to the scenario described in the text. In the Kamenetz Yeshiva, it was the *rosh yeshiva*, Rabbi Baruch Ber Leibowitz, who initiated and encouraged the escape to Vilna. See Yitzhak Edelstein, *Rabbi Baruch Ber Leibowitz* (Tel–Aviv, 1957), p. 46.

22. Letter of Zerach Warhaftig to the Jewish Agency, November 10, 1939, Central Zionist Archives (hereafter called CZA), S–26/1300; Arad/YVS, p. 203.

23. "The Relief Problem in Lithuania and Vilna Territory," report of Owen Norem to the Secretary of State, November 10, 1939, National Archives of the United States (hereafter called NA), 840.48 Refugees, 860 m. 48/27.

24. Letter of Rabbi Elchanan Wasserman to Moshe Blau, November 1, 1939, quoted in Netanel Katzburg Ed., *Pedut: Hatzala be–Yemei ha–Shoa: Mekorot u–Mechkarim* (Ramat–Gan, 1984), p. 16.

25. See for example the proposed budget of the *Vaad ha–Yeshivot* for the years 1937–1938 and 1938–1939, ACRC, file 380–4; Sursky, *Achiezer*, pp. 672–676.

26. Abundant evidence regarding the prominent role played by Rabbi Grodzinski

(1863–1940) in Orthodox life and his efforts on behalf of the yeshivot may be found in the collection of his letters regarding halachic and especially communal affairs. Sursky, *Achiezer*, pp. 111–232, 645–736.

27. Efraim Zuroff, "Rescue Via the Far East: The Attempt to Save Polish Rabbis and Yeshiva Students," *Simon Wiesenthal Center Annual*, 1, (Chappaqua, 1984), p. 173; Zerach Warhaftig, *Palit ve–Sarid be–Yemei ha–Shoa* (Jerusalem, 1984), p. 31.

28. "Report About The Conditions Of The Refugee Yeshivoth In Vilna," Archives of the American Jewish Historical Society, Brandeis University, Papers of the Council of Jewish Federations and Welfare Funds (hereafter called ACJFWF), I–69, Box 149.

29. For details on the prominent role played by Rabbi Eliezer Silver (1881–1968) in Orthodox life in America, see Aaron Rakeffet–Rothkoff, *The Silver Era in American Jewish Orthodoxy: Rabbi Eliezer Silver and his Generation* (Jerusalem and New York, 1981); Aaron Shurin, *Keshet Giborim* (Jerusalem, 1964), p. 207.

30. Rabbi Silver received Rabbi Grodzinski's appeal on September 14, 1939. Eliezer Silver, "Jewish Rescue Work in Our Time," in *Churbn un Rettung* (New York, 1957) (hereafter called Silver – VH), p. 21. This book is the official history of *Vaad ha–Hatzala* and its publication was commissioned by the rescue organization.

31. Appeals for aid were also addressed to Orthodox leaders in Eretz Yisrael. Cable of Rabbi Eliyahu Bloch to Agudat Yisrael (Jerusalem), November 9, 1939, AAYEY, file 62.

32. Cable of Rabbi Grodzinski to Central Relief, November 5, 1939, ACRC.

33. *Churbn un Rettung*, p. 153.

34. Silver–VH, pp. 21–22.

35. Ibid.

36. Shurin, *Keshet Giborim*, p. 259; *Encyclopedia Judaica*, vol. 14, p. 278.

37. Rothkoff, *Bernard Revel; Builder of American Jewish Orthodoxy* (Philadelphia, 1972), pp. 128–129.

38. Asher Z. Rand, ed., *Toldot Anshei Shem*, (New York, 1959), pp. 55–57.

39. "Vi'eeda Chatzi–Shnatit Shel Agudat ha–Rabbanim," *Ha–Pardes*, 13, no. 9 (Kislev 5700/December 1939), pp. 4–9. To the best of our knowledge, there is no official protocol of the convention at which *Vaad ha–Hatzala* was established, and thus we must rely on the convention resolutions, reports in the press, and the testimony of the participants for details on the events.

40. "The Resolutions of the Agudath Harabonim Convention," ACJFWF, I–69, box 149.

41. "Vi'eeda Chatzi–Shnatit Shel Agudat ha–Rabbanim," *Ha–Pardes*, 13, no. 9 (Kislev 5700/December 1939), p. 9; letter of Rabbi Simcha Wasserman to Abraham Horowitz, December 19, 1939, ACJFWF, I–69, box 149.

42. Fundraising appeals for *Vaad ha–Hatzala* were conducted in the following cities and states: Baltimore, Boston, Cleveland, Detroit, Indianapolis, New York, Philadelphia, Scranton, Washington, DC, California, Florida and Texas. "Avodat Vaad ha–Hatzala," *Ha–Pardes*, 13, no. 10 (Tevet 5700/January 1940), p. 8.

43. Marc Lee Raphael, "From Separation to Community: The Origins of the United Jewish Appeal," *Forum*, no. 37 (Spring 1980), pp. 61–65; and by the same author, *A History of the United Jewish Appeal 1939–1982* (Providence, 1982), pp. 1–11.

44. "Ve'eeda Chatzi-Shnatit Shel Agudat ha–Rabbanim," *Ha–Pardes*, 13, no. 9

(Kislev 5700/December 1939), 6.
45. "Vaad ha–Hatzala la–Yeshivot be–Airopa," *Ha–Pardes*, 13, no. 10 (Tevet 5700/January 1940), p. 4.
46. For a concise explanation of the religious component of Torah study, see *The World of the Yeshiva*, p. 116.
47. Rabbi Dr. Leo Jung was one of the Orthodox members of the JDC's Cultural Committee and became its chairman in 1941. Other Orthodox Jews who served on the committee were Rabbi Aaron Teitelbaum, Herman Hollander, and Peter Wiernik. See Jung's autobiography, *The Path of a Pioneer*, p. 171; Herman Hollander, *My Life and What I Did with It* (Jerusalem, 1979), p. 55.
48. For biographical data on the leaders of the JDC see Yehuda Bauer, *My Brother's Keeper: A History of the American Jewish Joint Distribution Committee 1929–1939* (Philadelphia, 1974), pp. 19–22.
49. "The Resolutions of the Agudath Harabonim Convention," ACJFWF, I–69, Box 149.
50. "Vaad ha–Hatzala la–Yeshivot be–Airopa," *Ha–Pardes*, 13, no. 10 (Tevet 5700/January 1940), p. 4.
51. Interview of the author with Jacob Hellerstein, recording secretary of the *Agudat ha–Rabbanim* from 1928 to 1972, November 29, 1973.
52. See above, Chapter 1.
53. See above, Chapter 1; *The World of the Yeshiva*, p. 41; Irving Bunim, who played an extremely active role in the *Vaad ha–Hatzala,* acknowledged that the fact that he had met Rabbi Aron Kotler when the latter visited the United States in 1935 motivated him to try to save him.
54. Silver–VH, pp. 21–22; Hellerstein interview.
55. Interview of the author with Rabbi Yitzhak Grozalsky, November 14, 1973; Hellerstein interview.
56. Hellerstein interview.
57. For details on Rabbi Silver's personality and communal activities, see Rakeffet-Rothkoff, *The Silver Era*, pp. 68–94; Menachem Glickman–Porush, *Ish ha–Halacha ve–ha–Ma'ase* (Jerusalem, n.d.); interview of the author with Rabbi Alex Wessfogel, July 22, 1973. On the differences between Rabbi Silver and Rabbi Henkin, see the interview by the author with Shmaryahu ha–Cohen Margalit, October 22, 1973.
58. On Rabbi Gordon's involvement in the establishment of the *Vaad*, see the interview by the author with Rabbi Simcha Wasserman, July 20, 1979.
59. Letter of Rabbi Simcha Wasserman to Abraham Holowitz, December 19, 1939, CJFWF, I–69, Box 149.
60. Ibid. Rabbi Wasserman wrote to Horowitz that because the *Vaad* was anxious not to adversely affect the JDC's fundraising, its campaign would be directed at the "regular contributors of the Yeshivoth" rather than to the general (Jewish) public.

Chapter 3

The Mission of
Dr. Samuel Schmidt

During the period in which the Emergency Committee for War-Torn Yeshivoth launched its initial activities, refugee rabbis and yeshiva students continued to arrive in Vilna—albeit in reduced numbers—despite numerous obstacles which made the journey perilous. During the brief Soviet occupation and the initial period of Lithuanian rule, travel between Eastern Poland and Vilna had been relatively unhampered, but by mid-November 1939 the new Soviet–Lithuanian border had been established and thereafter civilian travel between the two areas was subject to stringent regulations. Military patrols on both sides of the border sought to apprehend those attempting to cross illegally. Furthermore, the severe weather during the winter of 1939–1940, one of the most severe Europe had experienced, with temperatures dropping to 40^0 Centigrade below zero, made the escape to Vilna particularly dangerous. Nonetheless, hundreds of Jews, particularly rabbis and yeshiva students and members of the pioneer Zionist youth movements, succeeded in reaching Vilna, which had become a password for freedom among Polish Jews, even after the border was closed.[1]

The border crossings were to a large extent initiated and organized by emissaries sent from Vilna by the yeshivot and the Zionist youth movements, that had already reached the safety of Lithuania. They sought to encourage their students and members who were still in Soviet-occupied Poland to come to the neutral independent

Baltic republic, where they had established headquarters and, to a certain degree, resumed their activities and daily routine.[2]

The most popular route of escape was via the Polish town of Lida and the Lithuanian town of Eishishuk (Eisiskiai). Other routes were via Oshmiena or Shventzyan (Svencionys) or Novo-Shventzyan (Svencioneliai).[3] The border crossings took place at night in small groups of up to ten or fifteen people who were led across by a local guide (usually a non-Jew). On numerous occasions the refugees were betrayed by the guides, but until January 1940 they were usually released within a short time and were free to try again. In many cases refugees attempted to cross several times before they finally succeeded.[4] Thus during this period most of the considerable injuries and fatalities were caused by the unusually severe weather conditions.[5] By the end of 1939 approximately 2,100 yeshiva students as well as numerous rabbis[6] and about 1,500 members of the Zionist youth movements[7] had reached Vilna. Among them were almost the entire student body of nearly all the major Polish yeshivot: Mir, Kletzk, Kamenetz, Radin, Lomza, Bialystok ("Beit Yoseph"), Baranowitz ("Ohel Torah" and "Torat Chesed"), Slonim, Pinsk, Mezritch, Lubavitch, Ostrava, and Lutzk as well as students from Volozhin and Lublin.[8]

In January 1940, however, the Soviets made special efforts to hermetically seal the border, and those caught attempting to cross to Lithuania were sentenced to three to five years in labor camps. These measures severely curtailed the movement of refugees to Vilna, although it was not halted completely.[9] By this time, approximately 15,000 Jewish refugees from Poland had crossed into Lithuania.[10]

The continued influx of refugees to Vilna exacerbated the plight of the newcomers in the city and put an added strain on the relief organizations, which were already severely overburdened. Moreover, the Lithuanian government, which was concerned regarding the presence of so many Polish refugees in Vilna, decided to take special measures against the new arrivals. All refugees were obligated to register with the authorities, and those who could not prove that they had been in Vilna prior to its incorporation into Lithuania (on October 31, 1939) were not allowed to remain in the city. Refugees who were not Lithuanian citizens were given special passports certifying their status.[11] Moreover, on December 9, 1939, a special department (headed by Alekna) was established in the

Ministry of the Interior to handle all matters concerning the refugees. Its initial measures were designed to curtail the refugees' freedom of movement and reduce to a minimum the influence of the Poles in the city. In response, an umbrella organization of (local and foreign) Jewish agencies entitled *Ezrat Plitim* (Refugee Aid) was founded by Dr. Jacob Robinson—an eminent jurist who had headed the Jewish faction in the Lithuanian parliament[12]—in order to facilitate relief work and to create a unified Jewish representation which could negotiate with the government on the refugees' behalf. For example, *Ezrat Plitim* distributed the relief funds sent from abroad for the Polish refugees. The refugee rabbis and yeshiva students were represented on this committee by a member of the *Vaad ha-Yeshivot,* which played a major role in caring for their needs.[13]

Despite the physical hardships which the rabbis and yeshiva students suffered after their arrival in Vilna, most were engaged in intensive Torah study and had settled down to their usual routine within a relatively short time after their move to "the Jerusalem of Lithuania." Thus as early as mid-November 1939 Rabbi Eliyahu Bloch of the Telz (Telsiai) Yeshiva described the perseverance of the refugee yeshiva students in Vilna in glowing terms. Despite their suffering from "genuine famine," Rabbi Bloch noted that they were continuing their studies undaunted: "The voice of Torah is ringing frequently with all its force. The classes are being conducted regularly on schedule as if they [the yeshivot] were living tranquilly at home. This is the secret of 'The eternity of Israel will never lie.'"[14]

In January 1940, however, the Lithuanian government issued a decree forcing all refugees who had arrived in Vilna after its annexation by Lithuania to leave the city. The decree was designed to curtail the demographic and cultural supremacy of the Poles in Vilna, but its practical implications directly affected the Jewish refugees. As a result, most of the refugee rabbis and yeshiva students had to relocate within Lithuania proper.

While this move entailed various difficulties, the *roshei yeshiva* were not opposed to the "ruralization" decree because they thought that the atmosphere in the small towns would be more conducive to intensive study and therefore considered the move as ultimately beneficial for their students. In the words of Rabbi Grodzinski, who related the travails of the refugee yeshivot to Ashkenazic chief Rabbi Herzog: "The roshei yeshiva themselves want to leave [Vilna] because living in cities is spiritually difficult for the yeshivot, as in a small town they are not bothered and can therefore study with particular diligence."[15] In fact, two of the *roshei yeshiva*, Rabbi Finkel of Mir and Rabbi Kotler of Kletzk, had already arranged for the relocation of their schools even before the decree, since besides the spirituality considerations, they also sensed that the presence of large numbers of refugees in Vilna constituted a potentially dangerous situation.[16]

Thus during the initial months of 1940, many of the Polish yeshivot that had escaped to Vilna moved to small towns and villages in the Vilna district or in the area of pre-1939 Lithuania. The following table lists the yeshivot which left Vilna as well as their new locations:

Yeshiva and Number of Students	Relocation Site
Baranowitz ("Ohel Torah") - 145	Trakai/Semilishuk (Semeliskis)
Baranowitz ("Torat Chesed") - 49	Tavrig (Taurage)
Bialystok ("Beit Yoseph") - 186	Birzh (Birzai)
Kamenetz - 235	Rasein (Raseiniai)
Kletzk - 241	Janeva (Jonava)/Salok (Salakas)
Lomza - 125	Plungyan (Plunge)
Mezritch - 94	Nemenczyn
Mir - 273	Keydan (Kedainiai)
Pinsk - 128	Vilkomir (Ukmerge)
Radin - 198	Otyan (Utena) and Eishishuk (Eisiskiai)
Volozhin - 41	Zagare

The other yeshivot: Brisk (27), Grodno (75), Kollel Beit Yoseph (18 families - 75 people), Kollel Mir (22 families - 65 people), Lubavitch (43), Chachmei Lublin (63), Lutzk (43), Ostrava (57), Ostrow-Mazowietzki (42), Ramailes (53), Slonim (38), Warsaw-Beit Shmuel (40) remained in Vilna.

Of the 2,336 yeshiva students who had arrived in Lithuania by spring 1940 (when the ruralization decree was implemented), 1,476 left Vilna for sites in pre-1939 Lithuania, 621 remained in the city proper, and 239 relocated within the Vilna district.[17]

* * *

The implementation of the ruralization decree alleviated a pressing problem for the refugee students, who could now pursue their studies without fear of being expelled from Lithuania, but for most of the rabbis and students it did not constitute a long-range solution for the yeshivot. In fact, there were serious doubts as to whether Lithuania could serve as a temporary haven for any considerable length of time. With Lithuania sandwiched between Nazi-occupied Poland and the Soviet Union and coveted by both totalitarian regimes, its future as an independent republic did not appear promising. Thus the leaders of the refugee rabbis and yeshiva students continued to deliberate regarding the three major options that existed upon their arrival in Vilna: *aliyah* to Eretz Yisrael, emigration to the United States, or remaining in Lithuania (with the third alternative somewhat reinforced in the wake of the ruralization). The response of the leaders is of special importance in an analysis of the ultimate fate of the rabbis and yeshiva students and therefore merits further scrutiny.

During their first few months in Vilna, several *roshei yeshivot* made serious efforts to obtain certificates to enable their entire yeshivot to make *aliyah* to Eretz Yisrael. The most active in this respect was Rabbi Eliezer Yehuda Finkel of Mir. As early as November 7, 1939, he cabled the Central Relief Committee in New York to assist him in obtaining *aliyah* certificates,[18] and throughout the winter of 1939–1940 he continued his efforts to achieve this goal, often with the help of Rabbi Grodzinski, who tried to use his influence to mobilize various prominent rabbis in Eretz Yisrael to help.[19] In a letter to Moshe Shapiro of the executive committee of the Jewish Agency, Rabbi Finkel poignantly describes his chagrin upon learning that there were difficulties in implementing his plan to transfer the Mir Yeshiva to Eretz Yisrael: "With deep heartache I read of the difficulty in implementing this matter. There is no remedy for the severe wound of our people in the exile of the tents of Torah other than bringing them to our holy land and if G-d forbid there is no way to do so we are helpless and who knows what the terrible waves which strike us and undermine the existence of *yisrael sava* [Torah-true Judaism] will bring upon us on that day."[20]

Another *rosh yeshiva* who made similar attempts to obtain *aliyah* certificates for his yeshiva was Rabbi Aron Kotler of Kletzk. In late winter 1939–1940, for example, he wrote to the Jewish Agency asking for their help: "Our desire and the desire of hundreds of Torah students is to make *aliyah* to our holy land, to which the eyes of all Jews turn as to the only shining point for us in the world."[21] Rabbis Boruch Ber Leibowitz of Kamenetz[22] and Elchanan Wasserman of Baranowitz[23] were also interested in transferring their yeshivot to Eretz Yisrael, although the former, immediately after his arrival in Vilna, also cabled the Central Relief Committee to arrange to bring his yeshiva to the United States.[24] The general consensus among those *roshei yeshiva* who actively sought to leave Lithuania was that Eretz Yisrael was the preferred destination.

There were, however, those who thought that it would be best to remain in Lithuania. Rabbi Grodzinski, for example, supported this position, even though he tried to obtain visas to Eretz Yisrael for himself as well as for others.[25] He believed that Lithuania would remain neutral ("neither red nor black") and thus could serve as a haven for the refugee scholars.[26] In addition, he opposed the mass relocation abroad of all the Polish yeshivot, since he thought that some would have to return to Poland after the war to attend to the needs of Polish Jewry. Moreover, he opined that since there was little chance of obtaining the number of visas necessary to enable the yeshivot to relocate en masse, the schools would have to split up, and such a development he believed would undermine their existence.[27]

It is possible, however, that there was another practical consideration which motivated Rabbi Grodzinski's public stance against emigration. The Orthodox leader undoubtedly sought to prevent the spread of panic and despair among the refugees as well as among the local Jews, and this concern was also apparently a factor in his decision to publicly oppose mass emigration. In a letter to Rabbi Eliezer Silver in March 1940, he wrote, "Meanwhile, Torah [the yeshivot] is lying in the corner [Lithuania]."[28] Apparently Rabbi Grodzinski believed that the refugee rabbis and students were temporarily safe, although he no doubt realized that such a haven could turn into a trap (as was indeed the case for many of the Torah scholars). Rabbi Yoseph Shub, the secretary of the *Vaad ha-Yeshivot,* was also opposed to emigration at this point, and the public stance adopted by these leaders moderated communal pressure to leave.[29] It is not surprising, therefore, that during this period there seemed to be relatively little practical activity by the refugee yeshiva students related to immigration. Zerach Warhaftig, the religious Zionist leader who escaped from Poland to Vilna and headed the Palestine Office for Polish Refugees, was a frequent visitor to the yeshivot and his description of the atmosphere during the initial months of their stay in Lithuania is illuminating:

> The yeshivot quickly arranged themselves and resumed their regular, normal routines. Outside anxiety due to the rattling of sabres and the noise of bombs and inside a relaxed tranquil atmosphere and diligent learning. The living conditions were difficult. They ate bread with salt and drank water in small measure. The weather was very cold and the warmth provided by the heaters was insufficient. The external cold was overcome by internal warmth, by the fervor of learning, by the enthusiasm of the believers. A self-enclosed world, apathetic to worldly pleasures, immune to physical hardships. They respond to every problem or upsetting news item with greater diligence in their studies, with deeper delving, by clarifying and investigating questions which relate to eternal problems, which are above fleeting, temporal matters. On many occasions, I went into this or that yeshiva, not to study—I did not have the necessary time or emotional tranquillity for that— but to get my eyes' and heart's fill of the experience of casting aside the material and the temporary and of the spiritual uplifting above time and its ravages.[30]

Thus by early 1940 the yeshivot had succeeded in more or less recreating their original environment, a factor that to some extent mitigated the internal pressure to work for a long-range solution in the form of emigration. This was not the case, however, vis-à-vis the community rabbis, whose situation as refugees in Lithuania was quite different from that of the *roshei yeshivot* and yeshiva students. Cut off from their communities, they were unable to resume their normal duties and positions and consequently from the beginning of their stay in Lithuania they actively sought to emigrate, with Eretz Yisrael and the United States the preferred destinations. Several of these rabbis established an association called *Ichud Rabbanim Plitei Polin* (Union of Polish Refugee Rabbis) which attempted to obtain *aliyah* certificates and travel expenses. Among the leading community rabbis who escaped to Vilna were Rabbis Yitzchak Ze'ev

Soloveitchik (Brisk), Chizkiyahu Mishkowski (Krinki), Aryeh Shapiro (Bialystok), David Lifshitz (Suwalk), and Moshe Shatzkes (Lomza). In all, approximately fifty community rabbis found refuge in Vilna, including several who arrived with their entire families.[31]

While the yeshivot were reestablishing themselves, initially in Vilna and subsequently elsewhere in Lithuania, *Vaad ha-Hatzala* was taking its first steps to raise funds to alleviate their plight. Its initial activities were in accordance with the resolutions passed at the convention at which the rescue organization was founded. The months of Tevet and Shevat (December 13, 1939 to February 10, 1940) were designated for the campaign, and volunteer rabbis began fundraising activities all over the United States. Delegations of prominent rabbis visited such cities as Baltimore, Boston, Cleveland, Detroit, Indianapolis, New York, Philadelphia, Scranton, and Washington, DC, and the three Sabbaths of January 6, 13, and 20 were singled out for fundraising appeals.[32]

In various cities across the United States, regional campaigns were launched. In Chicago, for example, a Western Conference of rabbis and laymen convened on December 27, 1939, to plan the fundraising activities in that area. Among the resolutions passed at this meeting were that rabbis contribute a week's salary to the campaign, that laymen were called upon to donate ten percent of their yearly income, and that "poorer persons" were asked to give a sum equivalent to their earnings for a single day.[33] Special measures were taken to ensure the success of the campaign. For example, in November 1939 Rabbi Silver and the heads of the Central Relief Committee decided that no Orthodox representatives would be brought from abroad to raise funds in the United States during the emergency campaign.[34] Moreover, the various yeshivot whose students had escaped to Vilna, each of which had heretofore conducted its own separate fundraising drives in the United States, agreed to suspend their fundraising activities for the duration of the campaign.[35]

During the winter of 1939–1940, *Vaad ha-Hatzala* submitted its initial requests for allocations to local federations and welfare funds in various communities. This step aroused the anger of the JDC and ultimately led to the deterioration of the relations between the two agencies. Initially, however, the scope and negative effect (from the JDC's standpoint) of the *Vaad's* campaign were somewhat unclear, and thus whatever premonitions, reservations, and criticisms the JDC might have had vis-à-vis the *Vaad*, they were not aired publicly.

Thus, for example, in a special confidential bulletin issued on February 1, 1940, by the Council of Jewish Federations and Welfare Funds (and distributed to all its member agencies) regarding the activities of the *Vaad ha-Hatzala*, the JDC's stance was presented as follows: "The JDC feels that it is not in a position to approve or disapprove this effort. It has, however, always maintained that in order to avoid a multiplicity of fundraising drives, contributions for programs and projects subventioned by the major overseas organizations should be centralized through one agency."[36] As time went by and the *Vaad* put increased pressure on more and more federations throughout the United States, the JDC to some degree abandoned its restraint in dealing with this phenomenon, which constituted an extremely complex and delicate issue with significant communal implications.

The *Vaad* was well aware of the reservations about its fundraising activities and from the outset sought to reassure the leaders of the existing relief agencies that it had no intention of jeopardizing their ongoing fundraising campaigns. In his December 19, 1939, letter to Abraham Horowitz of the Central Relief Committee, Rabbi Wasserman noted that the *Vaad*'s work was a "one-time campaign to be carried out this winter" especially designed to meet this "newly created emergency." In addition, Wasserman emphasized that the *Vaad* would take specific steps to ensure that its work would not interfere with the United Jewish Appeal and would therefore "turn especially to the regular contributors of the yeshivoth," rather than to the general public.[37] In an interview conducted by the Council of Jewish Federations and Welfare Funds with Rabbi Silver and four other members of the *Vaad* in order to ascertain specific details regarding the rabbinic rescue campaign, the rabbis stressed the temporary nature of their work. In the bulletin subsequently issued by the Council regarding *Vaad ha-Hatzala*'s activities, this aspect was duly noted: "The committee emphasized the fact that this is a one-time campaign to meet an emergency situation."[38]

These reassurances notwithstanding, the seeds of the conflict between the *Vaad* and the JDC had already been planted as a result of the *Vaad*'s decision to turn to local federations and welfare funds for allocations, as well as the methods they used in doing so. In each community, local rabbis approached the welfare fund prior to the launching of the local campaign and presented the allocation figure that the *Vaad* considered appropriate for that community. If the welfare fund agreed to contribute that sum to the *Vaad's* campaign, no separate fundraising drive was launched.[39] These tactics, which were to spark acerbic controversies in numerous communities, were a constant source of friction between the *Vaad* and the JDC and local federations. The conflict became increasingly acute as time went by and the scope of the *Vaad's* relief activity overseas and fundraising campaigns in the United States considerably expanded.

* * *

On a practical level, the *Vaad* took two major steps during its first six months of existence. It sent an emissary to the Polish yeshivot in Lithuania to examine their situation firsthand and ascertain their needs, and it raised and transmitted financial assistance to these refugees. The individual chosen for the relief mission was Dr. Samuel Schmidt of Cincinnati, a personal friend of Rabbi Eliezer Silver and a veteran relief worker and communal figure. Trained as a public health specialist, Dr. Schmidt had served with the Zionist Medical Unit which operated in Palestine in 1918, had been a member of the JDC relief unit (headed by Dr. Boris Bogen) sent to Poland in December 1919, and from 1920 to 1923 directed the public health work of the JDC in Poland. Since 1927 he had been the editor of the Cincinnati English-language Jewish weekly *Every Friday* and was a prominent figure in that city's Jewish community. The only apparent possible reservation about his suitability for the task of *Vaad ha-Hatzala* emissary to the refugee yeshivot was the fact that prior to the journey he was, in terms of personal religious observance, far removed from the lifestyle and milieu of the Orthodox rabbis who had founded the *Vaad* and from those of the *roshei yeshiva* with whom he was to come into contact in Lithuania.

An active member of the socialist Poale Zion Zionist movement, Schmidt was indeed ostensibly ideologically far removed from Rabbi Silver's circles, yet he nonetheless was the Cincinnati rabbi's choice to undertake the mission, and he agreed to do so despite his initial hesitation.[40] Perhaps the fact that Schmidt had been born in Kovno in a traditional home and spoke fluent Yiddish made up for his lack of religious observance, as far as Rabbi Silver was concerned. According to Dr. Schmidt, it was an impassioned editorial in *Every Friday* regarding the tragedy of the uprooted yeshivot and his call for a modern-day Yochanan Ben-Zakai to rescue them that prompted

Rabbi Silver's offer. In any event, Schmidt met with numerous rabbis prior to his departure and decided that in order to succeed he had to conduct himself as an Orthodox Jew, which is what he did throughout the course of his mission (and following his return to the United States as well).[41]

Dr. Schmidt sailed from New York on February 8, 1940, aboard the SS *Bergensfjord* and arrived in Bergen, Norway, nine days later.[42] From there he traveled to Stockholm, where he met with Swedish Chief Rabbi Marcus Ehrenpreis,[43] and to Riga, where he conferred with the Lubavitcher Rebbe, Agudist politicians Dubin and Wittenberg, and the renowned historian Shimon Dubnow.[44] On February 27, 1940, he arrived by train in Vilna and on the next day met with Rabbi Grodzinski and JDC representative Moses Beckelman. The meeting with the elderly rabbi made an indelible impression on Schmidt and was the beginning of a particularly warm relationship between them, which considerably affected the *Vaad's* emissary and influenced his decision to maintain his religious observance after the completion of his mission. In a letter to his wife, Schmidt describes his emotions following his encounter with Rabbi Grodzinski:

> I spent a little more than an hour with Reb Chaim Ezer [sic]. He is a great man and as you know he is recognized as the greatest rabbi in our generation. I know that you will not make light of my sentimentality when I say that the trip with all the risks involved was worthwhile to be in his presence.... In the hour that I was with him I felt that Reb Chaim Ezer took me close to him and I was elated to be in such close presence with a holy man.[45]

Dr. Schmidt remained in constant contact with Rabbi Grodzinski throughout the course of his stay and did not make any significant decisions without first consulting the Vilna sage, who despite his extremely poor health played an active role in determining the policies of the *Vaad ha-Yeshivot* and the refugee Torah institutions. Needless to say, Dr. Schmidt discussed with him at length every issue of importance concerning the yeshivot.[46]

Shortly after his arrival in Vilna, Dr. Schmidt began visiting the various refugee yeshivot, beginning with those in the Vilna area. On March 3 he visited Brisk and Radin,[47] both of which were located in local synagogues. He conveyed the extremely positive impression these institutions made on him in a letter to his wife which was published as an editorial in *Every Friday*:

> A Jew with the ordinary five *"chushim"* (senses) can hardly appreciate the Jewish cultural reservoir in such Yeshivos. You must possess the true, basic, specifically Jewish sense to be able to comprehend the dynamic Jewish cultural current that is being generated and stored for future generations in these Yeshivos. It is this very current which is the driving power in all of us who are working for a positive Jewish life, even though some of us may be removed far, far from the source where this current is being generated.[48]

The sense of spiritual elevation that Dr. Schmidt derived from his meetings with Rabbi Grodzinski, and his visits to the yeshivot, remained with him throughout his trip and continued to influence him after his return to the United States. Already at this early point he believed that his mission had had a positive psychological effect on the refugees and particularly on the Orthodox leaders, even though he personally thought that "the spirit of despair noticeable almost everywhere" was not prevalent in the yeshivot.[49]

During his first week in Lithuania Dr. Schmidt also took steps to arrange for meetings with Lithuanian officials to iron out various difficulties regarding the status of several yeshiva students in the wake of the ruralization decree.[50] On March 6 he traveled to Kovno, where he met with government officials and discussed at length the nature and function of the yeshivot, attempting to present them as institutions of higher learning rather than rabbinical seminaries, in the hope that this approach might induce the Lithuanians to adopt a more positive attitude toward them.

During his visit to Kovno, Schmidt also visited two of the largest refugee Polish yeshivot: Mir, which was located in Keydan (Kedainiai), and Kletzk, which had moved to Janeve. He was extremely impressed by the diligence of the students. "In both," he wrote to his wife, "I found a remarkable devotion for the study of the Talmud. I could find no signs that either the spirit or intensity of devotion has been impaired by the terrible experience which they had to live through during the recent months."[51] The *roshei yeshiva* whom Dr. Schmidt met in Keydan and Janeve also made a strong impression upon him. He describes Rabbi Aron Kotler of Kletzk as follows: "He is indeed a most interesting person and considered the greatest Talmudic master of his own age. He is about 48 years, blue smiling eyes, small stature, powerful determination and penetrating vision." Another person who made a powerful impression upon Schmidt was the Kletzk *mashgiach* (spiritual supervisor) Rabbi Eliezer Shach, whom he described in a letter to his wife as follows: "in appearance, a typical bearded Japanese, at any rate Mongolian. A charming smile which just refuses to leave his countenance with penetrating jet black eyes. He left an indelible impression upon me and I lost no opportunity to keep him in my view all the time that I was in the *Yeshivo*."

During his visit to Keydan, Schmidt was hosted at a festive meal held in his honor by Rabbi Finkel, the Mir *rosh yeshiva*, during the course of which "the great heroism which *Harav* [the rabbi] Dr. Schmidt had displayed in coming here" was lauded. Dr. Schmidt found the appellation of *"Harav"* which Rabbi Finkel conferred upon him quite amusing, although by this point he was ready to admit that he was beginning to believe that he must have had a certain amount of *"zidkos"* (righteousness) in order to have had the privilege of being entrusted with such "a historic and important mission."[52]

During these initial visits, as well as in his talks with Rabbi Grodzinski, Schmidt broached the idea of establishing a unified committee which would serve as the authorized agency for the evaluation of the needs of all the yeshivot in Lithuania (refugee as well as local) and which would determine the distribution of the relief funds sent from abroad. Needless to say, such a step would be extremely beneficial for those involved in fundraising in the United States, as well as for the beneficiaries of the charity funds, but Schmidt nonetheless encountered serious opposition. In his own words, "This is not an easy matter here, the local patriotism of each yeshiva is strongly developed, a sort of an Alma Mater pride taking on manifestations of chauvinism in some cases."[53] Nonetheless, he maintained his effort on this issue, ultimately achieving a certain measure of success.

During his visit Dr. Schmidt did not confine himself to dealing with the yeshivot. An active member of Poale Zion in America, he met with Poale Zion leaders in Lithuania (local leaders as well as Polish refugees) and participated in several functions sponsored by the socialist Zionist party. The fact that he had come to Lithuania on behalf of the yeshivot was somewhat perplexing for some of his fellow Zionists, and there were occasions when Dr. Schmidt was presented to the public as an emissary of Poale Zion, with no mention made of his original mission.

The Cincinnati doctor lost no opportunity, however, to remind the members of Poale Zion that it was Orthodox rabbis who had sent him to Lithuania. Schmidt used this fact to stress the need for Jewish unity as well as to emphasize the importance of the yeshivot and to praise the rabbis for their openness and flexibility in choosing as their emissary a member of a party ideologically far removed from their own. Thus in a speech he made at a farewell party sponsored by Poale Zion in honor of those about to leave for Eretz Yisrael, Schmidt noted "that it was rather significant and full of meaning that the rabbis were first to think of sending someone here in these difficult times and that they should have picked a member of Poale Zion. I was certain we would have never chosen a rabbi as shaliach for us…. Am Yisrael means not only Poale Zion nor only the Zionists, but includes all Jews where the yeshiva men occupy a not insignificant place."[54]

While in Lithuania, Schmidt was also able to observe the plight of the rest of the Polish refugees and to scrutinize the work of the JDC, for whom he had high words of praise. In a letter to his wife he described the relief work done by the American Jewish relief agency: "The refugees were resurrected as it were through the assistance of the Joint. Had it not been for the money made available by the Joint at the very beginning I would have found 12,000 derelicts instead of human beings." Yet despite this assistance, the refugees felt insecure because of the precariousness of their situation in Lithuania. Many were panicky and sought to emigrate. "They fear," Schmidt wrote to the United States, "that the morrow may bring an abrupt end to their present comparative peace and safety and for that reason would like to run away somewhere as far from the Nazis, far from the Soviets."

Schmidt did not share the refugees' pessimistic view vis-à-vis future developments in Lithuania. He was fairly impressed by the manner in which the government was treating the Jews, given its proximity to Nazi Germany and Poland ("At a time when the odds are against us almost all over the world, we have the right to consider Lithuania as a mighty fine place for the Jew.") Moreover, he did not think Lithuania would be invaded, since the Russians needed the food produced there and knew that if they took over the country, there would be a famine. In Schmidt's opinion, the only danger was the possibility of war breaking out between the Nazis and the Soviets. As of mid-March 1940, however, he did not believe that would happen. "I have a strong intuition that Lithuania is destined to remain entirely undisturbed no matter how the war turns.... It does seem as though destiny itself had placed Lithuania as a haven of refuge for the yeshivos. In this little land, actually all of the yeshivos of Europe of any consequence are now located."[55]

Toward the end of March, Dr. Schmidt resumed his visits to the yeshivot outside of Vilna. On March 26 he visited the Kamenetz Yeshiva, which was located in Raseyn (Raseiniai), and several days later he went to Ponevitch (Panevezys) to visit the local yeshiva. He also attended to several matters related to his profession, taking steps to help ensure that the three cases of typhoid fever among the Mir Yeshiva students did not turn into an epidemic. He made sure the necessary vaccine was sent to the yeshiva in Keydan and gave the administrative director of the yeshiva detailed instructions on the necessary measures to be taken.[56] Schmidt, it should be noted, had brought along with him a large amount of vaccine, which he donated as a goodwill gesture to the Lithuanian Department of Health.[57]

Throughout his stay in Lithuania, Schmidt continued to be impressed by the manner in which the yeshivot had relocated there. In March 1940, for example, he wrote to Mrs. Schmidt:

> The heroism of the Yeshivo Bochurim in fleeing to Wilno to pursue their ideal cannot be overestimated. In general the way the yeshivoth managed to settle here is nothing short of a miracle. The yeshivoth themselves as an institution remaining untouched and unblemished, entirely immune to the ravages of time and events are a miracle. That some 2,400 yeshivoth men are studying with devotion and fervor in the various synagogues of towns throughout Lithuania having but recently escaped from such hell is a strong manifestation that we are a people of destiny. Were it not for Lithuania and the fact that Wilno was for a short period in the hands of the Soviets, most of the yeshivoth would have disintegrated.[58]

Besides his sense of admiration for the yeshivot as institutions and for the diligence and perseverance of their students, Schmidt was very much in awe of the *roshei yeshiva* and especially of Rabbi Grodzinski. Toward the end of his trip he wrote the following to his wife, in essence summarizing his response to his meetings with Rabbi Grodzinski and the *roshei yeshivot*:

> My meetings with Reb Chaim Ozer continue to inspire me and to stimulate within me new forces, new horizons or rather the horizons seem to recede at every meeting and my vision becomes keener.... What a holy man! What a fountain of wisdom! What a store of personal magnetism and human quality!... My visit to Ponievez and the brief intimate contact with the Ponievezer Rav has afforded me an additional exhilaration [sic]. He is a man of most warm human feeling and of sparkling wisdom in close contact with facts and realities as they exist.[59]

Dr. Schmidt had originally hoped to complete his mission in Lithuania by early April and return to the United States via Riga, Stockholm, Brussels, Paris, and Lisbon, flying back by clipper in time to arrive home for Passover. These plans did not materialize, however, since he missed the last plane from Stockholm to Western Europe and in the meantime the Nazis invaded Holland and Belgium. He therefore had to travel via Germany. This was possible for him to do as an American citizen, since the United States and Germany were not yet at war. Nevertheless it took several weeks to obtain the necessary German transit visa, so he returned from Sweden to Lithuania, where the wait would be "safer and less expensive" and where he would be able to utilize the time to complete various tasks connected with his mission.[60]

Upon his return to Lithuania, Schmidt resumed his visits to refugee and local yeshivot, met with American and British representatives as well as with Lithuanian government officials, and conferred frequently with Rabbi Grodzinski and various rabbis and *roshei yeshivot*. He divided the Passover holiday between Vilna and Kovno, anxiously awaiting the receipt of his German transit visa.[61] One of the highlights of his return visit to Lithuania was his meeting with Lithuanian Prime Minister Merkys and the Minister of the Interior. According to Schmidt, the Lithuanian head of state was not aware of the fact that so many yeshivot had found refuge in his country and was duly impressed by this phenomenon. He asked Schmidt to disseminate favorable propaganda in the United States regarding Lithuania since the government lacked the necessary funds to do so.[62]

During his meeting with the Minister of the Interior, Schmidt was able to arrange an entry visa to Lithuania for Rabbi Aaron Lewin (the "Reisha Rov," formerly a member of the Polish Sejm), who was living in Lwow and had been threatened with deportation by the Soviet authorities. He also was able to press for favorable treatment for the refugee yeshivot. According to Schmidt's account of the meeting, his host was quite responsive on that issue; Schmidt wrote that "despite some administrative difficulties which had to be carried through and which might have appeared unfriendly perhaps, he [the Minister] wanted me to know that the Lithuanian Government appreciated the great importance of the Yeshivoth and considered it a privilege to offer a place of refuge to all of these which constituted almost all the Yeshivoth of Europe."[63]

Dr. Schmidt was extremely pleased with the results of his meetings with government officials. In his reports back to Cincinnati he noted with a sense of satisfaction the results he thought he achieved: "All these official calls which I made have helped to create a better relationship and more respectful attitude towards the Yeshivos and Orthodox Judaism and in addition it has eased the contact with the government departments."[64] In another letter in the same vein, he ironically added, "I feel that as a result of my propaganda for the Yeshivos among these Lithuanian officials, they are beginning to evaluate the Yeshivos more than many of our Jews."[65]

During his return visit to Lithuania, Dr. Schmidt devoted considerable effort to the financial aspects of his mission. He worked hard to establish a unified committee to evaluate the needs of all the yeshivot (refugee and local) then in Lithuania and to oversee the distribution of the relief funds sent from abroad. Despite strong initial resistance by both Rabbi Grodzinski and the *roshei yeshivot*, Schmidt was able in early May, at a meeting he convened in Vilna, to obtain the unanimous consent of the latter to at least consider such a plan. The proposal Schmidt presented called for the establishment in America of a committee similar to the Vilna *Vaad ha-Yeshivot*. The difficult conditions in Lithuania apparently led to a softening of the once adamant opposition of the *roshei yeshiva*. They had serious apprehensions as to how funds would be raised for the yeshivot in the United States since the emergency fundraising drive launched by *Vaad ha-Hatzala* had ended. Thus by the time Dr. Schmidt left Lithuania, the consensus among the *roshei yeshivot* was that the proposal should be seriously discussed in America and, if conditions necessitated the formation of such a body, a plan to that effect should be drawn up and presented for their approval.

In the meantime Rabbi Grodzinski and the *roshei yeshivot* agreed upon a plan for the distribution of the funds transmitted from the United States: twelve percent of the total would be allocated to the Lithuanian yeshivot and distributed by the Kovno Rov (Rabbi Avraham Duber Kahana Shapiro). The remaining eighty-eight percent would be distributed among the refugee Polish yeshivot in the following manner:

> 50% (of the 88%) on a strict per capita basis
> 10% on the basis of quality and calibre
> 10% in accordance with "standards maintained"
> 15% to yeshivot with functioning offices in the United States
> 10% to yeshivot with representatives in the United States
> 5% would be set aside to correct any mistakes

This plan was approved at the Vilna meeting of the *roshei yeshivot*. The problem was, however, that before the details of the plan could be sent to the United States, some of the representatives of the yeshivot in America were given funds for their institutions in Lithuania not in accordance with this agreed-upon distribution plan. Thus some yeshivot with a smaller number of students received much more money than other schools with far more pupils. This development angered Rabbi Grodzinski, who instructed Schmidt to rectify the situation upon his return to the United States.[66]

Another area in which Dr. Schmidt was involved was the transfer and conversion into local currency of relief funds sent by *Vaad ha-Hatzala*. One of the most important tasks of his mission was to arrange for the conversion into Lithuanian lits at the best possible rate, of the dollars he brought with him and of other funds whose transfer he arranged. During his stay in Lithuania, Dr. Schmidt converted and distributed a total of $17,000 and also handled various transfer arrangements whereby funds donated to yeshivot in Lithuania were reimbursed by *Vaad ha-Hatzala* to individuals in the United States. Dr. Schmidt's financial activities deserve further scrutiny because they illuminate the various obstacles which the *Vaad* encountered in its efforts to transmit relief funds to the refugee yeshivot.

Dr. Schmidt arrived in Lithuania with $10,000 raised by the *Vaad ha-Hatzala*. There were two possible ways of converting the money into local currency: He could do so in a bank or via government channels at the official rate, or he could change the money on the black market, where the rate was considerably higher but the trans-actions were risky. The Lithuanian government was aware of the dilemma and therefore decided to offer a fifty percent supplement in lits above the official exchange rate for charity dollars sent from overseas. Schmidt took advantage of this offer and changed the $10,000 he brought with him via government channels at the rate of 13.3 lits per dollar, which apparently was approximately the same rate available on the black market.

In addition, he obtained $7,000 from individuals, $5,000 in lits and $2,000 in dollars. These funds were obtained through a transfer agreement whereby an individual in Lithuania gave Schmidt money and in return an agreed-upon sum was deposited by the *Vaad ha-Hatzala* in a U.S. bank account of a designated friend or relative, who cabled confirmation to the donor. These transactions had to be car-ried out with extreme caution, lest the government find out about them. In fact, several days before Schmidt left Kovno, one of the per-sons involved in such transfers was arrested. In addition, the utmost care had to be invested to ensure that the maximum rate was obtained. Schmidt related in his summary report that there had been "sincere criticism" of conversions made on behalf of the yeshivot "at rates far below the best rates." He related, moreover, that while he converted his dollars at well over 13 lits per dollar, by the time he left Lithuania the exchange rate had dropped to 10.5 lits for checks and 11.5 lits for cash. Thus timing was also of critical importance.

The extreme caution with which Dr. Schmidt carried out the pri-vate transfers of funds also stemmed from various difficulties in the United States. For example, the Cincinnati doctor received 67,500 lits from someone in Kovno in return for which the *Vaad ha-Hatzala* was to give $5,000 to a Mr. Kaplove in New Jersey. Kaplove cabled Kovno that instead of the money, he had been given dated checks from Rabbi Silver. Schmidt understood this development as an indi-cation that the *Vaad* was having difficulties raising money in the United States and therefore was hesitant about arranging additional transfers of this sort. Moreover, despite numerous inquiries to the main office in America, Schmidt was never able to receive a specific answer as to how much money he could exchange. Needless to say, this proved to be a serious handicap in his work in Lithuania. Despite the various problems, Schmidt was able, prior to his departure, to lay the groundwork for additional transfers of funds.

Another consideration that dictated caution was the fear—shared by Rabbi Grodzinski and Dr. Schmidt—that the JDC might reduce the allocation to the refugee yeshivot if they knew that they were receiving "substantial sums" from other sources. This was a distinct possibility, because when Schmidt arrived in Lithuania, the JDC subsidy for each student was 40 lits per month (exactly half of the sum Schmidt estimated was required for the monthly upkeep of one yeshiva student), but by the time he left it had been reduced to 32 lits per month; furthermore, there was talk of a further reduction since the government had stopped paying the fifty percent supplement for charity dollars from abroad. Thus Schmidt and Rabbi Grodzinski agreed at their first meeting that the financial aspects of the former's mission to Lithuania should not be publicized in any manner. This policy was strictly adhered to with the exception of the sums exchanged via government channels and a contribution of 1,000 lits which Schmidt made as a goodwill gesture to the student fund of the government university.

An additional issue which Dr. Schmidt dealt with in the course of his visit was immigration. He spoke to Rabbi Grodzinski several times about the possibility of transferring several of the yeshivot to the United States and Palestine (in accordance with the resolutions passed by the *Vaad ha-Hatzala*) but according to Schmidt, the Vilna Rabbi was skeptical about the possibility of success because of the numerous difficulties ("transport… permission… finances") involved in such a project. If immigration were a practical possibility, Schmidt noted in his summary report, "I am sure that Reb Chaim Ozer looked more favorable towards Palestine for such a transfer." Dr. Schmidt also discussed this topic with other *roshei yeshiva*, but at this point only two spoke to him seriously about transferring their institutions abroad. One was Rabbi Finkel of Mir, who, as was noted above, sought to relocate to Eretz Yisrael. The other was Rabbi Reuven Grazowsky of Kamenetz (who succeeded Rabbi Leibowitz when Leibowitz passed away in late 1939 after escaping to Vilna), who wanted to move his yeshiva to the United States.

While immigration was supposed to be quite high on Dr. Schmidt's agenda, one gets the impression from his reports that he devoted relatively little time to the issue, since the chances of arranging for the immigration intact of all, or even most, of the refugee yeshivot seemed very slim. Moreover, Rabbi Grodzinski, with whom Dr. Schmidt consulted on every issue and without whose approval he did not take any significant step, was extremely skeptical about immigration as a long-range solution for the refugee yeshivot.

In the course of his mission, Dr. Schmidt also met with the refugee community rabbis, who had organized separately under Rabbi Mishkowski of Krinki. In his summary report Dr. Schmidt described their plight in stark terms: "The situation of these rabbis is not a very happy one of course. Many of them enjoyed respectable and lucrative positions before the war and are now forced to live on charity pittance." The community rabbis asked Schmidt for financial assistance and help in immigrating to the United States. They claimed that the subsidy they received from the JDC was insufficient and asked that the *Agudat ha-Rabbanim* bring them to the United States. Schmidt requested that they fill out biographical questionnaires as preparation for immigration, and he gave these to Rabbi Silver upon his return. Rabbi Grodzinski, it should be noted, was opposed to giving funds to the community rabbis without express instructions to that effect from the United States, and therefore they did not receive any of the funds brought by Schmidt. The Cincinnati doctor did, however, bring their plight to the attention of their American colleagues upon his return.[67]

On May 29, 1940, Dr. Schmidt finally received his German transit visa in Kovno, and the next day he left Lithuania by train for Berlin. He stayed one night in "Naziland" and flew the next morning to Rome,[68] from whence he flew to Lisbon. He had hoped to be able to fly to the United States but was unable to do so, so he sailed on the SS *Washington,* which left Portugal on June 10, 1940,[69] arriving in New York eleven days later.[70]

Dr. Schmidt left Lithuania pleased with the results of his trip and fairly confident about the future of the yeshivot. He concluded his summary report with the following statement:

> My appearance in Lithuania raised the hopes of our people in a measure far beyond expectations. My mere presence there

contributed much toward raising the general morale and lent encouragement to all our institutions. The most recent events in Lithuania have no doubt produced changes which may seriously effect the future welfare of our Yeshivos. Yet I feel that there is no cause for despair. I am convinced that even in the future some satisfactory modus of existence will be found to enable the Yeshivos to continue in Lithuania, providing the necessary financial aid will be forthcoming from this country. One thing is certain, the study of Torah will never cease in Lithuania.[71]

Upon his return to the United States, Dr. Schmidt met with the leaders of the *Vaad ha-Hatzala* and reported at length on this mission at a meeting held in New York on July 2, 1940. He brought the *Vaad* complete lists of the refugee rabbis and yeshiva students in Lithuania,[72] told them of their plight, and praised their boundless *mesirut nefesh* (self-sacrifice) for Torah study. Schmidt also delivered a personal blessing from Rabbi Grodzinski to American Jewry in general and to the leaders of *Vaad ha-Hatzala* in particular, along with the Vilna rabbi's urgent request for increased aid to "save the Torah."[73]

By the time Dr. Schmidt returned from Lithuania, *Vaad ha-Hatzala* had considerably expanded its activities and had launched fundraising campaigns all over the United States. A significant portion of the *Vaad's* efforts were directed at federations and welfare funds, and this activity exacerbated its already tenuous relations with the Joint Distribution Committee and the Council of Jewish Federations and Welfare Funds. Throughout the winter of 1939–1940 and the following spring many federations appealed to the JDC and/or to the Council for guidance in dealing with the *Vaad*, whose demands for funds had sparked internal controversies in several communities.[74] In response, the Council sponsored a survey to examine the situation in sixteen cities whose welfare funds regularly contributed relatively large sums to the European yeshivot.

The responses indicated that with the exception of Kansas City, where the *Vaad* was not active at all, and of Cleveland, where the local federation had not been approached but an independent campaign among the Orthodox had been launched, the *Vaad* had used the same tactics in each community. The local federation had been approached, by the local Orthodox rabbi or by a delegation of rabbis from outside the city or by correspondence from the *Vaad's* main office in New York, and was presented with the following ultimatum: either the federation would allocate the sum designated by the *Vaad* as appropriate for their community or the rabbis would conduct a separate fundraising campaign.[75]

The demands made by the *Vaad* were viewed with alarm by the heads of the local federations, who found themselves in a difficult position. On the one hand, they usually were unable to raise enough money to deal adequately with all local and overseas needs. On the other hand, a separate appeal would only make matters worse by reducing the funds raised by the federation. Moreover, the Orthodox elements in several communities applied heavy pressure on the federation to accede to the *Vaad's* request, despite the fact that the figure demanded was usually extremely high and out of all proportion to the community's resources. The resulting conflicts were a source of concern to federation leaders, who sought to avoid internal strife which would undermine community unity and reduce their campaign income. They feared that this battle would be waged along ideological lines and would exacerbate intracommunal tensions. Thus, for example, Louis Greenberg, executive director of the Federation of Youngstown, Ohio, wrote two letters to the Council of Jewish Federations and Welfare Funds explaining the plight of his federation. On January 26, 1940, he wrote to Blanche Renard informing her that his federation had not acceded to the *Vaad's* demand:

> The enclosed situation is one which has led to considerable discussion in our community, on the basis that our Welfare Fund has denied an application to an agency performing a most vital Jewish function. Naturally in view of the fact that all elements in the community are represented in the Federation, the impression is broadcast that the Federation is manned by "assimilationists" hence does not give proper consideration to a vital orthodox Jewish function. As a matter of inter-public relations this is a rather nettlesome situation.[76]

A week later Greenburg further clarified the intracommunal developments in the wake of the *Vaad's* demands:

> You can readily understand the strength of such an emer-

gency campaign among orthodox subscribers in various cities. Many of these read Yiddish exclusively and are not sufficiently familiar with the fact that such agencies would be included in the scope of this appeal which are already beneficiaries of our and other federations and welfare funds. There is a great danger that such an appeal may increase, during a period of stress, the sectarian attitudes of orthodox and non-orthodox subscribers.[77]

In most of the communities, the response of the federation was therefore to negotiate with the rabbis and reach a compromise on the amount of the allocation, which was made on a one-time basis for this specific emergency and in most cases did not affect the federation's regular subvention to the European yeshivot. In this manner, the issue was settled in an amicable fashion and the problematics of a separate fundraising campaign were avoided.[78]

While the local federations were, in most cases, able to reach an agreement with the *Vaad*, the JDC and the Council of Jewish Federations and Welfare Funds were nonetheless perturbed by the *Vaad's* activities and tried to convince welfare funds to transmit their allocations to the refugee yeshivot in Lithuania via the JDC. In response to every inquiry regarding the *Vaad*, officials of both organizations pointed out the problematic aspects of the *Vaad's* activities and suggested alternate means of assisting the refugee Torah scholars. On February 8, 1940, for example, Blanche Renard, secretary of the Council of Jewish Federations and Welfare Fund's Committee on National Jewish Agencies, wrote to Louis Greenberg of Youngstown in response to the latter's inquiry and his suggestion that their appeal be "cleared through federation budgeting rather than in the form of an independent appeal."[79] Her response was very critical of the *Vaad*, and especially of Rabbi Silver, who, in her opinion, should have been more sensitive to the needs of the federations, in view of the fact that he was a member of the budget committee of the Cincinnati welfare fund. "The Emergency Committee, however, has not much sympathy for the difficulties of welfare funds and ... the drive was being undertaken without any consideration of the existence of welfare funds," she bitterly noted.

Renard's criticism of the *Vaad* was not limited to the internal, communal problems their demands had caused. The issue, in her opinion, was far more serious, since she considered the *Vaad* to be unsuited to carry out the task it sought to perform. In her words, "It is our feeling that the Union of Orthodox Rabbis is not equipped with sufficiently detailed and recent information regarding the status of European yeshivot to efficiently allocate funds to them."[80] Renard was also frank in the advice she offered the Toronto Jewish Welfare Fund. On April 1, 1940, she wrote them, in response to their query regarding the Emergency Committee for War-Torn Yeshivot, that the sums they had allocated for three European yeshivot that had escaped to Vilna should be sent via the JDC. Renard pointed out that there was no connection between the *Vaad's* one-time campaign and the regular allocations for the maintenance of the overseas Torah institutions (the funds allocated by Toronto were in the latter category), and therefore "It would seem that you would gain nothing by communicating with the Emergency Committee, whose plans at the moment seem not too definite...."[81]

Numerous requests for information on *Vaad ha-Hatzala* were directed to the JDC as well, and their response was similar to that of the Council of Jewish Federations and Welfare Funds. On April 24, 1940, for example, Henrietta Buchman, secretary of the JDC's Committee on Cultural Affairs, wrote to Elkan Voorsanger of the Milwaukee Jewish Welfare Fund, in response to his inquiry, that the JDC would be happy to transmit Milwaukee's allocation for the refugee yeshivot rather than having them send it through the *Vaad.* "Since Rabbi Grodzinski has for many years cooperated with the JDC in connection with the assistance the JDC extends to European yeshivoth, we could, if you so desire, transmit the $1,000 to our European office with instructions that the money be turned over to Rabbi Grodzinski for assistance to the Polish yeshivoth now in the Vilna area."[82]

This suggestion was only one of the means whereby the JDC sought to discourage welfare funds from contributing to *Vaad ha-Hatzala.* Another argument was that although the *Vaad* had originally been established to effect the relocation of the Polish yeshivot, a task which the JDC by its own admission was indeed unable to perform because of a lack of resources, it was in the meantime devoting all its funds to the maintenance of the refugee scholars, a function the JDC was already performing. For example, Henrietta Buchman wrote to Jacob Lightman of the Houston Jewish Community Council on April 10, 1940, noting that the JDC had already spent more than $450,000 for relief in Lithuania, some of which had been allocated to rabbis and yeshiva students. Moreover, she added, "As we understand it, the campaign for War-Torn yeshivoth has been launched to raise a fund, not for the care of Polish refugee students, but for the physical reestablishment of the former Polish yeshivoth which are now in temporary quarters in Lithuania."[83]

This theme was reiterated in extensive detail by Moses Leavitt, secretary of the JDC, in a letter to Rabbi Abraham Shaw of Baltimore, who had turned to the United Jewish Appeal after Rabbi Kalmanowitz made a speech on behalf of *Vaad ha-Hatzala*. (Rabbi Kalmanowitz had recently arrived in the United States from Vilna, where he had been in close contact with the refugee yeshivot.) In the course of his appeal for funds, Rabbi Kalmanowitz had claimed, according to Rabbi Shaw, that the refugee rabbis and students had been threatened by the Lithuanian government with deportation back to Poland if they could not produce maintenance guarantees of $500,000.[84] Leavitt's reply, while formulated in a diplomatic fashion, contradicted Kalmanowitz's claim in a clear-cut manner, noting that "an understanding has been reached with the authorities that refugees in Lithuania from the Nazi-held area of Poland, will not be compelled to return there against their will. Moreover, the *Vaad's* self-proclaimed goal," Leavitt noted, "was the relocation of the yeshivot which the JDC was already taking care of." In addition, in response to Rabbi Kalmanowitz's claim that the JDC did not oppose the *Vaad's* campaign, Leavitt concluded his letter with the following statement, which appeared in the report issued by the Council of Jewish Federations and Welfare Funds on the *Vaad ha-Hatzala* and which in essence summarized the official approach of the JDC and CJFWF:

> The Joint Distribution Committee, which contributes to most of the European yeshivoth through its Cultural Committee and other projects and which already has made grants to some of these agencies for emergency needs, has been asked to advise on this campaign. The JDC feels that it is not in a position to approve or disapprove this effort. It has, however, always maintained that in order to avoid a multiplicity of fund-raising drives, contributions for programs and projects subventioned by the major overseas organizations should be centralized through one agency.[85]

The message was quite clear. The JDC would not publicly oppose the *Vaad*, but there was every reason not to contribute funds to the *Vaad's* campaign since their efforts duplicated those of the JDC and caused confusion and internal strife.

The officials of the JDC and the Council of Jewish Federations and Welfare Funds did not confine their criticism to correspondence with local federations. On several occasions in the spring of 1940 they communicated with the *Vaad* and asked for clarification regarding what they considered to be the problematic aspects of the *Vaad's* activities. For example, on May 17, 1940, Carol Kuhn of the Council wrote to Rabbi Karlinsky of the *Vaad* regarding the use made by the rabbinic rescue organization of the funds they had raised up to that point.

> With the exception of the latter item [a special fund for the transfer of 400 students to Palestine] all funds appropriated seem to have been for relief and maintenance purposes. Since it is our understanding that the Joint Distribution Committee has appropriated large sums for this work, the appropriations of the Emergency Committee would seem to be duplicating this effort rather than working toward the permanent re-establishment of the yeshivoth. We had understood this latter to be the original aim of your committee. Could you let me know what the committee has been able to do or plans to do regarding this project?[86]

This letter was followed by a meeting on June 4, 1940, between Rabbi Kalmanowitz and JDC officials at which an attempt was made to achieve a *modus vivendi* between the two relief agencies. The results, however, were not satisfactory, as is indicated by a letter Henrietta Buchman wrote to Rabbi Karlinsky a week later. She noted that the JDC was fully aware of the information that Rabbi Kalmanowitz had presented on the plight of the refugee yeshivot in Lithuania and that it had already extended whatever aid it could to this group. "Of course the greater the contributions to the JDC, the greater will be the measure of aid we shall be in a position to make available to yeshivoth and rabbis, as well as for the many other urgent requirements not only in Vilna, but in all parts of the world." According to Buchman, the basic problem was, therefore, the structure of the existent fundraising framework of the American Jewish community:

Doubtless, you are aware that the JDC fundraising efforts are this year included in the United Jewish Appeal. The JDC is not conducting a separate campaign for funds. The UJA arrangement has been agreed upon to meet the expressed desire of Jewish communities throughout the country that to the greatest extent possible the confusion and irritation of separate appeals be eliminated, and to marshal all our forces in order that the greatest response may be had from the good people here who contribute the funds.

As we tried to make clear to Rabbi Kalmanowitz, the introduction of additional separate fundraising efforts serves only to confuse and irritate the Jewish communities in the country and cannot but reduce the contributions to the UJA. It seems to us, therefore, that it would be more advantageous to all concerned if the Orthodox leaders sponsoring your appeal would lend their active assistance to the UJA to help raise the funds so sorely needed for the activities which derive their major support from the organizations included in the United Jewish Appeal. Such cooperation, we feel certain, would increase the funds that would be available to the JDC, which in turn would then be in a better position to allot a larger measure of help for yeshivoth, as well as for other pruposes.[87]

We have no indication that the rabbis of the *Vaad* ever took Buchman's suggestion of joining the UJA seriously. On the contrary, the rabbis insisted on maintaining their independent framework and continued their appeals to local federations and welfare funds. In this context it should be noted that the criticism and skepticism regarding the *Vaad's* activities were not confined to the JDC and CJFWF and even existed in the Orthodox community. In February 1940, for example, *The Jewish Outlook*, the monthly of the Mizrachi Organization of America, expressed its support for the goals of the *Vaad ha-Hatzala* but questioned the need for the establishment of a separate organization and criticized its campaign tactics:

Could not the Joint Distribution Committee in spite of the heavy burdens it must now bear, better deal with the problem than a mere committee, however energetic and able, gotten up overnight? Could not sufficient pressure be brought upon the allocators of funds so that they recognize that the soul of a Jew needs feeding not less than his body, and that a hungry, homeless student or teacher is suffering doubly—in body and spirit? Second, is the method of campaigning the best that could have been evolved? If Weitzman could come for the cause of Palestine, and Nahum Goldman for the cause of the Congress, why could not one of the recognized sages and leaders of religious Jewry be with us here to guide, to direct and to inspire? This is by no means a reflection on the high caliber of those who are laboring in the campaign now. Their labors, however, would have been lightened and the results would have been more productive were such a personality among us now.[88]

Other Orthodox organizations, particularly those with more American-born (as opposed to immigrant) members, were hardly more enthusiastic in their support of the *Vaad* than was the Mizrachi. For example, both Young Israel and the Union of Orthodox Jewish Congregations (see Chapter 5) supported the rabbinic rescue organization, but at this point it ranked very low on their list of priorities and they devoted much more effort to encouraging their members to support religious Jewish education in the United States than to saving the premier Torah academies of Europe.[89]

Despite the *Vaad's* quarrels with the JDC and CJFWF and the lack of enthusiasm it engendered even in some Orthodox circles, the rabbinic rescue organization succeeded in raising approximately $100,000 by the end of June 1940. Of this sum, $50,300 was given to the New York offices of ten refugee yeshivot for transmission to their institutions (the sums based on previous budgets): Mir ($9,000); Kamenetz ($6,000); Radin ($5,000); Lomza ($6,000); Kletzk ($6,000); Bialystok ($4,500); Baranowitz ($5,000); Volozhin ($2,800); Slonim ($2,800); and Grodno ($3,200). Another $37,000 was sent to Rabbi Grodzinski, who worked out a distribution plan after consulting with the *roshei yeshivot* in Lithuania; the sums were to be allocated according to various criteria such as the number of students and the resources of the yeshiva (as outlined by Dr. Schmidt in his summary report on his trip to Lithuania). In addition, $5,000 was set aside for the transfer of students to Palestine,[90] and small sums were allocated for refugee students at Hungarian yeshivot ($1,000) and for the Torat Chaim Yeshiva in Warsaw ($1,200).[91] These funds were transmitted to the refugee yeshivot in Lithuania by means of the transfer arrangements described above, which had been worked out by Dr. Schmidt in the course of his mission.

While the sums raised by the *Vaad ha-Hatzala* during the period from fall 1939 to summer 1940 were much lower than the amount the rabbis had hoped to collect (the proclaimed goal was $500,000 for the relocation campaign, but in internal documents the figure cited was $250,000),[92] their campaign was fairly successful in light of the numerous obstacles they had to overcome. Moreover, any assessment of the public's response to the *Vaad ha-Hatzala's* campaign must take into consideration several additional factors. According to figures published in fall 1940, most of the funds raised by the *Vaad* during the initial year of its existence came from the Orthodox community. The balance, slightly more than seventeen percent of the money contributed to *Vaad ha-Hatzala*, were allocations from federations and welfare funds.[93]

We must keep in mind, however, that the *Vaad* was only one of numerous causes that appealed to Orthodox Jews in the United States for funds during this period. In addition to "American" causes such as the Interfaith Committee for Aid to Democracies (which assisted the British War Relief Society) and the Red Cross, there were Jewish causes such as the United Jewish Appeal and specifically Orthodox causes such as *Ezrat Torah*, yeshivot in America, the religious and charitable institutions of the ultra-Orthodox community in Palestine, and various emergency funds and refugee bureaus established by Orthodox groups. In view of the fact that so many organizations were competing for the limited charity dollars of American Orthodox Jews, the sums initially raised by *Vaad ha-Hatzala* were relatively large.[94]

Another factor to be taken into consideration is that the leaders of the *Vaad* did not devote themselves exclusively to fundraising for the rabbinic rescue organization. As leaders of other national Orthodox organizations, they could not allow themselves the "luxury" of working solely for *Vaad ha-Hatzala*. (Eliezer Silver was president of American Agudat Yisrael and Yisrael Halevi Rosenberg was president of *Ezrat Torah,* to cite two prominent examples.) Thus in Adar 5700 (March 11 to April 8, 1940) fundraising for the *Vaad* was temporarily suspended so that efforts could be devoted to raising funds for the United Jewish Appeal and *Ezrat Torah*.[95] On other occasions, the rabbis who headed the rabbinic rescue organization called upon American Jews to contribute to such causes as the

United Jewish Appeal,[96] a rescue campaign sponsored by the Lubavitcher Rebbe,[97] and a forest to be planted in Eretz Yisrael in honor of Rabbi Meir Berlin (under the auspices of the Mizrachi Organization of America).[98]

Another factor significantly affecting the *Vaad's* success during this period was the skepticism that greeted its establishment. The fact that several major Orthodox organizations initially questioned the need for its establishment or did not accord its efforts a high priority on their agendas undoubtedly hampered *Vaad ha-Hatzala's* activities. This problem was to some extent overcome during the spring and summer of 1940, however, because of other factors, such as the arrival in the United States of Rabbi Avraham Kalmanowitz, the president of the Mir Yeshiva, who was sent by Rabbi Grodzinski and Rabbi Shapiro of Kovno to attempt to secure aid for the refugee yeshivot.[99]

Rabbi Kalmanowitz was a well-known figure in the American Orthodox community. Since 1925 he had made periodic visits to the United States to raise funds for the Mir Yeshiva, and thanks to his efforts a network of supporters, as well as a New York office of the yeshiva, had been established.[100] He arrived in America in the winter of 1939–1940, after fleeing from Poland to Vilna with the Mir Yeshiva. From the time he reached the United States, he devoted himself almost completely to the rescue of the refugee yeshivot,[101] especially the Mir Yeshiva, with whom he maintained steady contact throughout the war.[102] Rabbi Kalmanowitz was a physically impressive individual (he had a long white beard and a saintly appearance), known for his ability to cry and faint at will, and his efforts on behalf of *Vaad ha-Hatzala* made a strong impact on the American Jewish community.[103] Moreover, the fact that he, who had personally participated in the flight of the yeshivot to Vilna and was an eyewitness to their plight in Lithuania, had dedicated himself to the cause of the *Vaad* helped the rabbinic rescue organization gain the support of the Orthodox public. This proved to be of essential importance in the ensuing months as events in Lithuania created a new crisis for the refugee rabbis and yeshiva students.

Notes

1. Arad/YVS, pp. 206–207; Joshua Lichtiger, *The Odyssey of a Jew* (New York, 1979); Ben–Zion Benshalom, *Be–Sa'ar be–Yom Sufa* (Tel–Aviv, 1944), pp. 152–153; Yitzhak Edelstein, "Be–Yemei Sufa," *Gal–ed*, 3 (1976), 335.
2. Zerach Warhaftig, *Palit ve–Sarid be–Yemei ha–Shoa* (Jerusalem, 1984), pp. 38–39. According to Rothstein in *Achiezer*, p. 726, Rabbi Grodzinski himself sent emissaries to occupied Poland to encourage rabbis and yeshiva students to come to Vilna. According to Rabbi Zelig Epstein, however, Rabbi Grodzinski opposed the move to Vilna, since he foresaw the Soviet occupation of Lithuania and knew that they prohibited emigration. Testimony (July 7, 1977) in possession of the author. For details on the emissaries sent by the Zionist youth movements see Yaakov Even–Chen, *Tenu'a be–Sa'arat Milchama* (Tel–Aviv, 1984), pp. 53–55, 80–82, 95, 127; Yehoshua Gilboa, *Lishmor la–Netzach* (Tel–Aviv, n.d.), pp. 20–24.
3. Arad/YVS, p. 206.
4. Testimony of Shalom Dorner, Archives of the Institute for Holocaust Research, Bar Ilan University (hereafter called BIA), Daled–3, p. 4; Tova Wiernik, for example, crossed the border successfully in late December 1939 on her sixth try! See her testimony in possession of the author; testimony of L. Bruk, Archives of Beit Lochamei ha–Gettaot (hereafter called ABLG), H. 478.
5. Lichtiger, *Odyssey of a Jew*, p. 74; letter of Dr. Samuel Schmidt to Mrs. Schmidt, February 20, 1940, Papers of Dr. Samuel M. Schmidt, American Jewish Archives, Hebrew Union College, Cincinnati. (Hereafter called SMS–AJA). Schmidt was sent by *Vaad ha–Hatzala* to Lithuania in early 1940 and heard first–hand from the refugees about the difficulties in reaching Vilna.
6. Letter of Rabbi Grodzinski to Dr. Cyrus Adler, December 31, 1939, Archives of the American Jewish Joint Distribution Committee (hereafter called AJDC), Vaad ha–Hatzala file.
7. Even–Chen, *Tenu'a be–Sa'arat Milchama*, p. 129.
8. Letter of Rabbi Grodzinski to Rabbi Yisrael Halevi Rosenberg, December 19, 1939, Papers of Rabbi Yisrael Halevi Rosenberg, Jewish Theological Seminary, New York City. (Hereafter called AYHR).
9. Testimony of Shalom Dorner, BIA, Daled–3, p. 4.
10. Warhaftig, *Palit ve–Sarid*, p. 28.
11. Edelstein, "Be–Yemei Sufa," pp. 337–338.
12. Dr. Robinson subsequently became one of the leading experts on the Holocaust. See "In Memoriam Jacob Robinson (1889–1977)," *Yad Vashem Studies*, XII (Jerusalem, 1977), p. 1.
13. Tzvi Barak, "Plitei Polin be–Lita ba–Shanim 1939–1941," *Yahadut Lita*, II (Tel–Aviv, 1972), p. 361; Yehuda Bauer, "Rescue Operations Through Vilna," *Yad Vashem Studies*, IX (Jerusalem, 1973) (hereafter caller Bauer/YVS), pp. 215–216; Yehuda Bauer, *American Jewry and the Holocaust; The American Jewish Joint Distribution Committee 1939–1945* (Detroit, 1981), p. 112; Rothstein, in *Achiezer*, p. 54.
14. Letter of Rabbi Bloch to Rabbi Blau, November 16, 1939, AAYEY, file 62.
15. Letter of Rabbi Grodzinski to Rabbi Herzog, January 26, 1940, Papers of Rabbi Yitzhak Halevi Herzog, Heichal Shlomo, Jerusalem (hereafter called AYHH), file of the letters of Rabbi Grodzinski. In Rabbi Kotler's words, the move would be bene-

ficial because "a town is more suitable for spirituality." See his letter to Rabbi Karelitz in Moshe Prager, "Roshei ha–Yeshivot she–Nimletu mi–Gay ha–Avadon ve–Lapid ha–Torah be–Yedeihem," *Beit Yaakov*, vol. XII, no. 3, p. 6.

16. "Bi'ayat ha–Plitim ha–Yehudim be–Lita," a report by Zerach Warhaftig, January 22, 1940, CZA, S–26/1300; letter of Rabbi Grodzinski to Rabbi Rosenberg, December 19, 1939, AYHR.

17. "Addresses of Lithuanian and Latvian Yeshivas and Polish Yeshivas in exile at [sic] Lithuania," ACRC, file 492–2; Chechik testimony; Rothstein, in *Achiezer*, p. 56; Warhaftig, *Palit ve–Sarid*, p. 141, based on a report that appeared in *Ha–Tzofe*, April 25, 1940.

18. Cable of Rabbi Finkel to the Central Relief Committee, November 7, 1939, ACRC.

19. Letters of Rabbi Grodzinski to Rabbi Herzog (November 15, 1939) and Rabbi Meier Karelitz (December 11, 1939), Sursky, *Achiezer*, pp. 225–227.

20. Letter of Rabbi Finkel to Moshe Shapiro, January 28, 1940, YVA, P–20.

21. Letter of Rabbi Kotler to the Jewish Agency, March 11, 1940, YVA, P–20.

22. Letter of Rabbi Grodzinski to Rabbi Herzog, November 15, 1939, Sursky, *Achiezer*, pp. 225–226.

23. Letter of Rabbi Eliyahu Bloch to Rabbi Moshe Blau, November 16, 1939, AAYEY, file 62.

24. Cable of Rabbi Leibowitz to the Central Relief Committee, November 7, 1939, ACRC.

25. Letter of Rabbi Blau to Rabbi Eliezer Silver, December 15, 1939, AAYEY, file 44. See note no. 19. Warhaftig, *Palit ve–Sarid*, p. 138.

26. Ibid., p. 45.

27. Ibid., p. 145; Report of Dr. Samuel Schmidt on his trip to Lithuania (1940) on behalf of *Vaad ha–Hatzala*, undated, SMS–AJA, microfilm no. 855.

28. Letter of Rabbi Grodzinski to Rabbi Silver, March 11, 1940, Silver Archives.

29. Hillel Zeidman, *Ishim she–Hikarti* (Jerusalem, 1970), p. 257; interview of the author with Rabbi Shimon Romm, July 27, 1977.

30. Warhaftig, *Palit ve–Sarid*, p. 142.

31. Ibid., pp. 136–137; letter of Rabbi Grodzinski to Rabbis Rosenberg and Teitelbaum, December 19, 1939, AYHR. Samuel Schmidt report on his trip to Lithuania, undated, SMS–AJA, microfilm no. 855. The desperation felt by the community rabbis is reflected in the fact that Warhaftig believed that they preferred to go to Eretz Yisrael, while Schmidt relates that they asked that the *Agudat ha–Rabbanim* bring them to the United States.

32. "Avodat Vaad ha–Hatzala," *Ha–Pardes*, 13, no. 10 (Tevet 5700/January 1940), 8.

33. Memo of A. M. Sirkin to Carol Kuhn, January 9, 1940, ACJFWF, I–69, box 149.

34. Letter of Rabbi Silver to Rabbi Moshe Blau, November 26, 1939, AAYEY, file 44. Blau, the leader of the Eretz Yisrael branch of Agudat Yisrael, had hoped to come to the United States to raise funds for his organization. Silver attempted to dissuade him from doing so because of the emergency campaign for the yeshivot.

35. "Emergency Committee. for War–Torn Yeshivoth under the auspices of the Union of Orthodox Rabbis," Budgeting Bulletin no. 77, February 1, 1940, p. 2, ACJFWF, Council of Jewish Federation and Welfare Funds reports: *Vaad ha–Hatzala*.

36. Ibid.

37. Letter of Rabbi Wasserman to Abraham Horowitz, December 19, 1939, ACJFWF, I–69, Box 149.
38. See note 35.
39. Ibid., pp. 1–2.
40. "Biographical Sketch," *Every Friday*, July 19, 1940, p. 7; *Churbn un Rettung*, pp. 161, 166–167, 174; letters of Dr. Schmidt to his wife, February–June 1940, SMS–AJA, microfilm no. 855.
41. Interview with Dr. Schmidt, Cincinnati, April 15, 1964 by Dr. Stanley F. Chyet and students of Hebrew Union College, SMS–AJA, tape recording no. 209.
42. Letter of Dr. Schmidt to Mrs. Schmidt, February 17, 1940, SMS–AJA, microfilm no. 855.
43. Letter of Dr. Schmidt to Mrs. Schmidt, February 20, 1940, SMS–AJA, microfilm no. 855.
44. Letters of Dr. Schmidt to Mrs. Schmidt, February 25 and 28, 1940, SMS–AJA, microfilm no. 855.
45. Letter of Dr. Schmidt to Mrs. Schmidt, February 28, 1940, SMS–AJA, microfilm no. 855.
46. Letters of Dr. Schmidt to Mrs. Schmidt, February 28 – June 2, 1940, SMS–AJA, microfilm no. 855.
47. The students of the Radin Yeshiva whom Schmidt met were approximately 100 boys who were waiting to move to Eishishuk, where the rest of their yeshiva had already been reestablished.
48. Letter of Dr. Schmidt to Mrs. Schmidt, February 28, 1940, SMS–AJA, microfilm no. 855; "Our Cultural Reservoir," *Every Friday*, April 19, 1940, p. 2.
49. Letter of Dr. Schmidt to Mrs. Schmidt, February 28, 1940, SMS–AJA, microfilm no. 855.
50. Ibid.
51. Letter of Dr. Schmidt to Mrs. Schmidt, March 8, 1940, SMS–AJA, microfilm no. 855.
52. Ibid.
53. Ibid.
54. Letters of Dr. Schmidt to Mrs. Schmidt, March 17 and 28, 1940, SMS–AJA, microfilm no. 855.
55. Letter of Dr. Schmidt to Mrs. Schmidt, March 17, 1940, SMS–AJA, microfilm no. 855.
56. Letters of Dr. Schmidt to Mrs. Schmidt, March 28 and April 7, 1940, SMS–AJA, microfilm no. 855.
57. Letter of Dr. Mickus, director of Health Department, Lithuanian Ministry of the Interior, to Doctors Hans Zinser and Harry Pilitz, March 28, 1940, SMS–AJA, microfilm no. 855.
58. Letter of Dr. Schmidt to Mrs. Schmidt, March 17, 1940, SMS–AJA, microfilm no. 855; "In the Land of War-Torn Yeshivoth," *Every Friday*, May 17,1940, p. 2.
59. Letter of Dr. Schmidt to Mrs. Schmidt, April 7, 1940, SMS–AJA, microfilm no. 855.
60. Letter of Dr. Schmidt to Mrs. Schmidt, April 14, 1940, SMS–AJA, microfilm no. 855.
61. Letters of Dr. Schmidt to Mrs. Schmidt, April 17 and 27, May 3 and 7, 1940,

SMS–AJA, microfilm no. 855.

62. Letter of Dr. Schmidt to Mrs. Schmidt, May 7, 1940, SMS–AJA, microfilm no. 855.

63. Letter of Dr. Schmidt to Mrs. Schmidt, May 3, 1940, SMS–AJA, microfilm no. 855.

64. Letter of Dr. Schmidt to Mrs. Schmidt, May 7, 1940, SMS–AJA, microfilm no. 855.

65. Letter of Dr. Schmidt to Mrs. Schmidt, May 3, 1940, SMS–AJA, microfilm no. 855.

66. Letters of Dr. Schmidt to Mrs. Schmidt, March 7 and June 2, 1940, SMS–AJA, microfilm no. 855; report by Dr. Schmidt on his trip to Lithuania, undated, SMS–AJA, microfilm no. 855.

67. Ibid.; letter of Dr. Schmidt to Rabbi Silver, June 6, 1940, SMS–AJA, microfilm no. 855.

68. Letter of Dr. Schmidt to Mrs. Schmidt, June 2, 1940, SMS–AJA, microfilm no. 855.

69. Letter of Dr. Schmidt to Mrs. Schmidt, June 10, 1940, SMS–AJA, microfilm no. 855.

70. Letter of Dr. Schmidt to V. Icikovic, June 28, 1940, SMS–AJA, microfilm no. 855.

71. Dr. Schmidt's summary report on his trip to Lithuania, undated, SMS–AJA, microfilm no. 855.

72. "Vaad ha–Hatzala," *Ha–Pardes*, 14, no. 4 (Tammuz 5700/July 1940), 3–4; "List of refugee yeshivot," undated, SMS–AJA, microfilm no. 855.

73. *Churbn un Rettung*, p. 177.

74. See, for example, the letters of Louis Greenberg (Youngstown, OH) to Blanche Renard, January 26, 1940; Elkan Voorsanger (Milwaukee) to the Council of Jewish Federations, February 6, 1940, both ACJFWF, I–69, Box 149.

75. "Emergency Committee for War–Torn Yeshivoth," Budgeting for Member Agencies, No. 86, issued by the Council of Jewish Federations and Welfare Funds, March 27, 1940; see also the responses of the following communities to the questions posed by the Council; Minneapolis; Springfield, MA; St. Paul, Omaha, Miami, Cleveland, Harrisburg, PA, Cincinnati, Tulsa, and Atlanta, ACJFWF, I–69, Box 149.

76. Letter of Louis Greenberg to Blanche Renard, January 26, 1940, ACJFWF, I–69, Box 149.

77. Letter of Louis Greenberg to Blanche Renard, February 2, 1940, ACJFWF, I–69, Box 149.

78. See note no. 75.

79. Letter of Louis Greenberg to Blanche Renard, February 2, 1940, ACJFWF, I–69, Box 149.

80. Letter of Blanche Renard to Louis Greenberg, February 8, 1940, ACJFWF, I–69, Box 149.

81. Letter of Blanche Renard to Florence Hunter, April 1, 1940, ACJFWF, I–69, Box 149.

82. Letter of Henrietta Buchman to Elkan Voorsanger, April 24, 1940, AJDC–VH.

83. Letter of Henrietta Buchman to Jacob Lightman, April 10, 1940, ACJFWF, I–69, Box 149.

84. Letter of Rabbi Shaw to Rabbi Jonah Wise, May 14,1940, ACJFWF, I–69, Box 149.

85. Letter of Moses Leavitt to Rabbi Shaw, May 16, 1940, ACJFWF, I–69, Box 149.

86. Letter of Carol Kuhn to Rabbi Karlinsky, May 17, 1940, ACJFWF, I–69, Box 149.

87. Letter of Henrietta Buchman to Rabbi Karlinsky, June 11, 1940, AJDC–VH.

88. "Distress of the Yeshivot," *Jewish Outlook*, 4, no. 6, (February 1940), p. 4.

89. Interview with Elijah Stein, financial secretary of the Young Israel movement, April 16, 1974; interview with Herman Hollander, a leader of American Mizrachi, December 18, 1973.

90. Memorandum of Carol Kuhn to Blanche Renard regarding the Emergency Committee for War–Torn Yeshivoth, July 5, 1940, ACJFWF, I–69, Box 149.

91. Letter of Carol Kuhn to Judah Shapiro, May 2, 1940, ACJFWF, I–69, Box 149.

92. The Decisions of the Allocations Committee Which Met on March 26, 1940, AVH; "Emergency Committee for War–Torn Yeshivoth under the auspices of the Union of Orthodox Rabbis," Budgeting for Member Agencies, No. 77, February 1, 1940, ACJFWF, CJFWF reports: *Vaad ha–Hatzala*.

93. "Status of East European Yeshivoth, Methods Of Transmitting Funds and Activities of Emergency Committee for War–Torn Yeshivoth (Replacing Bulletin #116)," Budgeting for Member Agencies No. 123, October 1940, issued by the Council of Jewish Federations and Welfare Funds, AVH.

94. For example, the 1941 budget of the Mizrachi Organization, which claimed a membership of 27,000, was $47,000. "1941 Convention," *Jewish Outlook*, 5, no. 10 (June 1941), pp. 10–11.

95. "Vaad ha–Hatzala la–Yeshivot di–Airopa," *Ha–Pardes*, 14, no. 1, (Nissan 5700/April 1940), 3, p. 5.

96. "Hachrazat Agudat ha–Rabbanim le–Teshuva vi–le–Tefila u–Tzedaka," *Ha–Pardes*, 14, no. 3, (Sivan 5700/June 1940), p. 2.

97. "Pidyon Shevuyim," *Ha–Pardes*, 14, no. 5, (Av 5700/August 1940), p. 9.

98. "To the Rabbis, Presidents and Officers of the Orthodox Congregations in the U.S.," *Jewish Outlook*, 4, no. 5, (January 1940), 8.

99. "Oreiach Gadol ve–Chashuv," *Ha–Pardes*, 13, no. 11, (Adar 5700/February 1940), p. 2.

100. Epstein, "Yeshivat Mir," pp. 114–115; interview with Rabbi Alex Weisfogel, executive–director of the Mir Yeshiva during the years 1940–1942, July 22, 1973.

101. Asher Rand, Ed., *Toldot Anshei Shem* (New York, 5710 [1950]), p. 117.

102. "Vaad ha–Hatzala," *Ha–Pardes*, 14, no. 6 (Elul 5700/September 1940), p. 27; for example, the cable of Rabbi Finkel to Rabbi Kalmanowitz, *Letters and Documents*, New York, n.d., p. 106.

103. Weisfogel interview; interview with Dr. Gershon Kranzler, executive secretary of Tzirei Agudat Yisrael, April 29, 1974.

Chapter 4

Visas to Curaçao and Rescue via the Far East

On June 15, 1940, Lithuanian independence came to an abrupt end as Soviet troops entered the Baltic republic and seized control (in accordance with the secret terms of the Molotov–Ribbentrop Pact of August 23, 1939). Two days later a Communist government headed by Justas Palesckis was established,[1] and on August 3, 1940, Lithuania was officially annexed by the Soviet Union and became a Soviet republic.[2] In the meantime, on July 1, the Soviets banned all organizations and political parties with the exception of the Communist Party,[3] and thus made clear their intention to apply in Lithuania the same stringent restrictions on Jewish education and culture as existed in the Soviet Union, even though these specific measures were not immediately instituted. Thus the refugee rabbis and yeshiva students in Lithuania found themselves in the same situation they had faced in September 1939 following the Soviet occupation of Eastern Poland. They knew that the yeshivot could not exist for long under Communist rule,[4] and so the Soviet annexation forced them to consider seriously the various means of leaving Lithuania. The problem was, however, that in the spring of 1940 there was no nearby convenient haven to escape to, as had been the case in fall 1939. Thus the escape to Vilna had not solved the problem but had merely postponed it. In the words of a popular joke which circulated at that time among the Jews in Lithuania, "We have been spared the death sentence but have been sentenced instead to life imprisonment."[5]

Within a few weeks after the Soviet takeover, the authorities began to close down Jewish educational institutions. In response, several of the yeshivot took steps aiming to preserve their schools. The students were split up into small groups and dispersed to near-by towns and villages in the hope that they would be less conspicuous and consequently less vulnerable. For example, the Mir Yeshiva, which had been ordered by the local Communists in Keydan to leave the city, split into four groups which went to Krakinova, Remigole, Shat (Seta), and Krok (Krakes). The *rosh yeshiva*, Rabbi Finkel, lived in Grinkishuk (Grinkiskis), where he and his secretary, Rabbi Epstein, coordinated activities, and the *mashgiach* (spiritual supervisor) went from group to group to give lectures and encourage the students.[6] The Kletzk Yeshiva, which had relocated in Jeneve, sent its students to Sluk (Salakas), Dusyat (Dusetos), and Dukshat.[7]

These steps did not, however, solve the major problem. By summer 1940 it had become increasingly obvious that the only possible means of preserving the yeshivot intact was emigration. The question was: emigration to where? The *roshei yeshivot* preferred Eretz Yisrael and the United States, but in both cases immigration policy precluded the transfer intact of all the yeshivot. In May 1939 the immigration of Jews to Eretz Yisrael had been limited by the infamous British White Paper to 10,000 per year for 1939–1944, plus an additional 25,000 refugees.[8] This figure however, was, divided into various categories based on professions and financial status, with rabbis and yeshiva students (categories B-2 and B-3)[9] accorded an extremely small number of visas. During April and May 1940, 32 rabbis were granted immigration certificates and there were months when the figure was even lower. Moreover, there were rabbis elsewhere who wanted to immigrate to Eretz Yisrael because their lives were in danger, and the few visas granted by the British could not all be sent to the refugee rabbis and yeshiva students in Lithuania.[10]

In this context it should be noted that during the entire period in which the refugee Torah scholars were in Vilna, efforts had been made, primarily by the chief rabbinate led by Ashkenazic Chief Rabbi Yitzhak ha-Levi Herzog and the leaders of local Agudat Yisrael, to obtain *aliyah* certificates for the refugee yeshivot. On February 6, 1940, Rabbi Herzog traveled to London to appeal to the British authorities to grant a special allotment of 1,000 visas for the refugee scholars as an emergency measure. According to Rabbi Herzog's proposal, the yeshiva students admitted to Eretz Yisrael would be granted tourist visas valid for five years (the usual tourist visa was for a maximum of one year) during which time they would complete their rabbinical training and at the end of which they would go abroad and serve in Diaspora communities. While in England, Rabbi Herzog also conferred with Ivan Maisky, the local Soviet ambassador, in an attempt to secure the necessary Soviet transit visas.[11]

Rabbi Herzog knew that the British would demand financial guarantees for the maintenance of these prospective immigrants, and so prior to his journey he had turned to the *Vaad ha-Hatzala*, Central Relief Committee and the JDC for assistance. On February 3, 1940, Rabbi Silver had cabled that the *Vaad* was willing to provide the necessary funds, and indeed a sum was set aside for this purpose.[12] Approximately two months later a special meeting of the major Orthodox relief agencies was convened in response to another appeal by Rabbi Herzog to Rabbi Silver for financial assistance. At the meeting the *Vaad* and Central Relief undertook to provide a monthly stipend of £4 per yeshiva student for four hundred students during the first two years after their arrival in Eretz Yisrael.[13] All this was not enough, however, since the British refused to make any special concessions and did not increase the number of visas.[14]

Despite the intransigence of the British and the fact that only a few of the *roshei yeshivot* were attempting to immigrate to Eretz Yisrael,[15] the chief rabbinate and the local branch of Agudat Yisrael continued their efforts to obtain certificates for all the refugee scholars, even though during the winter (1939–1940) and spring of 1940 it did not appear as if their immigration was a realistic possibility.[16] (Several hundred Polish refugees had managed to immigrate from Lithuania to Eretz Yisrael via Latvia, Sweden, and Western Europe in March 1940, but that route became too risky in the wake of the German occupation of the Benelux countries and France.)[17]

As far as immigration to the United States was concerned, the number of immigrants admitted yearly was determined by the quotas instituted in 1924. The annual quota for Polish immigrants was 6,524 (immigration applications were processed on the basis of the applicant's nationality, not his or her place of residence at the time of the application) and throughout this period the number of Polish citizens seeking to immigrate to the United States was much larger than the number of available places. Moreover, various government directives to the State Department officials who implemented U.S.

immigration policy made it extremely difficult for the applicants to fulfill the stringent requirements,[18] and thus the American option did not seem to be a realistic possibility for the masses of Polish refugee rabbis and yeshiva students. Indeed, despite the fact that *Vaad ha-Hatzala* had publicly proclaimed that one of its major goals was to bring some of the refugee yeshivot to the United States,[19] it initially devoted relatively little time and resources to practical efforts in this direction. Although the rabbis continually stressed the themes of rescue and relocation in their fundraising appeals, the funds raised by the *Vaad* during this period were allocated almost exclusively for the maintenance of the refugee yeshivot in Lithuania.[20]

In addition to the various problems involved in obtaining visas to Eretz Yisrael and the United States, there were numerous other obstacles to overcome before the refugees could leave the Soviet Union. For example, with the exception of the Mir Yeshiva, whose *rosh yeshiva,* Rabbi Finkel, had taken measures to ensure that valid passports were obtained for all his students,[21] practically none of the refugee rabbis and yeshiva students possessed the necessary travel documents. In addition, transit visas had to be obtained for each of the countries traversed enroute, transportation had to be arranged and paid for, and Soviet exit permits had to be secured.[22] These "technical" problems were magnified when the Soviets announced that the foreign embassies and consulates in Lithuania would have to cease operations by August 24, 1940.[23] The practical implication of this directive was that from that date on, all the contacts with the authorities in order to obtain the documents necessary for emigration would have to be conducted in Moscow, which was several hundred kilometers away. This new situation increased the feeling of hopelessness of the already-desperate Polish refugees in Lithuania.[24] Yet at this very point, when the future appeared so ominous and foreboding, a rescue possibility developed from a totally unexpected direction.

In early summer 1940 Nathan Gutwirth and Leo Sternheim, two Dutch Jews studying at Lithuanian yeshivot, applied to Jan Zwartendijk, the honorary Dutch consul in Kovno, for permission to enter one of the Dutch overseas colonies, since they could not return to their homes in Holland, which had been occupied by the Nazis in May 1940. Gutwirth and Sternheim had originally thought of going to Indonesia, but in the course of conversation they came up with the idea of going to Curaçao, an island in the Caribbean off the coast of Venezuela. Zwartendijk was willing to help, but since he was only an honorary consul, he turned to L. P. Decker, the Dutch (nonresident) ambassador to Lithuania, who was stationed in Riga, for permission to issue the visas. The latter informed Zwartendijk that Gutwirth and Sternheim did not require a visa to enter Curaçao, since permission was contingent upon the approval of the island's governor. Zwartendijk thereupon issued a document to that effect to the two yeshiva students in lieu of a regular visa.

Gutwirth and Sternheim told Zerach Warhaftig about the document they had obtained from the Dutch consul, and he suggested that they find out whether Zwartendijk would be willing to issue similar documents to non-Dutch citizens. In addition, Warhaftig advised that the "visa" be stamped into their passports and, to whatever extent possible, that it resemble an official visa. Zwartendijk agreed to the yeshiva students' request, on the condition that the individuals possess a valid passport and pay the regular fee for a visa, which was 11 lit (slightly less than $2). Moreover, he agreed to omit the paragraph that indicated that entry to Curaçao was dependent on the governor's approval. Thus the text of the visa issued by Zwartendijk was as follows: "The Dutch consulate hereby certifies that no visa is necessary for the entry of foreigners to Surinam, Curaçao, and other Dutch possessions in America."

Warhaftig informed the Polish refugees in Lithuania of this propitious development and hundreds applied to the Dutch consul for Curaçao visas. Time was running out, however, since the consulate had to cease operations—upon orders from the new Soviet authorities—by the end of August 1940. During the six weeks in which Zwartendijk was able to continue working (July 23 to August 31, 1940), he issued between 1,200 and 1,400 Curaçao visas to Polish refugees living in Lithuania. The only problem was that he was willing to issue visas only to those who possessed valid passports, and many of the refugees did not have the necessary documents.[25]

While it was absolutely necessary to obtain an end visa (a visa to a country willing to admit them on a permanent basis), this was only the first of numerous requirements that had to be fulfilled before prospective emigrants could achieve their goal. The next step was to choose an exit route and secure the necessary transit visas. The only feasible way of reaching Curaçao in the summer of 1940 seemed to be via the Far East, since most of Western Europe had already been occupied by the Nazis. Thus the refugees would have to travel across the Soviet Union and through Japan, and so Japanese transit visas had to be obtained.

They turned therefore to Sempo Sugihara, the Japanese consul in Kovno,[26] and applied for transit visas. Sugihara cabled Tokyo for instructions several times but did not immediately receive any reply. He was, however, very moved by the refugees' plight and therefore, on August 11, 1940, he began issuing Japanese transit visas to all applicants, even those who did not possess valid passports or Curaçao visas. Nine days later Sugihara received an urgent cable from the Japanese Foreign Ministry instructing him to immediately cease issuing Japanese visas, but he ignored his superiors' instructions and continued issuing transit visas until he left Kovno on August 31, 1940. By this time Sugihara, with the help of the consulate staff and a volunteer from the Mir Yeshiva especially enlisted for the task, had issued approximately 3,500 Japanese transit visas to Polish refugees, among them many rabbis and yeshiva students. He charged each applicant only 2 lit (approximately 33 cents) per visa and continued issuing documents even from the railway car in which he left Lithuania.[27]

Once Japanese transit visas had been obtained, the major remaining obstacle was securing Soviet exit permits. This issue was approached with extreme caution, since the Polish refugees were well aware of the Soviets' traditional reluctance to allow residents of the Soviet Union to leave the country. In his capacity as director of the Palestine Office for Polish refugees in Lithuania, Zerach Warhaftig played an instrumental role in these efforts. He met with Pijus Glovackas (Globetzki), the Deputy Prime Minister, as well as with Pozdniakov, the Russian representative in Kovno (whose task was to implement the incorporation of Lithuania into the Soviet Union), to attempt to secure their assistance. Warhaftig also tried to influence the latter with the help of his Jewish physician, Dr. Elchanan Elkes, a well-known Lithuanian Zionist leader.[28]

Globutzkius asked Warhaftig to submit a memorandum on the situation of the Polish refugees in Lithuania, as well as a list of those seeking to emigrate. The refugees viewed his request with a certain degree of suspicion, since they feared a Soviet trap, but Warhaftig nonetheless complied. With no small amount of trepidation, he submitted the memorandum and a list of approximately 700 prospective immigrants, including members of the pioneer Zionist youth movements, rabbis, and yeshiva students. (Heading the list were his own name and those of his immediate family.) As it turned out, the refugees' fears were unfounded. In early August 1940 Warhaftig was informed that a positive reply had been received from Moscow, paving the way for the emigration of the Polish refugees from Lithuania.[29]

All these events were the background for urgent efforts launched in Lithuania and abroad (primarily in the United States and Eretz Yisrael) to effect the relocation of the refugee yeshivot. Once a realistic possibility for emigration had been created—in the incongruous combination of Curaçao end visas, Japanese transit visas, and Soviet exit permits—the various groups attempting to assist the refugee Torah scholars intensified their efforts to achieve this goal.

* * *

These efforts were encouraged by the *roshei yeshivot* in Lithuania, who wrote to the leaders of the *Vaad* praising their initiative to effect the relocation of the yeshivot and comparing them to Rabbi Yochanan Ben-Zakai, who rescued numerous Torah scholars from the hands of the Romans at the time of the destruction of the Second Temple (70 C.E.). The *roshei yeshivot* in Lithuania stressed, however, that the relocation project must encompass all the yeshivot and should be done quietly, without any fanfare. From the letters received by Rabbis Silver and Rosenberg (the portion dealing with the relocation of the yeshivot was identical), it is obvious that the *roshei yeshiva* in Lithuania had coordinated their efforts on this issue.

In their letters to America, the *roshei yeshiva* did not explain their insistence that all the yeshivot be taken out together (each wrote that it was for "several very important reasons" but did not elaborate), nor is it entirely clear whether the reference to "all the yeshivot"[30] included the local Lithuanian yeshivot as well. Assuming that it did, the reason for this policy was probably twofold. The Lithuanian yeshivot feared that the relocation project might encompass only the Polish scholars and, realizing that they too had no future under Communist rule, they urged the *Vaad* to save them as well. The second possible reason was fear in the minds of the *roshei yeshiva* in Lithuania that yeshivot that had *roshei yeshiva* or representatives in the United States would get priority and that the rescue project might not encompass all the Torah scholars who sought to emigrate.

The *Vaad* was basically in agreement with the approach adopted by the *roshei yeshiva*. From its establishment, the *Vaad's* leaders had viewed the rescue of all the yeshivot as their special obligation, and at this point the rabbis certainly had no intention of minimizing their aims. On the contrary, their motivation after the Soviet occupation of Lithuania was even greater, because they assumed that the yeshivot would be closed down by the authorities and feared for the personal safety of the rabbis and students. The problem was, however, that the *Vaad* at this stage was neither financially nor technically able single-handedly to relocate to the United States all the yeshivot in Lithuania. Moreover, its initial efforts to obtain American visas for the refugee scholars had proven unsuccessful. An attempt to secure visas in conjunction with the establishment of a Yeshiva-in-Exile (patterned after the University-in-Exile which had been founded to absorb scholars forced to flee Nazi Germany), and a plan sponsored by *Agudat ha-Rabbanim* and Agudat Yisrael to bring rabbis to the United States to serve as pulpit rabbis, had both been rejected by the U.S. authorities.[31] Thus the rabbis were forced to seek the assistance of other American Jewish organizations, primarily the Joint Distribution Committee, whose resources, experience, and technical expertise in such matters were far greater than those of the *Vaad*.

The *Vaad's* request that the JDC help transfer the yeshivot en masse to the United States was not viewed favorably by the veteran Jewish relief organization. The JDC, whose leaders were extremely sensitive to Jewish–Christian relations and the public image of the Jewish community, was wary lest the arrival in the United States of thousands of East European rabbis and yeshiva students arouse a negative reaction. In the words of Moses Leavitt, the secretary of the JDC:

> It was obvious that this involved more than financial assistance. There were political and social and other implications in regard to the possibility of securing sufficient visas for admission of any appreciable number of these people to the United States, and the feasibility from the public relations angle of attempting to transplant close to 30 such institutions in the United States, involving 3,000 to 4,000 persons, was one that had to be seriously considered with other major organiza-

tions.[32]

Thus in early August 1940, leaders of the following major Jewish organizations were invited to a meeting with representatives of the *Vaad* and the JDC to discuss the *Vaad's* proposal: American Jewish Committee, American Jewish Congress, B'nai B'rith, HIAS, Jewish Theological Seminary, National Refugee Service, and the Zionist Organization of America. The meeting, on August 15, 1940, brought together almost all the leaders of the American Jewish defense and relief organizations, as well as of the Zionist movement and the Orthodox community. Among those who attended were: Paul Baerwald, Joseph Hyman and Bernhard Kahn (JDC); John L. Bernstein (HIAS); Nahum Goldmann (World Jewish Congress); Stephen Wise (American Jewish Congress); Henry Monsky (Bnai B'rith); Edmund Kaufmann (Zionist Organization of America); Alan M. Stroock (American Jewish Committee); Arthur D. Greenleigh (National Refugee Service); Aaron Teitelbaum (*Agudat ha-Rabbanim*); and Eliezer Silver (Agudat Yisrael). (The latter two were leaders of *Vaad ha-Hatzala* as well.)

The rabbis began by presenting their proposal to transplant to the United States the more than twenty Polish refugee yeshivot that had escaped to Lithuania, approximately 3,500 persons—*roshei yeshiva*, students, and the members of their families. The rabbis proposed that the State Department be approached to grant special visas for this group. There was considerable opposition to this project among the attendees. They questioned whether such an operation was feasible and, moreover, doubted whether its implementation was even desirable. The most prominent opponent was Rabbi Stephen Wise, who at that time was probably the most influential figure in the American Jewish community.[33] Wise believed that the absorption in the United States of perhaps three to five yeshivot would constitute an important contribution which American Jewry could make to Jewish culture, but that the resettlement of a larger number was simply not feasible. Moreover, he advised against bringing pressure to bear on the administration to grant visas for the entire group.

The rabbis obviously did not agree with Wise's approach, but neither side was able to convince the other. The practical result of the discussions was, therefore, the establishment of two subcommittees—a compromise of sorts which postponed a final decision pending further investigation of the issues. The first subcommittee was to determine the number of American visas which were required and to approach the State Department on this issue. The task of the second subcommittee was to raise the necessary funds to finance the immigration of those refugees for whom visas could be obtained.[34]

The differences of opinion between Wise and his supporters and the Orthodox rabbis were hardly surprising in view of the serious ideological differences between the two groups. It was, in essence, a reflection of the ongoing debate between the *Vaad* and the JDC. The Wise group, which represented the more established and acculturated elements of the community, were extremely concerned about American public opinion and therefore viewed with alarm the arrival of thousands of Polish rabbis and yeshiva students. The rabbis' primary consideration on the other hand, was the "holy" task of rescuing the Torah scholars. The social, public relations, and public opinion aspects of the issue were of little significance to the rabbis of the *Vaad* when the life's work of their mentors and colleagues hung in the balance. As firm believers in the primacy of Torah in Jewish life, they were convinced that the rescue of these scholars deserved top priority and were prepared to take whatever steps they considered necessary to realize their goal, ignoring or perhaps oblivious to the effect that such a development might have on American public opinion.

The ideological underpinnings of the *Vaad's* stance were clearly formulated in a public appeal for support written by Rabbi Jacob Levinson several months later in the rabbinic journal *Ha-Pardes*, which for many years served as the mouthpiece of *Agudat ha-Rabbanim* and consequently of *Vaad ha-Hatzala* as well:

> When we discuss the importance of the *Vaad ha-Hatzala* established by the *Agudat ha-Rabbanim* in America there are many people who do not fully comprehend its significance. The assumption exists that *Vaad ha-Hatzala* was created to save lives and is merely a matter of *pikuach nefesh* (saving those whose lives are in danger) or *pidyon shvuyim* (obtaining the release of those in captivity), and this mistaken assumption allows stubborn people to cast doubt upon the holy work because if we are merely dealing with saving lives, who is authorized to decide who gets priority, and to put the life of a rabbi and yeshiva student ahead of a *stam* (ordinary) Jew?
>
> The point of the matter is, therefore, that the work of this committee is a holy task upon which the future of the nation

is dependent because if we do not hurry while we are still able to save the remnant of the brilliant Torah sages and luminaries who are in desperate straits in tiny Lithuania, then not only the sages and *roshei yeshiva* are in danger, but our entire nation is in great danger as we will G-d forbid remain without a foundation and strength to continue our future existence and to continue the dynasty of the Torah and tradition which constitute the essence of our lives and without which "our nation is not a nation." When things were as they should be, the pipe of influence stretched from Europe via the wide sea to us, the Jews of America, and all our Torah possessions and all the loyal rabbis whom we have acquired in this country, all came to us from there. The *roshei yeshiva*, the Torah giants who spread the light of their Torah in the American yeshivot we have established here, are products of the yeshivot of Poland and Lithuania who devoted day and night to the study of Torah. Even after all the efforts which we have invested over the past years to establish important yeshivot, we still have not produced Torah sages and if G-d forbid the brilliant leaders and luminaries overseas will not find a secure haven in the United States, the only country in which we have been blessed by G-d with tranquillity, our future as the Jewish people, the people of religion and Torah is G-d forbid in danger. Therefore when we save a gaon [brilliant Torah scholar] and great sage, we are not only saving a soul but part of our nation, an organ upon which the soul is dependent, and when we bring from the lands of danger a few hundred yeshiva students who have absorbed the spirit and smell of Torah by eating bread and salt and drinking water in measure [a classical term for learning Torah under adverse physical conditions, a situation considered conducive to intensive in-depth Torah study] we are injecting new blood, live blood into the body of American Jewry to sanctify and purify the souls of people who have strayed from the path of the Torah.[35]

The rabbis of the *Vaad* did not, therefore, give up their hopes of relocating all the yeshivot. They participated in the work of the two subcommittees established at the meeting, probably hoping to convince them to support the *Vaad's* original proposal. The first subcommittee, however, adopted the approach advocated by Stephen

Wise and decided that the request submitted to the State Department should be for a minimum number of visas and that no attempt should be made to obtain approval for the entry of the entire group of rabbis and yeshiva students.[36] This decision was obviously a blow to the *Vaad's* chances of implementing its proposal, but they acquiesced in the hope that if these initial requests were approved, a means could ultimately be found to obtain all the necessary visas.

The first practical step taken was to send a delegation to Washington to meet with State Department officials. Rabbis Simcha Wasserman and Shalom Haymen of the *Vaad* were part of the delegation that met with Assistant Secretary of State Breckinridge Long, who was responsible for the Visa Division. After they brought the plight of the refugee scholars to his attention, Long responded by asking them to submit a list of rabbis whom they recommended for entry to the United States. The rabbis prepared two lists, one of 20 names and one of 100 names. At their next meeting, the Assistant Secretary of State accepted the longer list and promised to cable the American consul in the Soviet Union to ensure that the visas be granted. He also told the delegation that they should immediately instruct the prospective visa recipients to go to the U.S. consulate to receive the documents.

The rabbis received the good news on Friday evening, and despite the fact that the Sabbath had already commenced, they immediately cabled the rabbis in Lithuania whose names were on the approved list.[37] The willingness of the members of the *Vaad* to do so on the Sabbath is perhaps the most convincing indication of the extreme gravity with which they viewed the plight of the Torah scholars in Lithuania. Unless they considered the lives of the rabbis and students there to be literally in danger, they never would have performed an act which otherwise would have constituted a violation of the Sabbath. This case was the first example of a phenomenon which would occur several times in the course of the war and which served as an indicator of the rabbis' dedication to rescue activities.

The initial meetings with Breckinridge Long produced tangible results within a relatively short time. By September 18, 1940, 732 "alleged leaders of the intellectual thought of the Jewish religion and leading exponents of the Talmudic schools and colleges together with their families" had been approved by the Visa Division of the State Department for entry to the United States[38] and that figure subsequently rose to 1,200.[39] (The visas granted to the rabbis and yeshiva students, it should be noted, were not standard immigration visas but rather special emergency visas granted to European cultural, political, and intellectual leaders whose lives were in danger. The visas were issued under the terms of a special arrangement implemented under the auspices of the President's Advisory Committee on Political Refugees, headed by James Macdonald.)[40]

The initial success the *Vaad* enjoyed in its contacts with the State Department apparently softened even their erstwhile opponents in the Jewish community. In mid-December 1940 Stephen Wise headed a delegation to Washington (together with Aaron Teitelbaum on behalf of the *Vaad*) which met with Breckinridge Long and asked that an additional 3,800 rabbis, yeshiva students, and the members of their families be approved for entry to the United States. By this time, however, Long either had changed his policy or had reached the conclusion that the rabbis were trying to take advantage of the Department's "generosity," because the request was rejected. Long wrote in his diary, moreover, that he considered the request as "just a part of the movement to place me and the Department in general in an embarrassing position."[41] Long maintained his negative attitude toward the immigration of the larger group of rabbis and yeshiva students and subsequently rejected requests for additional emergency visitor's visas for them.[42] Thus this avenue of escape, which had originally proven quite promising, was eventually blocked. Nonetheless, the initial success helped enable numerous refugee scholars to leave the Soviet Union.

Much of the credit for the positive results achieved by the *Vaad* in Washington has been attributed to James Macdonald, chairman of the President's Advisory Committee on Political Refugees, who helped open many doors in the capital for the rabbis. It was he who introduced them to Breckinridge Long and helped obtain the initial several hundred emergency visas.[43] In this context, the extremely significant contribution made by the members of *Zeirei Agudat Yisrael*[44] to the work of the *Vaad ha-Hatzala* should be noted. This group, which constituted the young adults division of the Agudat Yisrael political party, was headed by Michael (Elimelech) Tress[45] and composed of approximately 2,500 young men, most of whom had been educated in the United States. They conducted a great deal of the political contacts maintained by the *Vaad* with the American authorities, and their assistance often proved invaluable to the

European born and -bred leaders of the rabbinic rescue organization, the majority of whom were unacquainted with the inner workings of the American government and almost none of whom thoroughly mastered the English language. The members of *Zeirei* frequently traveled to Washington to meet with congressmen and State Department officials and to arrange appointments for the leaders of the *Vaad ha-Hatzala*.[46] They were also to play a significant role in the *Vaad's* campaign to secure affidavits of financial support for prospective immigrants to America.

The second subcommittee established at the meeting of the representatives of the major Jewish organizations was entrusted with the task of raising the funds to cover the transportation expenses of the refugee Torah scholars. In the course of this subcommittee's deliberations, the representatives of the *Vaad* were forced to face the practical difficulties in implementing their original proposal. At the first meeting, held on October 8, 1940, Rabbi Teitelbaum spoke initially of providing funds for the immigration of 300 rabbinical leaders and 1,000 yeshiva students to the United States, but in the course of the meeting, "after a thorough discussion of the matter," he reduced the figures to 300 rabbis (who would be given first priority) and 500 students. Rabbi Teitelbaum proposed that the Orthodox groups in the United States provide fifty percent of the required sums—$200,000 of the required $400,000—with the rest of the funds provided by other interested organizations. (The representatives of Chabad (Lubavitch) presented a separate request, along similar financial lines, for the immigration to America of 156 rabbis and students from their institutions in Lithuania. It is not clear why this request was not incorporated into the proposal made by the *Vaad*.)[47]

Yet even Rabbi Teitelbaum's reduced proposal proved to be too ambitious, and so by the next meeting of the subcommittee, on October 21, 1940, he further lowered the proposed figures to 100 persons of "high rabbinical standing" which included the members of their families (a total of 25–30 families) and 100 older yeshiva students who were "threatened with expulsion to Siberia," making a total of 200 persons. The sums he requested from the non-Orthodox organizations for the immigration of this group amounted to $40,000, which was less than forty percent of the estimated overall costs of over $100,000. (Chabad also lowered its requests to 50 persons and $10,000, a reduction of more than two-thirds in both the number of immigrants and the funds sought.) The problem was, however, that at this point only B'nai B'rith was willing to make a firm financial commitment ($5,000); the other organizations had still not agreed to provide the necessary sums.[48] Moreover, the *Vaad* had to raise its share of the money, a task that would also prove somewhat difficult. Thus despite the *Vaad's* initial success in obtaining a considerable number of the necessary visas, the immigration of the refugee scholars was still uncertain; the lack of financial support from the American Jewish community threatened to undermine the success of the project.

* * *

In the summer and fall of 1940, while the *Vaad* was launching its initial efforts to obtain the support of the State Department, many of the Polish refugees in Lithuania attempted to obtain the necessary documents to enable them to leave the Soviet Union. Efforts in this direction, which had heretofore been sporadic and perhaps haphazard, suddenly assumed a fervent urgency in the wake of the Soviet invasion. Thousands of refugees turned to the Dutch and Japanese consulates as well as to the special offices opened by the Soviets to handle the requests for exit permits.[49] The situation of the rabbis and especially of the yeshiva students, was somewhat more complex than that of the other refugees (with the exception of the members of the Zionist youth movements), since the yeshivot as a rule operated as a unit in accordance with the policy established by the *roshei yeshiva*. Moreover, most of the students were financially dependent upon the yeshiva, so the success of their immigration efforts was to a large extent determined by the decisions made by their spiritual mentors. At this point, however, there were serious differences of opinion among the *roshei yeshiva* as to the best means of effecting emigration, a fact that was to have highly significant consequences on the fate of the refugee Torah scholars.

Prior to the Soviet occupation of Lithuania, several of the Polish *roshei yeshiva* had made efforts to obtain immigration visas—primarily to Eretz Yisrael and to a lesser extent to the United States—for themselves and their students. But little had been done in practical terms to advance this goal. While *roshei yeshiva* such as Rabbis Eliezer Finkel, Aron Kotler, and Boruch Ber Leibowitz had cabled or written to Rabbi Herzog, Agudat Yisrael, or the Jewish Agency

(Moshe Shapiro) in Eretz Yisrael or to the Central Relief Committee or rabbinic colleagues in the United States to ask for assistance in obtaining visas for their entire yeshiva,[50] hardly any of the *roshei yeshiva* had taken any practical steps to secure the necessary documents for all their students. They had made no attempt, for example, to obtain Polish passports for students who lacked them.

The only exception in this respect was Rabbi Finkel of the Mir Yeshiva. Even before the Soviets entered Lithuania, he had sent a student to Kovno to investigate the possibilities for immigration and subsequently issued instructions to obtain passports, visas, and exit permits for all his students. It should be noted, however, that even Rabbi Finkel had initially been reluctant to take concrete steps toward immigration; it was only after he had been convinced by several of this students, with the help of Zerach Warhaftig, who came to Keydan specifically for that purpose, that he issued instructions to that effect.[51] Warhaftig, the director of the Palestine Office for Polish Refugees in Lithuania, was extremely perturbed by the fact that the yeshivot were not taking the necessary steps to facilitate their emigration and spoke to Rabbi Grodzinski several times to convince him of the danger of the situation and the need for concrete action. The latter convened two conferences of *roshei yeshiva* to discuss this issue, but those assembled decided to oppose organized immigration and therefore nothing changed on a practical level as far as the rabbis and yeshiva students were concerned.[52]

When the Russians occupied Lithuania, the attitude of the *roshei yeshiva* changed as the need for immediate practical action to effect emigration became obvious. Moreover, an opportunity for escape materialized shortly thereafter in the form of the Curaçao end visas and Japanese transit visas. The problem was that many of the *roshei yeshiva* doubted whether these documents would really enable the yeshivot to emigrate. On the contrary, many of them feared that any attempt to leave the Soviet Union on the basis of visas would result in the deportation en masse of their entire yeshiva to Siberia.[53] In fact, skepticism regarding the ultimate value of these documents was fairly widespread. In the words of Rabbi Pinchas Hirshsprung, who was in Vilna at the time, the visas were regarded by many refugees as "a joke of sorts...or toilet paper."[54] Little wonder that many of the *roshei yeshivot* did not endorse this avenue of escape.

Once again, the only exception was the Mir Yeshiva, which in an organized manner sought to obtain Curaçao end visas and Japanese transit visas for the entire student body. During the summer and fall of 1940 Mir was the only yeshiva which, as a unit, took practical steps to obtain all the necessary documents.[55] Refugee yeshiva students from other yeshivot made similar efforts to obtain visas, but theirs was a personal initiative carried out individually without the approval of their *roshei yeshiva*—often, in fact, in direct contradiction to their instructions or advice.[56]

The task of obtaining the necessary visas became more difficult starting in fall 1940, when the foreign consulates in Lithuania were closed down by the Soviets. Hereafter, all visa requests had to be submitted to the consulates in Moscow, a policy that created all sorts of difficulties for the refugees, the least of which were logistic. The major problem was the fact that there was no guarantee that the Dutch and Japanese consuls in the Soviet capital would prove as cooperative as Zwartendijk and Sugihara had been. On the contrary, there was every reason to believe that no additional Curaçao or Japanese visas would be given, since in both cases the initiative had been personal. In fact, the Japanese had already ordered Sugihara to stop issuing visas even before he left Kovno.[57]

Thus it appeared that only those who had already obtained the necessary documents would be able to emigrate. There were, moreover, two additional obstacles which had to be overcome. Soviet exit permits had to be obtained and travel expenses had to be paid. The former problem was of considerable concern to the refugees; many of them feared a Soviet ruse and therefore refrained from applying for exit permits even though refugee leaders had been informed that emigration would be allowed. In this respect, the methods employed by the Soviet authorities in handling the requests for permits strengthened the refugees' apprehensions. For example, the special immigration offices opened by the Soviets to process the applications were located in the offices of the N.K.V.D. (secret police) in Vilna and Kovno. In addition, all prospective emigrants had to appear for questioning and fill out detailed biographical questionnaires time after time explaining at length why they sought to emigrate. Moreover, there were rumors that the N.K.V.D. had photographed all those waiting on line for visas at the Japanese consulate, and given the suspicion with which Soviets were traditionally regarded, it is hardly surprising that there were serious doubts in refugee circles regarding the wisdom of taking such a step.[58]

Rabbi Yoseph Epstein, Rabbi Finkel's personal secretary, described the mood and deliberations in the Mir Yeshiva and among the refugee yeshivot as follows:

> Every heart worried, who knows what the results of such requests could be? Among the refugees the fear of deportation to Siberia had already begun to gnaw away. What was missing, after all, just a request to leave the country and that was it. In those days, the mood in the yeshiva was extremely depressed. The requests for exit permits were going to be submitted this time not to a Lithuanian office under Soviet supervision but to the N.K.V.D. and who knows what "faults" would be found in the course of the N.K.V.D. interrogation of the applicants? It would be superfluous to stress how carefully the leaders of the yeshiva handled this matter. When the decision of the Mir students to submit the applications for exit permits became known to the other yeshivot it made a terrible impression. They truly feared that they were about to thereby bring utter devastation upon all the Torah scholars and hasten the end of the yeshivot."[59]

Moreover, the decision to submit applications had been reached in the Mir Yeshiva only after what was described by one participant as "an internal struggle within the yeshiva, differences of opinion, arguments against the administration [and] fears"[60] and by another as "enormous tension."[61] Thus the same factors that influenced various *roshei yeshivot* to oppose the attempts to obtain visas to Curaçao and Japan applied to the efforts to secure Soviet exit permits. Once again, only the Mir Yeshiva took practical steps in an organized manner to obtain the necessary documents.

The attitude of the *roshei yeshivot* was primarily a function of their deep distrust and fear of the Communist regime, a factor that significantly influenced their policy decisions in numerous instances. According to one source, a meeting of *roshei yeshivot* had been convened in Vilna in response to the initial Soviet request for the names of those seeking to emigrate and those assembled decided not to submit the names of any rabbis and yeshiva students.[62] If not for the fact that Warhaftig had been willing to submit his list, perhaps the Soviets would not have agreed to issue the exit permits.

Once Soviet permission for emigration had been obtained, the only remaining obstacle was the transportation expenses. Initially, railway tickets to Vladivostok could be purchased in rubles relatively cheaply, but within a short time the Soviets changed their policy and forced the refugees to buy their tickets at "Intourist," the official Soviet tourism agency. The practical implication of this step was that tickets had to be paid for in dollars and at the considerably higher tourist rate ($170 per person), despite the fact that it was illegal to possess foreign currency in the Soviet Union. This development complicated the plight of the refugees, most of whom were penniless to begin with. Thus many were forced to appeal for help from overseas to pay transportation expenses. Many of the rabbis and yeshiva students who sought to emigrate (primarily from the Mir Yeshiva) appealed therefore in the late summer and early fall of 1940 to the *Vaad ha-Hatzala* in the hope that the rabbinic rescue organization could provide them with the funds to pay for their trip to Japan.[63]

These requests put a severe strain on the *Vaad's* resources, which were not abundant despite moderate success in its initial fundraising activities. During this period, moreover, the *Vaad* continued to encounter considerable opposition from both the JDC and the Council of Jewish Federations and Welfare Funds, which were alarmed by the inroads made by the rabbinic rescue organization, especially among their own constituency—the local federations—and sought to minimize the allocations granted the *Vaad*. Thus in response to numerous inquiries concerning the *Vaad's* activities which were directed to the New York headquarters of the JDC and CJFWF during the summer and fall of 1940, the veteran relief agencies attempted to delegitimize the work of the rabbinic rescue organization.

The arguments presented by the JDC and CJFWF stressed two new major themes: the uncertainty regarding the continued existence of the yeshivot in Lithuania in the wake of the Soviet occupation, and the illegality of the methods used by the *Vaad ha-Hatzala* to transmit funds to the refugee scholars in distress. For example, in response to a letter from the Minneapolis Federation for Jewish Service asking whether it should transmit its allocation for the Torah scholars directly to Rabbi Grodzinski or via the *Vaad* or the JDC, Blanche Renard of the CJFWF listed the major arguments of the veteran relief agencies against the *Vaad's* activities. According to Renard, "the status of Lithuanian yeshivot is uncertain in view of the recent development," and therefore the JDC had temporarily stopped sending them any welfare fund contributions. Moreover, while the *Vaad* claimed to have a "means of conducting financial transactions which do not involve any actual exchange of money across borders," as far as the CJFWF was concerned, "The JDC states that the method used by the committee is illegal and unsafe at present. Furthermore, there is still the question of the actual existence of the yeshivoth."[64] A month later Henrietta Buchman of the JDC wrote in response to an inquiry from Indianapolis that while there had been no news of the yeshivot being closed down by the authorities, "their future is considered highly precarious." She noted, moreover, that State Department approval was now needed to transmit funds to Lithuania and that the JDC was not accepting any money for transmission to these yeshivot.[65]

The *Vaad* attempted to counter these arguments, both in its publicity and in meetings and correspondence with representatives of the veteran Jewish overseas relief agencies. On August 13, 1940, the *Vaad* published an advertisement in the Yiddish daily *Morgn Dzurnal* stressing the fact that they had recently received a direct communication from Rabbi Grodzinski to the effect that despite the Soviet occupation, the yeshivot continued to exist and that financial help was needed.[66] About three weeks later Rabbi Silver wrote to H. L. Lurie, executive director of the CJFWF, stressing the fact that, despite whatever had been publicized to the contrary, the yeshivot were still functioning and the funds currently being transmitted by the *Vaad* were even more critical than ever before, because the aid that the yeshivot had been receiving from the JDC had recently been drastically reduced. According to Rabbi Silver, the *Vaad* was about to embark upon a campaign to raise money for the transportation of the refugee scholars and thus the only sources of funds for the maintenance of the yeshivot during this period were the federations and welfare funds. He therefore asked Lurie to inform his members that the yeshivot continued to exist and were in urgent need of financial aid, which should be sent through the *Vaad ha-Hatzala*.[67]

On September 10, 1940, representatives of the JDC (Moses Leavitt and Henrietta Buchman), CJFWF (H.L. Lurie, Blanche Renard, George Rabinoff and Carol Kuhn), and *Vaad ha-Hatzala* (Rabbis Burak and Shulman) met to discuss the problem of the transmission of funds to overseas yeshivot. H. L. Lurie of the CJFWF began by posing a list of very pointed questions regarding the *Vaad's* ability to transmit funds to the yeshivot as well as its past activities.

(Among other pointed queries, he asked whether the *Vaad* could provide the CJFWF with a financial statement.) Rabbi Burak of the *Vaad* replied that the yeshivot continued to exist unmolested and he described the clearance arrangement used by both the *Vaad* and the American offices of the yeshivot to transmit funds to Lithuania.

Most of the ensuing discussion revolved around the legality of this method, with each side maintaining its traditional position. JDC secretary Moses Leavitt stated that he considered the *Vaad*'s clearance arrangement "dangerous and illegal as far as U.S regulations are concerned" and he emphasized "the danger to Jews from a public relations standpoint of acting counter to U.S. governmental regulations." As an alternative, he suggested that the *Vaad* and the *yeshivot* utilize a new government regulation allowing individuals in the United States to send up to $100 a month to individuals in Lithuania, provided certain residence and other qualifications could be met. The rabbis promised to investigate this possibility but at the same time made clear their basic position that "where lives are at stake, chances must be taken… legal or illegal." They noted, moreover, that without American support, the yeshivot would undoubtedly cease to exist.

While the meeting produced a possible alternative means of transmitting funds to Lithuania agreeable to both sides, it did not in essence solve the conflict between the relief agencies. No agreement was reached regarding the recommendation that the CJFWF would issue to the various welfare funds which, at their suggestion, had been withholding funds allocated for the yeshivot until an unquestionably legal method of transmission could be devised. The representatives of the *Vaad* urged the CJFWF to recommend that the funds be sent to the New York offices of the yeshivot and that the welfare funds not concern themselves with the means of transmission. H. L. Lurie opined, however, that the federations had a responsibility to see that their funds were handled properly.[68] Thus the issue remained a bone of contention between the relief agencies, and relations between them worsened as a result.

Throughout the late summer and fall of 1940 the failure to reach an agreement on the issue of the CJFWF recommendation was a source of continuous friction between the *Vaad* and the Council. Throughout this period the rabbis continued their attempts to induce the CJFWF to exert its influence upon its members to forward all outstanding allocations for the yeshivot directly to the

Vaad. The Council, however, did not yield. While it ostensibly presented the problematics of the *Vaad*'s clearance arrangement in a fairly noncommittal manner in official bulletins, it was far more forthright in its criticism of the *Vaad*'s methods in internal correspondence with local federations. Thus in a budgeting bulletin for member agencies issued in October 1940, the CJFWF stated that it was "not in a position to express an opinion"[69] on the *Vaad*'s clearance arrangement, but in a confidential letter to a local welfare fund, Blanche Renard clearly stated that "This method of transmission [employed by the *Vaad*] is not formally recognized and may be considered as irregular by the United States Treasury Department."[70] Moreover, in a letter written several weeks later to the Tri-State Coordinating Bureau (most likely an umbrella framework for several federations), Renard was even blunter in her criticism of the *Vaad*. She informed Norman Dockman of Pittsburgh that "confidentially we cannot recommend... the Emergency Committee for War-Torn Yeshivoth (because of method of transmission of funds)" [underlined in the original]. The CJFWF's negative view of the *Vaad* is emphasized by the fact that in the same letter Renard herself admits that at present "there is no alternative method by which welfare funds can send money to Lithuania."[71] The result therefore was, in effect, that each welfare fund had to make its own decision, although the fact that the Council was highly critical of the *Vaad*'s activities was undoubtedly quite significant.

The *Vaad*, needless to say, learned of the council's criticism of its activities and attempted to rectify what it considered to be the misunderstandings between the relief agencies. It protested "most emphatically" against the council's assertion that the clearance arrangement used by the *Vaad* was illegal. In a letter to the CJFWF, Rabbi Kalmanowitz explained that the method of transmission was "in full conformance with the federal regulations and does not violate the federal restrictions against the export of funds since no funds are sent out of the country." Kalmanowitz noted, moreover, that the position adopted by the Council was critical since the JDC had stopped all support two months previously and the only funds reaching the yeshivot were those provided by the *Vaad*. "Your responsibility is great and in this historic moment great care must be exercised lest an ill-advised word cause undue suffering to the Yeshivoth and three thousand students."[72] H. L. Lurie responded that the budgeting bulletin sent to the federations and welfare funds had been prepared with the cooperation of representatives of the *Vaad* and did not express any opinion on the legality of the transfer method and thus he attributed Rabbi Kalmanowitz's claims to a "misunderstanding."[73]

The *Vaad* did not accept Lurie's explanation, however, and quickly responded that from the beginning of the discussions regarding the text of the bulletin, it had sought to have the comment regarding the lack of formal recognition by the U.S. Treasury deleted. "We pointed out at that time," noted Rabbi Karlinsky, the secretary of the *Vaad,* "how many incorrect interpretations could be given to such a paragraph but to no avail. We want to emphasize that that [sic] it never had our approval and now we can state from actual experience that it has caused us great harm."[74] Rabbi Kalmanowitz also wrote to Lurie in the same vein, noting the crucial assistance provided for the refugee scholars by the *Vaad* and calling upon the Council to issue instructions to the federations to release the funds they had on hand for the Torah scholars.[75] In response, Lurie stated that the Council's function was purely as a "fact-finding and research service for our member agencies" and that it had no control over the individual federations and welfare funds, which were "entirely independent." He added that he had a "sympathetic interest in your [Rabbi Kalmanowitz's] activities and problems," and he asked for a list of the welfare funds that had sent contributions to the *Vaad* during October and November 1940, as well as of those that had withheld funds during that period.[76]

If the *Vaad* hoped that as a result of this correspondence the Council would urge its recalcitrant members to remit their outstanding allocations for the refugee Torah scholars to the *Vaad,* their optimism was ill-advised. (Interestingly, the *Vaad* sent the CJFWF a list only of those federations and welfare funds—thirteen in number—that had not yet fulfilled their pledges.)[77] There is no evidence of any attempt by the Council to encourage the federations to transmit their allocations for the yeshivot to the *Vaad.* On the contrary, Lurie continued to make clear his reservations regarding the *Vaad*'s methods, although his criticism was somewhat modified in the immediate aftermath of his exchange with Rabbi Kalmanowitz.[78]

The position adopted by the CJFWF and the JDC vis-à-vis the *Vaad*'s campaign and activities undoubtedly had its effect on the local federations and welfare funds, who in some cases withheld their allocations or attempted to transmit the funds via the JDC rather than via the *Vaad*. In order to illuminate the various problems the *Vaad* encountered in its campaign, as well as the manner in which the CJFWF and JDC affected the *Vaad*'s fundraising activities, let us examine in detail the cases of two middle-size Midwest Jewish communities: Indianapolis and Houston.[79]

In the summer of 1940, representatives of the *Vaad* visited Indianapolis and presented to the leaders of the local federation a demand for an allocation of $3,000. The latter refused to accede to this demand and offered $1,000, which was to include a $300 allocation to local Lithuanian yeshivot (Telz and Slabodka) and to Torah institutions in Rumania and Palestine. In response, the *Vaad* asked for an opportunity to present its case to the leadership of the federation and suggested that Dr. Samuel Schmidt, who had recently returned from his mission to Lithuania on behalf of the *Vaad*, be the invited speaker. On July 22, 1940, Schmidt traveled to Indianapolis and met with H. Joseph Hyman, the executive director of the federation, and addressed the members of the Budget Committee. According to Hyman, the federation had failed to achieve its campaign goals and therefore could not allocate the sum requested by the *Vaad*. The $1,000 being offered the *Vaad* was from a special emergency fund which was already "entirely depleted." Schmidt refused to accept this sum and urged the Budget Committee to increase the allocation in view of the emergency situation and the fact that "especially since the yeshivos were never given an adequate amount before [they should therefore] make up now for what they failed to do previously." Following deliberations, the committee decided to allocate the sum of $1,500, which was raised to $1,600 after negotiations among Schmidt, Rabbi Katz (a local rabbi), and the federation. Schmidt considered his mission successful and reported to the *Vaad* that he had left behind "a friendly atmosphere and good chances for further cooperation."[80]

Schmidt's optimism was apparently a bit premature, however. Three days after the Cincinnati doctor's presentation in Indianapolis, H. J. Hyman informed him that the board of the federation had decided to delay transmitting the sum allocated to the *Vaad*. In his words, "Since it is extremely questionable whether the Yeshivoth will continue to function in Lithuania and also whether it will be possible to evacuate them to the United States or Palestine, the Board felt that the $1,500.00 should be held in a trust fund here until when such time definite assurance could be given that the program of your Committee can be carried out."[81]

Schmidt was taken aback by the decision of the federation. He responded by reiterating his confidence in the *Vaad*'s leaders emphasizing what was, in effect, the rabbis' response to the claims posited on numerous occasions by the JDC and CJFWF. "Your proposed action," Schmidt wrote to Hyman, "in my estimation betrays a regrettable lack of confidence in the people at the head of the Emergency Committee. I am sorry to express myself so strongly, but it is the only interpretation I can give to your decision as I had occasion to remark during my talk before the committee. The difficulty is that most of us do not understand the Yeshivot people. I assure you that the money is greatly needed at this very moment, and furthermore, the Emergency Committee for War-Torn Yeshivos is fully competent to care for the funds in case something happens which may prevent its use for the present."[82]

On August 15, 1940, Schmidt again wrote to the Indianapolis federation urging them to remit "whatever money you have available for the yeshivoth" to the offices of the *Vaad*. Schmidt addressed the critical issue of the existence of the yeshivot by noting that he had just received a cable from Vilna with an appeal for help and that "the committee has been in constant contact with the Yeshivoth. These institutions are all functioning under more difficult conditions of course but they have not had the cooperation of the government which they previously enjoyed. I assure you that you need have no doubts as to the present functioning of the Yeshivoth."[83]

Schmidt's arguments did not convince the Indianapolis federation, which wrote to New York on August 29 and September 3, 1940, to seek the advice of the JDC and CJFWF. Both relief agencies presented a negative picture regarding existence of the *yeshivot* and the possibility of transmitting funds to Lithuania. On September 5, for example, Blanche Renard wrote to Hyman as follows:

> The problem of the European Yeshivoth is more difficult. We have been able to obtain very little specific information from the Emergency Committee for War-Torn Yeshivoth regarding the results of its campaign, how funds are reaching the Yeshivoth abroad, and what the status of the Yeshivoth is at present. With the European situation changing from day to day it is difficult to make any statement regarding the present or future existence of the institutions. Furthermore, as far as

transmission of funds are concerned, to remit money legally from U.S. to Lithuania, each transaction must be accompanied by a permit from the U.S. State Department, which, I understand, is difficult to obtain. Furthermore, on the other end, a permit must be obtained by the receiver in Lithuania from the Soviet government. As far as we know, the Emergency Committee for War-Torn Yeshivoth uses other means of making its funds available to Yeshivoth in Lithuania."[84]

Henrietta Buchman's letter was in a similar vein, and both advised Hyman to delay any decision until the special committee established to clarify the issue of the transmission of funds to overseas yeshivot had reached its conclusions.[85]

Hyman, however, was under pressure from the *Vaad,* which continued to press the Indianapolis federation to fulfill its pledge, insisting throughout that it was able to transmit the funds to the yeshivot in Lithuania. On September 26, 1940, he appealed again to Blanche Renard for an authoritative answer on the issues of the existence of the yeshivot and the possibility of transmitting funds to Lithuania.[86] Renard's response of October 1 clearly reflected the CJFWF's attitude toward the *Vaad ha-Hatzala.* She began by noting that both the JDC and the *Vaad* had informed the Council that the yeshivot were indeed functioning and then explained how the *Vaad's* clearance arrangement operated. She emphasized, however, that there were problems regarding this method of transmission, which was "not formally recognized and may be considered as irregular by the United States Treasury Department." Thus despite the fact that the responses to both of Hyman's questions were positive, the message, in effect, was negative. Moreover, Renard asked Hyman to consider the content of the letter as "strictly confidential [underlined in the original] since we believe it would be undesirable to publicize it," and copies of this missive were sent to every member of the CJFWF field staff.[87] The letter, it should be noted, had the desired effect: By November 25, 1940, the Indianapolis federation had still not fulfilled its pledge to the *Vaad ha-Hatzala.*[88]

The *Vaad* encountered similar problems in Houston. Their relationship with the local federation started on the wrong foot when the *Vaad* sent a fundraising delegation headed by Rabbi Kalmanowitz to that city in the middle of the local UJA campaign, despite requests by J. B. Lightman, executive director of the federation, to refrain from doing so.[89] In this case, the *Vaad* presented the federation with a *fait accompli*. When the federation protested the *Vaad*'s independent fundraising efforts, Rabbi Silver cabled that Rabbi Kalmanowitz was already on his way and his whereabouts were unknown, so his arrival could not be prevented or delayed. Silver promised Lightman, however, that Kalmanowitz would "consult and cooperate with you in every way."[90]

The federation refused to cooperate and threatened to stop the *Vaad*'s campaign in Houston. "If ... your delegation does come," Executive Director Lightman cabled Silver on April 3, "our committee and leaders advise that they will be completely out of sympathy with your cause and will definitely take measures to stop it in our city because we right now are in the midst of our important annual fund-raising appeal which includes such causes as yours."[91] The *Vaad*, on the same day, cabled Moses Feld, the president of the federation, as well as Lightman, in an attempt to calm the situation and assure them that Rabbi Kalmanowitz's activities in Houston would in no way prove detrimental to the UJA campaign. In addition, they noted the contributions raised by the rabbis' delegation in the nearby communities of Dallas and Forth Worth.[92]

Rabbi Kalmanowitz did indeed come to Houston with his delegation, which met with the Executive Committee and Committee on European, Palestinian and Some American Jewish Educational and Welfare Institutions and Organizations of the local federation. Despite an impassioned appeal by Rabbi Kalmanowitz on behalf of the Emergency Committee for War-Torn Yeshivot, the federation refused to make a definite commitment until the conclusion of its campaign. In a spirit of compromise, however, those assembled made a recommendation to the Budget and Allocations Committee that a minimum of $2,500 be granted to the *Vaad*, with the sum guaranteed by individual members of the community in the event that the federation could not fulfill this recommendation (if the campaign failed to achieve its goals).[93]

In reality, the problem facing the *Vaad* in Houston was not the amount of money raised by the campaign, but rather the question regarding the legality of the clearance arrangement used by the rabbis to transmit funds to Lithuania. In response to a letter from Rabbi Silver asking the federation to fulfill its recommendation and extend assistance to the refugee Torah scholars, Lightman replied that such a step could not be taken at that point in view of the complicated nature of the situation. "This whole problem has been gone into most thoroughly. Correspondence from the various Yeshivoth, from your organization and the Joint Distribution Committee, the Vaad Leumi, the Council of Jewish Federations and Welfare Funds and other organizations, were studied most carefully. The decision almost unanimously arrived at was that funds are to be held aside for the Yeshivoth until there was clear-cut advice from the national and centralized organizations through which and with which we work on these matters to the effect that we may make their funds available in a particular way."[94]

The extent to which the decision of the Houston federation had been influenced by the stance of the CJFWF is clearly reflected in a confidential letter which Lightman wrote to Rabbi Silver on October 23, 1940, in response to the rabbi's appeal that the federation funds allocated for the yeshivot be sent to the *Vaad*. Lightman pointed out that in reality no funds had yet been set aside for the yeshivot. "It is true that a recommendation had been made by our Yeshivahs Committee to the Budget Committee," he noted, "but this recommendation was not accepted. A sum of money was set aside for disposal by our Yeshivahs Committee, but that Committee, on advice received, has deemed it best to wait for the time being before making appropriations there...for European institutions."

This decision was based on the October 1940 bulletin issued by the CJFWF which Silver himself had adduced as proof that the situation had been clarified and that the funds should be forwarded to the *Vaad*. Lightman stressed, however, that in Houston their understanding of the bulletin was different. "It is true that the bulletin of the council does clarify the situation for the time being, but not leading to the conclusion that the funds be forwarded. Rather is the obverse conclusion the one that we have gathered from the bulletin." Lightman then quoted the portions of the bulletin that clearly indicate that the transmission of funds to the *Vaad* would prove problematic, concluding in brief, "We believe the entire matter speaks for itself."[95] The Houston federation was among thirteen welfare funds which as of late November 1940 had still not fulfilled their pledges to the *Vaad ha-Hatzala*.[96]

The difficulties the *Vaad* encountered in its dealings with the federations in Indianapolis and Houston were to a large extent a reflection of the differences in mentality and ideology between the rabbis of the *Vaad* and the professional leadership of the JDC and CJFWF both on the national and local levels. These differences and the neg-ative attitude toward the *Vaad* adopted by the rival Jewish relief agencies significantly hampered the rabbis' efforts to raise funds from local federations. Thus despite the fact that 36 federations had made allocations to the Emergency Committee for War-Torn Yeshivot by July 4, 1940, the total raised from this source was only $22,380, since so many of the contributions were relatively small. (The majority were for less than $500.)[97]

Luckily for the *Vaad*, however, it enjoyed far greater success with other sectors of the Jewish community. By mid-September 1940 the *Vaad ha-Hatzala* had raised $128,434, with an additional $15,500 in pledges still outstanding. The overwhelming majority of the funds ($88,230) had been transmitted to the Polish yeshivot in Lithuania with small sums set aside for the local Lithuanian yeshivot as well. Approximately 60% of this amount had been sent directly to the yeshivot and the remainder was transmitted to Rabbi Grodzinski for distribution as he saw fit. In addition, allocations were made for transportation from Poland ($6,000), for *Ezrat Torah* ($2,800), for refugee rabbis in Eretz Yisrael ($2,500), and for the shipment of old clothes to Vilna ($890). The sum of $4,820 was set aside for trans-portation of refugee scholars to Palestine and the outstanding pledges were ostensibly to be utilized for that purpose as well,[98] but in essence almost all the funds raised during the *Vaad's* initial year of existence were expended for the maintenance of the refugee schol-ars.

In the wake of the developments in Lithuania and the "creation" of concrete possibilities for the emigration of the refugee scholars, the *Vaad's* policy changed. Originally established for the express purpose of the relocation of the yeshivot, the *Vaad* decided hence-forth to devote its resources exclusively toward that goal. Thus in early November 1940 Rabbi Silver informed the CJFWF that from now on all funds designated for the maintenance of the yeshivot should be directed to the American offices of the yeshivot in Lithuania.[99] The *Vaad*, as he further clarified in a subsequent letter, "would like to make it absolutely clear that from now on the work of the Emergency Committee will be to provide tickets for the trans-portation of the thousands of scholars."[100] Thus approximately one year after its establishment, the *Vaad ha-Hatzala* began in earnest to fulfill its original purpose.

Notes

1. The Soviet takeover was preceded by a Russian ultimatum to the Lithuanian government on June 14, 1940, in which the latter were accused of signing a military pact with Latvia and Estonia in violation of the Soviet–Lithuanian defense treaty of October 10, 1939, and of arresting and torturing Russian soldiers in order to obtain information on Soviet military bases in Lithuania. The Russians demanded the establishment of a new government that would be "friendly" to the Soviet Union, the trial of Minister of the Interior Skucas and of Povilaitis, the chief of the Security Police, and the admission of an unlimited number of Soviet troops to Lithuania. Before the Lithuanian government could reply, Soviet forces invaded Lithuania and took over the country. Owen J. C. Norem, *Timeless Lithuania* (Chicago, 1943), pp. 174–175; Arad/YVS, p. 212.
2. Bauer/YVS, p. 219.
3. Arad/YVS, p. 212.
4. Dov Levin, "Chofesh Dati Mugbal ve–Al Tnai," *Sinai*, no. 79 (June–July 1976), p. 174.
5. Warhaftig, *Palit ve–Sarid be–Yemei ha–Shoa*, p. 118.
6. Yoseph Epstein, "Yeshivat Mir," in Mirsky, *Mosdot*, pp. 119–120; Elchanan Herzman, *Mofait ha–Dor; Ness ha–Hatzala Shel Yeshivat Mir* (Jerusalem, 1976), pp. 61–62.
7. Hillel Zeidman, "Yeshivat 'Etz Chaim' de-Kletzk," in Mirsky, *Mosdot*, p. 238.
8. Nathaniel Katzburg, "British Policy on Immigration to Palestine During World War II," in Yisrael Gutman and Efraim Zuroff, Ed., *Rescue Attempts During the Holocaust* (Jerusalem, 1977), p. 183.
9. Category B–2 was for religious functionaries, category B–3 was for students in rabbinical seminaries. Shulamit Eliash, "Hatzalat Yeshivot Polin she–Nimletu le–Lita be–Reishit ha–Milchama," *Yalkut Moreshet*, no. 32 (December 1981), p. 133.
10. The figures on visas granted to rabbis during April–May 1940 appear in AAYEY, file 120; letter of Rabbi Herzog to Mills (Commissioner of Immigration and Statistics), May 2, 1940, AAYEY, file 119.
11. Yaakov Goldman, "Rabbi Herzog's First Rescue Journey," *Niv ha–Midrashiya*, Winter 1964, pp. 5–7; Eliash, "Hatzalat Yeshivot," p. 137; Dina Porat, "Rikuz ha–Plitim ha–Yehudim be–Vilna ba–Shanim 1939–1941: Ma'amatzei ha–Yetzi'a," M.A. dissertation, Tel-Aviv University, 1973, pp. 59–60.
12. Eliash, "Hatzalat Yeshivot," p. 137. According to reports in the press, the *Vaad* had allocated $50,000 for this purpose, but financial documents indicate that the sum was initially $20,000 and was later reduced to $5,000. This was probably done due to the fact that Rabbi Herzog did not need the money because the visas were never granted. "Vaad ha–Hatzala la–yeshivot di–Airopa," *Ha–Pardes*, 14, no. 1 (Nissan 5700/April 1940), 3, 5; letter of Blanche Renard to Sol Stone, May 6, 1940, ACJFWF, I–69, Box 149; memo of Carol Kuhn to MW re Emergency Committee for War–Torn Yeshivoth, July 5,1940, ACJFWF, I–69, Box 150.
13. Cable of Central Jewish Committee and Rabbis Rosenberg and Teitelbaum to Rabbi Herzog, March 31, 1940, ACRC. Other groups that pledged support were the Chicago *Vaad ha–Yeshivot* (50 students for two years at $4 a month) and *Ezrat Torah*

(25 refugee rabbis and families).

14. Eliash, "Hatzalat Yeshivot," p. 140.

15. Letter of Zerach Warhaftig to Mercas Olami – Mizrachi, March 26, 1940 in Natanel Katzburg, Ed., *Pedut; Hatzala be–Yemei ha–Shoa, Mikorot u–Mechkarim* (Ramat–Gan, 1984), pp. 25–33.

16. Eliash, "Hatzalat Yeshivot," pp. 140–143; see, for example, the letter of Rabbi Moshe Blau to Mills, April 2, 1940, AAYEY, file 119.

17. Bauer, *American Jewry and the Holocaust*, pp. 115–116.

18. The most important of these directives was the "likely to become a public charge" clause, which gave consuls the right to reject an immigration application wherever the slightest doubt existed as to whether the applicant could successfully settle in the United States. Two detailed studies of U.S. immigration policy during this period are David S. Wyman, *Paper Walls; America and the Refugee Crisis 1938–1941* (Amherst, 1968); and Henry L. Feingold, *The Politics of Rescue; The Roosevelt Administration and the Holocaust 1938–1945* (New Brunswick, NJ 1970).

19. "The Plight of the Great European Yeshivos," *Every Friday*, December 8, 1939, p. 1.

20. Letter of Carol Kuhn to Rabbi Karlinsky, May 17, 1940, ACJFWF, I–69, Box 149.

21. Warhaftig, *Palit ve–Sarid be–Yemei ha–Shoa*, pp. 149–153; Epstein, "Yeshivat Mir," p. 121.

22. See note 15.

23. Several of the foreign representatives subsequently obtained permission to keep their offices open longer—initially until September 4, 1940, and later until November 4, 1940. The consulates that were willing to grant the refugees visas were, however, among those forced to cease operations in August. Warhaftig, *Palit ve–Sarid be–Yemei ha–Shoa*, p. 90.

24. The feelings of despair, it should be noted, were not confined to the refugee Polish yeshivot. The Lithuanian *roshei yeshivot* also viewed the future with grave apprehension and sought to arrange for the emigration of their institutions. See letter of Rabbi Katz (Telz Yeshiva) to Merkaz Agudat Yisrael in Eretz Yisrael, July 18, 1940, AAYEY, file 62.

25. Department for the Righteous Among the Nations, Yad–Vashem, File 977 (Zwartendijk); Testimony of Zerach Warhaftig, Oral History Division, Institute of Contemporary Jewry, Hebrew University, Jerusalem (hereafter called Warhaftig Testimony), interview No. 2, November 30, 1965, pp. 7–8; Warhaftig, *Palit ve–Sarid be–Yemei ha–Shoa*, pp. 101–105.

26. The main reason that Sugihara was sent to Kovno was apparently to collect information on the Wehrmacht. The Japanese did not explicitly trust the Nazis and feared that they would invade the Soviet Union without informing them beforehand. They therefore sent Sugihara to Lithuania to keep tabs on troop movements in Poland. Bauer/YVS, p. 219. For a comprehensive account of Sugihara's activities in Lithuania, including an attempt to analyze the motives for his assistance to the refugees see Hillel Levine, *In Search of Sugihara: The Elusive Japanese Diplomat Who Risked His Life to Rescue 10,000 Jews from the Holocaust*, New York et al., 1996.

27. Department for the Righteous Among the Nations, Yad–Vashem, file 1054 (Sugihara); Epstein, "Yeshivat Mir," p. 122. The Mir Yeshiva student did not know Japanese and consequently stamped many visas upside down. Mordechai Paldiel, "Hatzalat Alfei Plitim al–Yedei Me'atim Bodedim," *Yalkut Moreshet*, no. 40

(December 1985), pp. 157–160. Paldiel quotes an interview Sugihara granted many years after the war in which he explained his motivation for granting the visas: For two nights I could not sleep at all. I thought to myself, "As a consul I have the right to issue transit visas but not end visas. I cannot permit these people to die, people who come to seek my help with death staring them in the face. Regardless of the consequences I must act in accordance with my conscience."

28. Dr. Elkes later headed the Judenrat in the Kovno Ghetto. Leib Garfunkel, *Kovno ha–Yehudit be–Churbana* (Jerusalem, 1959), pp. 47–48.

29. Yaakov Edelstein, "Ha–Masa u–Matan ha–Rishon im Shiltonot Brit ha–Moetzot al Yetziat Yehudim mi–Russya be–Tekufat ha–Milchama," *Gesher*, no. 42 (March 1965), pp. 79–82; Warhaftig, *Palit ve–Sarid be–Yemei ha–Shoa*, pp. 118–121.

30. Letter of Rabbi Kotler to Rabbi Silver, July 7, 1940, Papers of Rabbi Eliezer Silver, Harrisburg, Penn. (hereafter called ESP); letter of Rabbi Wasserman to Rabbi Rosenberg, July 10, 1940, AYHR; letter of Rabbi Bloch (Telz Yeshiva) to Rabbi Dr. Bernard Revel (President of Yeshiva College), July 12, 1940, ESP. The author would like to thank Rabbi Dr. Aaron Rakeffet (Rothkoff) for providing access to the documents from the papers of Rabbi Silver.

31. Dr. Samuel Schmidt traveled to Washington in late July 1940 to meet with government officials to obtain their support for these proposals. See "Report of Samuel M. Schmidt on his trip to Indianapolis, Indiana and Washington D.C., July 25, 1940, SMS–AJA, microfilm no. 855.

32. Letter of Moses Leavitt to Samuel Goldsmith, January 27, 1941, AJDC–VH.

33. For Wise's role in the American Jewish community, see Melvin I. Urofsky, *A Voice That Spoke for Justice; The Life and Times of Stephen S. Wise* (Albany, 1982); David S. Wyman, *The Abandonment of the Jews; America and the Holocaust 1941–1945* (New York, 1984), pp. 69–70.

34. Letter of Moses Leavitt to Samuel Goldsmith," January 27, 1941, AJDC–VH.

35. Rabbi Jacob Levinson, "Chovat ha–Hatzala," *Ha–Pardes*, 14, no. 11 (Shevat 5701/February 1941), 11–12.

36. Letter of Moses Leavitt to Samuel Goldsmith, January 27, 1941, AJDC–VH.

37. Since the members of the delegation did not have any money with them (because the Sabbath had already begun), they gave their watches and jewelry as collateral until they could pay for the cables. *Churbn un Rettung*, pp. 203–205.

38. *Foreign Relations of the United States*, 1940, II (Washington, DC, 1957), 239–240.

39. *Churban un Rettung*, p. 205.

40. Wyman, *Paper Walls*, pp. 137–142.

41. Entry for December 12, 1940, *The War Diary of Breckinridge Long; Selections from the Years 1939–1944*, ed. Fred L. Israel (Lincoln, 1966), p. 161. Although Long has been severely criticized by every major historian who has examined the attitude of the Roosevelt administration towards the persecution of European Jewry because he staunchly opposed increased Jewish immigration and personally helped thwart several rescue schemes which could have saved thousands of European Jews, the Assistant Secretary of State was praised for his sympathetic attitude to the refugees in the history of *Vaad ha–Hatzala* published by the rabbinic rescue organization after the war. *Churbn un Rettung*, pp. 205–206. It should be noted, however, that the history of the *Vaad* appeared prior to the publication of the major studies by Feingold and Wyman, which exposed the critical and negative role played by Long

in determining the immigration policy of the Roosevelt administration.

42. Entry for December 23, 1940, Israel, *The War Diary of Breckinridge Long*, p. 165. A week later Rabbi Teitelbaum wrote to Long indicating that following his advice, the list of prospective visa recipients had been reduced from "3,800 students and 2,000 faculty members and refugee rabbis" to approximately 980 individuals "who are facing most hardship and danger." Letter of Rabbi Aaron Teitelbaum to Breckinridge Long, October 30, 1940, ACRC, file 492–2. There is no evidence of a positive reply to this appeal.

43. *Churbn un Rettung* lauded Macdonald's efforts on behalf of the *Vaad* and designated him as a *Chasid Umot ha–Ulam* (Righteous among the Nations); see p. 204.

44. The first branch of *Zeirei Agudat Yisrael* was founded on the Lower East Side of New York City in 1923. Originally the *Zeirei*, unlike the European branches of the Agudat Yisrael movement, devoted most of its efforts to social and educational programs rather than to ideological and political activities. In April 1939 the loosely allied branches of *Zeirei* in New York City established a national office and began organizing branches of the movement in several North American cities with large Jewish populations. This step marked the transformation of *Zeirei* from a federation of youth clubs to a full–fledged political movement. For many years, in fact, *Zeirei* fulfilled the function of the adult movement, which had difficulty establishing itself in America. George Kranzler, *Williamsburg; A Jewish Community in Transition* (New York, 1961), pp. 242–244.

45. Tress gave up a promising career as a business executive to devote himself to *Zeirei Agudat Yisrael*. It was he who transformed *Zeirei* from a small youth organization into a political movement. Ibid., pp. 253, 262. For a laudatory appraisal of Tress' leadership role in Zeirei Agudat Yisrael see Yonasan Rosenblum, *They Called Him Mike: Reb Elimelech Tress - His Era, Hatzala, and the Building of an American Orthodoxy*, Brooklyn, 1995.

46. *Churbn un Rettung*, pp. 201–205. Gershon Kranzler, "Setting the Record Straight," *Jewish Observer*, VII, no. 10 (November 1971), 9–14.

47. Letter of Bernhard Kahn to Henry Monsky, October 10, 1940, ACRC, file 492–2.

48. "Meeting of Finance Committee on Lithuanian Yeshivoth held on October 21, 1940, at the office of the J.D.C.," ACRC, file 492–2.

49. Department of the Righteous Among the Nations, Yad Vashem, files 977 (Zwartendijk) and 1054 (Sugihara); Baruch Oren, "Mi–Vilna Derech Yapan el ha–Olam ha–Chofshi," *Yalkut Moreshet*, No. 11, November 1969, p. 43.

50. See Chapter 3, notes 18–23.

51. Epstein, "Yeshivat Mir," p. 121; Warhaftig, *Palit ve–Sarid be–Yemei ha–Shoa*, pp. 149–150; interview with Rabbi Shimon Romm, July 27, 1977.

52. Warhaftig, *Palit ve–Sarid be–Yemei ha–Shoa*, p. 143.

53. Interviews with Rabbi Moshe Cohen (former student of the Kletzk Yeshiva), YVA, 0–3/3856, and Rabbi Shimon Romm (former student of the Mir Yeshiva). Many individuals who obtained Japanese visas subsequently tore them up for fear of being deported to Siberia. Interview with Rabbi Yaakov Nayman (former student of the Baranowitz Yeshiva), July 26, 1977.

54. Quoted in Warhaftig, *Palit ve–Sarid be–Yemei ha–Shoa*, p. 104.

55. Epstein, "Yeshivat Mir," pp. 121–123; Herzman, *Mofait ha–Dor*, p. 59.

56. Interview with Rabbi Moshe Cohen, YVA, 0–3/3856.

57. Department for the Righteous Among the Nations, Yad Vasehm, files 977 (Zwartendijk) and 1054 (Sugihara).
58. Oren, "Mi-Vilna Derech Yapan,", p. 43; Herzman, *Mofait ha–Dor*, pp. 59–63; interview with Rabbi Shimon Romm.
59. Epstein, "Yeshivat Mir," p. 123.
60. Ibid.
61. Herzman, *Mofait ha–Dor*, p. 65.
62. Yaakov Even–Chen, *Tenu'a be–Sa'arat Milchama* (Tel Aviv, 1984), p. 164.
63. Bauer/YVS, p. 221; Herzman, *Mofait ha–Dor*, p. 67; Epstein, "Yeshivat Mir," pp. 123–124.
64. Letter of Blanche Renard to Amos Deinard, August 5, 1940, ACJFWF, I–69, Box 149.
65. Letter of Henrietta Buchman to H. J. Hyman, September 5, 1940, AJDC–VH.
66. *Churbn un Rettung* , p. 185.
67. Letter of Rabbi Eliezer Silver to H. L. Lurie, September 5, 1940, ACJFWF, I–69, Box 149.
68. Representatives of the Federated Council of Palestinian Institutions also participated in the meeting. "Meeting Re Yeshivoth, September 10, 1940," September 18, 1940, ACJFWF, VH–600.
69. "Status of East European Yeshivoth, Methods Of Transmitting Funds and Activities Of Emergency Committee for War–Torn Yeshivoth (Replacing Bulletin #116)," Budgeting For Member Agencies, No. 123, October 1940, p. 2, AVH.
70. Letter of Blanche Renard to H. J.Hyman, October 1, 1940, ACJFWF, I–69, Box 149.
71. Letter of Blanche Renard to Norman Dockman, October 18, 1940, ACJFWF, I–69, Box 110.
72. Letter of Rabbi Kalmanowitz to the Council of Jewish Federations, November 5, 1940, ACJFWF, I–69, Box 149.
73. Letter of H. L. Lurie to Rabbi Kalmanowitz, November 6, 1940, ACJFWF, I–69, Box 149.
74. Letter of Rabbi Karlinsky to H. L. Lurie, November 8, 1940, ACJFWF, I–69, Box 149.
75. Letter of Rabbi Kalmanowitz to H. L. Lurie, November 8, 1940, ACJFWF, I–69, Box 149.
76. Letter of H. L. Lurie to Rabbi Kalmanowitz, November 18, 1940, ACJFWF, I–69, Box 149.
77. Letter of Rabbi Karlinsky to the Council of Jewish Federations and Welfare Funds, November 25, 1940, ACJFWF, I–69, Box 149.
78. See, for example, his letter to Elkan Voorsanger, November 22, 1940, ACJFWF, I–69, Box 149.
79. According to available statistics, there were approximately 10,850 Jews living in Indianapolis and 13,500 Jews living in Houston as of 1937. H. S. Linfield, "The Jewish Population of the United States," *American Jewish Year Book, 5707,* 46 (Philadelphia, 1944), 496.
80. Letter of H. J. Hyman to Samuel Schmidt, July 16, 1940; "Report of Samuel M. Schmidt on his trip to Indianapolis, Indiana and Washington, D.C.," July 25, 1940, SMS–AJA, microfilm no. 855.

81. Letter of H. J. Hyman to Samuel Schmidt, July 25, 1940, SMS–AJA, microfilm no. 855.

82. Letter of Samuel Schmidt to H. J. Hyman, June 29, 1940, SMS–AJA, microfilm no. 855.

83. On August 14, 1940, Rabbi Yoseph Shub of the Vilna *Vaad ha–Yeshivot* cabled Schmidt to inform him of Rabbi Grodzinski's death and to appeal for financial assistance. Schmidt immediately wrote to the Indianapolis federation asking them to fulfill their pledge to the *Vaad*. Cable of Rabbi Yoseph Schub to Samuel Schmidt, August 14, 1940; letter of Samuel Schmidt to Albert Goldstein, August 15, 1940, SMS–AJA, microfilm no. 855.

84. Letter of Blanche Renard to H. J. Hyman, September 5, 1940, ACJFWF, I–69, Box 149.

85. Letter of Henrietta Buchman to H. J. Hyman, September 5, 1940, AJDC–VH.

86. Letter of H. J. Hyman to Blanche Renard, September 26, 1940, ACJFWF, I–69, Box 149.

87. Letter of Blanche Renard to H. J. Hyman, October 1, 1940, ACJFWF, I-69, Box 149.

88. See note 77.

89. Letter of J. B. Lightman to Rabbi Silver, March 28, 1940; letter of Rabbi Silver to J. B. Lightman, March 31, 1940; cable of J. B. Lightman to Rabbi Silver, April 1, 1940, all ACJFWF, I–69, Box 149.

90. Cable of Rabbi Silver to J. B. Lightman, April 2, 1940, ACJFWF, I–69, Box 149.

91. Cable of J. B. Lightman to Rabbi Silver, April 2, 1940, ACJFWF, I–69, Box 149.

92. Cable of Rabbi Yisrael Rosenberg to J. B. Lightman, April 2, 1940; cable of Rabbi H. Raphael Gold to Moses Feld, April 2, 1940, both ACJFWF, I–69, Box 149.

93. Letter of J. B. Lightman to Rabbi H. Raphael Gold, April 4, 1940, ACJFWF, I–69, Box 149.

94. Letter of J. B. Lightman to Rabbi Silver, October 1, 1940, ACJFWF, I–69, Box 110.

95. Letter of J. B. Lightman to Rabbi Silver, October 23, 1940, ACJFWF, I–69, Box 110.

96. See note 77.

97. "Support Of Jewish Federations And Welfare Funds To The Emergency Committee For War–Torn Yeshivoth, March 15, 1939 [sic] to July 4, 1940," "Status Of East European Yeshivoth, Methods Of Transmitting Funds And Activities Of Emergency Committee For War–Torn Yeshivoth," Budgeting Bulletin for Member Agencies, No. 123, October 1940, p. 5, AVH.

98. "Emergency Committee For War–Torn Yeshivoth Financial Statement (Not Audited) For The Period March 15, 1939 to September 15, 1940," Budgeting Bulletin No. 123, October 1940, p. 4, AVH.

99. Letter of Rabbi Silver to the Council of Jewish Federations and Welfare Funds, November 5, 1940, ACJFWF, I–69, Box 149.

100. Letter of Rabbi Silver to the Council of Jewish Federations and Welfare Funds, December 5, 1940, ACJFWF, I–69, Box 149.

Chapter 5

The Tickets Campaign

The first refugee scholars who were able to obtain all the documents necessary to depart from Lithuania (end visa, transit visa, and exit permit) left in September 1940. They traveled by train via Minsk to Moscow, where they boarded the Trans-Siberian railroad. Ten days later they arrived in the Soviet Pacific port of Vladivostok, from whence they sailed to the Japanese port of Tsuruga.[1] In most cases the travel arrangements were handled by Intourist, the Soviet government tourism agency which demanded that the tickets be paid for in dollars at the highest possible price. As a result, the refugees were accorded first-class hotel accommodations and train tickets, creating a somewhat incongruous situation given the fact that most were leaving the Soviet Union virtually penniless. In some cases, individuals bought railway tickets to Moscow for rubles and there purchased train tickets to Vladivostok (also in rubles), thereby circumventing the foreign currency requirements, but such instances were the exception rather than the rule.[2]

The first Polish refugees reached Japan in October 1940. Upon their arrival in Tsuruga, they were met by representatives of "Jewcom," the Committee For Assistance To Refugees established by the minuscule Ashkenazic Jewish community of Kobe earlier that year.[3] Faced with the prospect of an influx of these refugees, the committee sought to assist them in their dealings with the Japanese government, provide them with material relief, and facilitate their emigration overseas. Jewcom paid the required $60 landing money per person for those who were unable to pay and covered the travel expenses from Tsuruga to Kobe, where the new arrivals were temporarily housed. Once the refugees had reached Kobe, Jewcom also had to provide them with food, housing, and medical care, since most had no funds and were unable to work while in Japan. Given the fact that 852 Jewish refugees reached Japan during the months October–December 1940, that task proved to be a formidable one for the small local Jewish community.[4]

Besides the financial burden of providing maintenance, initially for hundreds and later for thousands of transient refugees, Jewcom faced a more serious problem. Most of the Polish refugees had been allowed to enter Japan because they possessed genuine Japanese transit visas which had been obtained on the basis of the end visas to Curaçao. But the latter were basically worthless, and the former were valid for only 14 days, so it was obvious to the refugees, as well as to their benefactors from Jewcom, that a means would have to be found immediately to extend their stay in Japan. The dangers inherent in the situation were twofold. On the one hand, those who had reached Japan without genuine end visas in theory faced deportation back to the Soviet Union, unless they could find another country willing to admit them. On the other hand, the danger existed that even if those individuals were not expelled or deported, the Japanese authorities might bar the entry of additional refugees from the Soviet Union, thereby closing down an important rescue route.[5]

Jewcom turned for assistance to Setsuzo Kotsuji, a philo-Semitic Japanese Hebrew and Bible scholar who had previously worked for Japanese Foreign Minister Yosuke Matsuoka as an expert on Jewish affairs when the latter headed the South Manchuria Railway. Kotsuji initially obtained Foreign Ministry approval for the entry of several refugees who lacked Japanese transit visas, but ministry officials refused to allow those already in Japan on transit visas to extend their stay. In order to achieve this goal, Kotsuji appealed personally to Matsuoka, who explained that he could not officially accede to such a request but advised him to obtain the approval of the local police authorities in Kobe. The central government, Matsuoka promised, would simply ignore the refugees' presence, thereby in effect permitting their continued residence in Japan. Kotsuji obtained 300,000 yen from his brother-in-law and succeeded in bribing the Kobe police authorities to approve the extension of the refugees' transit visas. Their only condition was that the documents be renewed every fifteen days,[6] a relatively minor nuisance considering the dangerous alternatives.

Regardless of Kotsuji's success, the leaders of the Polish refugees realized that every effort had to be made to enable as many of the new arrivals to leave Japan as quickly as possible. Whatever hopes they had of increasing the number of refugees from Lithuania depended on their ability to ensure that those entering Japan could leave within a reasonably short time. In order to achieve that goal, Zerach Warhaftig, together with Yehoshua Bram of the General Zionists and Eliezer Szupakiewicz of *Poale Zion,* established a committee of prominent Polish refugees which was to function as a local Palestine Office. They set up headquarters in Yokohama (because of its proximity to the foreign embassies and consulates) and began efforts to get as many refugees as possible out of Lithuania, to facilitate the immigration of refugees to various havens and especially to Eretz Yisrael, and to prepare a contingency plan in case the refugees in Japan could not emigrate elsewhere. Once they began their activities, the committee was besieged with requests for Japanese visas from Polish refugees (and "local" Lithuanian Jews) in Lithuania, as well as from those groups in New York and Jerusalem that were trying to save them. Needless to say, many of these requests came from the *Vaad ha-Hatzala* and yeshiva circles in the United States and Palestine.[7]

The committee's first breakthrough came in mid-November 1940 in the course of negotiations regarding ship tickets with representatives of Nippon Yushen Kaisha (N.Y.K.), Japan's leading shipping line. Warhaftig and Szupakiewicz explained that they were anxious to arrange for the passage of refugees currently in Lithuania to Palestine and other destinations but were having problems obtaining Japanese transit visas. The representatives of N.Y.K., which was reputed to have enormous influence in government circles, undertook to arrange Japanese transit visas for all prospective passengers on the condition that the committee obtain the necessary end visas and make a $20 down payment on 500 tickets not later than December 31, 1940. The shipping company also agreed to immediately cable an initial list of 125 names to the Japanese consulate in Moscow indicating that tickets for these individuals had already been purchased on N.Y.K. and that the company was responsible for their maintenance in Japan prior to their journey to a final destination. In addition, N.Y.K sent the names of the prospective passengers to the Tokyo office of Intourist, which cabled its office in Kovno, and the committee also notified the individual refugees directly.

While this agreement ostensibly paved the way for the emigration of hundreds of Polish refugees from Lithuania, it did not entirely solve the problem, because the refugee committee in Japan lacked the funds to pay for the tickets. They therefore appealed to the major overseas Jewish relief agencies—the Jewish Agency, the Joint Distribution Committee, and World Jewish Congress—for assistance. The initial responses of these organizations were negative, however, and it appeared as if this rescue scheme would not be carried out. At least as far as the JDC was concerned, emigration from Lithuania based on Curaçao visas was considered a risky venture,[8] and the organization feared the consequences of the refugees' being stranded in Japan. In fact, in November 1940, JDC secretary Moses Leavitt had advised Moses Beckelman, his representative in Lithuania, against sending those with Curaçao visas to the Far East. Beckelman replied from Vilna that despite the problems that would result from the emigration to the Far East, the plight of the refugees was such that their welfare would be best served if they were able to leave Lithuania, even if it were only to Japan.[9]

The only organization that immediately indicated its willingness to help pay for the N.Y.K. tickets was the *Vaad ha-Hatzala*. Given its determination to rescue the refugee rabbis and yeshiva students from Soviet Lithuania, the *Vaad's* response was hardly surprising. This was, after all, the very *raison d'être* of the rabbinic rescue organization. In the words of Zerach Warhaftig, who was disappointed by the negative response of the major Jewish overseas relief organizations:

> The only public Jewish organization which grasped the importance of our proposal and in principle accepted it and indicated its willingness to participate in its realization was the *Agudat ha-Rabbanim* and its *Vaad ha-Hatzala*. The intense desire to save the yeshivot concentrated in Lithuania prompted them to seize upon any reasonable program. They exhibited an ability to raise money for this purpose and a readiness to act.[10]

The *Vaad's* activities in this context were undoubtedly motivated by the intense concern of its leaders regarding the fate of the yeshivot under Soviet rule. From past experience, most of the *roshei yeshiva* in Lithuania, as well as the rabbis in the United States, assumed that the days of the Torah academies in Lithuania were numbered and that special measures would be required to preserve their existence. In several cases the yeshivot, which had moved to small towns in the wake of the ruralization decree the previous winter, were forced to split up their students by moving them to several smaller villages in order to minimize their problems with the local authorities. For example, the Mir Yeshiva, which had relocated to Keydan (Kedainiai), left that town on August 5, 1940, and moved its students to Krakinove (Krekenava), Remigole (Ramygala), Shat (Seta) and Krok (Krakes).[11] The Kletzk Yeshiva, which had originally relocated to Janeva, sent its students to Salok (Salakas), Dusyat (Dusetos), and Dukstat.[12]

The problems facing the yeshivot were not only political, but also financial. During the fall of 1940, refugee rabbis and *roshei yeshiva* in Lithuania beseeched their American colleagues, and especially the leaders of the *Vaad ha-Hatzala*, for monetary help for their institutions as well as for assistance in emigrating abroad.[13] On October 2, 1940, for example, Rabbi Aron Kotler, the *rosh yeshiva* of Kletzk, wrote to Rabbi Yisrael Halevi Rosenberg in New York asking for financial assistance since "our Joint aid has already been stopped for three months." Rabbi Kotler indicated his disappointment, moreover, that while other groups had already received visas, travel documents had still not been arranged for himself and his students, a fact that left him "very very surprised regarding this negligence."[14]

Appeals such as this by a leading European *rosh yeshiva* spurred the *Vaad* to redouble its efforts on behalf of the refugee scholars. At the thirty-third annual convention of the *Agudat ha-Rabbanim,* which began on November 11, 1940, Rabbi Silver estimated that a million and a half dollars would be required for the relocation of the yeshivot, so it was obvious that special measures had to be taken.[15] The first step was administrative. On November 26 and 27 the leaders of the *Vaad* met at the offices of *Agudat ha-Rabbanim* and decided to expand the rescue organization's presidium. Rabbi Silver, who until then had served as sole president, was now joined on the presidium by Rabbis Joseph Konvitz of Newark, New Jersey, and Jacob Levinson of Brooklyn.[16]

The addition of Rabbis Konvitz and Levinson was particularly significant in view of the fact that both these prominent rabbis were active supporters of the religious Zionist Mizrachi movement.[17] Although *Vaad ha-Hatzala* had been established by the *Agudat ha-Rabbanim*, which was officially apolitical, the fact that Rabbi Silver was founder and president of American Agudat Yisrael, which opposed political Zionism, created problems for the rabbinic rescue organization. Thus the appointment of Rabbis Konvitz and Levinson not only expanded the *Vaad's* leadership, but also gave it a more "balanced" image and helped broaden its appeal. The rivalry between supporters of Mizrachi and Agudat Yisrael among the leaders of the *Vaad* was to surface from time to time, but efforts were made to separate rescue activities, on which a consensus existed among the rabbis, from the political and ideological issues on which there were differences of opinion. One means of achieving unity was to stress the supremacy of *Agudat ha-Rabbanim,* since all the leaders of the *Vaad*, regardless of political affiliation, were members of the rabbinic association.[18]

Another decision made by the *Vaad* in late November was to invite one of the European *roshei yeshiva* who were in the United States at the time to attend each of its meetings.[19] The presence of these Torah scholars would undoubtedly lend an important dimension to the discussions, but there was apparently a more prosaic reason for this step. One of the problems the *Vaad* faced in its fundraising efforts during this period was the attempts by representatives of various European yeshivot to raise funds in America on the their own. In the summer of 1940 Rabbi Silver had complained to Rabbi Rosenberg:

> Yesterday Rabbi Kalmanowitz, and Rabbi Greineman and Rabbi Wasserman visited here [in Cincinnati]. Today they left and Rabbi Kalmanowitz left for Chicago ...even though in my opinion it is not advisable to visit that city now and G-d forbid he is more likely to do harm than good. In general there is confusion regarding this matter. Everyone travels and speaks and brags about his deeds and lobbies and sends cables and tries to enlist support everywhere, which I fear will lead to bad results. In my opinion the *Agudat ha-Rabbanim* must take a strong stand to stop those who are confusing people and doing irresponsible things in order to prevent the cause from being ruined.[20]

Silver's complaint reflects the basic problematics of the *Vaad's* relations with the American offices of the refugee yeshivot. Throughout the first year of the *Vaad's* existence, the local offices of the yeshivot continued to raise funds, creating considerable confusion among those who sought to assist the refugee scholars. In fact, on November 5, 1940, *Vaad ha-Hatzala* informed various federations and welfare funds that henceforth it would confine itself exclusively to raising funds for the relocation of the yeshivot while the American offices would continue to raise funds for their maintenance.[21] Shortly thereafter, however, the *Vaad* took the above-mentioned steps designed to co-opt the refugee *roshei yeshivot* and less than two weeks later applied to the U.S. government for permission to transmit funds for the maintenance of the yeshivot in Lithuania.[22]

The rabbis never volunteered any clarification for the ostensible zigzag in their policy, but the most logical explanation is that it relates to their efforts to obtain allocations from federations and welfare funds. As long as the transfer of funds to Lithuania was prohibited by the U.S. government, the *Vaad* preferred to let the American offices handle such transactions or at least to indicate publicly that this was the case. Once the remittance of funds to Lithuania was approved, however, the *Vaad* immediately sought to utilize this channel to implement its own relief program. Ironically, the problems the *Vaad* encountered in its relations with the American offices of the yeshivot were quite similar to those the rabbinic rescue organization had created for the Joint Distribution Committee. There is, however, no evidence to suggest that the rabbis noted any similarity between the two situations or drew any conclusions therefrom.[23]

Having achieved a measure of unity on the fundraising for refugee yeshivot front, the *Vaad* intensified its efforts to assist the Torah scholars. On December 5 the *Agudat ha-Rabbanim* applied to the U.S. Department of the Treasury for a license to transfer funds to Lithuania for the maintenance of the refugee rabbis and yeshiva students.[24] The license, granted nine days later, allowed the rabbis to remit up to $15,000 to Moses Beckelman, the JDC representative in Vilna (or his substitute) for distribution among the rabbis and students.[25] Thus after using legally questionable methods to transfer funds to the beleaguered scholars in Lithuania during its initial year of operation, the *Vaad* was finally able to carry out these transactions with the approval of the American authorities.[26]

At the same time, the *Vaad* began to take practical steps to facilitate the emigration to the United States of rabbis and yeshiva students. Starting in early October, with the assistance of *Zeirei Agudat Yisrael*, Rabbi Silver began purchasing ship tickets for dozens of prominent rabbis and *roshei yeshiva* and their families, most of whom were in Lithuania. While the overwhelming majority were the leaders of the Polish refugee yeshivot (Rabbis Aron Kotler of Kletzk, Reuven Grazowsky of Kamenetz, Avraham Yaphin of Bialystok, and Shabtai Yogel of Slonim), the list also included such well-known rabbis as Menachem Zemba of Warsaw, who had remained in the Polish capital.[27] Most of the tickets were purchased with funds raised from American relatives and friends or by the local offices of the yeshivot, but in about one-quarter of the cases Rabbi Silver provided the necessary sums.[28] And while the entire operation was ostensibly carried out by *Zeirei* (even the correspondence was on their stationery), it was the *Vaad ha-Hatzala* that provided the financial support. The American-born or-educated young men of *Zeirei* facilitated the technical arrangements, at which they were far more adept than the immigrant rabbis of the *Vaad*, but the operation was essentially orchestrated, and to a certain extent financed, by the rabbinic rescue organization.[29]

In December 1940 the *Vaad* took another practical step to facilitate its immigration efforts. The rabbis decided to send a special emissary to the Far East to assist in obtaining U.S. visas for the refugee rabbis and yeshiva students in Japan. They thought it might be worthwhile to try from there to convince the U.S. authorities to grant more visas. The person chosen for the task was Frank (Efraim) Newman, a young businessman from New York who was friendly with Anshel Fink, a *Zeirei* activist involved in the *Vaad's* efforts to secure visas. Newman arrived in Japan on January 12, 1941, and within a short time began to coordinate his efforts with those of the representatives of the Polish refugees.[30]

The practical measures taken by the *Vaad* proved timely, since events in Lithuania had lent an added urgency to emigration efforts. On December 31, 1940, the Soviet authorities closed down all the foreign relief agencies and dissolved the existent refugee committees. More important, the refugees were given until January 25, 1941, to accept Soviet citizenship or be declared stateless.[31] The potentially dangerous implications of these decrees, which threatened to prevent emigration, prompted an increasing number of rabbis and yeshiva students to attempt to obtain the necessary travel documents. Whatever reluctance to emigrate or skepticism regarding the Curaçao visas or the escape route via Japan that had existed now dissipated in the wake of these decrees. On both sides of the Atlantic, a frantic search for end visas and transit visas was launched.

As might be expected, considerable efforts were invested in attempts to obtain those documents that had already proven their worth: end visas to Curaçao and Japanese transit visas. Regarding the former, two individuals who played a key role were Rabbi Shlomo (Wilhelm) Wolbe of Stockholm and A. M. de Jong, the local Dutch consul in the Swedish capital. A native of Germany who was studying at the Mir Yeshiva, Wolbe had been expelled from Poland in 1938 and had settled in Stockholm. Decker, the Dutch ambassador to the Baltic states, before his forced departure from the Soviet Union, had left instructions to direct visa requests to the Swedish capital; Wolbe was therefore inundated with appeals from his former yeshiva classmates to secure Curaçao visas for them. He approached De Jong, who proved to be particularly cooperative. Starting in January 1941 the Dutch consul issued 2,386 Curaçao visas for Polish refugees in Lithuania, among them approximately 1,000 rabbis and yeshiva students. Each visa cost 5 ½ Swedish crowns (the equivalent of slightly more than $1), sums that Wolbe raised locally.

De Jong, it should be noted, made a special effort to assist the refugees. Even on Sundays he came in to process applications and send out visas, and he often devised schemes to circumvent the obstacles created by the Soviets, who were constantly changing their requirements for exit permits. In fact, he volunteered to send visas by diplomatic cable to Intourist to accommodate Soviet demands and thereby facilitate the emigration of the refugees. When a group of students of the Mir Yeshiva were detained in Vladivostok by the local Japanese consul, who suspected that the Curaçao visas were not genuine, De Jong cabled him immediately to confirm the validity of the documents.

In addition to arranging visas to Curaçao, Wolbe also obtained several end visas to Haiti as well as a few Polish passports from Polish diplomats in Switzerland. The latter documents were particularly important for those refugees who lacked them. (Many yeshiva students either had left their passports at home when they escaped to Vilna or had never taken one out.) In several cases the

Polish passports were granted on the basis of the Curaçao visas Wolbe sent to his friend Elchanan Erlanger of Lucerne, who also sought to assist the refugee rabbis and students.[32]

In the meantime the refugees in Lithuania were trying to obtain Japanese transit visas from Japanese consuls in Moscow and other cities. While the Japanese diplomats in the Soviet capital were willing to issue transit visas to those whose names appeared on the lists submitted by the N.Y.K. shipping line, they refused to do so on the basis of Curaçao visas as soon as they discovered that such documents were basically worthless. The refugees thereupon began contacting Japanese consuls elsewhere, in the hope that they might be convinced to issue transit visas. Some of these requests, such as those directed to the consul in Chita, were apparently successful.[33]

In the United States *Vaad ha-Hatzala* was busy throughout this period attempting to raise funds to pay for the transportation of those refugee rabbis and yeshiva students who had succeeded in obtaining end visas and transit visas. The groundwork for the expansion of fundraising had already been laid at the meeting of the *Vaad* executive held in New York on November 26–27, 1940, at which Rabbis Konvitz and Levinson were added to the presidium.[34] The operative decisions made at that meeting to intensify fundraising bore fruit during the initial months of 1941 as the *Vaad's* campaign gained momentum.

The rabbis' efforts were concentrated primarily in the large metropolitan centers that had sizable Jewish communities. The key operatives were the members of *Agudat ha-Rabbanim* and leading Orthodox laymen. Delegations of prominent rabbis were sent to those cities with sizable Orthodox communities to assist their local counterparts in raising funds. Thus, for example, Rabbis Silver and Levinson headed the tickets campaign in New York, and the latter also traveled to Chicago to help establish an emergency fund headed by local rabbi Elazar Mushkin. A delegation of well-known rabbis from the East Coast headed by Bernard Levinthal of Philadelphia (former president of the *Agudat ha-Rabbanim* and a leader of the American Orthodox rabbinate for decades) traveled to Detroit to work with Rabbi Elimelech Wohlgelernter, and Rabbis Silver and Konvitz went to Miami to assist the local campaign. [35]

The *Vaad* sought to maximize its fundraising efforts by enlisting all the American Orthodox rabbis to participate in the tickets campaign. The rabbis were asked to organize activities in their own communities and were urged by the *Vaad* to contact, and if necessary even personally visit, congregation members who did not attend services regularly in order to encourage them to contribute. In addition, the rabbis were instructed to devote at least two to three weeks a year to visit communities in their area[36] in which there were no Orthodox rabbis, in order to reach as many individuals as possible. Special appeals were launched in synagogues all over the country. In New York City, for example, the Sabbath of Yitro (February 18, 1941) was set aside to raise funds for the *Vaad's* campaign.[37] In that city, which had the largest Orthodox community in the United States,[38] the rabbis established a campaign goal or "quota" of 500 tickets at $300 apiece.

The *Vaad* set ticket quotas for 87 cities and districts in 32 states. After New York, the rabbis expected the largest sums to be raised in Chicago (150 tickets or $45,000), and then Baltimore, the Cleveland area, Detroit, and Philadelphia (100 tickets each); and Boston and Pittsburgh (75 each); but even small communities such as Pensacola, Florida; Council Bluffs, Iowa; and Columbus, Georgia (5 tickets in each) were not ignored. According to the quotas established for each area, *Vaad ha-Hatzala* hoped to raise $788,400 or the equivalent of 2,628 tickets.[39]

The *Vaad* also sought to disseminate its message via the Orthodox press. In the Shevat 5701 (February 1941) issue of the rabbinic journal *Ha-Pardes*, for example, it published two full-page ads (one in Hebrew and one in Yiddish) pleading with Orthodox rabbis and laymen to provide funds. The first ad, entitled "Ve-Atem Tachrishun?" (And You Shall Remain Silent?), was directed primarily at Orthodox leaders and was signed by the three members of the *Vaad's* presidium and Rabbi Yisrael Halevi Rosenberg. The second ad, entitled "Helft Rattven di Torah" (Help Rescue the Torah) was signed by the same rabbis as well as Rabbi Levinthal (as honorary chairman), Rabbi Chaim Yitzhak Bloch (treasurer), and Hirsh Manishewitz (treasurer). The arguments marshaled by the rabbis to inspire the readers of *Ha-Pardes* reflected the *Vaad's* anxiety regarding the plight of the refugee Torah scholars and the enormous significance they attributed to their efforts to rescue them. In their words:

> American rabbis, where are you? Young and old lay leaders of synagogues where are you? Is this the time to sit idly by? Is this the time to remain silent?

The greats of our people are drowning at sea, are in captivity. The brilliant scholars of our generation and Jewish communal figures are fighting against the waves of annihilation engulfing all of Israel. They are stretching their weak hands to us, screaming through the tears, Save Us Brothers, Woe To Us To Have Suffered Such A Fate.

After all, thank G-d, we have means, visas from the government to bring them here. They, their families and students are turning to us, more than three thousand people calling to us for rescue in their hour of need.

Day and night we are engaged in rescue, to bring help and rescue to these unfortunates. We borrowed tens of thousands of dollars. Who can present all the details of the cables we receive daily with screams and horrible demands, a voice which pierces hearts. But we need money for tickets and expenses from there to Japan and Japan to here. We cannot rescue these unfortunates because of lack of resources and you remain silent?

Where is the fiery work to save the lives of the greats of our people. Help us! Hurry, shake up cities, spread the call in synagogues, demonstrate during the day, demonstrate at night, ring the bells in the ears of generous Jews. Open [their] hearts, yell, shout, go out to the markets and streets and announce [the campaign] for the ransoming of captives![40]

By the time the tickets campaign was launched, *Vaad ha-Hatzala*, or the Emergency Committee for War-Torn Yeshivot, as it was often still referred to, had acquired a fairly broad base of support in the Orthodox community. When it was established in late 1939 several important Orthodox organizations had been skeptical about the rabbis' insistence on setting up a separate relief and rescue organization for the refugee rabbis and yeshiva students,[41] but by early 1941 most of those doubts had dissipated. As a result, almost every major American Orthodox organization participated in the tickets campaign. Groups such as Young Israel,[42] the Union of Orthodox Jewish Congregations[43] and the Rabbinical Council of America supported the *Vaad's* fundraising drive and attempted to enlist the support of their members.[44]

This cooperation represented a turnabout not only in practical terms. These organizations, which to a large extent represented the native-born and/or-educated, more acculturated American Orthodox Jews, had been at odds for years with the leadership of *Agudat ha-Rabbanim,* which sought to maintain its hegemony in the Orthodox community despite far-reaching sociological and cultural changes. While the immigrant rabbis of the *Agudat ha-Rabbanim* functioned in accordance with traditional East European norms, which they considered binding, their younger, American-born and bred colleagues increasingly sought to establish new models to confront American realities.

Nowhere were these differences more pronounced than in the relations between *Agudat ha-Rabbanim* and the Rabbinical Council of America. In fact, the latter was established in 1935 primarily because of the differences between the graduates of American yeshivot and the leaders of the Orthodox rabbinic association, whose members had all been educated in Europe. Although *Agudat ha-Rabbanim* made several attempts during the two decades prior to World War II to open its ranks to graduates of the Rabbi Isaac Elchanan Theological Seminary of Yeshiva University and the Hebrew Theological College of Chicago, the rabbis produced by these institutions viewed the rabbinic association as being out of touch with American realities and unequipped to compete for the minds and hearts of American Jews against Conservative and Reform Judaism. Questions regarding cooperation with non-Orthodox Jews, mixed seating in the synagogue, and the active participation of nonobservant Jews in the services were hotly debated between the members of *Agudat ha-Rabbanim* and their American-educated colleagues and led to the establishment of the Rabbinical Council in 1935. Four years later negotiations were conducted regarding a possible merger between the two associations, but to no avail.[45] Despite these differences of opinion and outlook, the *Vaad* had approached the Rabbinical Council for help in raising funds almost immediately upon its establishment. While the members of the RCA were in theory willing to cooperate, they apparently did not become actively involved in such activities until early 1941, by which time *Vaad ha-Hatzala* had established its legitimacy and earned the support of practically the entire Orthodox community.[46]

Another modern Orthodox organization that provided active support for the tickets campaign was the Young Israel movement. Founded in 1912 by a small group of acculturated Jewish youth who wanted to remain Orthodox but sought to divorce themselves from the cultural milieu of their immigrant parents, Young Israel was dominated by its native-born, college-educated lay leadership. Its activists were not yeshiva graduates and usually refused to defer to immigrant Orthodox rabbis, who lacked secular education, were unsophisticated in American terms, and therefore were not particularly respected in the general community. If we add the fact that the movement sponsored social activities (such as mixed dancing), which were considered deviations from time-honored Orthodox norms, it becomes clear why the members of Young Israel were considered the least observant segment of American Orthodoxy.[47]

Given their ostensible lack of respect for the East European rabbis in the United States, the Young Israel's support for the *Vaad's* ticket campaign came as a pleasant surprise to the leaders of the rabbinic rescue organization. Their newfound appreciation for the Young Israel movement was expressed by Rabbi Silver in early 1941: "I convey most profuse gratitude for their loyal wholehearted cooperation and splendid work during the present rescuing campaign and I sincerely admire their efforts. As time goes on we are more convinced of your sincerity and conscientiousness in striving to elevate the ideals of true traditional Torah Judaism."[48] While Rabbi Silver viewed the Young Israel's active participation as an indication of increased ideological affinity between *Agudat ha-Rabbanim* and the lay Orthodox movement, there were other factors motivating the Young Israel's extensive support for the *Vaad's* campaign. One factor was the personal ties between the refugee *roshei yeshiva* and prominent American Orthodox Jews. Irving Bunim, one of the key lay leaders of Young Israel met Rabbi Kotler during the latter's visit to the United States in 1935. When he heard of the plight of the refugee rabbis and the fact that Rabbi Kotler was stuck in the Soviet Union, he helped activate the Young Israel movement for this cause.[49]

With the support of the somewhat disparate elements of American Orthodoxy assured, the *Vaad* sought to carry out the relocation of the refugee scholars stranded in Lithuania and the Far East. An important practical step to achieve that goal was taken on January 23, 1941, when Rabbi Silver signed an agreement with Thomas Cook and Sons—Wagon-Lits Inc. to handle all the travel arrangements for the rabbis and yeshiva students from the Soviet Union to the United States via Japan.[50] It is important to note here that U.S. immigration regulations forbade the entry of immigrants whose passage had been paid by an organization, and thus all travel

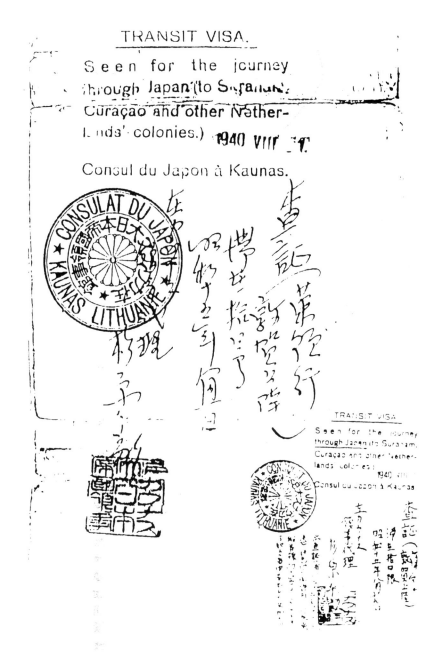

Japanese transit visa issued in Kaunas by Sempo Sugihara. (Simon Wiesenthal Center Archives)

Rabbi Avraham Kalmanowitz. (Orthodox Jewish Archives, Agudath Israel of America)

Japanese consul in Kaunas, Sempo Sugihara. (Simon Wiesenthal Center Archives)

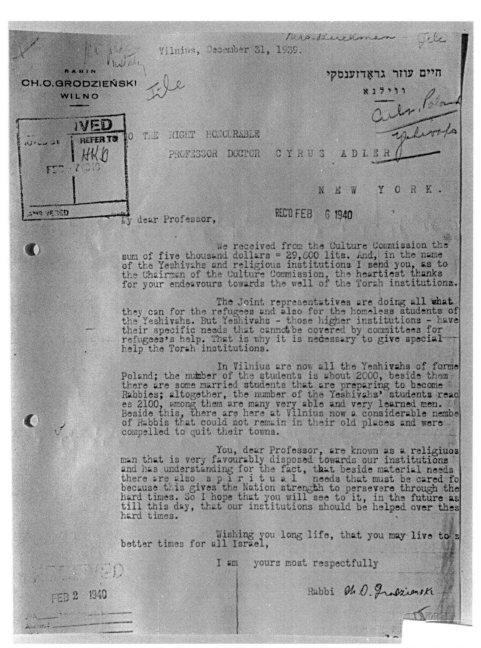

Vilnius, December 31, 1939.

RABIN
CH.O.GRODZIEŃSKI
WILNO

חיים עוזר גראָדזיענסקי
ווילנא

TO THE RIGHT HONOURABLE

PROFESSOR DOCTOR   C Y R U S   A D L E R

N E W   Y O R K .

My dear Professor,   RECD FEB 6 1940

        We received from the Culture Commission the sum of five thousand dollars = 29,600 lits. And, in the name of the Yeshivahs and religious institutions I send you, as to the Chairman of the Culture Commission, the heartiest thanks for your endeavours towards the well of the Torah institutions.

        The Joint representatives are doing all what they can for the refugees and also for the homeless students of the Yeshivahs. But Yeshivahs - those higher institutions - have their specific needs that cannot be covered by committees for refugees's help. That is why it is necessary to give special help the Torah institutions.

        In Vilnius are now all the Yeshivahs of former Poland; the number of the students is about 2000, beside them there are some married students that are preparing to become Rabbies; altogether, the number of the Yeshivahs' students reaches 2100, among them are many very able and very learned men. Beside this, there are here at Vilnius now a considerable nembe of Rabbis that could not remain in their old places and were compelled to quit their towns.

        You, dear Professor, are known as a religiuos man that is very favourably disposed towards our institutions and has understanding for the fact, that beside material needs there are also s p i r i t u a l   needs that must be cared for because this gives the Nation strength to persevere through the hard times. So I hope that you will see to it, in the future as till this day, that our institutions should be helped over thes hard times.

        Wishing you long life, that you may live to s better times for all Israel,

        I am   yours most respectfully

        Rabbi *Ch. O. Grodzienski*

FEB 2 1940

Letter of Rabbi Chaim Ozer Grodzienski to Dr. Cyrus Adler of the JDC appealing for aid for the refugee Torah scholars in Vilna, December 31, 1939. (JDC Archives, New York)

העלפט ראטעווען די תורה!

דער חורבן חתורה אין גרויס, די נשמה פון אידען איז די תורה הקדושה,
ואין לנו שיור רק התורה הזאת.

די ישיבות וועגען הרוב געוואָרען, טויזענדער תלמידי הכמים וענליזן נעבאַ
געלאָפען אין די וועלדער, א גרויסער טייל געפינען זיך אין ליטא, וייער ציל אין
עלעגד איז נרים, נאקעם און באַרוזים, אין גרעסטען הונגער־נויטה. גדולי ישראל
אדירי התורה, וואָגלען איבער שמעדם און דערפער, אנדערע זיינען פארשפאַרט
אין קאָנצענטראַציע לאַנערן, פילע האָבן זיך גערא טעוועטט ממש פון די נעגעל פון
מלאך המות, רח"ל.

שברעקט איס א ברידערליכע האנט מיר מוזען די ישיבת איינאָרדענען,
מיר מאַרען נישט לאָזן הונדערטער אין טויזענדער תלמידים אויסגעהן פון הנ־
גער. מיר מוזן אווגקשטעטלען צוריק דעם אור התורה, אנדערע ישיבות מוזען
אריבערגעפלהרט וערען אין ארץ ישראל, איינינע צו באטאַ דען אין ליטא, אין
אנדערע זוכן א פלאן אין גרימאַרלץ לענדער.

א קאמפיין צוריק אויפצובויען די הרב"ע ישיבות איז געעפענט געוואָרען
אין לאנד, דורך די אגודת הרבנים, וועמעס משטרמאַן איז הרב ר' אליעזר סילבער,
סינסינטי, פון די חברי הנשיאות פון אגוה"ר.

דער קאמפעין געהם יעצט אָן אין אל׳ע שטעדם אין אמעריקא, איבער'ן
גאַנצען לאנד.

רבנים, פרעזידענטען, בעאַמטע פון שוהלען! טהוט אייער
פליכט צו דער תורה! העלפט ראטעווען די מלחמה־געליטענע
ישיבות! מאכט אפיעלם אין אייערע שוהלען!

רעטונגם קאָמיטע פאר מלחמה געליטענע ישיבות

הרב אליעזר זילבער, משערמאַן   הרב חיים יצחק בלאך,
הרב ישראל הלוי ראזענבערג,   צבי חורש מאנישעוויטץ
הרב דוב ארי׳ לעווינטל,   — טרעזשזירערם

עהרעז־משערמאן

EMERGENCY COMMITTEE FOR WAR - TORN YESHIVOTH

Chairman, Rabbi El. Silver,

673 Broadway   New York, N. Y.

Phone GRamercy 7-7230

"Help Rescue The Torah". An appeal for funds by the Emergency Committee for War-Torn Yeshivoth. *Ha-Pardes*, Adar 5700/March 1940.

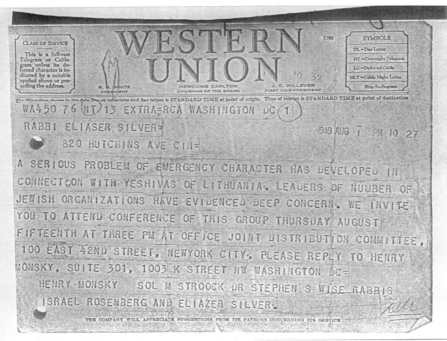

Invitation to Rabbi Eliezer Silver to attend a conference of American Jewish organizations convened to deal with the plight of the refugee yeshiva students in Lithuania, August 1, 1940. (Papers of Rabbi Eliezer Silver, American University)

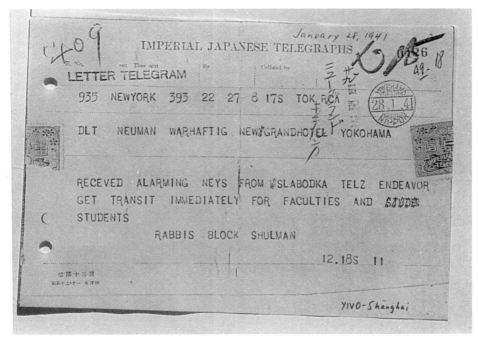

Appeal by Rabbis Block (Telz) and Shulman (Slabodka) to Frank Newman and Zerach Warhaftig in Japan to save their students, January 28, 1941. (YIVO Archives)

Mike Tress. (Orthodox Jewish Archives, Agudath Israel of America)

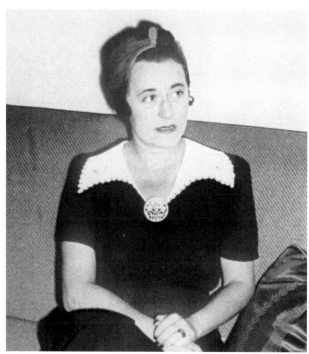

Laura Margolis, JDC emissary to Shanghai. (American Jewish Joint Distribution Committee Archives, Jerusalem)

MODERN TOURS INC.

38 CANAL STREET • NEW YORK
TELEPHONE WALKER 5 - 2456

NAME OF PASSENGER ___Isaac Welvel SOLOVEITSHIK___

Address ___Lithuania___

Accompanied by

1. ___ Age ___	4. ___ Age ___
2. ___ Age ___	5. ___ Age ___
3. ___ Age ___	6. ___ Age ___

EASTBOUND	WESTBOUND
Steamer___	Steamer___
Date___	Date___
Class___ Cabin___ Berth___	Class___ Cabin___ Berth___

Destination and Rate ___Transferred to Moscow through Cook's___ $ 200.00

Destination and Rate ___Cook's cable and transfer fee___ $ 11.00

Supplement___ $ ___

Revenue Tax___ Head Tax___ $ ___

French Port Tax $___ Italian Port Tax $___ Palestine Port Tax___ $ ___

DOCUMENTS: Passport___ $ ___

     Permit to Re-enter the U. S. A.___ $ ___

     Visaes:___ $ ___

___ $ ___

Baggage Delivery___ $ ___

    " Insurance___ $ ___

Travelers Cheques___ $ ___

Service It is understood that we reserve the right to
perform all, or part of the services herein
contemplated, through Thomas Cook & Son -
Wagon-Lits, Inc., and in that event, our
responsibility shall not extend beyond our
showing that such services were delegated
to Thomas Cook & Son - Wagon-Lits, Inc.

$ ___

TOTAL .. $ 211.00

P. R. No. . . . $ ___

BALANCE $ ___

P. R. No. ___

BALANCE . $ ___

Purchaser ___VAAD HAHATZALA___

___Per Rabbi El. Silver___

Payment by the *Vaad ha-Hatzala* for the travel of Isaac Welvel Soloveitshik from Lithuania to Japan, February 13, 1941. (*Vaad ha-Hatzala* Archives, Yeshiva University)

CBPO No. 127.
S. 1A.

Ref. N. IMMIGRATION 3595 **Shanghai Municipal Council.**

POLICE FORCE.
COMMISSIONER'S OFFICE.
P. O. BOX NO. 159

May 13, 1941.

CERTIFICATE.

THIS IS TO CERTIFY THAT THERE IS NO OBJECTION TO THE
ENTRY INTO THE INTERNATIONAL SETTLEMENT
OF SHANGHAI SOUTH OF SOOCHOW CREEK OF

Hirsz LEWINSOHN (N2bs)

MAY. 13 1941

Deputy Commissioner
Crime and Special Branches.
For Commissioner of Police.

(THIS CERTIFICATE IS VALID FOR **SIX** MONTHS FROM DATE OF ISSUE).

Osher Czeczyk

Shanghai Permit obtained for Hirsz Lewinsohn, May 13, 1941.
(Courtesy of Rabbi Asher Czeczyk)

A group of rabbis and rubbi-students leaving Shanghai on 29-9-41 by "Pres. Pierce" for Canada via San Francisco.

Name in full	Date of birth	Place of birth	Place of Residence	Arrival in Jap. in 1941
1. PUPKO GAGAN Frejda	3.1.1880	Lapy	Radun	
2. PUPKO GANGAN Aron	29.10.1910	Radun	"	24.2.-20.8.
3. GINSBERG chaim Berek	15.3.1890	Zdunska Wola	"	" "
4. JOGIEL Pierec	18.10.1894	Piaski	Dolhunowo	26.1. - 20. 9.
5. SOROCZKIN Boruch	23.1.1918	Zdziecol	Horodziej	24.2. - "
6. LEWIN Samuel Dawid	11.10.1911	Sambor	Luck	23.2. - "
7. LEWIN Markus	"	"	Rzeszow	14.3. - "
8. GOTTLIEB Kliezer Icchok	21.10.1918	Kolno	"	"
9. FASKOWICZ Boruch	31.8.1916	Pultusk	Opatow	13.2. - 30. 8.
10. HIRSZPRUNG Pinkas	13.7.1910	Dukla	Pultusk	5.3. - 20. 9.
11. LEW Josel Arja	10.3.1924	Kodin	Dukla	14.3. - "
12. SZTULMAN Dawid	5.9.1911	Wolomin	Brzesc	13.2. - 30. 8.
13. PIETRUSZKA Icek Jakub	8.10.1920	Makow	Wolomin	24.1. - 20. 9.
14. ROTENBERG Herszko	7.7.1911	Miedzyrzec	"	5.3. - 30. 8.
15. KRAMER Lajb	17.1.1918	Chelm	Warszawa	16.3. - "
16. HENDEL Icchok	20.11.1917	Kamerow	"	5.3. - 20. 9.
17. TENENBAUM Josef Mendel	22.7.1917	Kock	Otwock	14.2. - 30. 8.
18. SZTEJN Samuel	15.3.1914	Wiazn	"	" "
19. GERLICKI Moszek Eljasz	24.5.1915	Konskie	Wiazn	" "
20. KOTLARSKI Hersz Josef	20.10.1917	Adamow	Konskie	" 20.9.
21. RODAL Josek	1914	Przedburz	Otwock	" 30.8.
22. WAJNBERG Josef	1917	Janow	"	" "
23. GRYNGLAZ Mendel Wolf	1917	Lodz	"	" "
24. PORTNOJ Lejzer	1.3.1908	Brzesc	"	" "
25. BORENSZTEJN, Icek Nojach	10.1.1909	Kadzidto	Brzesc	24.1. - "
26. EPSTEIN Selig	25 years old	Slonim	Kadzidto	" "
27. LICHTIGER Szmuel	26 years old	Kobrin		20.9.
28. HERSZBERG, Abram-Mordko	24 years			" "
29. KOHEN Mojzesz	19 years	Warsaw		" "

List of yeshiva *leit* who left Shanghai on September 29, 1941 aboard President Pierce bound for Canada. (Archives of HICEM-Shanghai, JDC Archives, Israel)

Dutch honorary consul in Kaunas Jan Zwartendijk.
(Simon Wiesenthal Center Archives)

Frank Newman (*second from right*) meeting with Japanese Captain Koreshiga Inuzuka (*first from left*). Courtesy of Florence Newman, New York)

APPLICATION FOR A LICENSE TO ENGAGE IN A FOREIGN EXCHANGE TRANSACTION, TRANSFER OF CREDIT, PAYMENT, EXPORT OR WITHDRAWAL FROM THE UNITED STATES, OR THE EARMARKING, OF GOLD OR SILVER COIN OR BULLION OR CURRENCY, OR THE TRANSFER, WITHDRAWAL OR EXPORTATION OF, OR DEALING IN, EVIDENCES OF INDEBTEDNESS OR EVIDENCES OF OWNERSHIP OF PROPERTY.*

(To be executed and filed in triplicate with the Federal Reserve Bank for the district or with the Governor or High Commissioner of the territory or possession of the United States in which the applicant resides or has his principal place of business or principal office or agency. If the applicant has no legal residence or principal place of business or principal office or agency in a Federal Reserve district or such territory or possession the application should be filed with the Federal Reserve Bank of New York or the Federal Reserve Bank of San Francisco.)

To THE SECRETARY OF THE TREASURY
  Washington, D. C.

Sir:

I.

In accordance with Executive Order No. 8389 of April 10, 1940, as amended, regulating transactions in foreign exchange, etc., and the Regulations and Rulings issued thereunder, the undersigned hereby applies for a license to execute the transaction described below:

A. (1) The name of the applicant is Union of Orthodox Rabbis of United States ;

   (2) Applicant resides at or, in the case of a corporation, partnership, association or other organization, has its principal place of business at:

   673 Broadway, , New York , N. Y. , U. S. A. ;
   (Street)   (City)   (State)   (Country)

   (3) Applicant is and has been a citizen of.

   since.   :
        (Month)   (Day)   (Year)
   (4) The nationality** of the applicant is mostly U. S. Citizens.

   (5) Since 1902 the applicant has been engaged in the business of
   organization of Rabbis engaged in religious functions
                              (State nature of business)

B. The applicant desires a license in order to:
   (State in detail the nature, purpose and amount of the transaction, and the name, address, nationality** and extent of interest of every party, including the applicant, involved or interested in the transaction.)

*All definitions appearing in Executive Order No. 8389 of April 10, 1940, as amended, and the Regulations and Rulings issued thereunder shall apply to the terms employed herein.

**In the case of a corporation, partnership, or association, give country in which organized and indicate the approximate percentages of stock, shares, bonds, debentures, notes, drafts, or other securities or obligations of such organization owned or controlled, directly or indirectly, by a blocked country or one or more nationals thereof.

   To remit the sum of Five Thousand ($5000.00) to the Polish Embassy
   at Kuibyshev, U. S. S. R. for distribution among the Rabbinical students
   of Polish nationality now in the U. S. S. R. in the following provinces:
   Dzizak, Cardzou, Tchimkent, Kirize, Samarkand, Burbig, Chiatchewo, Bukhara,
   Altkrai, Dzambowl and Tashkent.

Applicant's No.

ORIGINAL

Application by the *Agudat ha-Rabbanim* to the US Treasury to transfer $5,000 to the Polish Embassy in the Soviet Union to assist Polish yeshiva students, August 12, 1942. (*Vaad ha-Hatzala* Archives, Yeshiva University)

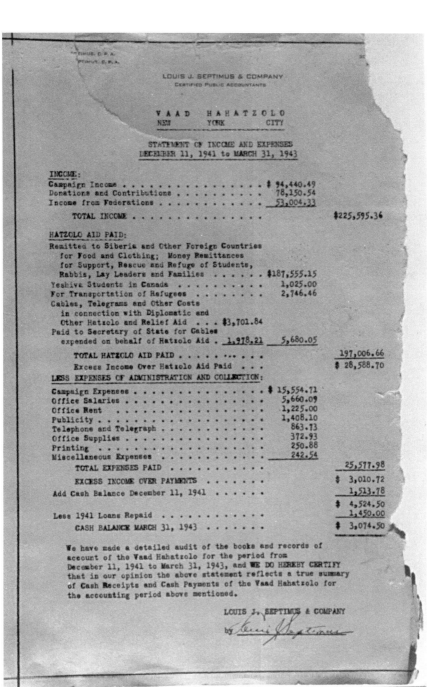

LOUIS J. SEPTIMUS & COMPANY
CERTIFIED PUBLIC ACCOUNTANTS

V A A D   H A H A T Z O L O
NEW   YORK   CITY

STATEMENT OF INCOME AND EXPENSES
DECEMBER 11, 1941 to MARCH 31, 1943

INCOME:

Campaign Income . . . . $ 94,440.49	
Donations and Contributions 78,150.54	
Income from Federations 53,004.33	
TOTAL INCOME	$225,595.36

HATZOLO AID PAID:

Remitted to Siberia and Other Foreign Countries
for Food and Clothing; Money Remittances
for Support, Rescue and Refuge of Students,
Rabbis, Lay Leaders and Families $187,555.15
Yeshiva Students in Canada 1,025.00
For Transportation of Refugees 2,746.46
Cables, Telegrams and Other Costs
in connection with Diplomatic and
Other Hatzolo and Relief Aid . . . $3,701.84
Paid to Secretary of State for Cables
expended on behalf of Hatzolo Aid . 1,978.21   5,680.05

TOTAL HATZOLO AID PAID 197,006.66
Excess Income Over Hatzolo Aid Paid . . . $ 28,588.70

LESS EXPENSES OF ADMINISTRATION AND COLLECTION:

Campaign Expenses . . . . $ 15,554.71
Office Salaries 5,660.09
Office Rent 1,225.00
Publicity 1,408.10
Telephone and Telegraph 863.73
Office Supplies 372.93
Printing 250.88
Miscellaneous Expenses 242.54
TOTAL EXPENSES PAID 25,577.98

EXCESS INCOME OVER PAYMENTS . . . . $ 3,010.72
Add Cash Balance December 11, 1941 . . . . . .   1,513.78

$ 4,524.50

Less 1941 Loans Repaid 1,450.00
CASH BALANCE MARCH 31, 1943 . . . . $ 3,074.50

We have made a detailed audit of the books and records of
account of the Vaad Hahatzolo for the period from
December 11, 1941 to March 31, 1943, and WE DO HEREBY CERTIFY
that in our opinion the above statement reflects a true summary
of Cash Receipts and Cash Payments of the Vaad Hahatzolo for
the accounting period above mentioned.

LOUIS J. SEPTIMUS & COMPANY

by

Statement of Income and Expenses of the *Vaad ha-Hatzala*, December 11, 1941 to March 31, 1943. (*Vaad ha-Hatzala* Archives, Yeshiva University)

Rabbi Aaron Milewsky.
(Courtesy of Aliza Milewsky Sofer, Jerusalem)

Rabbi Chaim Ozer Grodzinski.
(Orthodox Jewish Archives, Agudath
Israel of America)

Dr. Samuel Schmidt.
(Courtesy of Blessing Schmidt Sivitz,
Cincinnati)

Zerach Warhaftig.
(Courtesy of Dr. Warhaftig, Jerusalem)

Henrietta Buchman of the JDC and Gerhardt Riegner of the WJC. (American Jewish Joint Distribution Committee Archives, Jerusalem)

Moses Leavitt, JDC, New York (*standing*). (American Jewish Joint Distribution Committee Archives, Jerusalem)

Rabbi Eliezer Silver. (Orthodox Jewish Archives, Agudath Israel of America)

Rabbi Aaron Kotler. (Orthodox Jewish Archives, Agudath Israel of America)

expenses had to be covered by relatives or friends.[51] As it is, the *Vaad* tried to maximize fundraising from private individuals (especially relatives of the refugees),[52] so that it could use its resources for those who were totally dependent on the rabbinic rescue organization. It should be noted, however, that the exclusion of immigrants funded by organizations did not apply to recipients of the emergency visitors' visas granted through the efforts of the President's Advisory Committee on Political Refugees. Since many of the Torah scholars had been recommended for such visas,[53] the *Vaad* could cover their transportation expenses and openly raise funds for that purpose.

During the initial four mouths of 1941 *Vaad ha-Hatzala* began paying the travel costs of dozens of refugee scholars and their families who set out from Lithuania for the Far East. These trips were paid segment by segment at fixed prices. Thus, for example, many of the refugees traveled third class by train from Kovno to Moscow at $10 per adult and $5 per child. The train from Moscow to Vladivostok and steamer from the Pacific port to Tsuruga initially cost $110 for each adult ($55 for children). Steamer passage from Japan to the United States cost $100 per adult ($50 per child). Later the price from Moscow to the United States was raised from $210 to $257.50 for adults (from $105 to $202 for children), although in certain cases the prices were lower. In addition, in several cases the *Vaad* paid the Japanese maintenance fee of $60 per person as well as a head tax of $8 per arriving refugee, plus the cost of any cables sent.[54] The train tickets were obtained initially from Intourist by Thomas Cook and later by the Amalgamated Bank in New York, and the boat tickets were purchased at the New York offices of the N.Y.K. shipping line.[55]

By the end of April 1941 *Vaad ha-Hatzala* had raised $81,476.36 (and taken $4,503.96 in loans). Almost all of this sum was used to purchase railroad ($65,846.79) and steamer ($13,825) tickets. Upon closer examination, these figures give us significant insight into the degree to which the *Vaad* succeeded in enlisting public support for their campaign. First, the sums raised during the initial four months of 1941 were proportionally much higher than those raised the previous year. During all of 1940 the rabbis raised $142,715.29; if fundraising for 1941 had continued at the rate achieved during January–April, the 1941 figure would have been $244,429.08, or 69% higher. Also of interest is the relative success of the different methods used by the *Vaad* to raise money. Most of the funds were raised

by the independent appeals launched by *Vaad* activists in synagogues and among private donors. The largest sums were collected
in New York ($22,527.34, of which $6,705.50 was raised by the
Young Israel movement), Detroit ($10,500), Cincinnati ($10,025),
Baltimore ($8,921.55), Miami ($6,162), and Chicago ($6,100).[56]
While these figures are hardly surprising given the large Jewish communities in most of these cities,[57] it should also be noted that each
of these communities was visited by one or more of the *Vaad's* rabbinical leaders.[58]

While *Vaad ha-Hatzala* succeeded in considerably increasing its
income from its own appeals, it initially encountered serious difficulties in enlarging the allocations it received from local federations
and welfare funds. Whereas in 1940 the *Vaad* had obtained pledges
of $39,432.32 in allocations from 57 federations and welfare funds,
which constituted 27.6% of its total income, the figures for the initial four months of 1941 were considerably lower. During the period
from January 1 to April 29, 1941, *Vaad ha-Hatzala* received only
$9,253.34 from 10 welfare funds, a sum which constituted 11.3% of
its total income during those four months. There were also changes
in the attitudes of various federations. Toledo, for example, supported the tickets campaign although it had not previously granted the
Vaad an allocation, and Worcester, Massachusetts, substantially
increased its allocation in early 1941. On the other hand, there were
federations, such as San Francisco and Wilmington, that gave the
rabbis an allocation in 1940 but did not do so in 1941, or such as
Harrisburg, Pennsylvania, which in 1941 considerably reduced the
previous year's contribution.

One of the key factors was undoubtedly the timing of the tickets
campaign. While only ten federations had given the *Vaad* an allocation by the end of April,[59] the number of grants by community
fundraising drives rose significantly during the spring and summer.
By September the *Vaad* had already received allocations from 73 federations totaling $41,177.50,[60] a sum higher than the amount of
money it raised from federations during the entire previous year. It
should also be noted that in those communities in which the rabbis
received an allocation from the local federation they did not undertake independent local campaigns, a decision which in essence was a
financial gamble for the *Vaad*.

While timing undoubtedly influenced the response of local federations in early 1941, there were other factors at work as well. The

negative attitude of both the Joint Distribution Committee and the Council of Jewish Federations and Welfare Funds also certainly had a significant impact on numerous local communities, which either refused to grant the *Vaad* an allocation or donated less then the sum requested. In letter upon letter, officials of local federations appealed to the headquarters of the NCJFWF (and to a lesser extent to the JDC) for guidance regarding subventions to the refugee yeshivot and dealing with the rabbinic rescue organization.[61] In some cases, funds had been allocated for the Polish yeshivot but the money was not sent because of uncertainty as to the status (or even existence) of those institutions and the question of safe transmission.[62] Other federations that had been approached in the tickets campaign were unacquainted with the actual conditions in Europe and the Far East and with the activities of the rabbinic rescue organization, and so they sought guidance from the New York headquarters of the CJFWF and the JDC.[63] Invariably the requests for information were linked to the practical dilemmas which each community faced when confronted by the demands for allocations to the *Vaad ha-Hatzala* for the rescue of the Torah scholars.

Although CJFWF and JDC officials did not say so publicly, or even explicitly in correspondence with federations, they viewed the *Vaad's* fundraising efforts as detrimental to their own campaigns. Allocations to *Vaad ha-Hatzala* by local fundraising drives ultimately meant less income for the JDC, which bore the major burden of overseas Jewish relief and rescue work. In their opinion, the *Vaad's* efforts created a situation in which a specific group of Jews were accorded preferential treatment at the expense of other Jews. Thus throughout the tickets campaign, officials of the CJFWF and JDC tried very hard to discourage community fundraising drives from allocating funds to the rabbinic rescue organization.[64]

In polite, carefully formulated missives to local federation officials, Blanche Renard of the CJFWF and Moses Leavitt and Henrietta Buchman of the JDC marshaled numerous arguments to convince the communal fundraising agencies not to allocate funds to the *Vaad ha-Hatzala*. Although they never issued an outright condemnation of the rabbis' efforts, they made it clear that the *Vaad's* campaign created serious and complicated problems. In some letters Renard cited the confusion regarding the *Vaad's* aims and the fact that they had announced that they would no longer raise funds for the maintenance of the yeshivot, but were in fact doing so.[65] In response to other queries, Renard cast doubt on the number of visas the rabbis claimed they had and could obtain, as well as on the *Vaad's* statements regarding assistance being provided by the JDC for the transportation of the refugee scholars.[66] Throughout the period in question, Renard counseled the federations not to rush to transmit funds to the *Vaad*, but to wait until more information about its activities could be obtained.[67]

Moses A. Leavitt, the secretary of the JDC, adduced similar arguments to convince federation executives that the rabbis' efforts were at best misguided and in certain respects simply counterproductive. According to Leavitt, there was no realistic possibility of the *Vaad's* obtaining U.S. visas for 3,000 rabbis and yeshiva students, and thus its campaign goals were grossly inflated.[68] The JDC, moreover, had already allocated $175,000 for the transportation of Polish refugees via the Far East, half of which was earmarked for rabbis and yeshiva students. In view of the fact that the JDC was also paying for the maintenance of the refugees in Japan ($18,000 in March and $25,000 in April), the *Vaad's* efforts were, in effect, a luxury which the Jewish community could ill afford.[69] In his words to the secretary of the Jewish Welfare Fund of Chicago:

> While we all have the utmost sympathy in this problem, it is obvious that if a separate drive were to be launched, for every project which enjoys the interest and sympathy of special groups, it would cause untold confusion and defeat the very purpose of the Welfare Funds concept. Because the JDC makes allotments for these very projects, we have tried wherever possible to discourage direct applications to the Welfare Funds and communities in the United States on the part of separate groups.... We need hardly tell you that with the funds at our disposal, the JDC cannot do a 100% job in any field of activity, whether it be in relief or in emigration. In many sections, we are obliged to limit ourselves only to fractions of population and fractions of the problem. The same is true of what we are able to set aside for emigration purposes. The sums are woefully inadequate. If we had had at our disposal during 1940 $12,000,000 instead of roughly $6,000,000 we should, of course have been able to do twice as much, not only for the special projects in which special groups are interested, but for other vital programs of assistance in all parts of the world where

increasingly we have been called upon to give aid to unfortunate Jewish victims of the world disaster...

We all realize that we are living in an emergency and the problem is by meeting one emergency we may be ignoring dozens of others. Naturally, it is not the function of the JDC to sanction or veto separate appeals. The special groups insist on helping all of their own people to come to this country. They are not satisfied to do a partial job as the JDC is forced to do in all fields of its activity by reason of its limited means. Insofar as they can secure funds from their own groups here and are willing to make additional contributions over and above what they give to general relief needs, there can be no question of the propriety of their appeals for special purposes, but we have made clear to them that the JDC cannot approve any appeals they make to Welfare Funds for allotments for emigration work, since the JDC derives its support for its manifold activities, including emigration aid, from the same sources. The JDC cannot be quoted as encouraging any special campaign for purposes or programs in which the JDC itself is trying its hardest to be helpful. We cannot encourage competition with ourselves. But you must realize that insofar as we are not put into possession of adequate funds, special groups who get some of our help will try to secure additional amounts from you.[70]

Federation and welfare fund executives did not have to read between the lines of the letters from New York to understand the position of the CJFWF and the JDC. And while the official report issued in May 1941 by the former to its member agencies was much less judgmental in tone,[71] the bottom line was clear. It was the JDC that had covered the majority of the expenses of transporting the refugees from Lithuania to the Far East and beyond, as well as of maintaining them while in Japan, and therefore it deserved maximum support. The *Vaad ha-Hatzala* had played a role by providing information on prospective immigrants and to some extent had provided financial assistance for tickets, but its role in the rescue operation from Lithuania had undoubtedly been peripheral.

Under these circumstances the *Vaad* was hard pressed to convince the non-Orthodox elements of the Jewish community to support its activities. One unusual attempt to widen its base of support took place in February 1941, when the rabbinic rescue organization asked Dr. Louis Finkelstein, president of the Jewish Theological Seminary, the rabbinical school of the Conservative movement, to issue a statement endorsing their fundraising campaign.[72] Given the staunch opposition of *Agudat ha-Rabbanim* and its members to all non-Orthodox varieties of Judaism,[73] this surprising move indicates to what lengths the rabbis were willing to go to pursue their goals. In this case, however, their efforts were not particularly successful. Although Finkelstein did write a letter to Rabbi Levinson expressing support for the *Vaad's* goals, these comments were preceded by an explicit statement to the effect that the "JDC had done everything in its power for these scholars and has made every effort consistent with its limited resources and the many demands made upon them."[74] Finkelstein's recommendation was, in fact, similar in wording and content to the advice offered by the JDC to various federations,[75]—hardly surprising since Finkelstein consulted with JDC officials Joseph Hyman and Leavitt before writing the letter.[76]

Another indication of the rabbis' determination to maximize fundraising was the fact that at least on one occasion *Vaad* activists publicly drove on the Sabbath in order to solicit contributions. Rabbis Baruch Kaplan and Alexander Linchner traveled by taxi with Young Israel leader Irving Bunim at the behest of Rabbis Moshe Feinstein, Shlomo Heiman, and Shraga Feivel Mendlowitz to approach wealthy Jews in the Flatbush section of Brooklyn to donate funds.[77] The decision of these eminent rabbis to instruct observant Jews to commit an act which under normal circumstances would have been a grave violation of the Sabbath clearly shows how seriously the leaders of the *Vaad* related to the plight of the refugee scholars stranded in Europe.

* * *

While CJFWF and JDC officials were able to provide numerous details and statistics regarding the escape of the Polish refugees from Lithuania to the Far East, the picture they presented to federations and welfare funds was not complete. Nowhere was there any mention of the fact that in November 1940 Leavitt had advised Moses Beckelman, the JDC representative in Vilna, against sending refugees with Curaçao visas to Japan and that Leavitt had in fact attempted to halt the emigration of Jews from Lithuania.[78] Also ignored were the *Vaad's* efforts to assist the refugee scholars in obtaining the necessary travel documents (aside from U.S. visas[79]), although their role in providing maintenance funds for the yeshivot was mentioned. Even more important is the fact that at least to a certain extent the JDC's willingness to allocate so many resources for the rescue of the rabbis and yeshiva students should be attributed to the *Vaad's* efforts to focus the attention of the American Jewish community on their plight and to provide them with practical assistance. Although they constituted less than one-quarter of the Polish refugees in Lithuania and one-third of those who reached Japan,[80] the JDC set aside approximately half of the funds allocated for these refugees for the rabbis, yeshiva students, and their family members.[81]

This policy can be explained by the fact that the JDC sought to aid those who were able to emigrate from Lithuania regardless of their professions or ideological affiliations. If rabbis and yeshiva students were in a position to leave, they deserved JDC assistance. At the same time, one cannot ignore the fact that the ability of so many Torah scholars to depart from Lithuania was in no small measure due to the help they received from the *Vaad* and the American offices of the *yeshivot*. These aspects of the emigration picture, however were never brought to the attention of local federation officials by the CJFWF or the JDC.

On the other hand, the *Vaad's* claims regarding the scope and success of its activities were not always entirely accurate either. This was particularly true regarding the number of U.S. visas obtained. While the rabbis claimed that they had arranged visas for 3,000 individuals,[82] the actual figure was apparently much lower. The *Vaad* had indeed originally hoped to submit the names of some 10,000 Torah scholars and family members as candidates for special visas, but after meetings at the State Department it reduced its original list to 980. An additional several hundred names were subsequently submitted to the Visa Division for special consideration, but less than 1,000 names were actually recommended to U.S. consuls for positive consideration. Moreover, this step did not guarantee that each person recommended would be granted a visa, so in effect the number of rabbis and yeshiva students who actually received U.S. visas was even lower.[83]

Despite the *Vaad's* problems with the fundraising establishment of the American Jewish community, the rabbis were determined to press on to achieve their goals. They were greatly encouraged by the arrival in the United States in spring 1941 of several prominent Polish rabbis and *roshei yeshiva* who had emigrated from Lithuania via the Far East with the *Vaad's* help. The most prominent of the new arrivals was undoubtedly Rabbi Aron Kotler, the *rosh yeshiva* of the Etz Chaim Yeshiva of Kletzk, who was known throughout the Orthodox world as a brilliant Torah scholar and who had also for many years played an active role in communal affairs.[84] Other well-known *roshei yeshiva* who reached the United States at this time were Reuven Grazowsky of Kamenetz, Mendel Zaks of Radin, and Avraham Yaphin of Bialystok. Leading communal rabbis among the arrivals were David Lifshitz of Suwalk and Moshe Shatzkes of Lomza.[85] The *roshei yeshiva* who came to the United States had left the overwhelming majority of their students in Lithuania (only a few of the students from these yeshivot had reached Japan) [86] and were therefore very determined to become involved in the rescue efforts of *Vaad ha-Hatzala*.

Of the new arrivals the rabbi who was to play the most important role in the *Vaad's* activities was Rabbi Kotler. He landed in San Francisco on April 13 and, after stopovers in Chicago and Cincinnati, arrived eight days later in New York, where he was greeted by a crowd of thousands at Pennsylvania Station.[87] As soon as he reached New York, Rabbi Kotler became active in the attempts to rescue the Torah scholars in Lithuania and Japan.[88] His unflagging efforts on behalf of the *Vaad ha-Hatzala* added considerable prestige to the rabbinic rescue organization, and he emerged as one of its prominent leaders during the war years.[89]

While in Lithuania, Rabbi Kotler had deliberated whether or not to go to the United States without his students. The key factor in his decision to do so had been his hope of being able to work for their rescue more effectively from America.[90] Thus he arrived with a mission and wasted no time in attempting to transmit his message to American Jewry. One of his first public appearances was at the semi-annual convention of the *Agudat ha-Rabbanim* held April 29–30, 1941, at the Broadway Central Hotel in New York City. In an impassioned speech, Rabbi Kotler exhorted American Jewry, whom he labeled *she'arit ha-pleita* (surviving remnant), to come to the aid of the beleaguered Torah scholars. Besides being a forceful reminder that the objective for which the *Vaad ha-Hatzala* had been established had still not been fulfilled, Rabbi Kother's speech constitutes a succinct summary of the philosophy that united Orthodox rabbis, and especially *roshei yeshiva,* on both sides of the Atlantic:

> I am speaking to you on behalf of those whose voices you wanted to hear but are temporarily far away from here. The entire destruction came about because of the fulfillment of the verse "Jacob was left alone."[91] The yeshiva students are the only ones studying Torah today. The yeshivot in Lithuania continue to exist and the learning there goes on perhaps with even greater perseverance than before. But they are without status, without a candle to light the way, they have no means of preserving the body, and their soul is miraculously being strengthened. You must understand what the feelings are there, as they are viewed with suspicion by those in high places. But Torah is strengthening them and their faith is helping them not to fall into despair because they know that [in the Torah the phrase] "you shall stray" [from the Torah] is followed [by the phrase] "you shall be lost"[92] [from the land of Israel]. At the same time their hope in the surviving remnant—American Jewry—is that they will come to the rescue to save them, but it must be admitted that American Jewry has not fulfilled its obligation.[93]

After describing his painful departure from his students, who urged him to go to America to arouse the Jews there to work even harder to save the refugee scholars, Rabbi Kotler directed his message to American Jewry:

> Remember your great and sacred obligation during this terrible period. Previously when the curtain covering the holy ark was stabbed, blood started flowing; now the ark itself, the Torah scrolls and those who study Torah are bleeding. If, G-d forbid, our spiritual treasures over there will be destroyed, it will affect our own lives because we will miss those wells from which all the Jews, including those in America, have drawn. We cannot postpone the work. Every minute is valuable. Who knows what will happen in the future? The *Sefer Torah* is bleeding and it is up to you leaders of Israel to do everything possible to save the yeshiva students. Despite all the gratitude we owe *Agudat ha-Rabbanim* and *Vaad ha-Hatzala* I must state

that almost nothing has been done, we still have not fulfilled our obligation. Time is short and we must act immediately. Everyone must volunteer for this holy task.[94]

The arrival of Rabbi Kotler and other leading rabbis and *roshei yeshiva* in the United States not only marked the initial practical success of the *Vaad's* program but also helped infuse the rabbinic rescue organization with renewed vitality.[95] The rabbis of *Vaad ha-Hatzala* had proven that it was possible to rescue the Torah scholars from Lithuania, even if they had to be brought to the United States by a circuitous and highly unlikely route. The active participation of these rescued scholars in the *Vaad's* activities strengthened the status of the organization, especially among Orthodox Jews, and paved the way for its transformation into the full-fledged relief and rescue agency of American Orthodox Jewry.[96]

Notes

1. Warhaftig Testimony, interview no. 3, February 12, 1966, p.10
2. In order to ensure that the refugees would pay for their travel arrangements in foreign currency, the Soviets in Vilna and Kovno refused to sell train tickets for Vladivostok in rubles. Elchanan Herzman, *Mofait ha-Dor*, p.70; Yaakov Even–Chen, *Tenu'a be–Sa'arat Milchama*, p.170; Shmuel Soltz, *850 Yom Bein Aratzot u–Gevulot*, 1987, p.69.
3. Kobe was the center of what little Jewish life existed in Japan at that time. The community, which numbered several dozen families, was composed primarily of Sepharadim originally from Iraq and Iran, and Ashkenzim who had originally lived in Russia. Abraham Kotsuji, *From Tokyo to Jerusalem* (New York, 1964), p.160.
4. During this initial period most of the refugees who reached Japan were able to leave the country within a relatively short time, a factor that considerably eased the financial burden on Jewcom. As time went on, however, the number arriving increased substantially and the number of those able to leave declined sharply. See "Report Of The Activity Of The Committee For Assistance To Refugees The Jewish Community Of Kobe (Ashkenazim). July 1940 – November 1941" (Kobe, 1942), pp. 1–9 (Hereafter called Jewcom Report).
5. Ibid., pp. 19–30.
6. Kotsuji, *From Tokyo to Jerusalem*, pp. 161–166; David Kranzler, "The Japanese Ideology of Anti–Semitism and the Holocaust," *Contemporary Views on the Holocaust*, ed. Randolph Braham (Boston and The Hague: Dordrecht and Lancaster, 1983), p.101.
7. One of the main reasons for the numerous requests for Japanese visas was the fact that until December 1940 the Turkish consulate in Moscow refused to issue transit visas to individuals who had immigration certificates to Palestine. Therefore the only route available for those seeking to make *aliyah* was via the Far East— hence the need for Japanese transit visas. Zerach Warhaftig, *Palit ve–Sarid be–Yemei*

ha–Shoa, pp. 172, 180–187.

8. Ibid., pp. 193–195.

9. Leavitt not only advised Beckelman against emigration via Japan but actually tried to prevent HICEM from sending any refugees there. As far as the JDC was concerned, the problem was the high cost of maintaining the refugees in Japan ($500 per day), a responsibility which it assumed despite an already severely over-burdened budget. Bauer, *American Jewry and the Holocaust*, p. 122.

10. The *Vaad's* willingness to provide financial support for the N.Y.K. deal was not, as we shall see, unconditional. From the very beginning, the rabbis sought to limit their participation to the purchase of tickets for rabbis, yeshiva students, and the members of their families, a policy that reduced the scope of their assistance and upset Warhaftig. Warhaftig, *Palit ve–Sarid be–Yemei ha–Shoa*, p.195.

11. Yoseph Epstein, "Yeshivat Mir," in Mirsky, *Mosdot*, pp. 119–120.

12. Hillel Zeidman, "Yeshiva 'Etz Chaim' de-Kletzk," in Mirsky, *Mosdot*, p. 238.

13. See, for example, the letters of Rabbi Yitzhak Zeev Soloveitchik (September 23, 1940), Rabbi Avigdor Cyperstein (October 2, 1940), and Rabbi Henoch Eiges (November 14, 1940), all to Rabbi Yisrael Halevi Rosenberg, AYHR.

14. Letter of Rabbi Aron Kotler to Rabbi Rosenberg, October 2, 1940, AYHR.

15. Speech by Rabbi Silver at the annual convention of *Agudat ha–Rabbanim*, November 12, 1940, conference protocol p. 14, Papers of Jacob Hellerstein, secretary of *Agudat ha–Rabbanim*, in possession of the author.

16. "Minahaley Vaad Hatzala," *Ha–Pardes*, 14, no. 9 (Kislev 5701/December 1940), 15.

17. Rabbi Levinson succeeded Rabbi Meir Berlin as president of American Mizrachi in 1926 and held that post for two years. He later served as chairman of the Mizrachi's "Vaad Le–Chizuk ha-Torah ve–ha–Yahadut." Rabbi Konvitz was one of the leading rabbis in the United States who supported the Mizrachi movement. Aaron Pechenik, "Ha–Tenua Bein Shtei Milchamot," *Chazon Torah ve–Tziyon* (Jerusalem, 5720 [1960]), pp. 243–245; Aaron Rakeffet-Rothkoff, *The Silver Era in American Jewish Orthodoxy; Rabbi Eliezer Silver and His Generation*, p. 201.

18. See, for example, the letter of Rabbi Eliezer Silver to Rabbi Yisrael Rosenberg, December 20, 1941, Silver Archives.

19. "Aseifat Vaad Hatzala," *Ha–Pardes*, 14, no. 9 (Kislev 5701/December 1940), 14–15. Among the European *roshei yeshiva* who were already in the United States at this time were Rabbis Yechiel Gordon (Lomza), Mordechai Shulman (Slobodka), Eliyahu Bloch (Telz), and the president of the Mir Yeshiva, Rabbi Avraham Kalmanowitz.

20. Letter of Rabbi Silver to Rabbi Rosenberg, July 15, 1940, AYHR.

21. Form letter of Rabbi Eliezer Silver to federations and welfare funds, November 5, 1940, CJFWF, I–69, Box 149.

22. Letter of Rabbi Seltzer to the Foreign Funds Control of the U.S. Department of the Treasury, December 5, 1940, AVH.

23. In each relationship, the acute problem was one of priorities. Just as the American representatives of the yeshivot sought to provide as much relief as possible for the rabbis and yeshiva students of their institution, so too the *Vaad* wanted to accord priority to Torah scholars at the expense of the rest of the Jewish population in distress.

24. See note 22.

25. License NY–85939 issued by the Federal Reserve Bank of New York on behalf of the Secretary of the Treasury to the Union of Orthodox Rabbis of the United States, December 14, 1940, AVH. The license for the transfer was applied for by the rabbinical association rather than by the *Vaad*, because the former was an incorporated agency, one of the requirements to obtain permission for such a transaction. Letter of Blanche Renard to Reuben Resnick, December 27, 1940, ACJFWF, I–69, Box 149.

26. Budgeting Bulletin No. 123, October 1940, pp. 1–2, AVH; Throughout its initial year of operation the *Vaad* used a clearance arrangement based on the payment of funds in the United States in return for equivalent sums made available to refugee scholars in Lithuania. The leaders of the JDC refused to use such methods; in their opinion these violated the spirit, if not the letter, of U.S. regulations. For the same reason, they also refused to sanction the transmission of funds to Soviet Lithuania via Switzerland, a method used successfully by the Polish Relief Fund. See Bauer, *American Jewry and the Holocaust,* p.117.

27. Letter of Michael Tress to Modern Tours, October 16, 1940, Archives of Agudath Israel of America (hereafter called AAYA), file F – 3–3–5.

28. Undated summary of funds raised and amounts paid for ship tickets and cables to Modern Tours during the period from October 10 – November 28, 1940, AAYA, file F–3–3–5.

29. An examination of the 1940 budget of the Agudath Israel Youth Council will corroborate this analysis. The organization's total income for the year was $2,245.59 and its expenses were $2,903.26. Thanks to a subvention of $1,650 from Rabbi Silver, they were able to remain in the black. See AAYA, file 3–1–27.

30. Letter of Frank Newman to the author, February 5, 1975; "Mr. Ephraim Newman Arrives in Japan," *Orthodox Tribune,* February 1941, p.1.

31. Bauer, *American Jewry and the Holocaust,* p. 127.

32. See, for example, the letter of Rabbi Elchanan Wasserman to Wolbe in which he asks for the latter's help in obtaining a visa to Haiti, January 9, 1941, as well as other requests appended to the testimony of Rabbi Shlomo Wolbe and the testimony itself, Yad Vashem Archives 0–3/3044, pp. 1–2; statement by A. M. de Jong, file 377 of the Yad Vashem Department for the Righteous Among the Nations; Chaim Shapiro, "Escape from Europe: A Chronicle of Miracles," *Jewish Observer,* May 1973, pp. 22–23.

33. Warhaftig, *Palit ve–Sarid be–Yemei ha–Shoa,* pp. 184–185, 188.

34. The meeting of the executive was held shortly after the conclusion of the thirty-third annual convention of the *Agudat ha–Rabbanim,* at which a significant portion of the discussions dealt with the plight of the yeshivot and the urgent need for action to rescue athem. See the protocol of the convention, November 11–13, 1940, Hellerstein Papers.

35. "Vaad ha–Hatzala," *Ha–Pardes,* 14, no. 11 (Shevat 5701/February 1941), pp. 17–18.

36. "Skira al Odot Peulot Vaad ha–Hatzala mi–Yom Hitargenuto ad ata," *ibid.,* pp. 4–5.

37. "Michtav Vaad ha–Hatzala le–Chol Rabbanei New York," ibid., pp. 6–7.

38. There are no exact figures on the number of Orthodox Jews in the United

States, or their geographic distribution, but one of the most important statistics in this regard is the number of Orthodox rabbis. As of 1929, of the 313 members of *Agudat ha–Rabbanim*, 152 lived in New York City and 207 in the area from Boston to Baltimore. See Jeffrey S. Gurock, "Resisters and Accommodators: Varieties of Orthodox Rabbis in America 1886–1983," *American Jewish Archives*, XXXV, no. 2, (November 1983), 173–174.

39. "Ha–kvotes shel ha–Kartisim bi–Scoom 300 Dolar be–ad ha–Rabbanim ha–Rammim ve–Talmidei ha–Yeshivot lephi he–Arim," *Ha–Pardes*, 14, no. 11 (Shevat 5701/February 1941), 21–22.

40. The quote is from the ad in Hebrew which was ostensibly a personal appeal by the rabbis who headed the *Vaad*. Only the second ad was published under the name of the Emergency Committee for War-Torn Yeshivoth. See ibid., pp.2, 16. The figures presented in the ads are somewhat misleading. The thousand persons "presently in Japan" were not all rabbis and yeshiva students, but rather Polish refugees of whom at most several hundred were Torah scholars. From October 1940 until February 1941 a total of 1,208 refugees had reached Japan. See Jewcom Report, p. 8.

41. See Chapter 3, pp. 88–89.

42. Rabbi Joseph Konvitz, "Greetings," *The Young Israel Viewpoint*, March 23, 1941, p.34; Amos Bunim, *A Fire In His Soul; Irving M. Bunim 1901–1980; The Man and His Impact on American Orthodox Jewry* (Jerusalem and New York, 1989), pp. 75–92.

43. "Orthodox Union to Cooperate with Vaad ha–Hatzala," *The Orthodox Union*, March–April 1941, p.11.

44. The unity of the Orthodox community found temporary expression in the establishment of a "United Immigration Aid Council" by *Vaad ha–Hatzala*, the Union of Orthodox Jewish Congregations, Young Israel, and *Zeirei Agudat Yisrael*. Letter of Rabbi Simcha Wasserman to Rubin Sherer, March 13, 1941, AVH. Since there is virtually no documentation on the council and its activities, this was apparently a very short–lived initiative.

45. Gurock, "Resisters," pp. 135–141; Liebman, "Orthodoxy", p.32.

46. See, for example, "Special Meeting at the Yeshiva Building," November 29, 1939; the minutes of a meeting of the Executive Committee of the R.C.A. held March 6, 1940; minutes of the Executive Committee, February 5, 1941, all from the Archives of the Rabbinical Council of America. (Hereafter called ARCA).

47. In fact the Young Israel movement was publicly denounced at the 1934 convention of *Agudat ha–Rabbanim*. Its opponents often facetiously referred to Young Israel as a red heifer, which is able to purify the impure but in the process contaminates the pure. Bunim, *A Fire in His Soul*, p. 31; Liebman, "Orthodoxy," pp. 58–59.

48. Rabbi Eliezer Silver, "Greetings," *The Young Israel Viewpoint*, March 23, 1941, p. 35. Rabbis Silver, Konvitz and Levinson also publicly thanked the members of the Young Israel movement in *Ha–Pardes*, and especially its leader, Irving Bunim, for their active participation in the tickets campaign. In their words of praise, they made no allusion to any reevaluation of their previous criticism of the movement's apparent laxity in its observance of the ideals of "true traditional Torah Judaism." "Chevrat Young Israel be–New York," *Ha–Pardes*, 14 no. 11 (Shevat 5701/February 1941), 18–19.

49. Helmreich, *The World of the Yeshiva*, p. 41.

50. Letter of Rabbi Silver to H. G. Craddock, April 24, 1941; letter of I. Berman to Rabbi Silver, April 14, 1941, both AVH.

51. Letter of Samuel A. Halperin to Rabbi Eliezer Silver, January 2, 1941, Silver Archives; David Wyman, *Paper Walls: America and the Refugee Crisis 1938–1941,* pp. 141, 152.

52. See, for example, the cable of Rabbi Simcha Wasserman to M. D. Mirvis and his letter to Sam Borak, both February 12, 1941, and his letter to Mrs. Bloom, April 12, 1941, all AVH.

53. Letter of Elliot B. Coulter (Acting Chief, Visa Division, U.S. State Department) to Rabbi Aaron Teitelbaum, January 27, 1941, ACRC, file 492–2.

54. See, for example, the vouchers for the travel expenses of David Josel Chazanowicz and family (five persons), Szmuel Wolmark, Isaac Zilber, Jacob Sneidman, Icchok Rabinowicz, and others, paid in full by the *Vaad* on February 13, 1941 to Modern Tours as agents for Thomas Cook and Sons—Wagon–Lits, AVH. In most cases the maintenance fees and head tax were paid by "Jewcom." See Jewcom Report, p. 19.

55. Letter of I. Berman to Rabbi Eliezer Silver, March 20, 1941, AVH; "Memorandum [by Dr. Grubel] of conversation with Mr. Halpern of the Emergency Committee for War–Torn Yeshivos at 165 West 46th St.," April 21, 1941, ACJFWF, I–69, Box 150, VH reports, pp. 2–3.

56. "Emergency Committee For War–Torn Yeshivoth Vaad Hahatzala," Budgeting Bulletin B–27 of the Council of Jewish Federations and Welfare Funds, ACJFWF, CJFWF Reports, Vaad ha–Hatzala, pp. 4, 7–12.

57. Estimated Jewish populations for these cities as of 1937 were: New York, 2,035,000; Detroit, 90,000; Cincinnati, 21,800; Baltimore, 73,000; Miami and Miami Beach, 8,700; Chicago, 363,000. *American Jewish Yearbook,* 46 (Philadelphia, 1944), 496–497. Although Cincinnati had a relatively small Jewish community, the *Vaad's* success there can be attributed to Rabbi Silver's prominent role in communal affairs and his status in the city. Rakeffet, *The Silver Era in American Jewish Orthodoxy,* pp. 80–94.

58. Letters of Rabbi Jacob Levinson to Rabbi Eliezer Silver, February 4 and 7, 1941, Silver Papers at American University, Washington, DC; "Vaad ha–Hatzala," *Ha–Pardes,* 14, no. 11 (Shevat 5701/February 1941), 17–18.

59. CJFWF Budgeting Bulletin B–27, pp. 4, 7–12. The figures cited for welfare funds allocations represented funds pledged. By April 1941 some federations had still not transmitted the sums to the *Vaad.* See the letter of Rabbi Jacob Karlinsky to the Council of Jewish Federations and Welfare Funds, April 20, 1941, ACJFWF, I–69, Box 149.

60. "Support in 1941 from Welfare Funds and Independent Campaigns," submitted by *Vaad ha–Hatzala* to the Council of Jewish Federations and Welfare Funds, ACJFWF, CJFWF Reports, *Vaad ha–Hatzala.*

61. Among the federations that wrote to the NCJFWF during this period were: Louisville, KY (January 1, 1941); Duluth, MN (January 6 and April 29, 1941); Dallas (January 17, 1941); Kansas City, MO (January 20, 1941); Youngstown, OH (February 4, 1941); Cleveland (April 6, 1941); and Montgomery, AL (April 22, 1941). See ACJFWF, I–69, Box 149. Among the communities that wrote the JDC were Chicago (January 22, 1941), Omaha (February 5, 1941), and Rochester, NY (April 8, 1941), AJDC–VH.

62. See, for example, the letters of Anna Smith, executive secretary of the Jewish Welfare Federation of Duluth, Minnesota, to the Council of Jewish Federations and

Welfare Funds, January 6, 1941, and of Max Bretton, executive secretary of the Jewish Welfare Federation of Greater Kansas City to Blanche Renard, January 20, 1941, both ACJFWF, I–69, Box 149. While the sums allocated in Duluth were relatively small ($342 for 1939 and $705 for 1940), the Kansas City federation was holding $2,735 for European yeshivot, $1,000 for *Vaad ha–Hatzala,* and $3,145 for yeshivot in Palestine.

63. See, for example, the letters of Edward Kahan, secretary of the Atlanta Jewish Welfare Fund (January 22, 1941) and Morton Gottleib, executive director of the Richmond Jewish Community (April 1, 1941), both to Blanche Renard, ACJFWF, I–69, Box 149.

64. See, for example, the Leavitt–Goldsmith letter, January 27, 1941, AJDC–VH.

65. Letters of Blanche Renard to Anna Smith of Duluth (January 9, 1941) and to Louis Greenberg, executive director of the Jewish Federation of Youngstown (February 25, 1941), both ACJFWF, I–69, Box 149.

66. Letters of Blanche Renard to Edward Kahn (January 23, 1941) and to Louis Greenberg (February 25, 1941), ibid.

67. Letters of Blanche Renard to Anna Smith of Duluth (January 9, 1941), Jack Sher of Easton, PA (March 6, 1941); and Joseph Papo of Duluth, Minnesota (May 6, 1941), all ibid.

68. Leavitt–Goldsmith letter, January 27, 1941, AJDC–VH.

69. Letter of Moses Leavitt to Jacob Kammen, executive secretary of the United Jewish Welfare Fund of Rochester, April 14, 1941, AJDC–VH.

70. Leavitt–Goldsmith letter, January 27, 1941, AJDC–VH.

71. CJFWF Budgeting Bulletin B–27, May 1941, ACJFWF, CJFWF Reports, *Vaad ha–Hatzala,* pp. 1–3.

72. Letter of Dr. Louis Finkelstein to Joseph Hyman, February 13, 1941, AJDC–VH.

73. Gurock, "Resisters," p. 137.

74. Letter of Dr. Louis Finkelstein to Rabbi Jacob Levinson, February 15, 1941, AJDC–VH.

75. See, for example, the letters of Moses Leavitt to Samuel Goldsmith (January 27, 1941) and Jacob Kammen (April 14, 1941), both AJDC–VH.

76. Letter of Dr. Louis Finkelstein to Joseph Hyman (February 13, 1941) and to Rabbi Jacob Levinson (February 15, 1941), both AJDC–VH.

77. The story of the taxi ride is related in detail in Bunim's biography. According to this source, the event took place in November 1940, but that date is unlikely given the fact that the decision to launch the special fundraising initiative apparently was taken in the wake of the news that the Soviets had given the refugees the choice of taking Soviet citizenship or being declared stateless. The decision of the Soviet government was announced on January 1, 1941. Bunim, *A Fire in His Soul,* p.85.

78. Bauer, *American Jewry and the Holocaust,* p. 122.

79. The *Vaad* helped many rabbis and yeshiva students obtain Japanese transit visas on the basis of ship tickets purchased from the N.Y.K. line. In addition, the maintenance funds sent by *Vaad ha–Hatzala* to the yeshivot were undoubtedly also used to cover expenses incurred in obtaining transit visas and exit permits.

80. Approximately 3,000 of the 14,000 Polish refugees who escaped to Lithuania were rabbis, yeshiva students, and the members of their families. See CJFWF Budgeting Bulletin B–27, p. 6.

81. Ibid., p.3.

82. Letter of Rabbi Jacob Karlinsky to the CJFWF, February 14, 1941, ACJFWF, I–69, Box 149.

83. Letter of Rabbi Aaron Teitelbaum to Breckinridge Long, December 30, 1940, ACRC file 492–2; letter of Elliot B. Coulter to Teitelbaum, January 27, 1941; letter of Teitelbaum to Coulter, February 12, 1941; lists of rabbis and yeshiva students who were recommended for visas but had not received them, submitted to the State Department February 17, 1941, all ACRC, file 492–2. See also Wyman, *Paper Walls*, p. 140, for a case in which U.S. visas granted to 38 Polish rabbinical students who had reached Japan were canceled following a review of visa cases of individuals with first–degree relatives in Russia, Poland, or Germany.

84. Rabbi Kotler assumed the leadership of the Etz Chaim Yeshiva after his father–in–law, Rabbi Isser Zalman Meltzer, immigrated to Palestine. During the two decades in which he headed the yeshiva in Europe, Rabbi Kotler attracted many students from all over the world because of his original teaching methods. In addition, he was one of the leaders of *Agudat Yisrael* and served on its *Moetzet Gedolei ha–Torah* (Council of Sages), which made all the movement's policy decisions. See Aaron Shurin, *Keshet Giborim*, pp. 244–248.

85. "Vaad Hatzala," *Ha–Pardes*, 15, no. 4 (Tammuz 5701/July 1941), 3–4.

86. Unlike the students of the Mir Yeshiva, almost all of whom obtained the necessary travel documents and were thus able to leave Lithuania, very few of the students of the other yeshivot secured the visas and exit permits. As a result, the overwhelming majority of these students were still in Lithuania at this point, and few if any ever reached the Far East. Efraim Zuroff, "Rescue Via the Far East: The Attempt to Save Polish Rabbis and Yeshivah Students," *Simon Wiesenthal Center Annual*, I (1984), 167–168.

87. "Ha–Gaon R'Aron Kotler Shelita," *Ha–Pardes*, 15, no. 2 (Iyar 5701/May 1941), 2–3; "Rabbi Kotler Here," *Every Friday*, April 18, 1941, p. 3; "Rieziger Olam Yidn Kumt Bagrissen Kletzker Rosh Yeshiva Harav Aharon Kotler," *Morgn Dzurnal*, April 22, 1941, p. 1.

88. See, for example, his cables of April 27, May 5, and May 13, 1941, to Rabbi Ashkenazi in Shanghai regarding the efforts to rescue the yeshiva students still in Lithuania, AVH.

89. Bunim, *A Fire in His Soul*, pp. 96–112.

90. Alter Pekier, *From Kletzk to Siberia; A yeshiva bachur's wandering during the Holocaust* (New York, 1985), p.50.

91. Genesis 32:25.

92. Deuteronomy 11:16–17.

93. Protocol of the semiannual convention of *Agudat ha–Rabbanim*, Session B, April 30, 1941, p. 3, Archives of *Agudat ha–Rabbanim*. (Hereafter called AAH).

94. Ibid.

95. Bunim, *A Fire in His Soul*, p.88.

96. In the course of the war, various Orthodox groups founded special committees to raise funds to assist the Jews under Nazi rule, but all were relatively short–lived and none ever threatened the hegemony of *Vaad ha–Hatzala* in the American Orthodox community.

Chapter 6

Entry Permits to Shanghai

During January and February of 1941, Japan, which during the previous six months had served as a transit station for Jewish refugees from Central Europe on their way to havens all over the world, was suddenly inundated with hundreds of Polish Jews from Lithuania. And whereas almost all the refugees who had arrived from Germany in 1940 were able to depart relatively quickly,[1] most of the Jews from Lithuania had no such option. Having obtained Japanese transit visas on the basis of fictitious visas to Curaçao, they found themselves stranded in Japan with little hope of obtaining end visas. This situation not only seriously endangered the refugees already in Japan, but also threatened to induce the Japanese to bar the entry of additional refugees, cutting off one of the few proven emigration routes from Soviet Lithuania. Even if the Japanese did not deport the refugees already in Japan back to the Soviet Union, a decision to bar the entry of transient refugees in effect would mean that thousands of Polish Jewish refugees would be forced to remain in Soviet Lithuania.

Under these circumstances, the leaders of Jewcom and those active in the efforts to extricate Polish Jews from Lithuania began searching for alternate solutions. In a meeting of rescue activists held in Kobe on February 19, 1941, the consensus was that an attempt should be made to use the International Settlement of the nearby port of Shanghai instead of Japan as a temporary transit station. In addition, Anatol Ponevejsky, the president of Jewcom, raised the possibility of bringing refugees from Vladivostok directly to Shanghai. The reason was obvious. The only hope of obtaining addi-

145

tional Japanese transit visas was to move the refugees stranded in Japan elsewhere.[2] Otherwise, even those who possessed end visas (to Curaçao and other places) would be unable to leave, not to mention the plight of those who had still not obtained visas or exit permits.

The choice of Shanghai as a potential haven was dictated not only by geographic proximity but also by necessity. The International Settlement of the city, which was governed by a municipal council made up of the representatives of the foreign powers that had extraterritorial rights in the Chinese port, was one of the only places in the world to which Jews could still obtain entry. There was, moreover, an affluent and influential local Jewish community which could provide assistance in obtaining the necessary documents. While its resources had been strained by the recent influx of approximately 17,000 Jewish refugees from Central Europe, various community leaders were willing to help bring additional refugees to Shanghai.[3]

While the prospect of transferring the refugees from Japan to Shanghai offered hope to those still in Lithuania, many of the refugees already in Kobe staunchly opposed such a move. For example, the rabbis and students of the Mir Yeshiva tried extremely hard to convince Frank Newman, who had participated in the meeting of rescue activists and supported Ponevejsky's suggestion, not to proceed with the transfer plans. Shanghai's reputation as a "hellhole" scared them and they were determined to remain in Japan until they could emigrate as a unit to a safe haven. The fact that almost all the Mir students had reached Japan or were on their way there was also apparently a factor which influenced their particularistic approach.[4] Rabbi Kotler, on the other hand, most of whose students were still in Lithuania and lacked visas, advised Newman to proceed with the plan proposed by the local rescue activists.[5]

On February 25, 1941, Newman set out for Shanghai to attempt to obtain entry permits for the Jewish refugees in Japan as well as for those still in Lithuania. Shortly after his arrival in the Chinese port, he contacted Rabbi Mayer Ashkenazi, the spiritual leader of the local East European Jewish community, and enlisted his assistance.[6] On March 4, 1941, Zerach Warhaftig and Eliezer Szupakiewicz, leaders of the Polish refugees in Japan, arrived in Shanghai and joined forces with Newman and Ashkenazi.[7]

The rescue activists' efforts to obtain Shanghai permits became more urgent in the wake of new Japanese regulations made public in early March. Japanese consuls were instructed to refuse transit visas to individuals who lacked legitimate end visas. On March 5 Rabbi Kotler informed Newman and Rabbi Ashkenazi that groups of rabbis and yeshiva students who had reached Moscow on their way to the Far East were in danger of being sent back to Lithuania if they could not obtain the necessary documents promptly.[8] In addition, several refugee scholars who possessed end visas, among them a group of outstanding students from several yeshivot, had been detained in Kovno because of the new Japanese policy. In cable after cable, Rabbi Kotler and other leading *roshei yeshiva* urged Newman to obtain at least twenty Shanghai permits immediately in order to save this particular group.[9] In fact, because of this emergency, Rabbi Kotler, who was scheduled to leave Japan for the United States at that time, postponed his departure for several weeks.[10]

Newman returned to Japan in mid-March to attend to other emigration matters, while Warhaftig remained in Shanghai with Rabbi Ashkenazi and other local Jewish leaders and continued the efforts to obtain permits. Their campaign included negotiations both with the local Japanese authorities and with the Municipal Council of the International Settlement, which was headed by the British consul. The Japanese were represented by Naval captain Koreshige Inuzuka and Captain Onuki. The former was a prominent member of a group of Japanese officers and officials who had maintained extensive contacts with local Jewish leaders prior to the outbreak of the war and had been involved in proposed schemes for the large-scale resettlement of European Jewish refugees in Japanese-occupied Manchuria.

Despite Inuzuka's ostensible sympathy with the plight of the Jewish refugees,[11] and efforts by Newman and others to gain his support by various means,[12] the Japanese refused to grant a substantial number of permits to their area of the International Settlement. Since both the Chinese and the French also refused to admit large numbers of Jewish refugees, the only hope was to obtain permits from the Municipal Council. The latter agreed to grant the documents in question after the local Palestine Office (established at that time by Warhaftig and Szupakiewicz) provided maintenance guarantees of $30 per person and occasional additional payments. [13]

The refugees for whom the permits were requested were described to the Municipal Council as possessors of Palestine certificates who sought temporary entry to Shanghai in transit to their final destination. The fact that they ostensibly had no intention of staying in Shanghai was obviously a factor in the decision to admit them, but in reality this was not the case. The permits were, in fact, used to enable Polish refugees to leave Lithuania, whether they possessed Palestine certificates or not.[14]

It is not clear whether the Municipal Council realized that most of the permit recipients would be unable to leave Shanghai, if they did reach the Chinese port. In any event on March 22 Newman received word from Rabbi Ashkenazi that the first batch of permits had already been signed and sent to Moscow and Kovno. In addition, the Shanghai rabbi asked Newman to send him a new list of candidates for entry permits.[15]

Once the initial batch of permits had been obtained from the municipal authorities, several problems remained to be solved before the Torah scholars stranded in Lithuania could be rescued. The original plan called for the refugees to travel to China via Japan. The Japanese, however, continued to refuse to grant transit visas. Another, more serious problem involved the distribution of the permits. The original list had been compiled in the wake of an emergency situation. If there were, however, sufficient permits for other refugee scholars, and assuming all the recipients had an equal chance of emigrating, how were the permits to be distributed? What criteria were to be applied in determining which scholars, if any, deserved priority?

These were questions that had always existed vis-à-vis the *Vaad's* activities. Whether the rabbis had to compile a list of candidates for emergency visitors' visas to the United States or decide how much money to allocate for the rescue of specific individuals, such dilemmas were an integral part of their activities. Yet there is no documentation to indicate how those issues were dealt with in New York. In this case, however, there are numerous documents that help explain how rabbis and yeshiva students, among them prominent Torah scholars, confronted a complex dilemma with extremely prosaic implications. The fact that Jewish leaders, both inside and outside occupied Europe, were frequently forced to face such situations,[16] and that the decisions in this case ostensibly reflect the halachic approach as expounded by some of its most outstanding proponents, make this case worthy of further scrutiny.

The first response to the pressing question of rescue priority came from Rabbi Aron Kotler, who was undoubtedly the leading halachic authority among the refugee Torah scholars now in the Far East. In reply to a request by Rabbi Ashkenazi for a new list of candidates for permits, Rabbi Kotler answered on March 25 that the compilation of the list had been delayed pending the outcome of various other rescue initiatives, the results of which would determine which names would be submitted to the Shanghai authorities. According to Rabbi Kotler, that list would be compiled in accordance with the directives in the *mishnah* of the tractate *Horayot*[17] which is the classic halachic text on rescue priority and states as follows:

> A man must be saved alive [rescued] sooner than a woman and his lost property must be restored sooner than hers. A woman's nakedness must be covered sooner than a man's and she must be brought out of captivity sooner than he. When both stand in danger of defilement, the man must be freed before the woman.[18]

Rabbi Kotler's reply was conveyed in a letter to Rabbi Ashkenazi; it is not clear whether it was rendered as a binding halachic ruling, and to what extent it was publicized among the refugees in Japan. This fact will perhaps explain why, despite Rabbi Kotler's preeminent position in the yeshiva world, it appears that those who compiled the lists of candidates for Shanghai permits did not precisely follow the guidelines prescribed in *Horayot*.

Toward the end of March, word was received in Japan that another group of Polish refugee rabbis and yeshiva students were in extreme distress. They had arrived in Vladivostok on their way to Japan but had been detained by the Russians. The majority possessed end visas to Curaçao which had been obtained from A. M. de Jong, the Dutch consul in Stockholm, while others possessed visas to other countries. By this time, however, it was patently clear to the Japanese authorities that the people with Curaçao visas were not headed for the West Indies and they therefore barred the entry of any refugees who did not possess valid end visas. The Russians, in the meantime, had informed the refugees in Vladivostok that they would not be allowed to remain in the Pacific port indefinitely and threatened to send the entire group back to Lithuania if they were unable to leave by the end of March.[19]

Under these circumstances, the most logical solution was to attempt to obtain Shanghai permits, which would at least enable these refugees to leave the Soviet Union. This course of action was supported by the refugees themselves. Thus in late March Rabbi Yoseph Epstein, who was the personal secretary of the Mir *rosh yeshiva* and was among the refugees stranded in Vladivostok, appealed to his colleagues in Japan to try to obtain the necessary Shanghai documents for this group.[20] While his appeal undoubtedly introduced an added sense of urgency to the efforts to obtain Shanghai permits, the situation was further complicated several days later when word was received from New York that attempts by *Vaad ha-Hatzala* and *Agudat Yisrael* to obtain entry visas to South America were still pending because of a lack of funds.[21] A breakthrough on the Shanghai front had therefore become even more critical.

During the first half of April developments took place at a rapid pace. On April 7 Robertson, the deputy police commissioner, sent Rabbi Ashkenazi 35 entry permits.[22] At this point it had apparently been decided to send these visas to the refugee rabbis and students in Vladivostok rather than to those in Lithuania, but the rescue activists had still not obtained enough permits to save all the refugees stranded in the Pacific port. So on the same day, Rabbi Ashkenazi applied for ten additional permits for refugees in Vladivostok.[23] In the meantime, the permits already approved were submitted to Intourist Shanghai[24] which cabled the information to Intourist Vladivostok.

At this point the only problem remaining was transportation from Vladivostok, which proved to be quite difficult. There were no direct sailings from Vladivostok to Shanghai scheduled for the next two months, and since the only vessels that plied this route were cargo boats, there was no guarantee that passengers would be allowed on board.[25] The Russians, in the meantime, were adamant that a solution be found, and while it appeared that they would be willing to delay taking action for a few days, it was quite clear that they would not allow the refugees to remain in Vladivostok indefinitely.

On April 10 the refugees cabled Kobe that a ship would be sailing from Vladivostok directly to Shanghai on April 16. On the same day, the leaders of the refugees in Japan decided that the Shanghai permits would be allocated to the refugees stranded in Vladivostok (regardless of religiosity or ideological affiliation). Instructions to this effect were immediately transmitted to Rabbi Ashkenazi so that the permits could be cabled in time to Vladivostok to enable the refugees to sail on the ship.[26] The problem was, however, that the refugees lacked funds to pay for their passage. Thus on April 11 four of the leading refugee *roshei yeshiva* in Japan cabled the following appeal to *Tzeirei Agudat Yisrael* and *Vaad ha-Hatzala* in New York:

> Situation in Wladiwostocker hopeless sole rescue special ship Wladiwostok Shanghai immediately together with joint cable demanded sum Rabbi Ashkenazi Shanghai don't lin[g]er do all Jontef.[27]

Two days later Rabbi Aron Kotler arrived in the United States and immediately began mobilizing support for the rescue activities in the Far East. Within a matter of hours he secured a promise of $2,000 from Rabbi Eliezer Silver, and on April 15 he cabled Newman from San Francisco to instruct Rabbi Ashkenazi to expand his efforts to obtain Shanghai permits.[28]

On the following day Newman received word from Shanghai that a boat was scheduled to sail from Vladivostok to Shanghai on April 19. The fare was $32 per passenger, and the rescue activists asked Moses Beckelman of the Joint Distribution Committee to provide the necessary funds. When a positive response was not immediately forthcoming from the JDC, Rabbi Ashkenazi decided to pay for the passage of 49 persons (the number of rabbis, yeshiva students, and Orthodox Jews he thought were stranded in Vladivostok).[29]

On April 17 Newman received word from Shanghai that his contacts had indeed paid for 49 tickets. They had, moreover, supplied permits to all the refugees stranded in Vladivostok, regardless of religiosity or ideological affiliation.[30] Thus on May 1, 1941, the *Arktika* arrived in Shanghai from Vladivostok with 50 passengers (46 adults and 4 children) aboard, half of whom were rabbis and yeshiva students, members of their families, and other Orthodox Jews. These refugees were the first to utilize the Shanghai permits to leave the Soviet Union. Fifteen additional refugees stranded in Vladivostok were able to obtain entry to Japan on the basis of the Shanghai permits. Among them were the family of Rabbi Moshe Shatzkes, the rabbi of Lomza, Poland. It should be noted that the JDC later covered all the transportation costs of the voyage of the *Arktika*.[31]

In addition to his efforts to rescue the refugees stranded in Vladivostok, Rabbi Ashkenazi continued his attempts to obtain additional Shanghai permits for the rabbis and yeshiva students in Lithuania. By early April, 100 permits had been approved, but the rescue activists did not have the necessary funds to take possession of them. It was still not clear, moreover, whether the Soviets would allow the refugee (or other) Torah scholars to leave Lithuania on the basis of the Shanghai permits.[32] In addition, the problem of transportation had still not been solved. All the attempts to arrange passage by boat, for the refugees from Vladivostok directly to Shanghai or to secure permission for them to travel overland via Manchuria had been unsuccessful. Moscow had vetoed the proposal of a special boat and the efforts of Rabbi Ashkenazi, Newman, and local Jewish leaders in China regarding Manchuria had also failed.[33] Subsequent attempts by Jewcom to secure Japanese transit visas proved fruitless as well.[34]

Despite these problems, Rabbi Ashkenazi and the local refugee leaders continued their efforts to obtain additional permits, motivated by the numerous appeals for help from rabbis and yeshiva students in Lithuania. As soon as it became known that Shanghai permits could be obtained, the Torah scholars in Lithuania literally bombarded their friends and colleagues in Japan with requests for them.[35] As time went by, these appeals increased and the pressure for rescue intensified. Each yeshiva, organization, and interest group attempted to induce the refugee leaders to give them the number of permits necessary to save all "their" rabbis and students. Under such circumstances, obtaining the permits was only half the problem. Given the fact that the municipal authorities would obviously not grant permits for all the more than 1,500 yeshiva students still in Lithuania, it became clear that the distribution of the permits would pose an extremely complicated problem.[36]

Prior to his departure to the United States, Rabbi Aron Kotler had indicated to Rabbi Ashkenazi that the permits should be distributed in accordance with the directives in tractate *Horayot*, and he compiled a list of several hundred Polish refugee rabbis and yeshiva students who were to receive the first permits. The list was entrusted to Frank Newman, who delivered it to Rabbi Ashkenazi. The latter was supposed to submit the applications in strict accordance with the list prepared by Rabbi Kotler.[37]

In early April Rabbi Kotler left Japan, and a committee of refugee scholars was established to determine the distribution of the permits.[38] This step was taken apparently because, with Rabbi Kotler's departure, there was no rabbinic authority in Japan whose decisions on these matters of life and death would be accepted by all or even most of the rabbis and yeshiva students. Unless a recognized authority could be established by the representatives of all the yeshivot, it was obvious that bitter conflicts would erupt. Newman sought to assume this task, but he too left shortly thereafter for the United States. Despite his hopes of being able to arrange the distribution from New York, that did not prove to be the case.

Prior to sailing from Japan, Newman, in a letter to Tugendhaft, described the problems he feared would confront those in charge of distributing the permits:

> I find it necessary to make a little explanation about the many times I wrote you to see that you do not give special preference to any group. Unfortunately I cannot speak very clearly, but you understand. Anyway yeshiva people think first of yeshiva students and in composing the first list Rabbi Kotler could be depended upon implicitly. Now there is no one here with sufficient authority and roshei yeshiva will think first of their own yeshivot, then other yeshiva men and will never find place for other bnai Torah...
>
> I remind you again that immediately after I leave there will be a great problem for you to resist pressure from groups who want to "take over" the whole business. Please trust me and do not fall for any specious arguments.[39]

Newman's prognoses proved quite accurate. On April 28, for example, Rabbi Shmuel Szczedrowicki wrote to Rabbi Ashkenazi on behalf of the *Irgun ha-Yehudim ha-Hareidim be-Yapan* (Organization of ultra-Orthodox Jews in Japan) complaining that all the permits had been distributed to yeshiva students and none had been given to other religious Jews even though the names of several well-known public figures had been among those submitted to the rescue activists in Shanghai. Rabbi Szczedrowicki promised to send a list of permit candidates ranked according to the "degree of necessity" of rescue, but in the meantime he urged Rabbi Ashkenazi to secure per-

mits for Leib Mintzberg and Yaakov Trokenheim, who had represented Agudat Yisrael in the Polish Sejm, both of whom had escaped
to Vilna.[40]

Rabbi Szczedrowicki's appeal was one of many that Rabbi
Ashkenazi received during this period from the *roshei yeshiva* and
students of the various yeshivot. Two days later he received a letter
from Rabbi Avraham Yaphin, *rosh yeshiva* of "Beit Yoseph" of
Bialystok, which was typical of these requests. Rabbi Yaphin, one of
the leading Torah scholars in Japan at that time, began by praising
the students of his yeshiva who were so dedicated to the study of
Torah and bemoaning the fate of those still in Lithuania who were
presently threatened with the prospect of deportation to Siberia. He
complained that his yeshiva had not received a fair share of the permits (to date three rabbis and fourteen students had been granted
such documents) distributed in accordance with the list compiled by
Rabbi Kotler, and therefore asked Rabbi Ashkenazi for approximately 80 additional permits. According to Yaphin, the Shanghai rabbi
would certainly understand that his request was based on the prin-
ciples of *din* (religious law) and *yosher* (honesty) and therefore he
was certain that Rabbi Ashkenazi would comply with his appeal,
not only to fulfill the mitzvah of *pidyon shevuyim* (redemption of
captives), but also because the students of Beit Yoseph Bialystok
were so dedicated to Torah study.[41]

Rabbi Ashkenazi and his helpers also received numerous requests
for individuals other than rabbis and yeshiva students. For example,
some rabbis requested permits for relatives or for relatives of relatives.[42] These appeals were motivated by the fear of the fate that
would befall Orthodox Jews under the Soviet regime. It was obvious
to the refugees in Japan that even if the Nazis did not occupy
Lithuania, the conditions there would not be conducive to Jewish
religious life.[43]

As time went by, the concern of the refugee rabbis and yeshiva
students in Japan regarding the fate of their mentors and colleagues
in Lithuania steadily mounted. The scholars were deluged with
appeals for help from those they left behind,[44] and under such circumstances it was only natural that the pressure applied by each
yeshiva was intensified. The fact that attempts to secure entry to
alternative havens nearby, such as Harbin, were unsuccessful [45] also
contributed to the increased tension in the efforts to obtain
Shanghai permits.

On May 6, 1941, representatives of most of the rabbis and yeshivot in Japan met and established an official committee to deal with the Shanghai permits. This committee superseded the one founded a month earlier and immediately established itself as the representation of the refugee scholars in Japan. Its status derived from the fact that not only representatives of almost all the yeshivot had participated in its formation, but that it was headed by Rabbis Shatzkes, Yaphin and Lifshitz, the leading rabbinic figures in the Far East at that time.

According to the three rabbis, the committee's major objective was to compile the lists of those who would receive the Shanghai permits. Each list would be drawn up and approved by the representatives of the rabbis and the yeshivot and would be signed by the members of the executive committee. It was therefore imperative that neither the order of the list be changed nor any omissions be made. Rabbis Shatzkes, Yaphin, and Lifshitz urged Rabbi Ashkenazi to try to obtain the permits immediately, since it was truly a matter of *pikuach nefesh* (life or death). According to information received in Japan, the Russians were granting exit permits on the basis of the Shanghai documents, so the success of Rabbi Ashkenazi's efforts became absolutely critical. The rabbis advised the Shanghai rabbi that if he encountered financial difficulties, he should ask *Vaad ha-Hatzala* for assistance and they would do likewise.

On a practical level, the committee proposed that once a permit had been obtained, Rabbi Ashkenazi would inform Intourist Shanghai, which would in turn cable Intourist Kovno (or Riga or Moscow, depending on the case). The permit would be sent to the committee in Kobe, which would notify the recipient.[46] Meanwhile, the refugees in Japan were continuing their efforts to obtain a boat that would sail directly from Vladivostok to Shanghai. Their chances of success depended on the number of passengers. If enough refugees with Shanghai permits could reach Vladivostok, it was likely that a boat could be obtained.[47]

Before the new committee could submit its first list of permit candidates to Rabbi Ashkenazi, he sent them a list of the names that he had already submitted to the municipal authorities. Once again, there were those who were dissatisfied, among them members of the new committee, who protested privately to Rabbi Ashkenazi. (They apparently tried to do as much as possible on behalf of their colleagues before they were forced to accept the decisions of the committee.)[48]

One group whose requests posed a particular dilemma for Rabbi Ashkenazi was the Lubavitch Chasidim. They were not represented on the Kobe committee and therefore sent their own list to Shanghai along with a promise that their representatives in the United States would send funds to cover expenses.[49] We have no documentation that indicates how Rabbi Ashkenazi, who was a Lubavitch Chasid, reached his final decision, but we do know that quite a few Lubavitch students received permits to Shanghai.[50]

In mid-May Rabbi Ashkenazi sent the committee a summary of his efforts to obtain Shanghai permits. Up to that point 156 permits had been secured.[51] (This figure did not include the permits issued to the refugees who had arrived in Shanghai from Vladivostok in early May.) In addition, another 300 names had just been submitted to the authorities and he hoped that these individuals would be granted permits within two weeks. If all went well, it would be possible to obtain a ship to transport the refugees from Vladivostok directly to Shanghai.[52]

At this point however, there remained, two major problems to be solved. Most important was the fact that the outcome of the project was still uncertain. Despite rumors that the Soviet authorities were granting exit permits on the basis of the Shanghai documents,[53] there was no proof that this was indeed the case. Aside from the refugees who had arrived in Shanghai in early May, no one from Lithuania had reached the Chinese port on a permit, so any assessment regarding the value of the documents was at best speculation. Even some of those who were working to obtain permits had serious doubts as to the feasibility of the project. For example, Josef Tugendhaft, Rabbi Ashkenazi's assistant, wrote quite bluntly to the members of the Kobe committee on May 16 that a great deal of money had already been spent on the efforts to obtain permits and it was not such a good idea to throw away any additional funds on an "unknown" matter.[54]

The second problem involved the composition of the lists. According to Tugendhaft, almost everyone whose name had been on the original list compiled by Rabbi Kotler and submitted by Frank Newman either had already received a permit or was on the list submitted to the municipal authorities.[55] The *bnai Torah* committee, however, viewed the situation quite differently. On May 20 they complained to Rabbi Ashkenazi that 59 persons whose names were on the original list compiled by Rabbi Kotler did not appear on either of the lists they received from Shanghai. Since each of these was among "the most respected and important" Torah scholars, the situation had to be rectified immediately. According to the *bnai Torah* committee, merely including their names on a new list would not be sufficient. They were incensed because various changes had been made in the list, and they warned that such alterations could have grave consequences. In their words:

> The omissions and changes in the list we drew up are also likely to cause great damage since we arrange the names of the students in accordance with their importance and worth and when you issue a permit to a bad student while an important student has still not obtained one—this can cause chaos and confusion and lead to a discipline crisis in the yeshivot there [Lithuania] and therefore we asked you and requested that you keep to the order without changes and omissions.[56]

The Kobe committee had other complaints as well. Rabbi Ashkenazi had apparently accepted lists of permit candidates from various groups that were not represented on the *bnai Torah* committee. The latter were particularly upset by this phenomenon because in their opinion the "outside" lists included many individuals who had no reasonable hope of obtaining Soviet exit permits, which meant that life-saving documents were being wasted. (The Soviets had up to now granted exit permits only to Polish refugees. Former Lithuanian and Latvian citizens were refused permission to leave the Soviet Union.) The committee expressed its dismay and frustration regarding this development in the following terms:

> The committee therefore arranges on its present lists only those people for whom the possibility of exit is imminent, i.e. those who are not citizens there (only refugees) and who submitted requests for exit before February 10. In the second category are the refugees for whom unfortunately there is little hope at present.
> We, who were there not long ago, and who are in steady contact by letter with the yeshivot and their directors over there [Lithuania] know the details about the general situation there and the various details about the people in question. This is not true when marginal people submit the names of persons

for rescue. Therefore the learned rabbi, may he live a long and good life, will be so kind as to refuse all the requests of marginal people, which are not submitted via the committee, since they are likely only to waste permits and not benefit their possessors.[57]

The committee urged Rabbi Ashkenazi to continue his efforts to obtain permits. They were concerned because of Tugendhaft's doubts regarding the feasibility of the project and his intention to suspend operations until it became clear whether the refugees would indeed be allowed to leave Lithuania on the basis of the Shanghai permits. They condemned his proposal as an idea "which during normal times and in a normal country would be considered very strange [but which] under the present circumstances of time and place should not even be uttered." Mustering their powers of persuasion, they tried to convince Rabbi Ashkenazi that the rescue efforts had to continue:

> and what can be done today perhaps may not be at all possible tomorrow and if we do not prepare everything beforehand so that they will be ready for a propitious time in which exit permits will be granted (according to our information the time of this good will has still not ended but who knows how long it will last)—the danger exists that we will completely miss everything, G-d forbid. We must, therefore, not delay in obtaining more permits because the present time is suitable for fruitful work and let us not make accounts in matters concerning the rescue of the Torah and the *pikuach nefesh* of those who carry her flag and hopefully G-d will grant us success.[58]

Although the *bnai Torah* committee included representatives of almost all the yeshivot and rabbis—and on that basis demanded that their lists be accepted in toto by Rabbi Ashkenazi—there was one yeshiva that, even though represented on the committee, took independent steps to ensure that its students whose names had not been on the committee's lists would be granted permits. On May 20 Mayer Pantel and Zvi Milner of the Kamenetz Yeshiva wrote to Rabbi Ashkenazi to request that he immediately submit the names of David Epstein and Mordechai Weinberg, who were among the yeshiva's outstanding students but whose names had been left off the original list submitted by Frank Newman.[59] The *rosh yeshiva* of Kamenetz, Rabbi Reuven Grazowsky, who had already left for the United States, also asked Rabbi Ashkenazi to obtain permits for several of his students whose names had not been on the lists submitted to the municipal authorities.[60]

There were others who were dissatisfied with the decisions made by the Kobe committee. Rabbi Baruch Sorotzkin of the Telz (Telsiai) Yeshiva, which was located in Lithuania and many of whose students were Lithuanian citizens, as opposed to Polish refugees, bitterly protested that the committee, which was made up of representatives of the Polish refugee yeshivot[61] "did not want to recognize the right [of] our yeshiva, to obtain these visas and [was] unjustly applying stringent measures."[62] Moreover, in accordance with Rabbi Ashkenazi's instructions, Rabbi Sorotzkin had on several occasions appealed to the committee to arrange permits for Telz students, but his pleas had been ignored. His desperation, which is clearly evident in one of the final sentences of his letter, reflects the frustration of all the *roshei yeshiva* who were unable to obtain the coveted Shanghai permits for all their students: "Why should our yeshiva fare worse than other yeshivot and especially the heads and directors for our holy yeshiva and its best students who are truly exceptional in this generation?"[63]

As far as we know, the committee did not accede to Rabbi Sorotzkin's request. It was, in fact, precisely against such appeals that they had protested to Rabbi Ashkenazi. To support their stance, moreover, they apparently enlisted the support of the leaders of *Vaad ha-Hatzala.* Thus on May 27 Rabbi Kotler cabled Rabbi Ashkenazi that he should accept lists only from the *bnai Torah* committee.[64]

During the latter half of May Rabbi Ashkenazi continued his efforts to obtain permits[65] and appealed to New York for additional funds to finance his activites.[66] In the meantime, the Kobe committee received word that those individuals for whom Shanghai permits had been obtained and whose names had been cabled by Intourist were being allowed to leave the Soviet Union. Needless to say, this news motivated the committee to intensify its efforts to save the Torah scholars living under Communist rule, lest this "unnatural opportunity" for large-scale rescue be missed. At the same time, the committee was now forced to confront the dilemmas involved in drawing up a list of permit applicants. (The previous lists had been compiled by Rabbi Kotler and the first committee.) The methods chosen to deal with this problem are outlined in great detail in the letter to Rabbi Ashkenazi which accompanied the list (and which was signed by all the representatives on the committee).[67] The procedure for choosing the candidates was as follows:

> We did everything very seriously and very calmly in accordance with the instructions of the *roshei metivta* who were here recently *shelita* [may they be granted a long and good life]. The students were each given a specific ordinal number by the representative of their yeshiva according to their importance and the necessity of their leaving there. The sum total of those on the list of all the yeshivot and the list of the refugee rabbis and their families is more than 1,500. We decided in accordance with the instructions of the above-mentioned *roshei metivta shelita*—that every general list of permits which would be drawn up by us would include an exact proportion of each and every yeshiva according to the number of its students.
>
> This list which consists of 336 persons represents 20% of the total number of the students and rabbis on all the lists— thus 20% of the lists of each and every yeshiva were included in it. Small concessions were made only vis-à-vis the rabbis and their families who obtained slightly more than the 20% they deserved and in the case of the Grodno Yeshiva because of some important reasons.[68] We discussed every single detail very seriously and we did everything with the approval of all the members of the committee, so that any change or skipping whatsoever, putting those at the bottom of the list at the top, vice versa and the like is only likely to harm the matter and introduce confusion into this important work [because it will lead to] granting preferences to one yeshiva over another, saving the inferior [rabbis and students] before the elite, dividing a family into two…and in general weaken the work of our unified committee.[69]

This letter provides us with many details regarding the decision-making process, but it does leave several important questions unanswered. While we know that each yeshiva compiled its own list and that the key criteria were academic excellence and the degree of danger an individual was in, it is not clear in which order the various lists were taken. It can be assumed that the lists of the yeshivot were not taken en bloc, but rather that the first places were allocated to those in the first slot on each list, after which those in the second slot on each list were recorded and so on. The question remains, however, in which order were the various lists taken. Was this determined by lottery, the size of the yeshiva, or perhaps its reputation?

Another important point that requires clarification concerns Rabbi Kotler's letter to Rabbi Ashkenazi in which he indicated that the lists would be compiled in accordance with the directives in tractate *Horayot*. To what extent were these guidelines indeed followed by the *bnai Torah* committee? According to Rabbis Pantel, Milner, and Czeczyk, who were members of the executive committee, the criterion of academic excellence was taken into consideration in accordance with the *mishnah*.[70] But some of the other decisions taken by the committee do not appear to conform to the directives in *Horayot*. For example, the *mishnah* determined that in matters of life and death males should always be given rescue priority over females. Yet according to Asher Czeczyk, who compiled the list for the Radin Yeshiva, the wives and children of the *roshei yeshiva* were put at the top of the list, immediately after their husbands and ahead of all the students.[71] We do not know whether other yeshivot adopted the same policy (neither the original nor any copies of the master list have been found), but the decision by Radin appears to be in direct contradiction to the *mishnah*. Perhaps there was a subsequent rabbinic ruling that sanctioned the rescue of entire families as a unit, or could it be that the halachic injunctions were not strictly applied in this case due to the exigencies of the situation?

There is a possibility that Rabbi Kotler's decision to compile the lists in accordance with the *mishnah* in *Horayot* was not rendered as a halachic decision and was therefore not considered binding by the *bnai Torah* committee. While the committee indicated that its decisions were in accordance with the instructions of the leading rabbis who had recently been in Japan, they did not mention Rabbi Kotler's name. He left Japan relatively early and perhaps those who remained longer issued different instructions. Another possibility is that Rabbi Kotler never publicized his decision nor left instructions prior to his departure, that subsequent lists of candidates for Shanghai permits were to be compiled in accordance with the directives in *Horayot*. Unfortunately, the documents in our possession do not contain the answers to these questions.

In early June the situation remained the same. Rabbi Ashkenazi continued his efforts to obtain additional permits, while the *bnai Torah* committee in Kobe handled the contacts with Intourist and with those scholars still in Lithuania. In New York *Vaad ha-Hatzala* tried to raise the funds for the permits. These efforts soon became critical, since by mid-June all aspects of the rescue operation to Shanghai had been either delayed or completely halted because of financial difficulties. On June 9 Rabbi Ashkenazi cabled Frank Newman that 390 permits had already been received in Kobe and an additional 400 were needed but that he lacked the funds to pay for them even if they could be obtained.[72]

Five days later Ashkenazi cabled Newman that Intourist Kovno had asked their Shanghai branch to send 300 permits but that he did not have enough money to pay for the cables; he therefore urged Newman to rush funds to Shangahi.[73] On June 16 a similar appeal was cabled to *Vaad ha-Hatzala* by the *bnai Torah* committee, which warned the rabbis of the far-reaching consequences of the present financial crisis. Not only were they unable to cable the permits already in their possession to Kovno, but Rabbi Ashkenazi could not begin work to obtain permits for the 336 rabbis, yeshiva students, and family members whose names were on the master list they had just sent him. In short, the future of the entire project was in jeopardy.[74]

The difficulties were not only financial, however. The problem of transportation also remained to be solved. Both Rabbi Ashkenazi and Anatol Ponevejsky, the head of Jewcom, were searching for a solution but had not yet succeeded. Among the solutions considered were traveling via Japan, in which case Japanese transit visas or at least permission to switch boats in Japan would have to be obtained, or arranging a boat to sail directly from Vladivostok to Shanghai.[75]

On June 21, 1941, Rabbi Ashkenazi cabled Newman that Intourist Shanghai had already telegraphed 300 permits to the Soviet Union.[76] This meant, in theory, that if transportation could be arranged, these individuals could be rescued. At this point, however, external developments put an end to the plans to extricate the refugee Torah scholars from the Soviet Union to the Far East. On the next day, Germany invaded the Soviet Union and the systematic annihilation of European Jewry commenced. Although the *Vaad ha-Hatzala* had urged Rabbi Ashkenazi to secure more permits and had promised to send additional funds,[77] the Shanghai permits rescue initiative was, for all practical purposes, finished. With the invasion of the Soviet Union, the overwhelming majority of the Jews in Lithuania were trapped. Even those for whom permits had been obtained were unable to use them to escape to the Far East.[78]

How many people were rescued thanks to the Shanghai permits? The available documentation does not provide a clear-cut answer. After the war Rabbi Ashkenazi claimed that he had obtained 1,200 permits by the summer of 1941.[79] Yet at most only half of this total were in his possession before the German invasion of the Soviet Union, when rescue to Shanghai was still possible. We have concrete evidence regarding the rescue of only the 50 persons who arrived directly from Vladivostok in early May, and the fifteen refugees allowed to proceed to Japan at the same time. There is no record of any other refugees who left the Soviet Union on the basis of the Shanghai permits during this period.

Yet certain statistics indicate that the number of refugees who utilized the permits might have been larger. According to Jewcom, 860 Polish Jews had relocated to Shanghai by November 1941. Yet in 1942 there were 972 Polish Jews living in the city.[80] If we take into account that 29 Polish rabbis and yeshiva students immigrated to Canada in the fall of 1941 after being transferred from Japan to Shanghai,[81] we obtain a total of 141 Polish Jews who did not reach the Chinese port via Japan. If we subtract the 50 refugees who arrived from Vladivostok in early May, there were at least 91 Jews who reached Shanghai not via Japan and were perhaps able to utilize the permits.

Although the Shanghai permits rescue project did not fulfill the hopes of its initiators, it did achieve significant results. Besides helping to save dozens of refugees, it lay the groundwork for the relocation of the refugee Torah scholars stranded in Japan to Shanghai, a step that ultimately helped ensure their survival.

Notes

1. All 1,119 refugees who arrived in Japan from July 1 to September 30, 1940, stayed for only a brief period and had left the country by the latter date. Of the 852 refugees who arrived during October, November, and December, 693 were able to leave by the end of 1940. This situation changed dramatically in January and February 1941, when 1,325 Jewish refugees were admitted to Japan but only 383 left the country. See Jewcom Report, p. 9.

2. Entry of February 19, 1941, diary of Frank Newman, *Vaad ha–Hatzala* emissary to Japan. The diary was made available to the author by Dr. David Kranzler, whom the author wishes to thank for his assistance.

3. For details on Shanghai, its International Settlement, the local Jewish community, and the thousands of refugees who found a haven there see David Kranzler, *Japanese, Nazis and Jews; The Jewish Refugee Community of Shanghai 1938–1945* (New York, 1976). For many years the International Settlement of Shanghai was the only place in the world for which no entry visa was required, a fact that explains why thousands of Jewish refugees traversed half the globe to find refuge in the Chinese port. See also idem., "The Jewish Refugee Community of Shanghai 1938–1945," *Wiener Library Bulletin*, XXVI, no. 3/4 (1972/73), 28–37. In 1939 immigration to the International Settlement was limited to those who could deposit $400 as "guarantee money," individuals with job contracts in the city and intended spouses, or first–degree relatives of Shanghai residents. Idem. "Restrictions Against German Jewish Refugee Immigration to Shanghai in 1939," *Jewish Social Studies*, XXXVI, no. 1 (January 1974), 57–58.

4. Entry of February 19, 1941, Newman Diary. Throughout their stay in the Far East, the Mir Yeshiva sought to remain intact, and therefore in several cases individual rabbis and students who obtained visas to countries in North or South America did not utilize them. For details see Epstein, Mir, p. 127.

5. Newman was extremely critical of the "chauvinism and crass selfishness" of the rabbis and students of the Mir Yeshiva, who in his opinion refused to take into account the plight of the other refugees. The fact that Rabbi Kotler, whose Torah scholarship was renowned throughout the Jewish world, supported his view made it easier for Newman to reject the entreaties of Mir *rosh yeshiva* Rabbi Shmulewitz and his students. See the entries for February 19, 24, and 25 1941, Newman Diary. For the factors that influenced the practical steps taken by the rabbis and students of the various yeshivot to arrange for their emigration see Chapter 4 of this book. The main reason practically the entire Mir Yeshiva had been able to leave Lithuania, in contrast to all the other refugee yeshivot, was that its *rosh yeshiva,* Rabbi Finkel, had decided to obtain visas and exit permits for all his students in an organized fashion. Most of the other *roshei yeshivot* opposed the attempts to use Curaçao visas, because they feared that requests for Soviet exit permits would result in the en masse deportation of all the rabbis and students to Siberia.

6. Entries for February 25 and 29, 1941, Newman Diary.

7. Zerach Warhaftig, *Palit ve–Sarid be–Yemei ha–Shoa*, p. 229.

8. The individuals in question had obviously hoped to obtain Japanese transit visas in the Soviet capital but were unable to do so in the wake of the new Japanese regulations. Cable of Rabbi Kotler to Rabbi Ashkenazi and Newman, March 5, 1941, YIVO Archives, file 49; cable of group of refugees stranded in Moscow to Rabbis Kotler and Grazowsky, March 21, 1941, ibid.

9. Cables of Rabbi Kotler to Rabbi Ashkenazi and Newman, March 5, 13 and 16, 1941; cable of Rabbis Grazowsky and Zaks to Rabbi Ashkenazi and Newman, March 16, 1941, all ibid.

10. Cable of Rabbi Kotler to Rabbi Ashkenazi and Newman, March 12, 1941, ibid.

11. It was subsequently revealed that Inuzuka had written several anti–Semitic works under a psuedonym. For details on the naval captain and the other Japanese

officials involved in Jewish affairs during these years see Kranzler, *Japanese, Nazis and Jews*, pp. 169–174.

12. Newman gave Inuzuka a silver cigarette case with the inscription, "With thanks and admiration for your service to the Jewish people from the Union of Orthodox Rabbis of the United States and Canada, Purim 5701 (1941), Frank Newman." After the war Inuzuka was put on trial for war crimes committed while he was a commander of the Japanese Navy in the Philippines during 1943–1944, and he used the cigarette case as part of his defense. Warhaftig, *Palit ve–Sarid be–Yemei ha–Shoa*, p. 237.

13. Ibid., pp. 229, 238–239. These guarantees were in fact provided by the Shanghai Ashkenazi Jewish Communal Association. See note 15 below.

14. The maintenance guarantees were accompanied by guarantees by the Jewish Agency and the United Palestine Appeal to cover the transportation expenses to Palestine of all the emigrants who lacked sufficient funds. Letter of Shanghai Palestine Office to G. G. Phillips, March 18, 1941; cable of Warhaftig and Szupakiewicz to the Jewish Agency, March 18, 1941, both YVA, P–20/8.

15. Cable of Jeschiwah (code for Rabbi Ashkenazi) to Newman, March 22, 1941, YIVO Archives, file 49. According to Warhaftig, the first permits were only received on March 25, after the Shanghai Ashkenazic Jewish Communal Association assumed responsibility for the upkeep of 300 refugees from Poland during their stay in Shanghai on their way to Palestine. Letter of Godfrey Phillips to Warhaftig and Szupakiewiez, March 24, 1941, YVA, P–20/8; letter of B. Kopeliovich (Shanghai Ashkenazic Jewish Communal Association) to Phillips, March 24, 1941, YVA, P–20/8.

16. Among those forced to make such decisions were the heads of the Judenrats and rescue activists. Regarding the dilemmas faced by the former, see Isaiah Trunk, *Judenrat; The Jewish Councils in Eastern Europe Under Nazi Occupation* (New York, 1972), pp. 420–436; Leonard Tushnet, *The Pavement of Hell* (New York, 1974), pp. 52–53, 160–161, 169–170, 173–177, 185–186, 194–195. For the difficult decisions that had to be made by rescue activists, see for example the memoirs of Ruth Kluger-Aliav, *The Last Escape*, (paperback edition)(New York, 1973), pp. 126–129, 146–149. The painful dilemma of choosing candidates for rescue was referred to as *ha–bechira* (the choice or selection) by the agents of the *Mossad le–Aliyah Bet,* who arranged clandestine immigration to Palestine before, during, and after World War II. See also Dalia Ofer, *Derech Ba–Yam; Aliya Bet be–Tekufat ha–Shoa* (Jerusalem, 1988).

17. Letter of Rabbi Kotler to Rabbi Ashkenazi, March 25, 1941, Archives of Rabbi Meir Ashkenazi (hereafter called AMA), presently in possession of Rabbi Joseph David Epstein. The author wishes to thank Rabbi Epstein for his invaluable assistance in providing these documents.

18. It is interesting to note that the next *mishnah* states as follows: "A priest precedes a levite, a levite an Israelite, an Israelite a bastard, a bastard a *Natin* [descendant of the Gibeonites], a Natin a proselyte, and a proselyte a freed slave. This applies when they are all [otherwise] equal, but if a bastard is learned in the Law [*talmid chacham*] and a High Priest is ignorant of the Law [*am ha–aretz*] the bastard that is learned in the Law precedes the High Priest that is ignorant of the Law." Although this *mishnah* applies to the bestowal of honors and not to rescue priority,

the evidence seems to indicate that it influenced some of the decisions made by the rabbis. Tractate *Horayot*, chap. 3, *mishnayot* 7–8; translation from *The Mishnah*, trans. Herbert Danby (Oxford, 1933), p. 466.

19. Cable of Rabbi Shmulewitz to Newman, March 28, 1941, YIVO Archives, file 49; letter of Dov Amster to Warhaftig, March 28, 1941, YVA, P–20, file 8.

20. Rabbi Epstein's appeal was relayed to Newman by Rabbi Chaim Shmulewitz, who had assumed the leadership of the Mir Yeshiva following the immigration to Palestine of his father–in–law, Rabbi Eliezer Yehuda Finkel. See the cable of Rabbi Shmulewitz to Newman, March 27, 1941, YIVO Archives, file 49.

21. Unsigned cable from Brooklyn, New York, to Newman, March 31, 1941, ibid.

22. List of those granted permits to Shanghai signed by Robertson, Deputy Police Commissioner, Shanghai, April 7, 1941, AMA.

23. Letter of Rabbi Ashkenazi to Robertson, April 7, 1941, AMA.

24. Cable of Rabbi Reuven Grazowski to Newman, April 9, 1941, YIVO Archives, file 49.

25. Letter of Josef Tugendhaft to Newman, April 5, 1941, Personal Papers of Frank Newman (hereafter called Newman Papers). The author wishes to thank Mr. Newman for his assistance.

26. Letter of Zerach Warhaftig to Rabbi Ashkenazi, April 11, 1941, AMA.

27. Cables of Rabbis Shkopf, Grazowski, Shmulewitz, and Zacks to Anshel Fink (*Zeirei Agudat Yisrael*) and *Vaad ha–Hatzala*, April 11, 1941, AVH. The term *Jontef* (holiday) refers to the fact that Passover began the next day.

28. Unsigned cable [of Rabbi Kotler] to Newman, April 15, 1941, YIVO, file 49.

29. Unsigned cable from Shanghai (from Rabbi Ashkenazi or his assistant, Josef Tugendhaft, who for reasons of economy never signed his cables) to Newman, April 16, 1941, ibid.

30. Unsigned cable from Shanghai (from Rabbi Ashkenazi or Tugendhaft) to Newman, April 17, 1941, ibid. The decision to provide assistance to the non–Orthodox refugees was apparently quite difficult for Rabbi Ashkenazi and Tugendhaft, who viewed the rescue of the Torah scholars as their primary objective and therefore were reluctant to allocate resources for the rescue of others. Thus following the arrival of the boat from Vladivostok, Tugendhaft wrote to Newman, "Although the other group [of non–Orthodox refugees] cost us money, we were forced in the interest of the *bnai Torah* who were to be saved to undertake to pay these cost ourselves." Letter of Tugendhaft to Newman, May 4, 1941, Newman Papers.

31. Ibid.; letter of M. Birman to Moses Beckelman, May 8, 1941, AJDC, Shanghai. Birman wrote that 52 persons arrived, but the passenger list had only 50 names. See "List of recent arrivals," May 2, 1941, AJDC, file 461.

32. Letter of Warhaftig to Tugendhaft, April 14, 1941, AMA.

33. Letter of Warhaftig to Rabbi Ashkenazi, April 11, 1941, AMA.

34. Letter of Stolowy and Mapinsky (of Jewcom) to Rabbi Ashkenazi, May 1, 1941, AMA.

35. Letter of Warhaftig to Rabbi Ashkenazi, April 11, 1941, AMA.

36. See the letter of the unified committee of *bnai Torah* in Kobe to Rabbi Ashkenazi, May 28, 1941, AMA.

37. Letter of unified committee of *bnai Torah* to Rabbi Ashkenazi, May 20, 1941, AMA.

38. Cable of Mayer Pantel to Newman, April 11, 1941, YIVO, file 49.

39. Letter of Frank Newman to Josef Tugendhaft, n.d., AMA.

40. Letter of Rabbi Szczedrowicki to Rabbi Ashkenazi, April 28, 1941, AMA. The appeal was apparently successful because Mintzberg, his wife, and Trokenheim were among those for whom permits had been obtained by mid–May 1941. See the list of Shanghai Permits Received Already...May 16, 1941," AVH.

41. Letter of Rabbi Yaphin to Rabbi Ashkenazi, April 30, 1941, AMA.

42. Letter of Rabbi Moshe Shatzkes to Rabbi Ashkenazi, May 2, 1941, AMA.

43. As was noted above in Chapter 2, most of the Polish refugee Torah scholars who had escaped to Lithuania shortly after the outbreak of World War II had done so for fear of the Communists, not the Nazis.

44. Letter of Rabbis Shatzkes, Yaphin, and Lifshitz to Rabbi Ashkenazi, May 6, 1941, AMA.

45. Letter of Rabbi Aharon Kiseleff (Harbin) to Rabbi Zacks, May 5, 1941, Papers of Asher Czeczyk.

46. This cumbersome method was apparently chosen because the refugees in Japan were in contact with the rabbis and students in Lithuania and had the most up–to–date information on their whereabouts.

47. Letter of Rabbi Shatzkes, Yaphin, and Lifshitz to Rabbi Ashkenazi, May 6, 1941, AMA.

48. Letter of Rabbi Yaphin to Tugendhaft, May 12, 1941; letter of Mayer Pantel to Rabbi Ashkenazi, May 12, 1941; letter of Rabbi Shatzkes to Rabbi Ashkenazi, May 13, 1941, all AMA. Letter of Mayer Pantel to Zerach Warhaftig, May 14, 1941, YVA, P–20, file 3. Several attempts were also made to help individuals whose names had already been submitted by Newman but for whom permits had still not been obtained. See, for example, the letter of Rabbi Shatzkes to Rabbi Ashkenazi, May 13, 1941, AMA.

49. Letter from Kobe (illegible signatures) to Rabbi Ashkenazi, May 14, 1941, AMA.

50. "Shanghai Permits Received Already...May 16, 1941," AVH.

51. Ibid.

52. Among those for whom permits were received were 97 individuals whose names had previously been submitted by the refugee committee in Japan. Letter of Josef Tugendhaft (for Rabbi Ashkenazi) to Mayer Pantel, May 16, 1941, AMA.

53. Letter of Rabbis Shatzkes, Yaphin, and Lifshitz to Rabbi Ashkenazi, May 6, 1941, AMA.

54. Letter of Josef Tugendhaft to Mayer Pantel, May 16, 1941, AMA.

55. Ibid.

56. Letter of the unified committee of *bnai Torah* to Rabbi Ashkenazi, May 20, 1941, AMA.

57. Ibid.

58. Ibid.

59. Letter of Pantel and Milner to Rabbi Ashkenazi, May 20, 1941, AMA.

60. Letter of Rabbi Grazowski to Rabbi Ashkenazi, enclosed in Pantel and Milner's letter of May 20 (see note 59), AMA.

61. There was a representative of the Telz Yeshiva on the unified committee, but he represented only the students who were Polish refugees, not those who were Lithuanian citizens.

62. Letter of Rabbi Baruch Sorotzkin to Rabbi Ashkenazi, answered May 26, 1941, AMA.

63. Ibid.

64. Cable of Rabbi Kotler to Rabbi Ashkenazi, May 27, 1941, AVH.

65. Cable of Rabbi Kotler to Model, May 27, 1941, AVH.

66. Unsigned letter on stationery of Rabbi Ashkenazi's yeshiva (Yeshivat Mizrach ha–Rachok be–Shanghai) to Moses Beckelman, May 27, 1941, AMA.

67. The committee's executive committee consisted of the representatives of the Kamenetz (two), Beit Yoseph Bialystok, Radin, and Kletzk yeshivot and the association of rabbis. The other members of the committee (referred to as "the council") were the representatives of the following yeshivot: Brisk, Volozhin, Slonim, Lublin, Torat Chesed Baranowitz, Telz (refugees only), Mir, Grodno, Ramailes, Lomza, Pinsk, Ostrow, and Mezritch, and representatives of the *kollelim* and Beit Yaakov teachers. Letter of the unified *bnai Torah* committee to Rabbi Ashkenazi, May 28, 1941, AMA.

68. According to Rabbis Mayer Pantel, Zvi Milner, and Asher Czeczyk, who were members of the executive committee of the *bnai Torah* committee, the Grodno Yeshiva was granted a larger share of the permits because up to that point none of the rabbis and students from that yeshiva had been able to leave the Soviet Union. Letter of Mayer Pantel, Zvi Milner, and Asher Czeczyk to the author, May 25, 1977.

69. Letter of the unified *bnai Torah* committee to Rabbi Ashkenazi, May 28, 1941, AMA.

70. Letter of Rabbis Mayer Pantel, Zvi Milner, and Asher Czeczyk to the author, May 25, 1977.

71. Testimony of Rabbi Asher Czeczyk, recorded by the author, July 5, 1977.

72. Cable of Rabbi Ashkenazi to Frank Newman, June 9, 1941, AVH.

73. Cable of Rabbi Ashkenazi to Frank Newman, June 14, 1941, AVH.

74. Cable of Rabbis Szczedrowicki, Krawiec, and Pantel to *Vaad ha–Hatzala*, June 16, 1941, AVH.

75. Cable of Rabbi Ashkenazi to Frank Newman, June 14, 1941; cable of Anatol Ponevejsky to Jewcom, June 16, 1941, both AVH.

76. Cable of Rabbi Ashkenazi to Frank Newman, June 21, 1941, AVH.

77. One of the factors that lent an added sense of urgency to the efforts to obtain permits was the news that the Soviets had deported to Siberia various individuals active in Jewish life in Lithuania. Under these circumstances, the leaders of the *Vaad ha–Hatzala* feared that the yeshivot would be deported as well. See the cable of Rabbi Aaron Kotler (on behalf of *Vaad ha–Hatzala*) to Rabbi Ashkenazi, June 21, 1941, AVH.

78. For example, Rabbi Efraim Zar was among those for whom permits had been obtained by mid–May. He never reached Shanghai, however, but was murdered in Vilna, apparently in July 1941. See "Shanghai Permits Received Already May 16, 1941 Intourist Shanghai Notified Intourist Moscow, Kaunas and Riga," and "Report Submitted by Rabbi M. Ashkenazi on Aid given to European Refugees in Shanghai by *Vaad Hatzala*," February 19, 1948, both AVH.

79. "Report submitted by Rabbi M. Ashkenazi on Aid given to European Refugees in Shanghai by *Vaad Hatzala*," February 19, 1948, AVH.

80. Jewcom Report, p.22a; "Mispar Pleetei ha–Milchama ha–Polaneeym she–Hayu be–Shanghai," September 15, 1942, Yad Vashem Archives, M–2, 373.

81. "Vaad Hahatzala," Budgeting Bulletin No. B–13 of the Council of Jewish Federations and Welfare Funds, February 1942, AJDC-VH.

Chapter 7

Visas to Canada

During the spring of 1941 *Vaad ha-Hatzala* did not confine its rescue efforts to obtaining Shanghai permits. As far as the rabbis were concerned, the primary purpose of the Shanghai documents was to enable the Torah scholars to leave the Soviet Union, but their arrival in Shanghai, or even in Kobe, was by no means considered a satisfactory long-term solution. Thus the search for more secure havens, preferably in the Western hemisphere, continued and intensified as the war went on.

Among the rescue schemes initiated by the *Vaad* during this period was an attempt to secure visas to several South American countries. In May 1941 Dr. Samuel Schmidt, who had visited the refugee scholars in Lithuania on the *Vaad's* behalf in early 1940, was sent to Paraguay, Brazil, and Argentina to attempt to obtain immigration visas for the rabbis and yeshiva students in Lithuania, Japan, and China.[1] On May 29, Schmidt cabled Rabbi Silver from Asuncion, the capital of Paraguay, that visas could be obtained there and that he recommended sending funds to start the process, although he clearly realized that an element of risk was involved.[2] Although subsequent reports in the Orthodox press announced that 400 visas to Paraguay had been obtained and that a group of rabbis and yeshiva students were preparing to leave Kobe for Asuncion,[3] the project was never realized. The refugee scholars did not immigrate to Paraguay[4] and the plan formulated for the establishment of what was touted to be the first yeshiva in South America[5] were shelved.

A more successful rescue initiative was carried out in Canada with the help of the Polish government-in-exile, which as early as

July 1940 had asked the Canadian government to admit 2,000 Polish refugees and 100 Jewish children for the duration of the war.[6] Despite the opposition of Fredrick C. Blair, the director of the Immigration Branch of the Department of Mines and Resources, which implemented immigration policy, the Canadian government decided on January 21, 1941, to admit for the duration of the war 1,000 refugees of Allied nationality (who at that time were in neutral countries) on the condition that their governments pay for their transportation and guarantee their maintenance while in Canada.[7] Blair, who had been in charge of Canadian immigration policy since 1935, made no secret of his aversion to Jews and his opposition to their entry to Canada.[8] He feared that the majority of them would not leave the country after the war. In his estimation, some 80 percent of the refugees in question were Jews "who would all settle in our cities and engage in the same occupations as are followed by Jewish residents in Canada" and that they had every intention of remaining in Canada. From his point of view, the government was better off trying to persuade the refugees to go to the Belgian Congo.[9] Despite Blair's protestations, however, the Canadian government, at the behest of the British, agreed to grant entry to the Allied refugees.[10]

Once the Canadian government agreed in principle to the admission of Allied nationals, various important technical questions arose, the most critical of which was the distribution of the visas. When the British proposal was originally submitted to the Canadian government, it was believed that the refugees would be Polish, Czech, and Dutch citizens. As it turned out, however, the overwhelming majority of the potential candidates were Polish Jews who had reached Japan and Portugal.[11] Since the government was intent on maintaining what Blair euphemistically referred to as "a reasonable racial balance"[12] (i.e., limiting the number of Jews), the practical circumstances of the operation posed considerable difficulties. Despite numerous appeals by Viktor Podoski, the Polish consul-general in Ottawa, regarding the plight of the Polish refugees in Portugal who were facing internment, and the need to move the refugees out of Japan so that additional families in Eastern Poland could escape deportation to Siberia,[13] the wheels of Canadian immigration bureaucracy moved extremely slowly. Blair carefully supervised the selection process and insisted that the Allied governments live up to their financial obligations in this respect; as long as that was the case, none of the refugees succeeded in entering Canada.[14] Thus despite the fact that the Cabinet had officially approved the entry of 79 Polish refugees from Japan on February 11, 1941,[15] it was months before any would actually reach Canadian soil.

In early spring 1941 the Polish government-in-exile was still having difficulties providing the financial guarantees and therefore turned to local Canadian Jewish organizations for assistance. On April 22, 1941, a delegation of the Federation of Polish Jews in Canada, headed by national executive secretary Mordechai Peters and his brother Shimon Petrushka, met with Dr. Tadeusz Brzezinski, the Polish consul in Montreal, who informed them that the Canadian government planned to allow the entry of 1,000 refugees who were Allied nationals. Brzezinski anticipated that most of those admitted would be Poles and was certain that about half of the Poles would be Jews. He explained that financial guarantees were required and asked his guests for their help.[16]

The Polish request was the first indication Canadian Jewry had that the government was contemplating the admission of Polish Jewish refugees to Canada, and it galvanized the Jewish community into action. In this regard the United Jewish Refugee and War Relief Agency, the Canadian affiliate of the Joint Distribution Committee and the relief arm of the Canadian Jewish Congress, was the key organization. Created in 1939 and directed by Montreal lawyer Saul Hayes, it represented Canadian Jewry on all refugee and relief matters vis-à-vis the Canadian authorities.[17] At the meeting with Brzezinski, the delegation from the Federation of Polish Jews indicated that the Jewish community would provide help regarding the necessary guarantees,[18] but in reality it had no authorization or power to do so. They immediately turned therefore to the United Jewish Refugee and War Relief Agency, with which they were affiliated, to provide the necessary assistance.[19]

At this point it was still not clear exactly what guarantees were being demanded by the Canadian authorities, and the United Jewish Refugee and War Relief agency set out first to determine the extent of the obligations required by the government.[20] At the same time, the news regarding the possible entry to Canada of Polish Jewish refugees spread throughout the Jewish community, which responded with offers of assistance and money.[21] Blair, who was wary of these developments, refused to meet with a delegation of the Jewish community on this matter and angrily wrote to Podoski that

Brzezinski had raised false expectations in the Jewish community. In addition, he made clear that only a small number of Jewish refugees in Japan would be admitted and that the guarantees had to be provided by governments, not private agencies. In his words, "Unless this is clearly kept in mind, a great deal of confusion is going to arise, which will make our administration of this problem much more difficult than it now is."[22]

Indeed, as the number of Polish Jewish refugees in Japan rose to over 1,500, Blair became increasingly fearful of attempts by Jewish organizations to facilitate the entry of all of them, a prospect he obviously found extremely unappealing. (When the Canadian authorities originally agreed to admit 1,000 Allied refugees then in neutral countries, they thought there were only 50 Polish refugees in Japan.) Thus on May 8, 1941, he warned Undersecretary of State for External Affairs N. A. Robertson "that a desperate effort is now being made in Japan to get the door open for these 1,500 Jewish refugees" and asked that every effort be made to ensure that the Canadian Legation in Tokyo not grant visas to individuals who did not meet the requirements set down by the immigration authorities.[23]

In the meantime, Canadian Jewish organizations, primarily the United Jewish Refugee and War Relief Agency and the Federation of Polish Jews in Canada, continued their efforts to determine the extent of the guarantees required by the government and to enlist community support. Hayes, Peters, and Petrushka met with Podoski and Brzezinski on May 6 and heard from the Polish consul-general that guarantees of $300 per year per refugee for two years were required. Since Podoski wanted to obtain entry visas for 100 Polish Jews from Japan, guarantees of $60,000 would be necessary. Podoski explained that Blair would not be satisfied with guarantees from private agencies, since in his experience they did not always live up to their obligations; therefore the guarantees would have to be given to the Polish government, which in turn would submit them to the Canadian immigration authorities. In addition to an unequivocal statement that the organizations would provide the maintenance guarantees, they would also have to submit documentation on the sources of their income in order to convince the Canadian government that the refugees would not become public charges following their arrival in Canada.[24]

At the meeting, Podoski also raised another serious potential problem involving the identity of the refugees. Blair had already told him that he expected the percentage of Jews in this group to be equivalent to the percentage of Jews in the Polish population, which was approximately 12%. Given the fact that the overwhelming majority of the Polish refugees in Japan were Jews, such a stipulation was patently unfair. Podoski promised that he would obtain visas for about 100 Jews, even though that figure constituted a much higher percentage of Polish citizens to whom Canadian entry permits would be granted.[25] Indeed, throughout the spring and summer of 1941 Podoski tried to increase the number of Polish refugees in general, and Jewish refugees in particular, who were admitted to Canada—an effort that brought him into direct conflict with Blair.

It was at this point, in early May 1941, that word reached yeshiva circles in New York that there was a possibility of obtaining entry visas to Canada for the refugee Polish rabbis and yeshiva students in Japan. The leaders of *Vaad ha-Hatzala*, led by Rabbi Avraham Kalmanowitz, immediately launched a campaign to ensure that as many rabbis and yeshiva students as possible would be granted visas. Their first step was to get the New York representatives of the various refugee Polish yeshivot to prepare affidavits indicating their readiness to provide whatever financial guarantees were necessary. (The *Vaad* also submitted its own affidavit, as did the *Agudat ha-Rabbanim*.[26]) In addition, a delegation of rabbis headed by Rabbi Kalmanowitz traveled to Ottawa and met with Podoski on May 12 to present their case for the admission of 102 persons—primarily rabbinical students and rabbis, but five female teachers and several children and wives as well.

Podoski's initial reaction was negative, since he and Blair had discussed the entry of 70 refugee scholars out of the 79 visa recipients who would initially be admitted. Rabbi Oscar Fasman of Ottawa, who conducted the negotiations with the Polish consul on behalf of the rabbis, attempted to convince Podoski to submit the list anyway, stressing the necessity of saving religious refugees, who were likely to suffer the most if deported by the Japanese back to the Soviet Union. Podoski reluctantly agreed, although he doubted whether Blair would accept the list in its entirety. In his opinion, the rabbis were better off sending all the names to the Polish ambassador in Tokyo. Fasman was opposed to such an idea, because he feared that it was designed to enable Podoski's colleagues in Japan "to make a few dollars" (from bribes,[27] a clear-cut indication that he did not trust the Polish consul's integrity and motives).

The actual list was presented to Podoski two days after the meeting, in the wake of lengthy consultations among the rabbis. Special efforts were made to include rabbis and students from all the various yeshivot, since it was clear that not all the refugee scholars could be brought to Canada. In fact, one of Rabbi Kalmanowitz's main fears was that if the entire list of 102 was not accepted, it was possible that rabbis or students from certain yeshivot would be rescued, because the list was arranged in alphabetical order (not by institution). Under such circumstances, Kalmanowitz contemplated submitting separate lists for each yeshiva.[28]

The list that Fasman submitted to Podoski was not the only one presented to the Polish consul at this time. On May 14, two days after Podoski met with the rabbis, Mordechai Peters of the Federation of Polish Jews in Canada sent him a list of 133 Polish Jewish refugees in Japan. Noting that the Polish consul had already accepted Peters' contention that prominent persons deserved special consideration, he urged Podoski to accept this entire list since "It is of the utmost importance for Jewish religious and cultural life that these people be saved." The largest representation on the list were rabbinical students (76), with places also allotted for rabbis (2), teachers (9), journalists (4), communal leaders (2), and others. Five of the candidates had relatives in Canada and were therefore also included on the list.[29] This list was, in fact, almost identical to the one presented by the rabbis, with the addition of about thirty non-Orthodox refugees chosen by the Federation of Polish Jews in Canada. In that respect, the rabbis had the unqualified support of the Federation which backed their demand that rabbis and yeshiva students be accorded priority in the granting of Canadian visas.

If these lists had been submitted by Podoski and accepted by Blair, perhaps the selection process would have gone smoothly, but that was not the case. On May 15 Podoski cabled Peters that he could only accept a list of 70 persons, and the UJRWRA, which had been approached by Kalmanowitz to give official authorization to the rabbis' list, put pressure on the Federation of Polish Jews to cooperate in compiling a different list. The Federation, which was an affiliate of the UJRWRA, apparently did not have much choice in the matter; as a result, Peters was forced to write to Podoski to cancel his original list of 133 and to turn the choice of visa candidates over to the Polish embassy in Tokyo and the local Jewish committee. Even worse from the rabbis' perspective was the decision made by a joint committee of the UJRWRA and the Federation of Polish Jews that preference would not be given to Torah scholars, but rather to those who would otherwise be stranded without an emigration destination and, where possible, to those with relatives and friends in Canada.[30]

To further complicate matters, Podoski informed Peters and Fasman that Polish Ambassador to Japan Romer now expected about 500 non-Jewish Polish refugees to apply for immigration to Canada, so he could hope for only 70 visas for all categories of Jews. Fasman, who was heartbroken over this turn of events, blamed Petrushka for convincing Rabbi Kalmanowitz to try to get the approval of the UJRWRA for the rabbis' list. Fasman had originally told him to immediately submit the names to Podoski, but Kalmanowitz had followed Petrushka's advice, since the latter never imagined that the UJRWRA could so easily overrule the decision of the Federation of Polish Jews. In Fasman's words, "Rabbi K. may not be as ethical as you would wish, but he is a prophet by virtue of intelligence and experience."[31] Thus, ironically, when the *Vaad* chose to operate together with the official community organizations, it was forced to pay a heavy price.

These negative developments did not deter the *Vaad* and its local supporters, who continued their efforts to have as many rabbis and yeshiva students as possible admitted to Canada. On May 18 Rabbi Fasman, who led the local efforts upon Rabbi Kalmanowitz's departure from Ottawa, wrote to Saul Hayes to try to convince him to allocate all the 70 Canadian visas to refugee Torah scholars. After asserting that the rabbis and students had no realistic hope of entering the United States (an argument Hayes used to limit the number of visas allotted to the group), Fasman tackled the critical issue of rescue priority head-on. In his words:

> The seventy embody a wealth of Jewish sacred learning, the like of which can no longer be duplicated, now that European Yeshivoth are closed. In these people we have that intense tradition of Torah which buoyed up the spirit of Israel. Thus, we are saving not only people, but a holy culture which cannot be otherwise preserved. When the United States admitted Einstein, and not a million other very honest and good people who asked for admission, the principle was the same. It is cer-

tainly horrible to save only a few, but when one is faced with
a problem of so ghastly a nature he must find the courage to
rescue what is most irreplaceable.

Fasman, moreover, did not limit himself to ideological arguments.
He also had some practical reasons. He noted that Podoski believed
that Blair would prefer the refugee scholars for three reasons. They
were not suspected of Communists leanings, they were likely eventually to leave Canada for other destinations, and their presence in
the country would attract American philanthropy. Fasman even suggested that the *Agudat ha-Rabbanim* provide the financial guarantees
to the Canadian government instead of the UJRWRA.[32]

Hayes, needless to say, never accepted this proposal, which in
effect would have robbed his organization of any say in determining
the identity of the prospective immigrants to Canada and other
related matters. He did however, meet with Rabbi Kalmanowitz,
Fasman, Petrushka, Peters, and several others to work out a viable
compromise which could be presented by the Jewish community to
the Polish authorities. By this point it was clear to the Jewish leaders that only 70 Canadian visas were available for Polish refugees in
Japan and therefore a list was compiled which included 50 refugee
scholars and 20 others.

In the meantime, Blair notified Podoski that the Canadian government considered the Poles responsible for the financial guarantees, that the government was willing to admit 68 Polish refugees
who were to be recommended by the local Polish Embassy in Japan,
and that appropriate instructions would be cabled to the Canadian
Chargé d'Affaires in Tokyo.[33] To be on the safe side, the Federation
of Polish Jews on May 21 cabled the Polish embassy in Tokyo two
lists, one of 70 persons as agreed upon with Podoski, and an additional list of 13 names in case any of the original list were rejected
for any reason by the Canadian authorities. Four days later, the
Federation cabled 12 more names to the Polish embassy in Tokyo for
the same reason.[34]

Throughout this period, it should be noted, *Vaad ha-Hatzala*
actively cooperated with the Federation of Polish Jews,[35] with
whom they obviously had much more in common than with the
leaders of the United Jewish Refugee and War Relief Agency. The latter were particularly perturbed by the efforts of the Federation to
handle refugee affairs, which they considered their exclusive

domain. In correspondence, Saul Hayes wrote to his colleagues that they will "have to clip its [the Federation's] wings as we have already done when it enters this work," and he bitterly complained "that at least one-quarter of my time is spent on my own constructive work and the balance repairing the damages done by others, which, if proper consultation had been made in the beginning would have obviated illogical and foolish situations."[36]

In this respect, the *Vaad's* active involvement was hardly welcomed by the UJRWRA, which viewed the rabbis' activities as superfluous interference causing more damage than good.[37] Given that attitude, it is hardly surprising that the *Vaad* continued its independent efforts in Canada, cooperating whenever possible with the Federation of Polish Jews. Its relationship with the UJRWRA was analogous to the *Vaad's* troublesome relationship with the Joint Distribution Committee. In both cases, *Vaad ha-Hatzala's* efforts to obtain a maximum number of visas and assistance for refugee rabbis and yeshiva students ran counter to the policy of the organized Jewish community and led to friction between the two groups.

In the meantime, Polish Consul-General Viktor Podoski was continuing his efforts to increase the number of Polish refugees admitted to Canada. On May 26 he wrote to Blair, offering to provide financial guarantees for 41 additional Polish citizens stranded in Japan. Podoski specifically noted the plight of the refugee rabbis and yeshiva students and asked the director of the Immigration Branch to increase the number of Polish refugees to be admitted from 79 to 120.[38] Blair acceded to the request, but not for humanitarian reasons. It seems that the Canadian chargé in Tokyo had, despite Blair's best efforts to reduce the number of refugees admitted, granted visas to more than 79 Polish refugees, and consequently it was decided to raise the figure of those admitted to 120 (to cover those who had already arrived and those who had already set out).[39]

In describing the situation, Blair left nothing to the imagination in terms of his response to the efforts of *Vaad ha-Hatzala* and others to facilitate the entry to Canada of Polish-Jewish refugees. After receiving several cables regarding this matter which were intercepted and brought to his attention by Canadian censorship, Blair wrote to Stone of the Ministry of External Affairs:

> This correspondence reminds me a good deal of what I have seen on a farm at hog feeding time when they are all trying to

get their feet into the trough. It is perfectly evident from what we have now on file that a group of Jewish people in the United States are trying to get a lot of rabbinical students into this country who were refused admission to the United States and they are very anxious to shove certain ones forward to be sure that they will get into this list.[40]

This clearly explains Blair's request that Podoski not inform the Jewish organizations of the addition of 41 more visas, lest "this would be regarded as an evidence that the door can be shoved open if they push hard enough,"[41] and lest his department be subjected to increased pressure.

In early June the delicate relations between the local Jewish groups dealing with this matter became even more strained as Saul Hayes attempted to assert UJRWRA hegemony. In a letter to Podoski, he told the Polish consul that his organization was the sole agency that could provide the financial guarantees and, as such, demanded to be fully apprised of all the relevant details. While the Federation of Polish Jews was an affiliated agency, which as far as the UJRWRA was concerned could do exploratory work, it was not a refugee organization and its decisions in financial matters were certainly not binding on Canadian Jewry.[42]

Podoski, who had enough trouble dealing with Blair, let alone being involved in internal Jewish squabbles, made clear to Hayes that he wanted no part of the dispute. At the same time, however, he did insist that Hayes send him an unequivocal undertaking to provide financial guarantees for "seventy Jewish refugees now in Japan, plus such additional numbers as may be admitted later."[43] Hayes immediately sent Podoski a letter which included the requested guarantees,[44] but the lack of unity among the Canadian Jewish organizations continued to plague their well-intentioned efforts. The Federation of Polish Jews regarded the efforts to obtain Canadian visas for Polish refugees as its area of interest and expertise, while the UJRWRA refused to allow them to dominate or even play a leading role in the project.[45] Given the close cooperation between the *Vaad ha-Hatzala* and the former in choosing the prospective visa recipients, it was obvious which side the rabbis supported.[46]

By mid-June 1941 the situation had become even more complicated. Despite the efforts of the *Vaad* and the Federation of Polish

Jews to obtain the maximum number of Canadian visas for the Torah scholars, no rabbis or yeshiva students were among the 79 Polish citizens who were granted entry to Canada. The Japanese authorities were now threatening to deport to Shanghai all the refugees who could not emigrate, a step the *Vaad* feared would seriously jeopardize the refugee scholars. With the United States practically off limits to the rabbis and yeshiva students because of a new American regulation barring the entry of any refugees who had first-degree relatives living under Nazi occupation, it became even more urgent to obtain Canadian visas.[47] Given Blair's persistent efforts to keep the number of Jewish refugees admitted to a minimum[48] and the internal squabbles in the local Jewish community,[49] the rabbis and their Canadian allies faced a difficult uphill battle.

In the meantime, the UJRWRA and the Federation of Polish Jews took steps to solve their differences and reach a *modus vivendi* which would enable them to work together. On June 22, 1941, Canadian Jewish Congress President Sam Bronfman, Lazarus Phillips, and Saul Hayes met with Peters and Wolofsky of the Federation at the latter's home and agreed to establish a special committee composed of two representatives each from the Central and Eastern regions of the Canadian Jewish Congress, one representative from its Western region, and two persons designated by the Federation of Polish Jews, to handle the negotiations regarding the Polish refugees. Thus both organizations would continue to play an active role on the issue but would be able to do so together. Podoski, whose complaints regarding the confusion caused by the strife between the organizations were a major factor in bringing about the agreement, was duly informed of this development by both sides,[50] and he immediately renewed his efforts to increase the number of Polish refugees from Japan to Canada.

On June 26 he wrote to Blair asking for 80 additional visas for Polish refugees in Japan, basing his request on the fact that not a single rabbi or yeshiva student had received a visa. According to Podoski, his recommendations on behalf of the scholars reached the Polish Ambassador in Tokyo after all the visas had already been distributed by Canadian Chargé d'Affaires McGreer to other persons. He therefore asked Blair to allot 80 visas specifically for Polish rabbis and yeshiva students in Japan out of the original allotment of 1,000 visas which the Canadian government had set aside for Allied nationals. Knowing that Blair wanted to disqualify the prospective refugees by claiming that they had no real interest in coming to Canada but rather sought to enter the country to facilitate their subsequent move to the United States, Podoski assured the Director of Immigration that that was not the case and specifically undertook to guarantee the maintenance of the refugee scholars. He also assured him that he had already obtained an extension for their stay in Kobe from the local Japanese ambassador, who had promised Podoski that the refugees would not be deported from Japan until July 25, 1941, at the earliest.[51]

The UJRWRA, it should be noted, was by this point also in favor of granting priority to at least a token number of rabbis and yeshiva students. Miffed by the fact that none of those recommended for entry to Canada by the Canadian Jewish organizations had been granted visas, they attempted via Ignacy Schwarzbart, the Jewish representative in the Polish parliament-in-exile in London, to induce the Polish government to apply pressure on its embassy in Japan to accept those chosen by the UJRWRA together with the Federation of Polish Jews. This included a token number of rabbis and yeshiva students, whose total exclusion until now was, in Hayes's view, "a serious situation in view of the fact that a section of our population is anxious to have a number proceed to Canada and the plight of these in Japan will be tragically serious if they are not moved."[52]

Blair, needless to say, was hardly impressed by the newfound unity in the Jewish community. He maintained his staunch opposition to the entry of additional Jewish refugees who, in his opinion, would have much preferred to immigrate to the United States and who indeed made "frantic efforts" to do so but were unsuccessful. In his words: "...we have come to the conclusion rightly or wrongly that the interest in Canada of these rabbinical students arises only because they have failed to get into the United States. The Jewish population of this country is not sufficient to absorb a group of 80 rabbis or rabbinical students and I sincerely regret after going into the matter as carefully as we can, we have reached the conclusion that this movement cannot be approved."[53]

In the wake of Blair's refusal to grant the visas, Podoski immediately approached Dr. H. L. Keenleyside, Assistant Undersecretary of State for External Affairs, who agreed to speak to the Director of Immigration and promised a favorable result. Two days later, on July 11, the Polish consul hosted Hayes, Wolofsky, Petrushka, and Peters at the consulate to discuss the issue and seek ways to convince the

Canadian government to accede to his request regarding the refugee Torah scholars. In his opinion, the key factor was to persuade the authorities that under no circumstances would the refugees become public charges. To achieve that end, he suggested that the UJRWRA formally declare its willingness to establish a special center in Montreal for the refugee yeshiva students.[54]

A letter along these general lines was indeed presented, but other lobbying efforts were also made. On July 24, for example, Peters took Elya Chazan, a Polish refugee yeshiva student who had arrived in Montreal from Japan on his way to the United States only a day previously, to meet with Dr. Keenleyside in Ottawa. The latter had asked to meet what Peters referred to as "a specimen of a yeshiva Bochur," and Chazan's arrival in Canada was therefore extremely opportune. The meeting apparently went very well, because the senior Canadian official not only told Peters that both he and Acting Undersecretary of State for External Affairs Robertson did not share Blair's opposition to the entry of the refugee rabbis and yeshiva students, but that the two of them would do their utmost to see that they were admitted to Canada.[55]

This was particularly encouraging news in view of the alarming cables received from Japan that week by various Orthodox organizations in the United States as well as the Federation of Polish Jews in Canada.[56] According to the refugees, they could all obtain visas to the British dominions (Canada, Australia, and South Africa) through the local Polish embassy, if the Joint Distribution Committee provided the necessary financial guarantees for their maintenance.[57] Upon receipt of this news, the leaders of *Vaad ha-Hatzala* immediately enlisted the entire Orthodox community to apply pressure on the JDC. At a meeting on July 28 at the Hotel Pennsylvania in New York, representatives of all the major Orthodox organizations supported the *Vaad's* demand that the JDC facilitate the emigration of the refugee Torah scholars. (Among those in attendance were representatives of *Agudat ha-Rabbanim*, *Agudat Anshei Chesed Chabad*, Agudath Israel Youth Council of America, Central Organization of Agudath Israel of America, Central Relief Committee, *Hapoel Ha-Mizrachi* of America, Mizrachi Organization of America, National Council of Young Israel, Union of Chassidic Rabbis of America, Union of Orthodox Jewish Congregations of the United States, and *Vaad ha-Rabbanim* of New York.) In a memorandum subsequently submitted to the JDC, the organizations stressed that from their point of view the rescue of the Torah scholars was "the primary duty" of the American Jewish relief organization. At the same time they promised that they would do "all in their power to fully aid, maintain and lighten the responsibilities of the Joint Distribution Committee as soon as the Talmudical students, Deans and Rabbis reach the shores of the continent."[58]

These efforts obviously had some effect. On July 31 Sam Bronfman, who a day earlier had asked to meet the Minister of Mines and Resources Thomas Crerar to discuss the entire range of problems regarding Jewish immigration to Canada,[59] requested that the meeting deal exclusively with the plight of the refugee rabbis and yeshiva students. Bronfman explained that he sought to discuss "the immediate possibility of offering these learned people sanctuary in Canada for the duration of the war" since according to the information he had just received, "the lives of many Rabbis and seminary students are in jeopardy and unless asylum is offered to them at once their fate will beggar description."[60] Five days later Robertson and Keenleyside met with Blair to discuss the issue, but the latter stubbornly resisted their suggestion that 80 of these scholars be admitted, claiming that "it was an old habit on the part of these people to ask for a number which was far below the number they hoped to get, and once they got the door open they would never be content until they got the whole group in which we know is true from other sources." Faced with a stalemate, the officials agreed to defer a decision until Crerar met with a Jewish delegation three days later.[61]

On August 8, 1941, Crerar and Blair met with a high-level delegation of Jewish representatives who sought to influence the government to allow the entry of additional Jewish refugees to Canada. The first item on the agenda was the proposal to admit 80 refugee rabbis and yeshiva students. As usual, Blair tried his best to sabotage the proposal by various means, but this time he failed. After a fairly lengthy discussion, Crerar agreed that if the Polish consul-general had indeed promised that the refugee scholars would be admitted and if such a list as well as appropriate guarantees were provided, the Canadian government could increase the number of visas to 200 and thereby offer a haven to 80 rabbis and yeshiva students. Efforts by members of the delegation to increase this number further to include all the Torah scholars stranded in Japan were not successful; even delegation members acknowledged that there were limits beyond which it was not reasonable to ask for government assistance.[62]

Once government approval had been obtained for the 80 scholars, a race against time began to implement the decision. Within several days, a list of 80 rabbis and yeshiva students and 14 alternates was compiled by the leading *roshei yeshiva* affiliated with the *Vaad ha-Hatzala* and was submitted to the Polish ambassador in Tokyo with the approval of the Federation of Polish Jews and UJRWRA.[63] Blair, in the meantime, maintained a vigilant guard to ensure that the visas were allocated only to bona fide rabbis and yeshiva students and that no one who was still on the waiting list to enter the United States would be admitted. He also made note of every piece of information regarding Jewish refugees who served as spies (in the Far East and elsewhere) that might strengthen his case against their entry.[64] It was due to Blair's obvious opposition and stringent application of the regulations that both the *Vaad ha-Hatzala* and the *Agudat ha-Rabbanim* submitted affidavits in late August to Moses Leavitt of the JDC, Hayes, and Peters to confirm that all the visa recipients were Torah scholars who were personally known to the heads of the *Vaad*, were pro-Allies, anti-fascist, planned to remain in Canada for the duration of the war, and had no intention of seeking admission elsewhere.[65]

Once such bureaucratic obstacles had been surmounted, there were still serious technical problems to overcome. In regard to the financial guarantees, the *Vaad* and yeshiva circles had undertaken to cover maintenance costs, while the JDC was going to cover the transportation expenses of those whose relatives were unable to pay.[66] At this point, however, the main problem was transportation. By late August 1941 many of the Polish refugees in Japan had been deported to Shanghai, but there were no boats sailing directly from the Chinese port to Canada.[67] Thus during the final week of August and the initial weeks of September, M. Birman, who headed the Shanghai branch of HICEM,[68] which handled the transportation arrangements on behalf of the JDC, spent countless hours attempting to come up with the quickest and safest route. One of the routes considered was via Batavia, Indonesia, and Australia. Another was via the United States. In each case, the appropriate transit visas had to be obtained as well as tickets.[69]

By mid-September 1941 it became clear that the best route to travel was via the United States. Transit visas were obtained there and cabled to Shanghai, and reservations for an initial group of 41 were made aboard the SS *President Pierce*, which was scheduled to sail at the end of September. The problem was, however, that in 1941 Yom Kippur was on October 1, and that meant that the refugee scholars might have to fast two whole days instead of one, since their route crossed the International Date Line. As a result, 16 of the 41 prospective passengers announced categorically that they refused to sail on *President Pierce*.[70] The members of this group were all students of the Mir Yeshiva, whereas most of those who agreed to sail despite the Yom Kippur problem were students of other yeshivot.

According to HICEM director Birman, while the rabbis and students who agreed to sail were certainly not any less religious than those from Mir, the latter adopted a "firm and independent attitude" since they were the recipients of special aid from American Jewish Orthodox organizations and were not dependent on local assistance. The fact that both Canadian visas and U.S. transit visas had been obtained for them, an almost unheard-of phenomenon in those days, also strengthened their independent stance. The students from Kletzk, Lublin, Lubavitch, Slabodka and Telz, on the other hand, were totally dependent on assistance from the local relief committees and they therefore "eagerly seized the opportunity to leave our city, deciding at the same time to keep two days Yom Kippur on the steamer."

Thus on September 30, 1941, at 4:20 A.M., the SS *President Pierce* set out from Shanghai to San Francisco with 29 recipients of the Canadian visas set aside for Polish refugee rabbis and yeshiva students. In effect, the group consisted of 4 rabbis (aged 25–61), 23 students (aged 17–33, mostly from yeshivot other than Mir), and the widow and son of renowned Torah scholar "the Chofetz Chaim"[71] (Rabbi Yisrael Meier Kagan, who headed the Radin Yeshiva and was world famous for his halachic treatises). The trip to the United States was without incident, and the group traveled by train from San Francisco to Canada, entering at Sarnia Port on October 23, 1941.[72]

In the meantime 51 refugee rabbis and yeshiva students who possessed Canadian visas were still in Shanghai and their emigration prospects were getting slimmer by the day. By October the only shipping companies operating out of Shanghai were the Java China Line and the American President liners. The former, which sailed only as far as Australia, refused to sell tickets to holders of Canadian visas unless they had in hand tickets from Australia to Canada— which were practically impossible to obtain since there was no regular service between the two countries—or had a guarantee from an Australian or American organization for the full cost of the tickets. The only other way to purchase tickets from them was to deposit $200 per passenger,[73] which, given the erratic sailing schedule, was a calculated risk. As far as the American line was concerned, their next boat was only scheduled to sail from Shanghai at the end of October or beginning of November and they refused to sell HICEM third-class tickets, which meant that the transportation expenses would be much higher than expected.[74] Under these circumstances, every possible ship and route were explored, but problems mounted daily as U.S.–Japanese relations deteriorated.[75]

In early November 1941 the situation looked very bleak. American-bound steamers no longer entered Shanghai and it was almost impossible to book passage on those leaving from Manila, because the dates of departure were not known far enough in advance to enable the refugees to arrive in the Philippines on time. To further complicate matters, there were no third-class tickets available on these boats, and it was extremely difficult to obtain even second-class tickets. In addition, for the refugees to be able to travel from Manila, they had to obtain transit visas for both the Philippines and the United States. Yet despite these difficulties, HICEM hoped to send them to the Philippines as quickly as possible in the hope that they would ultimately be able to reach Canada from the port.[76] Those plans never materialized, however, and so despite subsequent efforts by Rabbi Kalmanowitz, *Vaad ha-Hatzala*,[77] and others, the 51 refugee rabbis and yeshiva students who possessed Canadian visas were forced to remain in Shanghai for the duration of the war.

Although only a relatively small fraction of the Polish refugee Torah scholars stranded in the Far East were brought to Canada in the fall of 1941, the rescue of the 29 rabbis and yeshiva students constituted an important victory of the *Vaad ha-Hatzala*. Once again, they had proven the validity of their *raison d'être*. Indeed, without their active involvement as a lobby on behalf of the Torah scholars, it is highly unlikely that any would have been admitted to Canada. And while it is true that the refugees in Shanghai were not living under Nazi occupation, nor were they subjected to systematic annihilation, the conditions under Japanese rule were quite harsh, with consequent limited loss of life. At the same time, the *Vaad* could never have achieved even partial success without the support of the

local established Jewish community. In this respect, their cooperation with the Federation of Polish Jews in Canada was a key factor,
since the latter played an important role in convincing the UJRWRA
to support the *Vaad's* demands that rabbis and yeshiva students be
accorded priority. Had the *Vaad*, with the active assistance of the
Federation of Polish Jews, not insisted on adopting such a policy, it
is most likely that no refugee rabbis or yeshiva students would have
been admitted to Canada in 1941.

Notes

1. "Rabbi Silver at Shevuoth Services," *Every Friday*, May 30, 1941, p. 2; letter attest-
ing to the fact that Dr. Schmidt was proceeding to Paraguay and other South
American countries as a representative of the Union of Orthodox Rabbis of the
United States and Canada, May 16, 1941, AAH.
2. Cable of Schmidt to Rabbi Silver, May 29, 1941, Silver Archives.
3. "Paraguay Issues Yeshiva Visas," *Orthodox Tribune*, August, 1941, p. 1.
4. According to the statistics issued by Jewcom, only two Polish refugees emigrated
to Paraguay. Kobe Report, p. 22b.
5. "Paraguay Opens Doors To 400 Refugees," *Orthodox Youth*, August 1941, p. 1. The
reason the project was dropped is not entirely clear. We do know that despite the
fact that visas were available for at least all the students of the Mir Yeshiva, Rabbi
Kalmanowitz opposed the idea. Cable of Rabbi Chaim Shmulewitz to Rabbi Eliezer
Finkel, July 26, 1941, AYHH, file 8.
6. Irving Abella and Harold Troper, *None Is Too Many*: *Canada And The Jews of Europe
1933–1948* (Toronto, 1982), p. 77.
7. Memorandum of Blair to Crerar, February 11, 1941; cable of Canadian Secretary
of State for External Affairs to Canadian Charge d'Affairs, Tokyo, March 8, 1941,
both Canadian National Archives (hereafter called CNA), RG 76, Vol. 441, file
673931.
8. On Blair's anti–Semitism and staunch opposition to the entry of Jews to Canada
see *None Is Too Many*, pp. 7–8, 19–28, 54–56.
9. Ibid, p. 80; Blair to Crerar, February 11, 1941, CNA, RG 76, Vol. 441, file 673931.
10. Letter of Acting Undersecretary for External Affairs N. A. Roberton to Viktor
Podoski, March 14, 1941, ibid.
11. Letter of Mordechai Peters (Federation of Polish Jews in Canada) to Lazarus
Phillips, April 25, 1941, Archives of the Canadian Jewish Congress. (Hereafter called
ACJC).
12. Letter of Blair to Podoski, March 26, 1941, ibid.
13. Letters of Podoski to Blair and Robertson, February 19, 1941; letter of Podoski
to Robertson, April 19, 1941; cable of Secretary of State for External Affairs to High
Commissioner for Canada (London), April 23, 1941, all ibid.; Abella and Troper,
None Is Too Many, p. 81.
14. Blair memorandum to Crerar, April 23, 1941, CNA, RG 76, Vol. 441, file 673931.
15. Letter of A. Henry, Secretary to the Cabinet War Committee, to Blair, February
14, 1941, ibid.

16. Letter of Peters to Phillips, April 25, 1941, ACJC; diary of Saul Hayes, entry for April 29, 1941, ACJC, files of the United Jewish Refugee and War Relief Agency (hereafter called UJRWRA), file 174.

17. With the ascension of Samuel Bronfman to the presidency of the Canadian Jewish Congress in January 1939, that organization began to play a much more active role in the efforts to enable the entry of Jewish refugees to Canada. See Abella and Troper, *None Is Too Many*, p. 57.

18. Letter of Mordechai Peters to Lazarus Phillips, April 25, 1941, ACJC.

19. Saul Hayes diary, April 29, 1941, ACJC, UJRWRA file 174.

20. Ibid., entries of April 29, May 1 and 2, 1941.

21. Abella and Troper, *None Is Too Many*, p. 82.

22. Letter of Blair to Podoski, May 2, 1941, CNA, RG 76, Vol. 441, file 673931.

23. Letter of Blair to Robertson, May 8, 1941, ibid.

24. Saul Hayes diary, May 6, 1941, ACJC, UJRWRA file 174.

25. "Memorandum [of Federation of Polish Jews in Canada] Regarding Permission to Enter Canada of Polish–Jewish Refugees From Japan and Elsewhere," May 6, 1941, ACJC, UJRWRA file 174. At this point, Podoski thought that about 500 Polish refugees from Japan would be brought to Canada. See his letter to Peters, May 8, 1941, ibid.

26. See, for example, the affidavit signed by Alex Weisfogel on behalf of the Kamenetz Yeshiva, May 8, 1941, the undated affidavit of Rabbi Jacob Karlinsky on behalf of the Emergency Committee for War Torn Yeshivoth, and the affidavit of Rabbis Y. H. Rosenberg and Y. L. Seltzer on behalf of the Union of Orthodox Rabbis of the United States and Canada, May 8, 1941, all ACJC.

27. Letter of Rabbi Oscar Fasman to Mordechai Peters; letter of Rabbi Kalmanovitz to Simcha Petrushka, both May 14, 1941, ACJC.

28. Letter of Rabbi Kalmanowitz to Petrushka, May 14, 1941, ACJC.

29. Letter of Peters to Podoski, May 14, 1941, ACJC.

30. Letter of Peters to Podoski, May 15, 1941; Saul Hayes diary, May 15, 1941, both ACJC, UJRWRA file 174; letter of Rabbi Fasman to Petrushka, May 16, 1941, ACJC.

31. Letter of Fasman to Petrushka, May 16, 1941, ACJC.

32. Letter of Fasman to Hayes, May 18, 1941, ACJC, UJRWRA file 174.

33. In reality, the number of available visas was only 68, since 11 Polish refugees had already arrived in Canada from Japan and they were reduced from the original allotment of 79, but Jewish leaders still thought the number of available visas was 70, which was the figure quoted by Podoski in correspondence with Peters. Letter of Blair to Podoski, May 19, ACJC; letter of Secretary of State for External Affairs to the Canadian Charge in Tokyo, May 20, 1941, CNA, RG 76, Vol. 441, file 673931; Saul Hayes diary, May 20, 1941, ACJC, UJRWRA file 174; letter of Peters to Podoski, May 20, 1941, ACJC; letter of Podoski to Peters, ACJC, UJRWRA file 174.

34. Cables of Federation of Polish Jews to Polish Embassy, Tokyo, May 21 and 25, 1941, CNA, RG 76, Vol. 441, file 673931.

35. Cable of Rabbi Kalmanowitz to Rabbi Szmulewitz, May 25, 1941, ACJC.

36. Memo of Hayes to L. Rosenberg, May 22, 1941, ACJC, UJRWRA file 174.

37. Letter of Hayes to R. L. Zion, May 28, 1941, ibid.

38. Urgent letter of Podoski to Blair, May 26, 1941, ACJC.

39. Letter of Blair to Robertson, May 27, 1941, CNA, RG 76, Vol. 441, file 673931.

40. Letter of Blair to Stone, May 28, 1941, ibid.
41. Letter of Blair to Podoski, May 28, 1941, ibid.
42. Letter of Hayes to Podoski, June 3, 1941, ACJC, UJRWRA file 174.
43. Letter of Podoski to Hayes, June 4, 1941, ibid.
44. Letter of Hayes to Podoski, June 5, 1941, ibid.
45. Letter of Peters to Podoski, June 6, 1941; letter of Hayes to Sam Bronfman, June 7, 1941, both ACJC, UJRWRA file 174.
46. Saul Hayes diary, June 6, 1941, ibid.
47. Letter of Podoski to Blair, June 26, 1941, CNA, RG 76, Vol. 441, file 673931; cable of Jewcom to Jewish Immigrant Aid Society, June 17, 1941; cable of Union of Orthodox Rabbis and Rabbi Kalmanowitz to Federation of Polish Jews, June 18, 1941, both ACJC.
48. See, for example, letter of Blair to Robertson, June 11, 1941; letter of Blair to Podoski, June 13, 1941, both CNA, RG 76, Vol. 441, file 673931.
49. Memorandum of UJRWRA by Saul Hayes, June 18, 1941, ACJC, UJRWRA file 174.
50. Saul Hayes diary, June 22, 1941; letter of Peters to Podoski, June 24, 1941; letter of Hayes to Podoski, June 26, 1941, all ACJC, UJRWRA file 174.
51. Letter of Podoski to Blair, June 26, 1941, CNA, RG 76, Vol. 441, file 673931.
52. Memo of Saul Hayes to National Officers regarding the present status of the Polish Jewish Refugee Movement , July 9, 1941, ACJC, UJRWRA file 174.
53. Letter of Blair to Podoski, July 8, 1941, CNA, RG 76, Vol. 441, file 673931.
54. Letter of Peters to Lazarus Phillips, July 23, 1941, ACJC.
55. Letter of Peters to Phillips, July 30, 1941, ibid.
56. See, for example, cable of Jewcom (Kobe) to Federation of Polish Jews, June 24, 1941, ibid.; cable of Union Rabbis Yeshivas Rabbi Kalisz to Michael Tress and Meier Schenkolewski of Agudat Yisrael Youth, July 25, 1941, AAYA, file 3–6–1.
57. Cable of Union Rabbis Yeshivas Rabbi Kalisz to the *Agudat Ha–Rabbnim*, July 24, 1941, AAH.
58. Memorandum to the Joint Distribution Committee, July 29, 1941, Silver Archives.
59. Memorandum by Sam Bronfman to Thomas Crerar, July 30, 1941, CNA, RG 76, Vol. 441, file 673931.
60. Letter of Bronfman to Crerar, July 31, 1941, ibid.
61. Blair "Memorandum For File," August 5, 1941, ibid.
62. Blair "Memorandum For File," August 9, 1941, ibid.
63. Cable of Hayes to Polish ambassador, Tokyo, August 14, 1941, ibid.;"letter of Meyer Klein to Zerach Warhaftig, August 11, 1941; letter of Petrushka to Yaakov Greenberg, August 11, 1941, both YVA, P–20, 2.
64. Letter of Blair to Podoski, August 14, 1941; Blair, "Memorandum For Files," August 15, 1941, both CNA, RG 76, Vol. 441, file 673931.
65. Letter of Rabbi Seltzer to Saul Hayes and Moses Leavitt, August 25, 1941, AAH; letter of Hayes to Podoski, and letter of Rabbi Seltzer to Peters, both August 25, 1941, CNA, RG 76, Vol. 441, file 673931; letter of Rabbi Levinson to Leavitt, August 26, 1941, AJDC–VH.
66. Letter of Leavitt to Paul Veret (Omaha), August 27, 1941, AJDC–VH.
67. Letter of Birman to JDC, New York, August 26, 1941, files of the correspon-

dence between HICEM and JDC, 1941–1942 (hereafter called HICEM–JDC files).

68. HICEM was an acronym of HIAS (Hebrew Sheltering and Immigrant Aid Society), ICA (Jewish Colonization Association), and Emigdirect, three Jewish migration associations which were merged together in 1927. HICEM was established to handle Jewish emigration to destinations other than the United States and Palestine. Yitzhak Mais, "HICEM," in *Encyclopedia of the Holocaust* (New York, 1990), pp. 657–658.

69. Letter of Birman to JDC, New York, September 2, 1941, HICEM–JDC files.

70. Letter of Birman to JDC, New York, September 26, 1941, HICEM–JDC files.

71. The 80 visas were originally supposed to be distributed as follows: Mir (44), Lubavitch (9), Kletzk (6), Kamenetz (6), Lublin (6), Radin (2), Bialystok (2), Telz (1), Kollel (2), Rabbis (2). When the initial arrangements were made for the first 41 scholars to sail to the United States, 16 visas were given to students of the Mir Yeshiva and the rest were distributed among the other yeshivot. Only three students from Mir utilized the visas, whereas all those from the other yeshivot sailed on the *President Pierce* despite the Yom Kippur problem; letter of Rabbi Levinson to Leavitt, August 26, 1941, AJDC–VH; Yoseph Epstein, "Yeshivat Mir," p. 127; letter of Birman to JDC, New York; cable of HICEM Shanghai to JDC, New York, both September 30, 1941, HICEM–JDC files; departmental file no. 673931, October 24, 1941, CNA, RG 76, Vol. 441, file 673931.

72. Letter of Kilbreath to District Superintendent of Immigration, Eastern District, January 26, 1942, ibid.

73. Letter of Birman to JDC, New York, October 5, 1941, HICEM–JDC files.

74. Letter of Birman to JDC, New York, October 10, 1941, ibid.

75. See, for example, letters of Birman to JDC, New York, October 16, 26, and 28, 1941, all HICEM–JDC files; press release of UJRWRA, submitted to Canadian Jewish press, November 6, 1941, ACJC.

76. Letter of Birman to HIAS and JDC, New York, November 7, 1941; two letters of Birman to JDC, New York, both November 13, 1941, HICEM–JDC files.

77. See, for example, the cable of British Chief Rabbi Hertz to Canadian Prime Minister Mackenzie King, December 7, 1941; letter of Blair to Podoski, December 13, 1941, both CNA, RG 76, Vol. 441, file 673931.

Chapter 8

Relief to Central Asia and Shanghai

During the summer and early fall of 1941 the Japanese authorities, frustrated by the inability of the remaining Jewish refugees to leave the country, deported them to Shanghai. The process, which was initiated in August[1] and lasted until October, encompassed 1,098 Jews, of whom at least 860 were of Polish origin, among them more than 400 rabbis, yeshiva students, and family members.[2] The relocation of these refugees created new problems for the overburdened relief agencies functioning in Shanghai, which had already absorbed some 20,000 German and Austrian refugees.[3] And while the rabbis and yeshiva students were not responsible for the major problems that plagued the local Jewish relief efforts, their arrival did create additional complications.

Prior to the arrival of the first Polish Jews in Shanghai in the spring of 1941, local relief efforts had been coordinated by the Committee for the Assistance of European Jewish Refugees in Shanghai (known as CFA) headed by Michel Speelman and Ellis Hayim. Established in October 1938 in the wake of the large influx of refugees from Central Europe, the CFA represented the refugees vis-à-vis the local authorities and oversaw the collection and distribution of relief funds, providing a wide range of services for the needy newcomers, including food, housing, and medical care. Its funds were provided by overseas Jewish relief agencies, such as the JDC in the United States and the Council for German Jewry in Great Britain, in addition to money raised locally. Formed to coordinate

191

the activities of various relief agencies and thereby eliminate duplication and increase efficiency, the CFA rapidly become the dominant
force in relief affairs for the Jewish community of Shanghai.[4]

As long as the refugees arriving in Shanghai were from Central
Europe, the CFA continued to maintain its preeminent position in
the field of refugee relief. In the spring of 1941, however, the first
Polish refugees landed in the Chinese port and a new situation was
created. A group of local Jews of East European origin joined to provide suplementary assistance for these newcomers and established
the "Committee for Assistance of Jewish Refugees from Eastern
Europe" (known as East Jewcom or EJC). From the very beginning
East Jewcom encountered difficulties with the CFA, because it
refused to unequivocally accept the latter's hegemony in relief
affairs and because it provided assistance solely for the Polish
refugees, help that ostensibly enabled its recipients to maintain a
higher standard of living than their Central European co-religionists.

Although there were legitimate practical reasons for the stance
adopted by the EJC,[5] the CFA nonetheless strongly opposed East
Jewcom's efforts. Thus, for example, the CFA tried to force all the
Polish refugees to accept housing in its refugee homes (where the
costs of upkeep were considerably cheaper) and attempted to force
East Jewcom to bear exclusive responsibility for the new arrivals,
even though the latter had made clear that it merely sought to com-
plement the assistance provided by the CFA. The JDC, which
attempted to mediate between the two committees in the hope of
creating a unified relief framework, realized early on that such an
idea was impossible to implement and agreed to work with both the
CFA and the EJC, stepping in when necessary to settle disputes.

Under these circumstances, the arrival of the refugee rabbis and
yeshiva students in the summer and fall of 1941 further complicated an already delicate situation. The CFA and EJC were, in fact,
embroiled in one of their typical disputes when the refugee scholars
began arriving in Shanghai and therefore none of the necessary
preparations for their absorption were made. As a result, temporary
housing under very difficult conditions was initially arranged in an
old synagogue, and only thanks to Rabbi Ashkenazi's persistent
efforts did the CFA agree to provide subsidies for food and rent at
the equivalent of $5 (U.S.) per person per month.

This level of assistance was not considered sufficient by some of
the refugee scholars, however. The Mir Yeshiva, for example, which

continued to exist as a separate entity, initially demanded $7 per person per month plus clothing and medical care from local JDC representative Laura Margolis. And while this demand was summarily rejected, the refugee scholars' insistence on maintaining their unique lifestyle of intensive Torah study was accepted, even though Margolis, who was an American-bred and-educated social worker, had her doubts whether such a policy was justified under the circumstances. In her opinion, the refugee scholars, especially those from the Mir Yeshiva, had "no conception of realities, limitations or of anything else except their own immediate problem," but she did acknowledge that this insistence on a lifestyle of prayer and study was universally accepted by the Jewish community and consequently by the JDC as well.[6] In fact, the JDC played a major role in arranging suitable housing for the rabbis and yeshiva students in accordance with their demands,[7] and provided most of the funding for them through local relief agencies.[8]

Despite this assistance, the rabbis and yeshiva students still found it necessary to appeal to *Vaad ha-Hatzala* for additional help. The higher costs of kosher food and the difficult physical conditions they had to live under prompted desperate appeals by Rabbis Ashkenazi and Shmulewitz to New York.[9] In response, the *Vaad* sent close to $7,000 to the refugee scholars during the period prior to the outbreak of the war in the Pacific,[10] a sum practically equivalent to the assistance they received from the JDC through the CFA and EJC. (As Polish refugees they received $5 per person per month, or $2,250 for the entire group of 450.[11] Assuming this aid was granted upon the arrival of the refugees, which began in August, but taking into account that some of the group arrived only in September and others in October, the sums are approximately equal.)

Throughout this period, efforts continued to arrange for the emigration of the Torah scholars abroad, as it was obvious that Shanghai was hardly an optimal haven.[12] Much work was invested, for example, in the attempts to arrange transportation for the 80 scholars who had been granted Canadian visas in August 1941. As was noted above, a first group of 29 left Shanghai aboard *President Pierce* on September 30, 1941,[13] but 51 others remained behind. HICEM and the JDC attempted to arrange transportation as well as the necessary visas for this group,[14] but various complications delayed the refugees' departure. By the time all the necessary arrangements had been made for them to depart Shanghai for Manila on December 11,

1941,[15] the Japanese had attacked Pearl Harbor and the trip had to be cancelled.[16]

The war in the Pacific put an end to whatever hopes there were for the continuation of the emigration of refugee rabbis and yeshiva students via and from the Far East. With the exception of a few who managed to reach England and Palestine by a circuitous route via Mozambique in 1942,[17] the rest of the refugee scholars residing in Shanghai were forced to remain there for the duration of the war. America's entry into World War II marked the end of the first phase of the activities of the *Vaad ha-Hatzala* and is therefore an appropriate point at which to summarize to what extent the rabbinic rescue organization achieved its original goal of rescuing the refugee rabbis, yeshiva students, and the members of their families who escaped from Poland to Lithuania in 1939–1940.

While such a summary is extremely important in terms of assessing the *Vaad's* achievements and in determining the veracity of its claims against the JDC, it must be stated at the outset that it is difficult at this point to determine exact figures for several of the key questions. Let us begin by attempting to determine how many *roshei yeshiva*, administrators, students, community rabbis, and their family members escaped from Poland to Lithuania following the Soviet invasion. This is perhaps the easiest question to answer since there are relatively minor discrepancies among the various estimates. According to the figures of the *Vaad ha-Hatzala*, it assisted 2,654 such persons during 1940–1941, plus approximately 1,400 rabbis and students in the Lithuanian yeshivot whose situation was considerably different from that of the Polish refugees but who also nonetheless were considered prospective emigrants by the Vaad.[18] According to JDC statistics, the number of Polish refugee rabbis and yeshiva students who escaped to Vilna was 2,611, with no specific mention of family members,[19] who apparently were also included in this figure.

The next question is how many of the refugee scholars were able to leave Lithuania following its occupation by the Soviets. In early January 1942, in response to an inquiry by the Council of Jewish Federations and Welfare Funds for a report to its constituent agencies, the *Vaad* claimed that 1,302 of the 4,000 prospective emigrants it had registered in early 1941 had already been resettled in the United States (273); Palestine (250); Canada (29); Shanghai (550); and Persia, India, Latin America, and Australia (200).[20] However, the JDC, which was asked by the CJFWF to respond to the *Vaad's* claims, did not accept these figures. Henrietta Buchman insisted that the figure for Shanghai be reduced to 450 and noted that although they were willing to concede the numbers on the other countries, these too were "open to question." In fact, in the wake of the JDC's comments regarding Canada, the number for that country had been reduced from "does not exceed 50" to the precise figure of 29. Even more important, the JDC insisted that it receive due credit as the major supporter of the emigration and maintenance of the refugee scholars, with the *Vaad's* role recognized as secondary. In Buchman's words, the CJFWF report on the *Vaad's* activities should read: "By far the largest sums required for the maintenance and transportation of the yeshiva people were provided by the Joint Distribution Committee. The *Vaad ha-Hatzala* merely supplemented the amounts made available by the JDC and the other organizations mentioned above."[21]

A careful examination of the available evidence seem to indicate that the figures presented by the *Vaad* were misleading, if not outright falsifications, and that Buchman's protestations were for the most part justified. In this regard, there are two major questions that must be answered. How many rabbis, yeshiva students and family members emigrated from Lithuania? Who paid for their transportation and maintenance expenses?

The overwhelming majority of the Polish refugees who succeeded in leaving Lithuania did so via the Far East, almost all passing through Japan. It is not clear, however, exactly how many emigrated via this route. In a 1942 report by Jewcom there are three different figures on the number of Polish Jews who passed through Japan, ranging from 2,074 to 2,178 (out of a total of 4,608 Jewish refugees).[22] A report by Dr. Moshe Moiseef, the representative of the World Jewish Congress in Japan, lists the number of Polish refugees as 1,962 out of 4,664.[23] In summation, while it is impossible to determine the exact number of Polish refugees, it is reasonable to assume that approximately 2,000 to 2,200 reached Japan during 1940–1941.

Having established the general scope of the emigration of Polish Jews via Japan, the next problem is to determine the number of refugee Torah scholars and family members. This is more difficult because, although there are exact statistics on the number of rabbis and yeshiva students, there is no information on how many wives and children were part of the group. Thus the figure of 79 rabbis and

341 yeshiva students of Polish origin which appears in the Jewcom report must be taken as a minimal number, to which we have to add 6 rabbis and 18 yeshiva students of non-Polish origin and an unspecified number of wives and children (most of whom were no doubt classified by Jewcom as "without profession").[24]

Only the Mir Yeshiva emigrated in its entirety, and among the rest of the refugee scholars the percentage of rabbis and *roshei yeshiva* (as opposed to students) was relatively large, which meant a higher number of wives and children. (Many of the rabbis and *roshei yeshiva* emigrated with their families, whereas the yeshiva students were invariably single.) Thus it would be reasonable to add approximately 150 persons to the figure of rabbis and yeshiva students, making a total of 600 yeshiva *leit* (individuals connected to the yeshiva in some way) who reached Japan. This is based on the assumption that about 50 of the rabbis were accompanied by an average of three family members, and it is confirmed by JDC estimates.[25] To this figure we must add approximately half of the 50 refugees who reached Shanghai directly from Vladivostok through the efforts of Rabbi Ashkenazi and Newman (the others were neither rabbis nor yeshiva students nor family members).[26] In summation, it appears that approximately 625 rabbis, *roshei yeshiva*, administrators, yeshiva students, and family members escaped from Lithuania to the Far East.

The next question is how many of these refugee scholars emigrated prior to the outbreak of the war in the Pacific. Available documentation indicates that the yeshiva community in Shanghai numbered approximately 450 throughout the war,[27] so it would appear that some 175 individuals managed to emigrate from the Far East before December 1941. We know that 29 scholars departed from Shanghai to Canada on September 30, 1941,[28] so we can safely assume that approximately 145 rabbis, yeshiva students, and family members emigrated to other destinations, with the overwhelming majority going to the United States and a small minority to Palestine.[29]

Even if we add the rabbis and yeshiva students who emigrated to the United States and Palestine via European routes (at most a few dozen, but probably fewer),[30] total figures are much lower than the 1,302 whom the *Vaad* claimed to have resettled. There is no evidence regarding any appreciable number of refugee Torah scholars resettled in Persia, India, Australia, or Latin America, for example, and the figures given for both the United States and Palestine appear to be considerably higher than they actually were. In fact, if we examine the financial expenses of this operation, it is obvious that the *Vaad* could not have possibly resettled the number of refugee scholars whose emigration it claims to have arranged.

According to certified financial statements submitted by the *Vaad*, from January 1, 1940, to December 10, 1941 (the period during which the refugee scholars emigrated from Lithuania,) the rabbinical rescue organization spent $97,052 on the transportation of rabbis, yeshiva students, and the members of their families.[31] Given the fact that it cost $180 for an adult to travel by train from Kovno to Vladivostok and from there by boat to Tsuruga, and that a ship ticket from Japan to the United States cost an additional $100,[32] it becomes clear that the figures presented on resettlement cannot possibly be accurate. Just the trip to the Far East for the 625 who we know left Lithuania would have cost approximately $103,500. (This is based on the assumption of 525 adults paying $180 apiece and 100 children paying half that price.)

If we add the cost of transporting approximately 200 of the scholars to the United States, Canada, and Palestine,[33] it becomes clear that the *Vaad* obviously did not cover all the transportation expenses of even a considerable percentage of refugees whose rescue it had helped facilitate. These sums were, in fact, covered by the JDC, which spent close to $175,000 during this period on what Henrietta Buchman referred to as "the Lithuanian emigration project," plus relatively large sums for the maintenance of the refugees in Japan. (By May 1941 the maintenance expenditures had reached $25,000 per month.[34]) Obviously not all of this was spent on the Torah scholars, but since they constituted about 30% of the refugees who reached the Far East, they obviously were the beneficiaries of a significant portion of this aid.

We see, therefore, that despite promises by the *Vaad ha-Hatzala* that they would cover the transportation expenses of the refugee rabbis and yeshiva students, time and again the rabbis were forced to ask the JDC for funds.[35] At some point, in fact, the JDC obligated itself to cover 80 tickets to the United States and Palestine for refugee scholars, which were utilized by such rabbinic luminaries as Rabbis Aron Kotler, Mendel Zaks, and Avraham Yaphin [Jofen], who emigrated to the United States and Eliezer Finkel and Shabtai Yogel who went to Palestine.[36] The fact that it was the JDC that funded the passage of several individuals whose rescue was undoubtedly considered by the *Vaad ha-Hatzala's* founders to be their crowning achievement, underscores one of the more problematic aspects of the activities of the rescue organization whose goals were obviously beyond its means.

This problem is also clearly seen in the case of those who emigrated to Canada. Despite promises by the *Vaad* to contribute $300 per month toward their maintenance, they provided only $900 total (as opposed to over $8,000 provided by the United Jewish Refugee and War Relief, a JDC affiliate). The latter had provided the Canadian government with guarantees for the maintenance of the scholars based on the promises of the *Vaad ha-Hatzala,* which assumed responsibility for covering all the costs or for raising the necessary funds from other (Orthodox) organizations.[37]

Nonetheless, the *Vaad* achieved important successes in its efforts to rescue the elite of the Torah world. Beyond the considerable financial assistance to the yeshivot, (over $200,000 for maintenance and transportation during 1940–1941),[38] the *Vaad*, by focusing on the plight of the refugee Torah scholars, made sure that they were accorded high-level treatment by the Jewish community. There were indeed those, like Harry Miller of the Jewish Federation in Chattanooga, Tennessee, who when approached by the *Vaad* for a contribution, questioned the priority afforded the rabbis and yeshiva students; in his words, "As far as I am personally concerned, I cannot see any reason on earth why these yeshiva students should be singled out for rescue any sooner than many others who lived in Europe, for a life is a life and the life of any layman is just as sweet to him as the life of a Yeshiva student."[39] But despite such protestations, the *Vaad*, through the persistence and dedication of its leaders and supporters, was able to provide significant assistance for the refugee Torah scholars and facilitate their rescue in considerably greater numbers than otherwise would have been the case.

The *Vaad* did not complete its goal of relocating all the yeshivot, but it was not for lack of effort. Nor could it ultimately be blamed for the lack of foresight exhibited by leading Torah sages who forbade, or at least discouraged, their students from obtaining Curaçao and Japanese visas of dubious validity or worth. Perhaps most important was the fact that the plight of these refugees did not exist in a vacuum but was only one of numerous causes that had to be dealt with on an emergency basis.[40] This is of course the reason why the founders of the *Vaad* thought that their step was justified, whereas the leaders of the JDC responded in a negative manner. The begrudging cooperation between the two agencies yielded partial success which ultimately satisfied no one, but it resulted in a significant achievement in terms of rescue.

* * *

Even before the emigration routes to North America became impassable with the outbreak of the war in the Pacific, *Vaad ha-Hatzala* found itself facing another serious problem. In the fall of 1941 the *Vaad* began receiving appeals for help on behalf of rabbis and yeshiva students who were living under extremely difficult conditions in the Soviet republics of Central Asia.[41] Most of them were among the 7,000 Jews arrested and/or deported by the Soviets from Lithuania in June 1941 during the week prior to the Nazi invasion. Others were apparently among the hundreds of thousands of Jews deported from eastern Poland or among those who had escaped to the Soviet interior during the initial days following the outbreak of the war between Germany and the Soviet Union. The deportees were initially sent to labor camps (those arrested) and rural settlements (those exiled) in Siberia and the regions near the Arctic Circle, where the living conditions were extremely harsh. Besides being forced to do difficult physical labor ten to twelve hours a day, the deportees suffered from malnutrition and a lack of adequate housing, clothing, and medical treatment.[42]

The plight of Alter Pekier of the Kletzk Yeshiva was typical of the students deported from Lithuania to the Soviet interior. He had escaped to Vilna with his fellow yeshiva students in October 1939 and subsequently moved with the entire yeshiva to Janeva not far from Kovno. Following the Soviet occupation of Lithuania in June 1940, the yeshiva split into three groups, and in August Pekier and his brother Berel moved with a group headed by the *rosh yeshiva*, Rabbi Aron Kotler, to the town of Salakas, where they remained for close to a year. On June 6, 1941, the yeshiva students were summoned to the office of the local Soviet official and asked whether they wanted to apply for Soviet citizenship. All but two replied in the negative.

The next day those who had refused were informed by Jewish Communists that they had to report to the local official again. There they were processed for the trip to Siberia. They were then transferred by bus to Dukst, where they were put into a boxcar which held 35 persons and was sealed from the outside. (The sanitary facilities were a hole in the floor.) The train finally left Dukst on June 17, 1941, traveling via Svencionys to the old Russian border, which they crossed at Naujoji Vilnia four days later. From there they traveled via Minsk (where the men were separated from the women and children), Smolensk, Saratov, Ufa, Omsk, Novosibirsk, Tomsk, and Krasnoyarsk, arriving on July 6, at Labor Camp Number 7, 7 kilometers from Resheti between Krasnoyarsk and Irkutsk. The conditions in the camp were extremely harsh. The inmates, most of whom were non-Jewish Lithuanian businessmen and intellectuals, were forced to do such backbreaking tasks as uprooting trees, laying railroad tracks, sawing lumber, and transporting huge logs from place to place. Despite the difficult conditions, the rabbis and students tried their best to continue to observe Jewish rituals and traditions.[43]

The plight of the Polish deportees changed drastically after the Nazi attack on the Soviet Union, which led to a turnabout in Soviet–Polish relations. The two countries, which had been in a state of war since the Soviet invasion of Eastern Poland in 1939, became allies, and in the wake of the signing of the Sikorski–Stalin Agreement on July 30, 1941, Polish citizens in the Soviet Union were granted official pardons on August 12, 1941, and their release from detention began. Because of technical difficulties and wartime conditions, however, it took weeks and in some cases months for the process to be implemented throughout the Soviet Union. Thus in certain places the deportees were already released in September 1941, while in others the inmates were only granted freedom in 1942.[44]

Upon their release, many of the Jewish deportees traveled south and settled in the republics of Uzbekistan, Turkmenistan, Tadzikistan, Kazakhstan, and Kirgizia, and especially in the cities of Bukhara, Samarkand, Dzhambul, Chimkent, and Kokand. They preferred these locales because of the warmer climate, the more abundant food supply, and the fact that they were far away from the front and closer to the Soviet border. Despite the relative improvement in the conditions, the plight of the refugees remained extremely difficult. By November 1941 there were several hundred thousand Polish refugees in southern Central Asia, most of them homeless, unemployed, and without any means of support. To make matters worse, they were not the only ones seeking shelter in that area; there were numerous Soviet citizens fleeing the front as well, basically for the same reasons. In fact, the Soviet authorities even attempted to force the Poles to remain where they were, but the refugees contin-ued to stream southward, anxious to leave the camps and the harsh winter far behind. The situation was particularly difficult for the Jewish refugees in the cities, who suffered from discrimination in food distribution and employment.[45]

Despite the extremely harsh conditions, the rabbis and yeshiva students attempted to stick together and maintain some semblance of their original lifestyle. They urgently appealed to the leaders of the *Vaad ha-Hatzala* and the American offices of the yeshivot for assistance, and the former convened a special meeting on December 9, 1941, at the Broadway Central Hotel in New York City to deal with their plight.[46] It was decided that the *Vaad* should launch a nationwide campaign on behalf of the beleaguered refugee Torah scholars in the Soviet Union and send a representative to meet with them, assess their needs, and conduct relief work for this group. The leaders of the *Vaad* also voted to enlarge the presidium from three to five members, adding Rabbis Yisrael Halevi Rosenberg and Yechiel Mordechai Gordon to the triumvirate of Rabbis Silver, Konvitz, and Levinson. In addition, Rabbis Zev Gold of the Mizrachi, Yehuda Seltzer of *Agudat ha-Rabbanim,* and Kamenetz *rosh yeshiva* Reuven Grazowsky were elected as vice-presidents of the rabbinic rescue organization.[47]

The participation of leaders from disparate elements in the Orthodox community underscores the almost unanimous support[48] which the *Vaad* had secured by this point. At the same time, it is important to acknowledge the dominant role played by the *Agudat ha-Rabbanim* in the rabbinic rescue organization. Practically every officer of the *Vaad* was at least a member, if not a leader, of the rab-binic association, and it was the rank and file of the *Agudat ha-Rabbanim* who did most of the *Vaad's* fundraising throughout the United States. And although several key leaders of the *Vaad*, such as Rabbis Silver (Agudat Yisrael), Levinson (Mizrachi), and Rosenberg (*Ezrat Torah*), were also leaders of other Orthodox organizations, their preeminent role in the *Vaad's* activities was primarily a result of their status as leaders of the *Agudat ha-Rabbanim*, and so they opposed attempts by the political organizations to increase their influence in *Vaad ha-Hatzala* at the expense of the rabbinic association.[49]

In fact, during the early years of *Vaad ha-Hatzala* its officers often preferred to approach government officials as leaders of the Union of Orthodox Rabbis of the United States and Canada, which was of established public standing while the *Vaad ha-Hatzala* was still relatively unknown.[50] As time passed, and the *Vaad* achieved a measure of success, its activities eventually assumed priority for those involved, who increasingly neglected other organizational responsibilities. This was particularly true of Rabbi Silver, who was accused time and again of ignoring his obligations as president of American *Agudat Yisrael* in favor of his efforts on behalf of the refugee Torah scholars.[51]

The participants in the meeting also said a special prayer for the welfare of the United States, which had just officially entered World War II, and they sent a telegram of encouragement to President Roosevelt. In addition, Rabbi Silver delivered a patriotic speech calling upon every Orthodox Jew in America to "manifest his love for the government and the country."[52] Although the leaders of the *Vaad ha-Hatzala* were willing without hesitation to circumvent U.S. government regulations that they felt unfairly hampered the *Vaad's* attempts to assist or rescue the refugee scholars, the rabbis' loyalty to the United States was never in doubt. They considered themselves lucky to be living at that time in the United States and were therefore anxious to contribute their share to the war effort. Thus the *Vaad's* leaders and supporters participated in numerous campaigns to sell U.S. bonds, called upon their congregants to enlist in the armed forces, and offered special prayers for a speedy American victory.[53]

In the wake of the December 9 meeting, *Vaad ha-Hatzala* began a threefold effort to assist the refugee Torah scholars in the Soviet Union. The *Vaad's* fundraising campaign was redesigned to focus on this new problem, means were sought to send these refugees aid as quickly as possible, and attempts to arrange the evacuation of this group were also undertaken. In each of these spheres, however, the *Vaad* encountered serious difficulties, which in essence were interrelated.

From the very beginning of its attempts to assist the scholars in Central Asia and Siberia, the *Vaad* had to contend with the opposition of the JDC, which had severe doubts as to the validity of such a campaign. By mid-January 1942 the JDC had already reached an agreement with the Soviet authorities and the Polish Red Cross for the distribution of relief to the Polish refugees in the Soviet Union, including rabbis and yeshiva students. According to the terms of the agreement, American supplies, clothing, medicines, and concentrated foods were to be shipped on Russian transports or Russian chartered boats (free of charge and without customs) to the Polish embassy in the Soviet Union, which would distribute the goods through local committees it had established for this purpose. Several outstanding Jewish leaders had already been appointed to serve on these committees, and the Polish government had assured the JDC that there would be no discrimination against Jews in the distribution of the relief.[54]

An initial sum of $100,000 had been allocated by the JDC for this purpose, and from their point of view the *Vaad's* efforts were a duplication of their own, since the rabbis and yeshiva students would be among the beneficiaries. Therefore JDC officials believed that the *Vaad* had no justification for appealing for funds from "the same sources… from which the JDC receives its contributions." If, on the other hand, the *Vaad* could raise funds from "their own orthodox circles in ways which will not affect the fund-raising campaigns of the communities from which the JDC receives its incomes, there can be no objection to having additional funds made available for whatever purposes they may have with regard to the particular persons in whom they are interested."[55]

The *Vaad* rejected this criticism, claiming that since the JDC's aid was distributed on a nonsectarian basis to 2 million Polish refugees in the Soviet Union, there was no way that sufficient relief could be provided for the refugee scholars, who had special needs (kosher food) requiring additional assistance. In addition, the *Vaad's* goal, it should be noted, was not merely to ensure the physical survival of the Torah scholars, but to enable them to continue their studies uninterrupted as if there were no war.

The *Vaad* had therefore undertaken a program of sending clothing as well as money directly to the rabbis and yeshiva students in Siberia and Central Asia. There was an additional complication, however, because the American offices of the yeshivot whose students had been exiled to the Soviet Union (Bialystok, Kletzk, Kollel Kovno, Telz, Baranowitz, Kamenetz, etc.) were also collecting funds for this purpose. The *Vaad* clarified, therefore, that its campaign was primarily for those students from yeshivot that did not have offices in the United States (Pinsk, Brisk, Mezritch, Vilkomir, etc.) as well as for refugee rabbis not affiliated with yeshivot, and also to supplement the funds raised by the American offices of the other yeshivot. In its literature the *Vaad* stated that it "had at no time the purpose or the desire to usurp the work of the individual offices of the yeshivot. The large sums required during the emergency periods could not be supplied by the *Vaad ha-Hatzala* and could at best but supplement the funds raised by the individual offices from their friends, patronizers and annual donors."[56]

It is not clear to what extent the *Vaad's* explanations were accepted by the American offices of the yeshivot, but they certainly were unacceptable to the JDC, which continued to present the efforts of the rabbinical rescue organization as largely a duplication of their own and consequently superfluous. In letters to federations seeking advice on whether to allocate funds to the *Vaad*, the message from JDC headquarters was unequivocal: "The JDC cannot veto or approve the fund-raising campaigns of any of the separate groups, which out of an interest in special problems, desire to do a 100% job. We must take the position, however, that they should not appeal to the same sources for income that the JDC does and at the same time expect the JDC to carry the major part of the burden in the same area, in addition to all the other responsibilities we are called upon to shoulder."[57]

Needless to say, this attitude angered the leaders of the *Vaad,* who complained bitterly to the JDC and sought clarification. In the words of Rabbi Silver:

> One would suspect from the contents of that letter [to Philip Bernstein of the Cleveland federation] that it is your earnest desire to "pick a quarrel" with the Vaad Hahatzala and the Orthodox Rabbinnate of the United States and Canada. May I say that we notice a tendency on your part to minimize the work of the Vaad Hahatzala, leaving the erroneous impression that the JDC takes care of everything and of everybody.
>
> As you well know we could come out with weighty counter charges of instances where the JDC has appropriated sums of money originally designated for the Vaad Hahatzala.... There are other criticism that should we come out publicly with it would not add to the prestige of the JDC. We refrain from doing so because we value greatly the work of the JDC. With

all its faults, the JDC is doing a tremendous job and we over-
look the shortcomings.

However, we feel that we are entitled the same consideration. You know that the Vaad Hahatzala reaches places and
extends relief and rescue work where the JDC cannot or will
not go. Why, then, those letters to the Jewish Communities?[58]

In late May, Rabbi Silver again complained to the JDC in the
wake of statements made by Joseph Hyman about the *Vaad's* activities and reiterated his original request for a meeting to clarify the
issues under contention.[59] The JDC agreed and on June 4, 1942,
Rabbis Silver and Yisrael Rosenberg met with J. C. Hyman and
Henrietta Buchman in New York. Although there is no protocol of
the meeting in the archives of either organization, the positions presented were clearly outlined in a subsequent exchange of letters
between the participants. Rabbis Silver and Rosenberg wrote a fairly sharp letter to Hyman on June 9, which they began by accusing
the JDC and the CJFWF of conveying the impression "that the work
of the *Vaad ha-Hatzala* merely grants insignificant aid to individual
Rabbis and students." The rabbis then presented their case to justify the *Vaad's* activities, noting on the one hand their unique concern
for the welfare of the yeshivot and on the other the fact that the aid
they were sending to the refugee scholars in the Soviet Union and
Shanghai was absolutely essential for their continued existence. In
their words:

> Orthodox Rabbinate in particular, as well as traditional
> Jewry at large, have a keen interest not only in saving the lives
> of the individual, which in itself is of the utmost importance,
> but to rescue the student bodies as a whole, and afford them
> the opportunity to continue their learning under all circum-
> stances. The Yeshivoth have shown their self sacrifice in the
> last two years of their exile. Under the most difficult condi-
> tions they have not given up their studies. We cannot fail them
> now....
> Do you propose to disregard the cables from Turkestant
> [sic], Samarkand, Tchimkant, Buchara, Mirka, Kardiz,
> Dzizhak, Obyatcheva, and Nihzna Michave where groups of
> 60 to 80 students have already formed their Yeshivoth as above

mentioned? And do you actually believe that the support given them by the Vaad Hahatzala is of no consequence? Are we to believe that the statement by various Welfare Funds, namely, that the Vaad Hhatzala [sic], including its leaders, is under suspicion and does not deserve the support of American Jewry, came as a result of information conveyed by you. We trust that it is not so.[60]

At the JDC the tone of the *Vaad's* letter was hardly appreciated. On June 15 Buchman called Rabbi Rosenberg to warn him that if the rabbis did not retract the letter, the JDC could respond in a manner "which would not be helpful" to the *Vaad*. Rosenberg was not in, but Buchman conveyed the message to Joseph Hellerstein, the secretary of the *Agudat ha-Rabbanim*, who promised to speak to Rabbis Rosenberg and Silver and get back to her.[61] The result of this exchange was a revised version of the original, which, although dated June 9, was sent to the JDC a week later.[62] The second version was more restrained in its criticism of the JDC and concluded with the request that, "In fairness to the leaders of the Vaad Hahatzala, who were always loyal friends of the JDC and admirers of its colossal relief work, and for the good of the institutions and rare intellectual scholars for whom we are laboring, we would appreciate having your objective opinion on the work of the Vaad Hahatzala."[63]

In his response, Hyman reiterated the basic position of the JDC but also included one new and very significant element. He began by stressing the fact that his organization viewed itself as responsible for all of European Jewry, but in view of the limited funds at its disposal ($5 million to $5.5 million) was unable to "meet in toto or 100% any of the requirements that are so close to the needs and to the heart of Jewish life." Thus it was understandable, in Hyman's opinion, why organizations such as the *Vaad* deemed it necessary to launch special campaigns.

This was the first time that a prominent JDC leader acknowledged the basic validity of the *raison d'être* of the *Vaad ha-Hatzala*, confirming that the rabbinic rescue organization was engaged in worthwhile relief activities and was supplying aid that the JDC was unable to provide. According to Hyman:

Certainly the Joint Distribution Committee, outside the general funds that it can disburse on an equal plane for all victims, for all refugees, for all sufferers, and to a limited extent to cultural institutions, has no means for extending special, intensive aid to maintain the several yeshivoth in exile, which we understand from you, have been re-established in the various Soviet Russian provinces—Siberia, Turkestan, Bukhara, Samarkand, and in other areas. The Joint Distribution Committee, through its general relief program, can reach only those primary elementary needs which go toward maintaining the very life and existence of numbers of the refugees, among whom are included rabbis and religious functionaries.

The field of special interest to which the Vaad Hahatzala has dedicated itself is therefore in effect not merely a supplementation of the relief work rendered by the Joint Distribution Committee, but it goes further than that—it sets up as a definite goal the maintenance and the saving of the Jewish yeshivoth in exile and of the great teachers who preserve the Jewish tradition. That is true with respect to the situation of the yeshivoth in Shanghai, that is true in regard to the preservation of the yeshivoth in other areas where the Vaad Hahatzala states it has established contact with groups of the yeshivah leaders.[64]

As significant as this admission was, even more important was the fact that this new attitude was reflected in the responses the JDC sent to local federations inquiring about the rabbinic rescue organization. In late June, for example, Moses Leavitt sent Hyman's letter to a community leader in Philadelphia and added: "We feel that the Vaad Hahatzala has a valid claim for community support, since whatever they are doing to extend aid to refugee yeshivoth and their students, is done on the basis of keeping alive traditional cultural-religious institutions. The funds they make available are over and above the sums which we are able to provide for the maintenance of needy refugees, including the yeshivah groups."[65] Hyman reiterated the JDC's new position in August 1942 in response to a query from the Louisville Conference of Jewish Organizations, which had established a committee to investigate the claims of the *Vaad ha-Hatzala* regarding the war-torn yeshivot.[66] Although the Joint was sending relief to the Polish Jewish refugees in the Soviet Union, its activities had "no connection to the purely religious program of the perpetuation of traditional Judaism and the aid to the teachers of the yeshivoth who were forced to flee from Poland. To that extent we are not doing what the *Vaad Hahatzala* is seeking to do in Siberia on behalf of the yeshivoth teachers and students there."[67]

This change of attitude toward the *Vaad* was predicated by two developments. One was the growing realization by the leaders of the JDC that their organization was simply unable to cope with the growing overseas needs of Jews in distress, especially in the Soviet Union, where numerous technical difficulties were hampering relief activities.[68] The other was their recognition that among the refugees were specific groups which deserved special assistance. Thus, for example, in early June 1942 the JDC acceded to a request by the Jewish Labor Committee for a special allocation of $2,500 to a group of 200 outstanding refugee Jewish labor leaders stranded in the Soviet Union. (The group was already being assisted by the Jewish Labor Committee, which had also raised funds in the United States on their behalf.) Although there was considerable opposition to the request by members of the Emergency Administrative Committee who viewed this allocation as a dangerous precedent, funds were granted (although less than had been requested).[69]

In effect, the plight of these labor leaders was similar to that of the refugee scholars supported by the *Vaad*: An existent American Jewish organization was supporting their claim that they deserved priority and was raising funds on their behalf. In their case as well, the local organization had a measure of fundraising success but was forced to turn to the JDC for additional assistance. But whereas the JDC allocated funds at the request of the Jewish Labor Committee, who considered themselves "very close to the JDC,"[70] such was not the case vis-à-vis the rabbis of the *Vaad ha-Hatzala*. Even after the validity of the rabbinic rescue organization's program had been acknowledged, there apparently still was a residue of skepticism and dissatisfaction. Hyman, in his letter to the Jewish leaders in Louisville, injected an element of doubt regarding the veracity of the *Vaad's* claims, stating that he knew of no way to check their activities. Thus he advised the local Jewish leaders to make their decision on the basis of their confidence in the good faith and responsibility of the leaders of "the Vaad Hahatzala movement," adding that normally the JDC would conduct an inquiry but under the current circumstances it was "impractical" to do so. [71]

In the meantime, during the spring and summer of 1942, the *Vaad* continued to send funds (via American Express)[72] and parcels (of food and clothing with the Jewish Labor Committee)[73] from the United States directly to the refugee scholars in Central Asia. The rabbis also sought alternative relief routes to increase the aid to the Soviet Union. One such route was via Eretz Yisrael (Palestine). In July 1942 Rabbi Silver sent Rabbi Chizkiyahu Mishkowski in Jerusalem $2,000 and a list of 113 refugee rabbis, yeshiva students, and their families in Central Asia to whom food parcels should be sent.[74]

As time went on, this route was to prove increasingly important, and Rabbi Mishkowski (who had been a rabbi in Krinki, Poland, and emigrated to Palestine in April 1941)[75] was to play a key role in these efforts. Initially, however, the results of the relief efforts from Palestine were uncertain (by late August the rabbis had still not received any proof that the parcels had reached the refugee scholars), so the *Vaad* decided to send funds through the Polish government-in-exile. In late August 1942 the *Agudat ha-Rabbanim* applied for a license to send $5,000 to the Polish Embassy in the Soviet Union for distribution among the refugee scholars,[76] and this sum was sent to the Polish Ministry of Finance in New York on September 23.[77]

By this time, the *Vaad* had collected the names of several hundred refugee Torah scholars who had organized themselves into yeshiva-like groups in various locations in Central Asia. By June 1942 Rabbi Silver wrote to a federation requesting an allocation for about "100 or more rabbis and students organized in a yeshiva in Samarkand, 80 or more in Abeytchev, 60 or more each in Mirki [Merke] and Nisi-Michaev, 40 or more in Buchara, 35 or more in Michaev and 30 or more in Djijeck [Dzizhak]."[78] About a month later the rabbis sent a telegram to Polish President Sikorski, naming the heads of the groups functioning as yeshivot in Central Asia, and requesting aid for 250 Torah scholars in six locations, not all of which had been listed by Rabbi Silver.[79]

These figures, however, were much lower than those quoted by the *Vaad* in its public appeals, in public meetings, and in information given to the CJFWF. Time and again the *Vaad* quoted the figure of 3,000 refugee scholars, which was based on the erroneous assumption that if 1,202 of the 4,000 people who registered as prospective immigrants in Lithuania were resettled, the rest must have been evacuated to Siberia.[80] Wishful thinking, groundless optimism, and good fundraising strategy appear to have combined to produce this inflated figure. There is no doubt, however, that by the summer of 1942 the *Vaad* knew of at least several hundred refugee Torah scholars who had organized into groups in various locations in the Soviet Union, and as time went by more and more names reached the *Vaad's* offices.

The *Vaad ha-Hatzala* did not confine its activities on behalf of the scholars in Central Asia to sending relief. As early as August 1941, Orthodox leaders began efforts to evacuate this group from the Soviet Union.[81] These activities were conducted primarily by British Chief Rabbi Joseph Hertz and Ashkenazic Chief Rabbi of Eretz Yisrael Yitzhak ha-Levi Herzog, since the project was based on the evacuation of the scholars to Palestine. These plans were thwarted, however, by the steadfast refusal of the Soviets to allow their exit and the difficulties in obtaining the necessary Palestine certificates. When the Soviets finally allowed the exit of a limited number of Poles in July 1942 (primarily those serving in the Anders Army), only a few well-known rabbis such as Rabbi Hager and Rabbi Halberstam of Cracow were allowed to join them.[82] Despite these initial setbacks, the leaders of the *Vaad*, assisted by prominent rabbis elsewhere in the world, especially Rabbis Hertz and Herzog, continued their efforts to bring the scholars stranded in the Soviet Union to relative safety.

Besides assisting the rabbis and yeshiva students in the Soviet Union, the *Vaad ha-Hatzala* also continued its relief program for the Torah scholars in Shanghai. Here too the difficult physical conditions made life extremely problematic for the scholars, who sought to maintain their unique lifestyle. In Shanghai as well, legal and technical difficulties made the transmission of relief extremely difficult and created serious obstacles for the *Vaad's* relief program. In this case, after the outbreak of war in the Pacific, the transfer of funds to Japanese-occupied territory was prohibited by the Trading with the Enemy Act. As a result, untold difficulties were created for the Jewish refugees in Shanghai who had to a large extent been dependent on aid from the United States.

The JDC, which bore the major burden of refugee relief in Shanghai, solved the problem by raising funds locally in return for the promise of repayment in dollars after the war or "at such time that it would be legal and feasible to do so." Thus JDC officials approved loans of $180,000 for six months starting in December 1941, enabling their local representative Laura Margolis to maintain the JDC's aid program at its previous level.[83] While the promise of repayment was sufficient to induce local residents to grant loans to the JDC, it was apparently not good enough to convince enough people to assist the refugee rabbis and yeshiva students. The *Vaad ha-Hatzala* therefore agreed to deposit these amounts in dollars in U.S. bank accounts immediately upon receiving word that the funds had been pledged. There were, however, legal and technical problems regarding these transactions. First of all, there was no direct contact between the United States and Shanghai and, even if such contact existed, such an arrangement was of dubious legality since it violated the spirit, if not the letter, of U.S. wartime regulations.

The *Vaad* solved this problem by establishing contact with the refugee scholars via neutral countries. By January 1942 the rabbis had renewed communications with Shanghai via Rabbi Aaron Milewsky[84] of Montevideo, Uruguay, and Rabbi Wilhelm Wolbe[85] in Stockholm. During the first three months of 1942 the *Vaad* maintained contact with Shanghai via both these channels, but starting in April all communications were sent via Rabbi Milewsky.

Once this communication channel had been firmly established, a means had to be found to conceal the true content of the messages, which violated American regulations. A special code based on the first chapter of Exodus was devised. Each of the patriarch Jacob's sons listed as having gone down to Egypt was given a numerical value in ascending order: Reuven, Shimon, Levi, Yehuda, Issachar, Zevulun, Binyamin, Dan, Naftali, Gad and Asher. Reuven became the code for $100, and each name after that represented an additional $100. In addition, various terms such as "skins," "bales," and "rabbis" were used to refer to money, and Hebrew words were often substituted for numbers.[86]

Thus, for example, on January 16, 1942, Rabbi Chaim Shmulewitz, the head of the Mir Yeshiva in Shanghai, cabled Rabbi Milewsky instructing him to cable Rabbi Kalmanowitz in New York that "Ponevejskys Epsteins Shmoinogud visit Feldman 235 West 29." The explanation of the message is as follows: David Ponevejsky (a resident of Shanghai) is willing to give the refugee Torah scholars $8,000 (*shmona* is the Hebrew word for the number eight) in return for the same amount which was raised in Chicago by Rabbi Efraim Epstein. In order for the transaction to be carried out you are to give the said sum to Aaron Feldman, whose address is 235 West 29th Street, New York City.[87]

Confirmation of the transaction and instructions regarding the distribution of additional funds raised were contained in Rabbi Kalmanowitz's reply, which was cabled by Rabbi Milewsky on January 22, 1942:

> Aron well. Stop. Epstein regards everybody Stop. Also brothers Gud [sic] Reuben regards Mirsky Yisochor Kotler regards Kletzker Judah Grosovski regards Kamienietzky Shimon regards Telz Lubliner Beth Jacob Rabonim. Everybody Reuben regards Nawaredok Slonimer. All well cable health[88]

The instructions from *Vaad ha-Hatzala* were as follows: The money has been deposited as per your request ("Aron well"). The $8,000 raised by Rabbi Epstein is to be distributed to all the refugee Torah scholars ("Epstein regards everybody"). In addition, the following sums were raised on behalf of the various yeshivot: $1,100 ("Gud Reuben") for the Mir Yeshiva ("Mirsky"); $500 (Yisochor) for the Kletzk Yeshiva ("Kotler regards Kletzker"); $400 ("Judah") for the Kamenetz Yeshiva ("Grosovski regards Kamienietzky"); $200 ("Shimon") each for the students from Telz, Lublin, Beth Jacob girls' school, as well as for rabbis; and $100 ("Reuben") for the yeshivot of Navardok and Slonim.

In this manner, tens of thousands of dollars were turned over to the rabbis and yeshiva students in Shanghai during the war. By the summer of 1942, $22,000 in relief had been arranged.[89] However, a change had to be made in the communication channel when Uruguay declared war on Japan. Starting in spring 1942 all messages to and from Shanghai were transmitted by Rabbi Milewsky via Argentina with the help of Rabbi Zev Hillel Klein, the leader of the Mizrachi in Buenos Aires.[90]

In addition to these funds, small sums raised in Argentina[91] and Uruguay[92] were sent to Shanghai via Switzerland. In addition, Heinrich Erlanger of Lucerne, Switzerland, a former student of the Mir Yeshiva, raised funds and maintained contact with the refugee scholars during this period.[93] These funds together with the assistance of the JDC enabled the refugees in Shanghai to maintain their unique lifestyle despite the difficult conditions under which they lived.

During the spring and summer of 1942, while the *Vaad* was focusing its attention exclusively on the welfare of the refugee scholars in the Soviet Union and Shanghai, the implementation of the Final Solution was rapidly intensifying. Large-scale deportations were carried out from the Warsaw Ghetto and numerous other locations; newly constructed death camps at Treblinka, Sobibor, and Belzec stepped up operations; and the stranglehold of the Nazis on thousands of Jewish communities was intensified. These developments were still unknown in the United States, however, and as a result the *Vaad ha-Hatzala*, as well as other American Jewish organizations, continued their regular activities, unaware of the scope of Nazi atrocities and the urgent need for emergency rescue initiatives.

Notes

1. Unsigned letter of Jewcom to Laura Margolis, August 12, 1941, AJDC, file 462.
2. Jewcom Report, p. 22a; David Kranzler, *Japanese, Nazis and Jews*, p. 358.
3. "Statement of the Chairman to the JDC Executive," September 11, 1941, AJDC, file 462.
4. *Japanese, Nazis and Jews*, pp. 93–95
5. Since the Polish Jews refused to be housed in the CFA-sponsored "refugee homes," which they considered substandard, their living costs (which included medical aid provided gratis at the refugee homes) were naturally higher. Another factor affecting the amount of money required for these refugees was the *kashrut* requirements of the Orthodox, who constituted a significant portion of the new arrivals. If we add the aid provided exclusively for German refugees by the International Committee for Granting Relief to European Refugees (the Komor Committee), we see that in reality the level of assistance provided for both groups was approximately equal. Ibid., pp. 91, 349–350. See also the letter of A. Oppenheim (EJC) to Speelman explaining the attitude of the Polish refugees, October 2, 1941, AJDC-VH.
6. Letter of Laura Margolis to Robert Pilpel, October 26, 1941, AJDC, file 462; Kranzler, *Japanese, Nazis and Jews*, pp. 349–351
7. The Mir Yeshiva, which constituted the majority of the yeshiva group, insisted on being housed together, and the appropriate arrangements were eventually made to do so. See letter of Margolis to Pilpel, October 26, 1941, AJDC, file 462; "Minutes of Meeting Held in Mr. Speelman's Office Between East Jewcom and CFA," October 29, 1941, AJDC, file 462; Elchanan Herzman, *Mofait ha–Dor*, p. 85.
8. Efraim Zuroff, "Rabbis' Relief and Rescue: A Case Study of the Activities of the *Vaad ha–Hatzala* (Rescue Committee) of the American Orthodox Rabbis, 1942–1943," *Simon Wiesenthal Center Annual*, Vol. III, 1986, p. 125.
9. See, for example, cable of Rabbis Ashkenazi and Shmulewitz to Rabbi Silver, August 27, 1941; cable of Rabbi Ashkenazi to Rabbis Silver and Kotler, October 22, 1941, both AVH. It is interesting to note that the Mir Yeshiva initially refused to accept the leadership of Rabbi Ashkenazi and conducted its own negotiations with the JDC and local relief agencies. Letter of Margolis to Pilpel, October 26, 1941, AJDC, file 462. Similar appeals for assistance were also directed to the JDC. See cables of Rabbi Finkel to JDC, August 28, 1941, and of Rabbi Ashkenazi and *Vaad ha–Yeshivot* to the JDC, September 4, 1941, both AJDC, file 462.

10. Prior to the entry of the United States into World War II, the *Vaad* sent $6,915 to the refugee scholars in Shanghai. "Vaad *ha–Hatzala* [sic] Statement of Income and Expenses January 1 to December 10, 1941," AVH.

11. Letter of Margolis to Pilpel, October 26, 1941, AJDC, file 462.

12. In fact many of the Polish refugees considered themselves to be in transit in Shanghai, expecting to be able to emigrate. See the letter of Speelman to the secretary of the JDC (New York), October 4, 1941, AJDC, file 462.

13. See Chapter 7.

14. Letter of Phillip Freider (Manila) to Margolis, November 12, 1941; letter of Margolis to Pilpel, November 14, 1941, both AJDC, file 462.

15. Cable of Margolis to JDC (New York) November 24, 1941, AJDC, file 462.

16. "American Relief Workers, Representing JDC In Shanghai, Doubt They Can Leave" (press release), December 8, 1941, AJDC, file 462.

17. Interview with Rabbi Shimon Romm, July 27, 1977, in possession of the author. Rabbi Romm was among the yeshiva students who escaped to Vilna and subsequently made it to Japan thanks to a Japanese transit visa and a visa to Curaçao. He was deported to Shanghai in August 1941 and a year later was one of a small group of Allied citizens who were allowed to leave in the framework of a diplomatic exchange conducted under the auspices of the Polish authorities. The group was supposed to travel to London, but in Mozambique Romm requested permission from the local British consul to utilize his certificate to Palestine and subsequently arrived there on October 10, 1942.

18. "*Vaad ha–Hatzala*: A Factual Record," undated appeal for funds, Papers of Eliezer Silver at American University, Washington, DC; the figure of 4,000 "Yeshivoth people" also appears in "*Vaad ha–Hatzala* (Emergency Committee For War–Torn Yeshivoth)," a memorandum prepared by the Council of Jewish Federations and Welfare Funds (CJFWF) based on information supplied by *Vaad* officials, January 14, 1942, AJDC, file 360.

19. Bauer/YVS, p. 215

20. "Vaad ha-Hatzala," CJFWF memo, January 14, 1942, AJDC, file 360, p. 1. The figure of 4,000 prospective emigrants obviously included the Lithuanian rabbis and yeshiva students.

21. Letter of Buchman to Isaac B. Seligson (CJFWF), January 16, 1942, AJDC, file 360. Although the text provided by Buchman did not appear verbatim in the CJFWF report, it clearly stated that the JDC had provided most of the funds to cover the expenses for the maintenance and transportation of the refugee Torah scholars. See "Vaad ha–Hatzala," Budgeting Bulletin B–13, February 1942, AJDC-VH.

22. The Jewcom Report lists the number of Polish Jews as 2,178 (p. 8), but in the statistical breakdowns according to sex (p. 12a) and occupation (p. 13a) their number is listed as 2,074, and according to the emigration statistics (p. 22a) there were 2,111 Polish Jews who left Japan from July 1940 until November 1941.

23. "Situation of the Jewish Refugees in Japan," a report sent to the World Jewish Congress by its representative in Japan, Dr. Moshe Moiseeff, June 7, 1941, YVA, P–20, file 3.

24. Jewcom Report, p. 13a.

25. Letter of Moses Leavitt to Paul Veret (Omaha), August 27, 1941, AJDC, file 360.

26. See Chapter 6.

27. Estimates for the members of this group range from slightly under 400 (Polish sources) to slightly over 500 (*Vaad* sources), but figures based on assistance provided indicate that the number of refugee scholars was in the vicinity of 450. See Polish statistics (on the period until September 18, 1942), YVA, M–2,373. In CJFWF bulletin B–49 on the activities of the *Vaad,* there is mention of 512 persons rescued from Poland and Lithuania and stranded in China, but the number resettled in Shanghai through the *Vaad's* efforts is listed as 450; "*Vaad ha–Hatzala,*" CJFWF Bulletin B–49, June 22, 1943, AJDC, file 361. According to JDC Executive Vice–Chairman J. C. Hyman, "the 450 yeshivah people in Shanghai are receiving from JDC funds $5.00 per person monthly." See his letter to Dr. Maurice Taylor, December 10, 1941, AJDC, file 462.
28. See Chapter 7.
29. The United States admitted the largest number of Jews emigrating from Japan (532 Polish Jews, 1,246 Jews from Germany, and 186 classified as "others"), or almost half of the total. See Jewcom Report, p. 22a. The report is replete with mathematical and statistical errors but nonetheless presents an accurate overall picture. According to the figures compiled by Shmuel Graudenz, who served as the coordinator of the Palestine Office in Shanghai, 20 rabbis and 8 yeshiva students were among the 262 who made *aliyah* from January 1 to October 31, 1941, Zerach Wahraftig, *Palit ve–Sarid, be-Yemei ha-shoa,* pp. 275–276.
30. A few prominent rabbis and *roshei yeshiva* reached the United States via Western Europe, such as Rabbi Abraham Kalmanowitz of Ticktin, Poland, who had been closely affiliated with the Mir Yeshiva for years, and Rabbis Eliyahu Meyer Bloch and Chaim Mordechai Katz of the Telz Yeshiva. See "Oreiach Gadol Ve–Chashuv," *Ha–Pardes,* 13, no. 11, (Adar 5700/February 1940), 2; "Aseifat *Vaad ha–Hatzala,*" *Ha–Pardes,* 14, no. 9, (Kislev 5701/December 1940), 14–15. Among the *roshei yeshiva* who emigrated to Eretz Yisrael via Turkey were Rabbi Eliezer Finkel of Mir and Eliezer Shach of Kletzk. *Palit ve–Sarid,* pp. 152–153, 216. According to Warhaftig, the latter reached Eretz Yisrael via Japan, but that is not the case.
31. According to the *Vaad's* records, it spent no funds on transportation until 1941. Until then *Vaad ha–Hatzala* spent most of its money assisting in the maintenance of the yeshivot. "Emergency Committee for War-Torn Yeshivoth Vaad ha–Hatzala," Budgeting Bulletin B–27 of the CJFWF, May 1941, p. 4; "Vaad ha–Hatzala," CJFWF Memorandum, January 14, 1942, p. 4, AJDC, file 360.
32. "Memorandum; The Work Of The *Vaad ha–Hatzala* And Its Relation To The Joint Distribution Committee," undated (approximately mid-1942), AVH. The figures of $180 for the trip from Lithuania to Japan and an additional $100 for the voyage from Japan to the United States are also confirmed by the ticket receipts from Modern Tours, although in some cases the entire trip cost $267.50 and not $280; February 13, 1941, AVH.
33. We know that there were only 4 children among the 50 refugees who reached Shanghai directly from Vladivostok on May 1, 1941, so the estimate is based on approximately 50 families with children out of 85 rabbis who reached Japan. See "List of recent arrivals, May 2, 1941, AJDC, file 461.
34. Letter of Buchman to Nathan Padgug, August 7, 1941, AJDC, file 360; *Aiding Jews Overseas; report of the AJJDC Inc. for 1940 and the first 5 months of 1941,* New York, 1941, p. 39.

35. See, for example, "Memorandum" of Buchman to J. C. Hyman and Dr. Joseph Schwartz, July 7, 1941, AJDC, file 360; letter of Hyman to Rabbi Albert Gordon, September 4, 1941, AJDC, file 360.

36. Letter of Rabbi Simcha Wasserman to Dr. Bernard Kahn, January 19, 1942; response of Kahn to Wasserman, January 22, 1942, both AJDC, file 360.

37. Letter of Buchman to *Vaad ha–Hatzala*, April 17, 1941; letter of Buchman to Joseph Talamo, May 28, 1941, AJDC, file 360.

38. According to the figures on the *Vaad*, published by the CJFWF, the rabbinic rescue organization spent $96,730 on the maintenance of the yeshivot in 1940 and $120,227 for transportation (70%) and maintenance (30%) in Lithuania and Japan in 1941 prior to December 10. See CJFWF Budgeting Bulletin B–27, May 1941, p. 4, ACJFWF, VH reports; Budgeting Bulletin B–13, February 1942, p.4, AJDC–VH.

39. Letter of Miller to Buchman, June 14, 1941, AJDC–VH.

40. See, for example, a very bitter letter (one of many) from Rabbi Moshe Blau of Agudat Yisrael in Palestine in which he complains about the lack of assistance his organization has received from Rabbi Eliezer Silver, who, besides being the leader of *Vaad ha–Hatzala*, also headed the American branch of Agudat Yisrael. Letter of Blau to Jacob (Yaakov) Rosenheim, July 25, 1941, AAYEY, file 14.

41. The information regarding the plight of the refugee scholars reached the *Vaad* from the Soviet Union directly as well as via Palestine. See, for example, the cable of Isaak Burland, who was in Turkmenistan, to Rabbi Londinski, November 24, 1941, AVH. Letter of Rabbi Chizkiyahu Yoseph Mishkowski to Rabbis Silver and Kotler, November 9, 1941, AVH. Rabbi Mishkowski mentions a list of more than 200 rabbis, yeshiva students, and activists in his possession. Earlier Rabbi Herzog had sent a smaller list of rabbis and yeshiva students in the Soviet Union to British Chief Rabbi Hertz in the hope that he could secure exit permits for them. Letter of Rabbi Herzog to Rabbi Hertz, September 29, 1941, and reply of H. Pels (on behalf of Rabbi Hertz) to Rabbi Herzog, December 11, 1941, both AYHH, file 8.

42. Yoseph Litvak, *Plitim Yehudim mei–Polin be–Brit ha–Moetzot 1939–1946*, Jerusalem, 1988, pp. 18, 70, 128–148. Shimon Redlich, "The Jews Under Soviet Rule During World War II," unpublished doctoral dissertation, New York University, 1968, p. 60; Dov Levin, "Arrests and Deportations of Lithuanian Jews to Remote Areas of the Soviet Union, 1940–1941," *Crossroads*, no. 11, 1984, pp. 85–86.

43. Alter Pekier, *From Kletzk To Siberia; A yeshiva bachur's wandering during the Holocaust* (New York, 1985), pp. 32–71.

44. Litvak, *Plitim*, pp. 171–74; Edward J. Rozek, *Allied Wartime Diplomacy; A Pattern in Poland* (New York, 1958), pp. 50–67. In Labor Camp No. 7, for example, three refugee Polish yeshiva students were released on August 30, 1941, whereas more than 50 others were not released until October 1941. *From Kletzk to Siberia*, pp. 71–78.

45. Litvak, *Plitim*, pp. 184–185; Eliyahu Dobkin, "Report Concerning the Refugees Arriving in Teheran," September 24, 1942, Part I, p. 1, YVA, M–2/343; Redlich, pp. 81–83.

46. See the invitation to the meeting, December 1, 1941, AVH.

47. "Aseifat Vaad ha–Hatzala," *Ha–Pardes*, 15, no. 10 (Tevet 5702/January 1942), 2–3, 5.

48. Despite the prominent role of Mizrachi leader Rabbi Levinson in the leadership

of the *Vaad*, there were those in the Mizrachi movement who were critical of the *Vaad's* attitude toward their organization. See the letter of Leon Gellman (president of American Mizrachi) to Rabbi Karlinsky, December 11, 1941, AVH.

49. See the letter of Rabbi Silver to Rabbi Rosenberg, December 20, 1941, AYHR.

50. This was especially true of Rabbi Yisrael Halevi Rosenberg, who was a dominant leader of the *Agudat ha–Rabbanim* for many years. During his term as president he established contacts with many congressmen and public figures and became one of the best–known Orthodox leaders in the United States.

51. See, for example, the letters of Rabbi Moshe Blau to Jacob Rosenheim, October 2 and December 29, 1941, AAYEY, file 16; and the letter of Rosenheim to World Aguda, April 27, 1942, AAYA, file 2. According to Rosenheim, Rabbi Silver was interested only in *Vaad ha-Hatzala*, rabbis, and yeshiva students, and as far as he was concerned, the needs of other Orthodox Jews could be handled by the general relief organizations.

52. "Aseifat Vaad ha-Hatzala," *Ha-Pardes* 15, no. 10 (Tevet 5702/January 1942). 2–3, 5.

53. See, for example, the speeches by Rabbis Rosenberg, Silver, and Levinson at the *Agudat Ha–Rabbanim* convention in Atlantic City, NJ on June 22–24, 1942. Protocol of the convention, AAH. See also "Rabbi Silver Offers Special Prayer," *Every Friday*, December 19, 1941, p. 8.

54. Letter of Buchman to Seligson, January 16, 1942, AJDC, file 360.

55. "*Vaad ha-Hatzala*," Budgeting Bulletin B–13, of the Council of Jewish Federations and Welfare Funds, February 1942, pp. 3–4, AJDC–VH.

56. Ibid., p. 2; "*Vaad ha-Hatzala*," January 1942, p. 3, ACJFWF, I–69, Box 150, VH reports.

57. Letter of Buchman to Philip Bernstein (Cleveland), May 14, 1942, AJDC–VH; see also letter of Buchman to Joseph Talamo (Worcester), May 28, 1942, ibid., file 360.

58. Letter of Rabbi Silver to the JDC, May 11, 1942, AJDC–VH.

59. Letter of Rabbi Silver to Moses Leavitt, May 26, 1942, AJDC–VH.

60. Letter of Rabbis Rosenberg and Silver to J. C. Hyman, June 9, 1942, AJDC–VH.

61. Handwritten notes of Buchman in the margin of the letter of Rabbis Rosenberg and Silver, ibid.

62. Letter of Joseph Hellerstein to Buchman, June 16, 1941, AJDC–VH.

63. Letter of Rabbis Rosenberg and Silver to Joseph Hyman, June 9, 1941 (revised version), AJDC, file 360.

64. Letter of Hyman to Rabbis Rosenberg and Silver, June 18, 1942, AJDC–VH.

65. Letter of Leavitt to George Sherman, June 25, 1942, AJDC, file 463.

66. Letter of Rabbi Charles B. Chavel and Charles Strull to Hyman, August 20, 1942, AJDC, file 360.

67. Letter of Hyman to Rabbi Chavel and Strull, August 27, 1942, AJDC–VH.

68. See, for example, the minutes of the JDC Executive Committee meeting of June 17, 1942, pp. 4–8, AJDC, file 422.

69. "Minute," Meeting of the Emergency Administration Committee, May 27, 1942, AJDC, file 421; ibid. for June 2, 1942, AJDC, file 422.

70. Ibid. p. 2.

71. Letter of Hyman to Rabbi Chavel and Strull, August 27, 1942, AJDC–VH.

72. Letter of Rabbi Reuven Levovitz to the Foreign Control Division of the Federal Reserve Bank, August 24, 1942, AVH.

73. Letter of Tamar Kosher Meat Company to *Vaad ha–Hatzala*, June 9, 1942; letter of Jacob Pat, executive–secretary of the Jewish Labor Committee to Rabbi Kalmanowitz regarding the 134 parcels of food which the JLC sent to Russia on behalf of the *Vaad*, June 23, 1942, both AVH.

74. Cable of Rabbi Silver to Rabbi Mishkowski, July 10, 1942, and to Rabbis Herzog and Mishkowski, July 13, 1942, both AVH.

75. Letter of his son Rabbi David Mishkowski to the author, 23 Adar 5735 (March 6, 1975).

76. Letter of Rabbi Levovitz to the Foreign Control Division of the Federal Reserve Bank, August 24, 1942, AVH.

77. "Application For A License To Engage In A Foreign Exchange Transaction...," March 4, 1943, AVH.

78. Letter of Rabbi Silver to Rabbi Chavel, June 12, 1942, AJDC, file 360.

79. Cable of *Agudat ha–Rabbanim* (Rabbis Silver and Rosenberg) and deans of Polish rabbinical colleges (Rabbis Kotler and Kalmanowitz) to Ignacy Schwarzbart, July 8 and 11, 1942 (same cable), YVA, M–2/560.

80. "*Vaad ha–Hatzala*," Budgeting Bulletin B–13, February, 1942, p. 2, AVH; "Kriya Nilhava mi–Vaad ha–Hatzala," *Ha–Pardes*, 16, no. 3 (Sivan 5702/June 1942), 4; "Bichiyot ve–Yilalot be–Lishkat" Vaad ha–Hatzala, *Ha–Pardes*, 16, no. 4, (Tammuz 5702/July 1942), 3–4.

81. Cable of Rabbis Herzog and Kahane to Dr. Schwarzbart, August 11, 1941, YVA, M–2, 322.

82. "Report to the Jewish Agency" by Eliyahu Rudnitzki, September 8, 1942, YVA, M–2, 343.

83. Moses Leavitt, "Memorandum On The Refugee Situation In Shanghai," June 17, 1942, AJDC, file 463.

84. See, for example, cable of Rabbi Kalmanowitz to Rabbi Milewsky, January 21, 1942, AVH. Rabbi Milewsky had studied in the yeshivot of Grodno and Slabodka and was the unofficial leader of the Orthodox community in Uruguay.

85. Cable of Rabbi Kalmanowitz to Rabbi Wolbe, January 22, 1942, AVH.

86. Interview of the author with Rabbi Milewsky, September 1, 1975, YVA, 0–3/3554.

87. Cable of Rabbi Shmulewitz to Rabbi Milewsky, January 16, 1942, Archives of Rabbi Aaron Milewsky (hereafter called AMA); Milewsky interview.

88. Cable of Rabbi Kalmanowitz to Rabbi Milewsky, January 22, 1942, AMA.

89. Letter of Rabbi Milewsky to *Vaad ha–Hatzala*, October 23, 1942, AMA.

90. Milewsky interview.

91. Letter of Rabbi Klein and Y. Chidekel to Rabbi Milewsky, June 1, 1942, AMA.

92. Letter of Erlanger to Rabbi Milewsky, June 21, 1942, AMA.

93. Letter of Erlanger to Rabbi Milewsky, July 23, 1942, AMA.

Chapter 9

News of the Final Solution and Attempts to Achieve Unity

Toward the end of the summer of 1942 the news from Europe regarding the Jews under Nazi occupation became increasingly alarming. The details of numerous mass murders seemed to lend credence to indications that European Jewry might be facing total annihilation as a result of an unprecedented, carefully planned onslaught of violence against them. These reports reached American Jewish organizations in different ways and from various sources. Both the *Vaad ha-Hatzala* and *Agudat Yisrael* received such information at this time, prompting a fundamental, albeit temporary, change in the tactics adopted by various key Orthodox organizations vis-à-vis their non-Orthodox counterparts.

If until now leading Orthodox organizations, such as *Vaad ha-Hatzala, Agudat ha-Rabbanim* and *Agudat Yisrael,* had pursued an independent course of action regarding rescue initiatives, it was now obvious that the situation required cooperation with the rest of the community. Given the enormity of the tragedy, the Orthodox activists realized that they could not handle a catastrophe of such proportions with their limited means and so they sought to work with the entire American Jewish community. Yet the task of achieving communal unity for rescue proved to be far more difficult than the rabbis and Orthodox activists originally supposed. And even the unprecedented threats facing European Jewry could not, as we shall see, convince the disparate elements of American Jewry to unite for this purpose.

219

* * *

On September 3, 1942, Sylwin Strakacz, the Polish consul general in New York, telephoned *Aguda* activist Dr. Isaac Lewin that he had received an urgent cable at the consulate for Jacob Rosenheim, the leader of world *Agudat Yisrael*, who was then living in New York. The cable was from Isaac Sternbuch, an Orthodox Jew living in Montreux, Switzerland, who headed HIJEFS, an organization he and his wife Recha had established to assist in relief and rescue activities, and which specialized in assisting religious Jews.[1] The message had been sent via the Polish diplomatic channels in order to speed its delivery and avoid possible censorship. Strakacz read the contents to Lewin and sent the text the same day. Sternbuch's cable, which was based on communications he had received from occupied Poland,[2] read as follows:

> According to recently received authentic information, the German authorities have evacuated the last Ghetto in Warsaw, bestially murdering about one hundred thousand Jews. Mass murders continue. From the corpses of the murdered, soap and artificial fertilizers are produced. The deportees from other occupied countries will meet the same fate. It must be supposed that only energetic reprisals on the part of America could halt these persecutions. Do whatever you can to cause an American reaction to halt these persecutions. Do whatever you can to produce such a reaction, stirring up statesmen, the press, and the community.
>
> Inform Wise, Silver, Lubavitcher, Einstein, Klatskin, Goldman, Thomas Mann and others about this.
>
> Do not mention my name. Please acknowledge receipt of the present dispatch.[3]

Sternbuch apparently doubted that his cable would reach its destination as quickly as he hoped, so on the same day he called Rabbi Avraham Kalmanowitz at the *Vaad ha-Hatzala*. According to the testimony of Kalmanowitz's assistant Alex Weisfogel, the rabbi fainted in the middle of the conversation and Sternbuch delivered the rest of the horrible news to Weisfogel himself.[4]

This was the first confirmation regarding the systematic annihilation of Polish Jewry and the dangers faced by all Jews in occupied

Europe. When it reached the Orthodox circles in the United States, it galvanized the rabbis and activists into action. Rosenheim immediately cabled the contents of the cable to President Roosevelt "in the name of the Orthodox Jews all over the world" and proposed, in addition to Sternbuch's suggestions, that the United States initiate a joint intervention of all the neutral countries in Europe and the Americas to express their deep moral indignation."[5] In addition, despite his feeling of being "physically broken down from this harrowing cable,"[6] the elderly *Aguda* leader contacted Rabbi Kalmanowitz and other Orthodox leaders, as well as the individuals listed in Sternbuch's cable.[7] Rosenheim also asked Lewin, who served as the liaison between Orthodox circles and the Polish diplomats in the United States, to ask the embassy to arrange a meeting with President Roosevelt via the State Department.[8]

On the next day, September 4, Lewin called the Polish embassy in Washington and spoke to Minister Plenipotentiary Michal Kwapiszewski regarding the possibility of arranging such a meeting for Rosenheim. The Polish diplomat replied in writing the same day that Polish ambassador Ciechanowski supported such an initiative and in fact had already spoken to Roy Atherton of the State Department regarding the destruction of the Warsaw Ghetto. Atherton had informed him that the information had already reached the American authorities in early August, but they had so far been unable to confirm its authenticity and so had neither publicized the reports nor officially responded to them. Atherton was ready, however, to meet with Rosenheim to discuss steps the government might take once the news was confirmed.[9]

In the meantime, Rabbi Kalmanowitz had already begun on the previous day to notify Jewish leaders regarding the terrible news from Poland and to arrange meetings with various personages. Among those he spoke to was Rabbi Stephen Wise, leader of the American Jewish Congress and the World Jewish Congress and the undisputed leader of American Jewry.[10] Kalmanowitz asked Wise to meet with Orthodox leaders as soon as possible, and the two agreed to meet the following day at the offices of the *Agudat ha-Rabbanim* on the Lower East Side of New York City.

Thus on September 4, Rabbis Kalmanowitz, Silver, and Aron Kotler joined with Rosenheim to meet with Stephen Wise, who was accompanied by Dr. Aryeh Tartakower and Dr. Leon Kubowitzki of the World Jewish Congress. The rabbis were extremely shaken by the news from Sternbuch and demanded that the information be fully publicized in order to mobilize the community for concerted action. Wise, however, was much more cautious, claiming that they needed further confirmation before the details of the murders were released to the media. What he apparently did not reveal to the rabbis,[11] was that Sternbuch's cable had been preceded by another telegram originally sent from Switzerland which included a similar, albeit slightly different, message regarding the atrocities in Eastern Europe.

One week earlier, on August 28, Wise had received a communication from MP Samuel Sydney Silverman, leader of the British section of the World Jewish Congress, with a message from Gerhardt Riegner, the World Jewish Congress's representative in Switzerland. Riegner had sent the cable on August 8 in Geneva to American consul Howard Elting, Jr., and subsequently to his British counterpart. It indicated that Riegner had received information from a generally reliable source to the effect that a plan for the mass annihilation of European Jewry was being considered by Nazi leaders and that its implementation was planned for the coming fall. Among the methods discussed was the use of prussic acid, and according to the informant, the killings would be carried out somewhere in Eastern Europe.

Wise's caution most likely stemmed from the attitude of the State Department officials. After receiving the cable from Geneva, which was transmitted by Elting along with an endorsement of Riegner, they had decided not to pass it on to the American Jewish leader. This was the reason that Wise only learned of its contents on August 28 when he received Silverman's cable. Riegner had asked the Jewish member of parliament to "Please inform and consult New York," and Silverman did so without the knowledge of the U.S. State Department, which had in effect censored Riegner's message from Switzerland. (The British Foreign Ministry had also had reservations about transmitting the cable to Silverman but, after a week of deliberations, delivered it along with the advice that they had no information that would confirm its contents.)

On September 2, 1942, Wise sent Silverman's cable to Undersecretary of State Sumner Welles, unaware that the State Department already had a copy of Riegner's original message. Wise wrote that Riegner was a reliable person ("not an alarmist") and suggested that the information be brought to President Roosevelt's attention and that the American minister in Switzerland meet with Riegner to determine whether he had any additional information regarding the Nazis' plans. Welles phoned Wise the next day and asked him not to publicize the information until the State Department could confirm its authenticity.[12] It is probably for that reason that Wise did not reveal it to the rabbis. In fact, he apparently tried to play down the reports, although in theory he could have considered Sternbuch's cable a confirmation of the information from Riegner.[13]

Another problematic issue at the meeting related to what response the community should adopt if the news from Switzerland did prove accurate. The representatives of the World Jewish Congress suggested such actions as protest meetings and a march on Washington, but the Orthodox representatives were at this point adamantly opposed to such measures. According to Kubowitzki's account of the meeting, they responded to these suggestions in the harshest terms imaginable:

> You are the grave-diggers of our people. You have chosen to antagonize Hitler. You proclaimed a boycott against Germany, you published strongly worded resolutions. Hitler is not the first Haman in our history. The experience of centuries has taught us how to deal with Haman. Stop your provocations! Let us rescue our people through our tested methods.[14]

The Orthodox representatives believed that quiet behind-the-scenes lobbying (*shtadlanut*) would prove more effective than the standard mechanisms of modern political protest.[15] Ironically, within approximately a year the tables would be turned, with the Orthodox organizations sponsoring a protest march by hundreds of rabbis in Washington and the leader of the World Jewish Congress working behind the scenes to mitigate its impact.

Despite these differences of opinion, Wise agreed to the rabbis' suggestion that he convene a meeting of the leaders of the major American Jewish organizations to discuss the community's response to the news from Switzerland. Thus, on September 5, 1942, he invited more than thirty Jewish leaders to a "special meeting" to be held the next day "of leading Jewish bodies to consider together action which can and should be taken" in the wake of the receipt of "horrifying news of mass massacres of Jews... information so appalling and implications for future so grave...."[16] In the meantime, Rosenheim and other Orthodox leaders met on September 4 with James G. Macdonald, chairman of the President's Advisory Committee on Political Refugees, who had previously assisted the *Vaad ha-Hatzala* in efforts to rescue numerous refugee rabbis and yeshiva students to the United States. Macdonald, who was on good terms with Eleanor Roosevelt, sent her a copy of the cable received from Switzerland, as well as a message indicating that he thought it important that she be aware of this information.[17]

On September 6, 1942, leaders of 34 leading American Jewish organizations met at the offices of the World Jewish Congress in New York to share the news from Europe and discuss what steps should be taken. Among the Orthodox participants were Jacob Rosenheim, Isaac Lewin, and Meier Shenkolewski representing *Agudat Yisrael*, as well as Rabbi Kalmanowitz and Shabse Frankel, an activist layman, representing the *Vaad ha-Hatzala*.[18] There are conflicting reports on whether Wise revealed the contents of Riegner's cable at the meeting,[19] but Sternbuch's message was definitely presented. Wise demanded, however, that the news from Europe be kept secret until he could obtain official confirmation from the State Department. In fact, according to various sources, he even accused the Orthodox groups of spreading atrocity propaganda or horror stories.[20] Given the information already at Wise's disposal, such charges hardly seem justified, but on the other hand his doing this might have been a tactic to ensure that the Orthodox, who had difficulty accepting the decision to maintain silence, would keep their word.

At this meeting a bitter argument also erupted between the representatives of the *Agudat ha-Rabbanim* and the Jewish Labor Committee, with the former attacking the latter for publicly supporting underground activity and guerilla warfare. Another issue of contention was the advisability of threatening the Germans with reprisal attacks; the Orthodox representatives vehemently opposed such an approach, according to a report by one of the participants at the meeting.[21]

Another practical decision made at the meeting was the establishment of an ad hoc committee headed by Stephen Wise to monitor the situation and decide policy in the interim. It was initially made up of representatives of the American Jewish Congress, B'nai B'rith, Jewish Labor Committee, and *Agudat ha-Rabbanim*, and it held its first meeting three days later. At that meeting Wise revealed the contents of the cable from Riegner which he had received via Silverman and it was decided to send a delegation to Washington to meet with State Department officials and request that the government attempt to determine what was happening in Poland. On September 10 Sumner Welles met with a delegation of Jewish leaders and agreed to initiate an investigation. During this period Wise also met with Treasury Secretary Robert Morgenthau, whom he asked to inform President Roosevelt about the news, as well as with other leading personages and State Department officials.[22]

In the meantime, Orthodox activists in the United States received additional information regarding the murders in Europe via Sternbuch in Switzerland. In letters written in veiled language using Yiddish terms, J. Domb, Sternbuch's informant, transmitted messages which clearly indicated that almost all the Jews of Warsaw were being murdered. For example, in a letter that was dated September 4, 1942, (but which arrived several weeks later) he wrote:

> I spoke to Mr. Jaeger. He told me that he will invite all relatives of the family Achenu (with the exception of Miss Eisenzweig from Warsaw) to his countryside dwelling Kever. I am done here. I feel lonely. As to the Citrus fruit, I hope I will receive them in time, but I do not know whether I will then find any of my acquaintances. Uncle Gerush also works in Warsaw. His friend Miso works together with him and is a very diligent worker.... Please pray for me.

Once the Yiddish words are translated, the message becomes crystal clear: Based on information received from Nazis (*Jaeger*, hunter), all the Jews (*Achenu*, our brothers) with the exception of the iron workers (*Eisenzweig*) are being sent to their deaths (*Kever*, grave). By the time of the Sukkot holiday celebrated in the fall (when a citrus fruit, etrog, is used in the ritual prayers) it is not clear whether any of the Jews will still be here. The deportations (*gerush*) are proceeding apace in Warsaw and the number of deaths (*Miso*) is steadily rising. In a letter dated September 12 Domb wrote that *achenu* had died and that there was no one left to use the citrus fruit. [23]

As additional details on the murders reached Orthodox circles in the United States, the commitment to preserve public silence on this issue became increasingly difficult to maintain. The rabbis and activists found themselves in an increasingly untenable position as they learned more and more details regarding the mass annihilation of European Jewry. On the one hand, they believed that the decision to refrain from publicizing the news of the murders was not only a mistake, but an example of gross negligence on their part, a betrayal of their function as Jewish leaders. On the other hand, they along with the rest of the organized Jewish community, had undertaken to refrain from publicizing the information until it could be authenticated. Moreover, any group that did not observe the ban would be ostracized, and so the leaders of the *Vaad ha-Hatzala*, *Agudat ha-Rabbanim*, and *Agudat Yisrael* felt compelled, at least initially, to maintain silence. Regardless of the impact of the terrible news, they did not feel sufficiently strong to be able to break ranks with the American Jewish leadership.[24]

Even this restraint had its limits, however, and after approximately two months *Aguda* activist Dr. Isaac Lewin broke the silence. In an article entitled, "The Catastrophe of European Jewry and Its Impact in America," which appeared in the Kislev 5703 (November 1942) issue of the Agudist Yiddish-language monthly *Iddische Shtimme*, he revealed, albeit in relatively vague terms, the events that had transpired over the past two months. According to Lewin's account, he received the first news regarding the mass murders (the details of which he did not elaborate) in early September 1942, but the American Jewish leadership decided at that point to refrain from publicizing the reports. Despite the fact that every attempt to verify the news yielded additional details on deportations, mass murder, and the like, the leaders of the American Jewish organizations continued to maintain silence.

Lewin bitterly attacked this policy, which he described as contrary to the leaders' "Jewish and human obligations." He called upon the Jewish organizations to publicize the news at least in the Jewish press and begin to take concrete action to save Jewish lives. Lewin called upon Stephen Wise and Nahum Goldmann, who headed the ad hoc committee to monitor developments and who had been meeting in Washington with U.S. officials, to enlist other Jewish organizations, such as *Agudat ha-Rabbanim* and *Agudat Yisrael*, in their lobbying efforts and to establish a permanent Jewish delegation or presence in the American capital. Convinced that concrete measures could save lives, Lewin implored the leaders of American Jewry to begin such efforts immediately. In his words:

We must not forget for a minute our brothers and sisters in the Nazi hell!

Jews are still alive in Poland! We don't know where, we don't know how many. But it is criminal to despair regarding their fate. Every day is significant, every minute is valuable....

At this time every person who sits idle, even for an hour, is responsible for the lives of those who can still be saved.

We ask the leaders of the Jewish organizations in America: What will you answer when you will be held accountable? *What will you answer when you are asked what you did when the blood of your brothers flowed ceaselessly?* [emphasis in original][25]

Lewin's impassioned plea, published in a relatively obscure journal with an extremely limited circulation, obviously had no effect on the policy of the American Jewish leaders. In fact, it was not reprinted in any of the other Jewish press, not even in the Orthodox newspapers and journals. Although various accounts were published regarding the murder of European Jews, primarily in Poland, none indicated that the Nazis had embarked upon a plan for the total annihilation of all the Jews in Europe.[26]

It was only after U.S. Undersecretary of State Summer Welles summoned Wise to Washington on November 24 to confirm the reports from Europe that the American Jewish leader convened a press conference to reveal the information already in his possession. Wise told the reporters that according to sources confirmed by the State Department 2 million Jews had already been murdered in a campaign to wipe out European Jewry. Eighty percent of the half million Jews originally living in Warsaw had already been annihilated, and the Nazis were in the process of deporting Jews from all over Europe to Poland to be killed. This news received fairly extensive coverage in the general press and was supplemented by reports from Great Britain and Palestine. Needless to say, it was covered far more extensively in the Jewish press.[27]

That night Wise returned to New York, and on the next day he met with the members of the ad hoc committee of Jewish leaders that had been established at the September 6 meeting. The committee at this point consisted of representatives of the American Jewish Committee, American Jewish Congress, Jewish Labor Committee, B'nai B'rith, World Jewish Congress, Synagogue Council of America and *Agudat ha-Rabbanim*. In the wake of the confirmation of the news from Europe, the committee agreed upon a five-point plan of action designed to publicize the news as widely as possible in the hope of arousing public opinion: (1) holding a press conference by Stephen Wise (which was held that afternoon); (2) sending a cable request to 500 newspapers to publish editorials condemning the murders; (3) cabling several hundred prominent non-Jews to issue statements regarding the atrocities; (4) calling for a worldwide day of mourning and prayer to be observed on Wednesday, December 2, 1942; and (5) attempting to arrange a meeting with President Roosevelt to discuss the plight of European Jewry. One of the Orthodox representatives proposed that the day of mourning be observed during Chanukah, but his proposal was opposed by Rabbi Aron Kotler, who explained that such a step would be interpreted as an admission that the situation of European Jewry was totally hopeless and that would be counterproductive.[28]

The arrangements for the meeting with President Roosevelt were handled by a special subcommittee, which was first convened by Stephen Wise five days later at the offices of the American Jewish Congress. By this time Wise had been informed by the State Department that President Roosevelt was prepared to meet a small delegation of Jewish leaders, but the composition of the group had to be determined. After much discussion, it was decided that the delegation would include the presidents of the four major defense agencies—Stephen Wise of the American Jewish Congress, Maurice Wertheim of the American Jewish Committee, Henry Monsky of B'nai B'rith, and Adolf Held of the Jewish Labor Committee—as well as presidents of the Synagogue Council of America (Rabbi Israel Goldstein) and of the *Agudat ha-Rabbanim* (Rabbi Yisrael Halevi Rosenberg).

Two days later Wise wrote his "Dear Boss" letter to Roosevelt imploring him to meet with the delegation regarding "the most overwhelming disaster of Jewish history." Noting Hitler's decision to annihilate all the Jews in Nazi-occupied Europe and the "indisputable" figure of 2 million Jews murdered, Wise expressed the hope that the President would "speak a word which may bring solace and hope to millions of Jews who mourn and be an expression of the conscience of the American people." Being aware that Roosevelt was not enthusiastic about such a meeting, Wise concluded his letter with a reminder that there might be negative repercussions if the President did not agree to meet with the Jewish delegation. In his words, "It would be gravely misunderstood, if despite your overwhelming preoccupation, you did not make it possible to receive our delegation, and to utter what I am sure will be your heartening and consoling reply."[29]

On December 2, 1942, the same day that Wise wrote to Roosevelt, Jews the world over observed the day of mourning and prayer which had originally been proposed by the *Agudat ha-Rabbanim* on the basis of a suggestion by Palestinian (Ashkenazic) Chief Rabbi Yitzhak ha-Levi Herzog. The day was observed throughout the United States and in 29 other countries, with the focal point in New York City, which had the world's largest Jewish community. The Yiddish newspapers appeared with black borders, special prayer services were held in the afternoon in synagogues, special radio programs were broadcast, and a ten-minute work stoppage was observed by hundreds of thousands of Jewish labor union members as well as numerous non-Jews.[30]

The "Day of Mourning and Prayer" was followed by a meeting of the delegation of Jewish leaders with President Roosevelt, on December 8, 1942, at the White House. The participants were the leaders of the four major defense organizations and Rabbi Rosenberg of the *Agudat ha-Rabbanim*. (Israel Goldstein was unable to participate.) At the meeting Wise read a letter from the ad hoc committee which stressed the need for immediate action to save European Jewry; he asked the President to issue warnings that those involved in the murders would be prosecuted and to establish a commission that could collect and publicize information on Nazi crimes against civilians. He also submitted a 20-page memorandum entitled "Blueprint for Extermination," which summarized the available data on the murders country by country.[31] Roosevelt agreed to issue a warning regarding war crimes and assured the delegation that the government would do whatever it could to "be of service to your people in this tragic moment."

The meeting was followed by a press conference at which Wise distributed copies of the delegation's letter to the President and the memorandum summarizing the information on the annihilation of European Jewry. He noted, moreover, that the President had authorized him to say that Roosevelt had been profoundly shocked to learn that 2 million Jews had already been murdered, and those responsible for these crimes would be held accountable. This press conference marked the completion of the ad hoc committee's plan of action, and Wise therefore initiated its dissolution.[32] In effect, the only official framework within the American Jewish community for unified action now no longer existed. Despite the fact that the mass murder of European Jews was proceeding at an accelerated pace, such a framework would not be created until more than three months later. Once again, extremely valuable time was being squandered because of the inability of American Jewish organizations to unite for rescue activities.

Although Orthodox organizations were active in the efforts to organize an effective response to the increasingly harrowing reports emanating from Europe, the news of the mass annihilation of European Jewry had little immediate impact on practical rescue activities launched from the United States. Although a few rabbis as early as November 1942 called for practical steps to deal with the emergency in Nazi-occupied Europe,[33] the *Vaad ha-Hatzala* did not at first alter its rescue policies. On the contrary, during the fall and winter of 1942–1943 it continued to focus its primary efforts on assisting the refugee scholars in Central Asia and Shanghai. This policy was clearly reflected at the *Vaad's* annual conference, held in New York City on January 5–6, 1943. Not one of the resolutions passed at the conference called for any practical measures to expand the scope of the *Vaad's* rescue activities beyond its original mandate. In this respect, it was Rabbi Eliezer Silver who, in his opening address, set the tone for the conference. According to the Cincinnati rabbi, dwelling on the plight of European Jewry at this point would distract those assembled from the major task at hand. In his words:

> ...we are all broken-hearted and know of the troubles which have befallen European Jewry and this meeting was called for great and mighty deeds. We must raise the maintenance— bread to eat and clothes to wear—and most of all, we need large sums because we have promises that we will be able to transfer those in Shanghai and those in Siberia to Eretz Yisrael and South Africa. This is the greatest work and we need one and a half million dollars to achieve it.[34]

Although the conference ultimately decided to reduce the goal of the *Vaad's* campaignby half, the policy he advocated was accepted without dissent. The efforts of the rabbinic relief organization would continue to be devoted exclusively to the rescue of the refugee Torah scholars in Central Asia and Shanghai.[35]

Given the fact that it was now reasonably clear to the leaders of the *Vaad* that European Jewry was facing mass murder, if not total annihilation, how could they justify such a policy? There were five major reasons that the news from Europe did not bring about an immediate change in the *Vaad's* activities. The first is that the rabbis, like the other American Jewish leaders, had not yet internalized the implications of the information regarding European Jewry. At this point, not a single American Jewish organization had reoriented its practical policies to respond to the new emergency. To the extent that such changes were ultimately made, they were instituted months later.[36]

The second reason is that the *Vaad's* leaders were convinced that the yeshiva *leit* in Siberia and Central Asia, as well as in Shanghai, were in danger of dying of starvation. This was certainly the case for those in the Soviet Union, but it was also to a lesser extent, true of those living under Japanese occupation.[37] While dying of starvation may have been less shocking than being murdered in a gas chamber, the result was certainly the same.

The third reason was that the *Vaad* did not consider its task complete until the refugee scholars had been brought to places where they could resume their full-time Torah study under reasonable conditions. The Soviet Union and Japanese-occupied Shanghai could hardly be considered satisfactory in that respect.

The fourth reason was that the leaders of the *Vaad* had always regarded the rescue of the rabbis and yeshiva students as their personal responsibility. They realized that in the wake of the revelations regarding the destruction of European Jewry, it was more than likely that the plight of the refugee scholars who were not under Nazi occupation would henceforth be accorded a very low priority in the distribution of relief funds, a situation alluded to by Rabbi Silver in his opening address.[38]

The final reason was practical. In view of the limited funds at the *Vaad's* disposal and its consistent inability to raise enough money to carry out its entire program, it was simply unfeasible for the organization to assume additional responsibilities. This reality was clearly reflected in the fundraising goals set at the conference, as well as in Rabbi Silver's highly critical remarks regarding American Jewry's failure to provide the *Vaad* with the funds it needed to perform the tasks at hand. In Rabbi Silver's opinion, both the rabbinate and the entire community bore part of the blame for the fact that so many

Jews, and especially Torah scholars, had not been rescued, because the *Vaad* could have saved them had they had sufficient resources. The community could therefore not claim that "their hands had not spilled this blood."[39] They should make every effort to raise funds for the *Vaad*. In his words:

> A campaign to raise three quarters of a million dollars was announced at this meeting. This is a small minute sum compared to our needs. Let our rabbis and public figures everywhere take note of the great responsibility resting upon us, and let them volunteer for the holy work of *Vaad Hatzala*. We must not sit idle and watch the holy be devoured, G-d forbid. The blood of our brothers and sisters is crying out to us from the earth which was cursed by G-d.[40]

The feeling that the community should be doing more than it was was not confined to practical issues such as fundraising. There were also religious issues which came to the fore time and again as the situation in Europe worsened. For example, in conjunction with the decision of *Agudat ha-Rabbanim* to set aside December 2 as a special day of mourning (and fasting), *Ha-Pardes* issued an impassioned call to the community and especially to Reform Jews to repent and adhere to Orthodox Jewish practice. The journal, which for many years served as the unofficial mouthpiece of *Agudat ha-Rabbanim*, had on numerous occasions since the outbreak of the war called upon American Jews to return to religious observance,[41] but this was the first time that its appeal specifically targeted Reform Jews. In the rabbis' minds, the fate of the Jewish people was directly linked to the level and extent of Jewish observance, and therefore in the wake of the new circumstances in Europe they were ready to appeal even to their staunchest ideological enemies in order to alleviate the plight of European Jewry. In the words of the appeal:

> ...hell is open under our feet and now is a time for prayer and lamentation. We address ourselves to those who are close and those who are far—the Reform members of our people. Please have mercy do not stand aside any longer. Fast and accept the responsibility of being one people with us—observe the laws of the true Torah, get rid of the foreign Gods. Clear your tables

of forbidden foods, observe the Sabbath and pray to *Ha-Shem*, the god of the heavens. Get rid of the foreign clothes from your temples and return to *Ha-Shem*. Let us open the gates of mercy together and shout out to the G-d of Israel—Look we are one people, one Torah, one G-d.[42]

This call for renewed Jewish observance was also reflected at the *Vaad's* conference, where the rabbis responded in theological terms to the catastrophic news from Europe. After listening to a hair-raising letter ostensibly written on behalf of 93 students of the Beit Yaakov women's seminary in Cracow who preferred to commit suicide rather than be violated in Nazi brothels,[43] Rabbi Moshe Shatzkes proclaimed:

> We believe in G-d and his Torah, and we are not questioning the severity with which the Jewish people are currently being judged, nor do we question the anger; and we pray and appeal to G-d with all our soul and might that he show us his countenance and hear our cries and will promptly bring about the salvation of the Jewish people in our time and will take revenge on all our enemies.[44]

Fortified with their steadfast belief in the righteousness of their cause and the necessity of the work of the *Vaad ha-Hatzala*, the rabbis set out to achieve their practical financial goals. From the time of U.S. entry into World War II until the end of March 1943 the *Vaad ha-Hatzala* raised $225,595.36[45] which was proportionally only slightly higher than the amounts raised prior to that date ($145,372.26 for the period January 1–December 10, 1941).[46] More than half of the funds were utilized to send relief to the refugee scholars in Siberia and Central Asia ($118,555), while most of the rest of the relief funds disbursed were directed to the rabbis and yeshiva students in Shanghai ($69,000).[47] Despite intensive efforts by the rabbis,[48] the *Vaad's* campaign was adversely affected by the same problems that had plagued their efforts from the very beginning: the limited appeal of their cause and their problematic relations with the JDC. Although the latter had begrudgingly admitted in the late spring of 1942 that the *Vaad's* efforts were not entirely duplicating their own, JDC officials as well and those of the Council of Jewish Federations and Welfare Funds continued to discourage local federations from allocating funds to the *Vaad ha-Hatzala*.[49]

In mid-February, for example, Rabbi Eliezer Silver sent the Federation for Jewish Service of Omaha, a request for financial assistance, accompanied by a report of the *Vaad's* recent activities and needs. According to Rabbi Silver, the latter could not, however, "convey to you those cumulative abstract values of spiritual and cultural worth, the result of centuries of devoted work of great Rabbis and Talmudic scholars who are being saved directly through our efforts. Those values must be felt and cannot be stated in words."

The proverbial "bottom line" was financial. The *Vaad* estimated that the Omaha community should contribute a minimum of $3,500 to its campaign, and it threatened to conduct a separate fundraising campaign if the local federation refused to cooperate.[50] Paul Veret, the director of the Omaha federation, wrote to the JDC and CJFWF asking for information on the *Vaad,* specifically raising the issue of whether the rabbinical rescue organization was duplicating the efforts of the JDC. He also asked for the latest figures on the allocations the *Vaad* had received from federations.[51]

Veret received responses from both Isaac Seligson of the CJFWF and Henrietta Buchman of the JDC. The former letter was somewhat noncommittal ("your community must determine whether it desires to allocate funds for the yeshivoth groups or whether it is of the opinion that the yeshivah problem in Siberia is part of the Jewish refugee problem which the JDC is attempting to alleviate"),[52] as was ostensibly Buchman's. But although she did not directly attack the *Vaad,* her detailed analysis of the JDC's relief activities on behalf of the Polish refugees in the Soviet Union and Shanghai left little room for doubt that in her mind the JDC was far more deserving than the *Vaad ha-Hatzala* of the support of the Omaha Jewish federation.[53]

Ultimately the *Vaad* received $1,000 from Omaha,[54] but the negative attitude of the major American Jewish fundraising agencies undoubtedly significantly reduced the funds raised by the rabbinic rescue organization and severely hampered its ability to carry out its relief and rescue programs. In fact, in 1942, of 128 welfare funds that submitted detailed reports of their allocations, 42 contributed a total of $23,010 to the *Vaad ha-Hatzala.* Although this constituted a substantial increase over the previous year (during which 22 of 93 reporting welfare funds contributed $14,225),[55] it still constituted a distinct minority of the local federations and reflected the reluctance of the great majority to support the *Vaad ha-Hatzala's* particularistic program.

Notes

1. For biographical information on the Sternbuch family and details regarding HIJEFS (*Hilfsverein fur Judische Fluchtlinge in Shanghai*) see Joseph Friedenson and David Kranzler, *Heroine of Rescue: The incredible story of Recha Sternbuch who saved thousands from the Holocaust* (Brooklyn, 1984).

2. A major source of information was a Polish Jew named J. Domb, who was living in Warsaw. Since he was recognized as a Swiss citizen by the Nazis, he was not forced to live in the ghetto and was able to communicate with the Sternbuchs. See ibid., pp. 90–91.

3. Isaac Lewin, "Attempts at Rescuing European Jews with the Help of Polish Diplomatic Missions during World War II," *The Polish Review*, Part I, XXII, no. 4 (1977), p. 5.

4. Amos Bunim, *A Fire in His Soul*, p. 108; Friedenson and Kranzler, *Heroine of Rescue*, p. 92.

5. Cable of Jacob Rosenheim to President Roosevelt, September 3, 1942, NA, European War 748.00716.

6. David S. Wyman, *The Abandonment of the Jews; America and the Holocaust 1941–1945* (New York, 1984), p. 45.

7. David Kranzler, *Thy Brother's Blood; The Orthodox Jewish Response During the Holocaust* (Brooklyn, 1987), p. 91.

8. David Kranzler, "Orthodox Ends, Unorthodox Means; The Role of the Vaad Hatzalah and Agudath Israel during the Holocaust," in Seymour Maxwell Finger, ed., *American Jewry During the Holocaust*, 1984, p. 3.

9. Isaac Lewin, "Attempts At Rescuing European Jews With The Help Of Polish Diplomatic Missions During World War II," *The Polish Review*, Part II, XXIV, no. 1 (1979), pp. 46–47.

10. For details on Stephen Wise's preeminent role in the American Jewish community see among many others Melvin Urofsky, *A Voice That Spoke for Justice; The Life and Times of Stephen S. Wise* (Albany, 1982).

11. Kranzler, *Thy Brother's Blood*, pp.92, 295. According to Orthodox sources, they were never informed by Wise about Riegner's cable. Lewin, for example, claimed in 1947 that Riegner's cable reached Wise only after the September 6 meeting of leaders of American Jewish organizations. "Ver hat upgehalten di rettungsarbeit far eiropishe idin," *Morgen Dzurnal*, November 23, 1947. Wyman claims that Wise did convey the contents of the cable to Rosenheim (Wyman, *Abandonment of the Jews* p. 46), but it appears that this was not divulged until September 9 to the members of an ad hoc committee established on September 6 by a meeting of representatives of more than 30 American Jewish organizations.

12. Ibid., pp. 43–45; Yehuda Bauer, "When Did They Know?" *Midstream*, XIV, no. 4 (April 1968), 51–58.

13. Kranzler, *Thy Brother's Blood*, p. 92.

14. Aryeh Leon Kubovy, "Criminal State vs. Moral Society," *Yad Vashem Bulletin*, no. 13 (October 1963), p. 6. Kubovy refers to a meeting held in 1942 "with leading Orthodox rabbis and with heads of Polish and Lithuanian Yeshivot who had reached the United States via Siberia" following receipt of an "alarming cable telling of massacres of Jews in Eastern Europe," an obvious reference to the September 4 meeting

at the offices of the *Agudat ha–Rabbanim*. In reality, only one of the rabbis at the meeting (Rabbi Aron Kotler) arrived via Siberia.

15. Friedenson and Kranzler, *Heroine of Rescue*, p. 93; "Orthodox Ends Unorthodox Means," p. 3.

16. *Heroine of Rescue*, p.94.

17. Wyman, *Abandonment of the Jews*, p. 46.

18. The only major American Jewish organization that did not participate was the American Jewish Committee, which claimed that its leadership was out of town but that they were interested in being informed of the proceedings. See the "highly confidential" memo by David Wertheim of *Poale Zion* to members of his movement, circular no. 27, September 9, 1942, Archives of the World Jewish Congress (hereafter called AWJC) at the American Jewish Archives, Cincinnati, file D92/1; Friedenson and Kranzler, *Heroine of Rescue*, p. 94.

19. According to a memo from David Rosenblum to Maurice Wertheim of the American Jewish Committee regarding this meeting, mention was made of information about the deportation and massacre of Jews in Warsaw which had been received by the State Department from the U.S. consul in Switzerland. Similar information received by the *Agudat ha–Rabbanim* was also noted, but there was no mention of any discussion of Riegner's cable. Memo of Rosenblum to Wertheim, September 9, 1942, (hereafter called Archives of the American Jewish Committee at YIVO Archives AAJCom), RG 347.1.29, Box 33, file Poland 1942. Urofsky claims in *A Voice That Spoke for Justice*, pp. 318–322, that Wise revealed the contents of Riegner's cable and his promise to Welles at a meeting convened by the American Jewish Congress, but he is likely referring to a subsequent meeting, on September 9. In Wyman, *Abandonment of the Jews*, p. 46, Wyman also claims that Wise shared the information regarding Riegner's cable, but there are others who dispute this point. See, for example, Kranzler, "Orthodox Ends Unorthodox Means,"p. 3.

20. Friedenson and Kranzler, *Heroine of Rescue*, p. 94; Kranzler, *Thy Brother's Blood*, p. 93.

21. Wertheim memo, September 9, 1942, AWJC, D92/1; Kranzler, *Thy Brother's Blood*, p. 93.

22. Memo of Rosenblum to Wertheim, September 9, 1942, AAJCom, RG 347.1.29, box 33, file Poland 1942. Wise had already contacted Supreme Court Justice Felix Frankfurter on September 4 and had asked him to inform President Roosevelt about Riegner's cable. Urofsky, *A Voice That Spoke for Justice*, pp. 318–322; Wyman, *Abandonment of the Jews*, pp. 46–47; Friedenson and Kranzler, *Heroine of Rescue*, p. 94.

23. Letter of J. Domb to Elias Sternbuch, September 12, 1942, WAYA, Jerusalem, file 2; Friedenson and Kranzler, *Heroine of Rescue*, pp. 91–92.

24. Ibid., pp. 94–95.

25. Yitzhak Lewin, "Di Katastropha phun Airopaischen Idintum un ihre Apklang in Amerika," *Iddische Shtimme*, Kislev 5703 (November 1942), quoted in Yitzhak Lewin, *Churbn Airopa* (New York, 1947), pp. 32–35.

26. See, for example, the *Morgan Dzurnal* of September 20, 1942, which reported that a Swedish businessman traveling in Poland had learned that half the Jews in the ghettos of Warsaw, Lodz, Cracow, and Lvov had been murdered. Wyman, *Abandonment of the Jews*, p. 47.

27. Press release of American Jewish Congress, November 26, 1942, AWJC, D92/3;

Wyman, *Abandonment of the Jews*, p. 51; Haskel Lookstein, *Were We Our Brothers' Keepers?*; *The Public Response of American Jews to the Holocaust 1938–1944* (New York and Bridgeport, 1985), pp. 110–128.

28. Diary entry of Arieh Kubowitzki, November 25, 1942, in Myriam Kubovy, "Ultimate Rescue Attempts: Collection of Documents from the World Jewish Congress Archives in New York," Manuscript in Yad Vashem Library, 2^0 79–741, p. 16; Wyman, *Abandonment of the Jews*, pp. 51–71. Wyman lists *Agudat Yisrael* as a member of the ad hoc committee, but it was *Agudat ha–Rabbanim* that represented American Orthodoxy in this case.

29. Ironically, Wise did not mention the inclusion of Rabbis Goldstein and Rosenberg in the delegation, which according to his letter would include representatives of "the American Jewish Committee, American Jewish Congress, and B'nai B'rith." Rafael Medoff, *The Deafening Silence; American Jewish Leaders and the Holocaust* (New York, 1987), p. 100. See also Edward David Pinsky, "Cooperation Among American Jewish Organizations in Their Efforts to Rescue European Jewry During the Holocaust, 1939–1945," doctoral dissertation submitted to New York University, 1980 p.189; Wyman, *Abandonment Of the Jews*, p. 72.

30. Ibid., p. 71; Kranzler, "Orthodox Ends Unorthodox Means," p. 3; Eliyho Matzozky, "The Response of American Jewry and Its Representative Organizations Between November 24, 1942, and April 19, 1943, to Mass Killing of Jews in Europe," unpublished masters thesis, submitted to Yeshiva University, 1979, p. 12.

31. "Memorandum Submitted to the President of The United States," December 8, 1942, AWJC, D115/12.

32. Press release of the American Jewish Congress, December 8, 1942, AWJC, D92/2; Wyman, *Abandonment of the Jews*, pp. 72–73; Arthur Morse, *While Six Million Died: A Chronicle of American Apathy* (New York, 1967), p. 28.

33. "Aseifat Agudat ha–Rabbanim," *Ha–Pardes*, 16, no. 9 (Kislev 5703/November 1942), 3.

34. "Seder ha–Aseifa Shel Vaad Hatzala," *Ha–Pardes*, 16, no. 10, (Tevet 5703/December 1942), 8.

35. "Hachlatot Aseifat Vaad Hatzala," ibid., pp. 7–8.

36. Most of the steps taken by Jewish organizations in this early period related primarily to publicizing the plight of European Jewry. See, for example, Wyman, *Abandonment of the Jews*, pp. 70–73.

37. For the difficult conditions of the refugee scholars see Kalman Goldwasser, *Phun Der Veisl Bizen Teich Kizel–Su* (Paris, 1972), pp. 140–150. See also the letter Rabbi Grazowski received from Siberia in which he was informed that eleven students of the Kamenetz Yeshiva had died from the severe conditions. "Michtav Ayom ve–Nora," *Ha–Pardes*, 17, no. 4 (Tammuz 5703/July 1943), p. 4. For the conditions of the Torah scholars in Shanghai, see Kranzler, *Japanese, Nazis and Jews*, pp. 378–381.

38. See note 34.

39. The verse quoted by Rabbi Silver (Deuteronomy 21:7) is the declaration made by the elders of the place of habitation closest to the site where a corpse is found and there is no evidence regarding the identity of the murderer. The elders thereby publicly absolve themselves of responsibility for the murder that took place in their vicinity.

40. "Aseifat Vaad Hatzala," *Ha–Pardes*, 16, no. 10 (Tevet 5703/January 1943), 6.

41. See, for example, "Le–teshuva, vi–tefilla u–tzedaka," *Ha–Pardes*, 14, no. 4 (Tammuz 5700/July 1940), pp. 2–3; "Hachrazat Agudat ha–Rabbanim le–Yehudei Amerika," *Ha-Pardes*, 14, no. 7 (October 1940/Tishrei 5701), p. 2; "Ta'anit tzibur olami," ibid., 16, no. 6 (Elul 5702/September 1942), 3–5.

42. "Ta'anit tzibur olami," *Ha–Pardes*, 16, no. 9 (Kislev 5703/December 1942), 2.

43. It is not certain that this incident which has already become part of Holocaust "mythology"—streets being named for the 93 young female martyrs—actually took place. For a historical study of this "event," see Judith Tydor Baumel and Jacob Schachter, "The Ninety–three Bais Yaakov Girls of Cracow: History or Typology," in *Reverence, Righteousness, and Rahamanut*, ed. Jacob J. Schacter (Northvale, NJ 1992), pp. 93–130.

44. "Aseifat Vaad Hatzala," *Ha–Pardes*, 16, no. 10 (Tevet 5703/January 1943), 6.

45. "Statement Of Income And Expenses December 11, 1941 to March 31, 1943," AVH.

46. "Statement Of Income And Expenses January 1 to December 10, 1941," AVH.

47. "Statement Of Income And Expenses December 11, 1941 to March 31, 1943," AVH.

48. See the numerous letters by heads of local federations to the JDC and CJFWF seeking guidance on how to respond to the *Vaad's* appeals for allocations. AJDC, files 361 and 423; CJFWF, I–69, Box 110.

49. See, for example, the letters of Moses Leavitt and Henrietta Buchman of the JDC to the directors of local federations, AJDC files 360, 361, and 463, and of I. B. Seligson of the CJFWF, ACJFWF, I–69, Box 110.

50. Letter of Rabbi Silver to the Federation for Jewish Service, Omaha, undated but included in a letter of February 19, 1943, ACJFWF, I–69, Box 110.

51. Letter of Paul Veret to George Rabinoff, February 1943, ACJFWF, I –69, Box 110.

52. Letter of Isaac Seligson to Paul Veret, February 24, 1943, ACJFWF, I–69, Box 110.

53. Letter of Henrietta Buchman to Paul Veret, February 25, 1943, AJDC, file 361.

54. "List Of Allocations By Welfare Funds For Fiscal Year Beginning January – May 1943," 1944 Budgeting Bulletin For Member Agencies No. B–16, June 1944, p. 5, AJDC, file 362.

55. Letter of M. Freund (CJFWF) to Hans Lamm (Kansas City Jewish Welfare Federation), July 27, 1943, ACJFWF, I–69, Box 150.

Chapter 10

Internalization of the Disaster and a Change in Perspective

While the *Vaad ha-Hatzala* was attempting to intensify its fundraising activities in early 1943, the leaders of American Orthodoxy were facing new political developments which forced them time and again to reassess their relationship with the rest of the community. Until the summer of 1942, they had for the most part refrained from participating in the unsuccessful efforts to unite American Jewry for political action against the Nazi regime,[1] but this situation changed in the wake of the cables sent from Switzerland by Riegner and Sternbuch. It now became clear that the plight of European Jewry constituted a unique emergency which required extraordinary measures.

Under such circumstances, the natural tendency was to attempt to unite the community, a response strongly supported by Orthodox leaders.[2] The first step was to establish a temporary committee, headed by Stephen Wise, which publicized the information on the annihilation of European Jewry and organized the delegation of Jewish leaders which met with President Roosevelt in the White House on December 8, 1942. Although the committee was disbanded by Wise less than a week after this meeting,[3] its establishment represented a trend which was to intensify as the mass murder of Jews in Europe continued.

These developments also had an impact on the leaders of the *Vaad ha-Hatzala,* who had heretofore worked primarily on behalf of the refuge rabbis and yeshiva students. As time went on, they became increasingly involved in political activities designed to unite American Jewry in order to facilitate rescue efforts, among other goals. This development also marked the increased involvement of the leaders of *Agudat Yisrael,* primarily Jacob Rosenheim and Dr. Isaac Lewin, both of whom had emigrated to the United States from Europe after the outbreak of World War II.

The first initiative to unite American Jewry following the publication of the news regarding the Final Solution was taken by Henry Monsky, the president of B'nai B'rith. On January 6, 1943, he invited representatives of all the major American Jewish organizations to a conference to formulate postwar policy and deal with the issue of Palestine. The conference was held on January 23–24, 1943, at the William Penn Hotel in Pittsburgh, 32 of the 34 organizations invited sent representatives. (The two that declined were the American Jewish Committee and the Jewish Labor Committee.)[4]

Although Orthodox leaders did not play any role in convening the Pittsburgh conference, they supported Monsky's initiative; both *Agudat ha-Rabbanim* and *Agudat Yisrael* sent three representatives to participate in the deliberations.[5] The problem, from the point of view of the Orthodox delegates, was that the conference, which had originally been convened to deal with postwar problems, especially the Palestine issue, was ignoring the most pressing Jewish issue: the rescue of European Jewry. Thus while they were willing to support the creation of an American Jewish Assembly representing the American Jewish community, the Orthodox representatives, and especially Dr. Isaac Lewin of *Agudat Yisrael,* insisted that rescue be put on the agenda. In fact, even though it was fairly clear from the outset that the aim of the organizers was primarily to advance the Zionist goal of establishing an independent Jewish state in Palestine, the non-Zionists among the Orthodox (i.e., the representatives of *Agudat Yisrael)*[6] were willing to cooperate, if this new framework were utilized to facilitate rescue activities. Thus the primary demand made by Lewin and others was that rescue efforts be included as part of the mandate of the organization.

Lewin also attempted to moderate the resolution on Palestine in order to facilitate the participation of the American Jewish Committee and the Jewish Labor Committee, which had declined the invitation because they opposed the efforts to establish an independent state in Palestine. (The American Jewish Committee in principle also opposed the idea that the Jews in the United States constituted a separate political entity.) Lewin argued that adding rescue activities to the agenda would encourage the participation of these two major organizations; he also pressed for use of the term Jewish "homeland" instead of "commonwealth" in the resolution, for the same reason. His efforts were to some small extent successful, helping to pave the way for negotiations between the conference organizers and the American Jewish Committee and Jewish Labor Committee. As a result of these talks, the latter two agencies ultimately joined the efforts to establish the new umbrella organization, which was to be renamed, at the request of the American Jewish Committee, the American Jewish Conference.[7]

The efforts of Lewin and his colleagues at Pittsburgh to make rescue the key issue were basically unsuccessful, although they did force it onto the agenda. The Orthodox leaders therefore realized that they could not limit their rescue work to the activities sponsored by the American Jewish Conference. Thus in mid-February 1943 they established the "Council of Jewish Organizations for the Rescue of the Jews in Europe," a temporary committee to initiate political activities to facilitate rescue efforts. Headed by Rabbi Yisrael Rosenberg and created under the auspices of the *Agudat ha-Rabbanim*, the Council included representatives of the veteran rabbinic association, its younger counterpart the Rabbinical Council of America, Mizrachi, *Agudat Yisrael*, Young Israel, and the newly established Council of Grand Rabbis.[8] (The latter, which was established in early 1943, was in essence a Chasidic version of the *Vaad ha-Hatzala*. Founded by the Boyaner Rebbe, Mordechai Shlomo Friedman, and others who believed that a separate organization was required to deal exclusively with the rescue of Chasidic rebbes, it attempted to duplicate the *Vaad's* practical and fundraising successes.)[9]

The efforts to unite these Orthodox organizations had begun at least as early as December 1942 but had encountered serious difficulties. Rosenheim wrote bitterly to a colleague that in the course of the negotiations, the Mizrachi was mobilizing their indescribable *sinas chinam* (baseless hatred) to "drive Agudat Yisrael into a corner."[10] Although this rivalry between the Orthodox political parties was to continue,[11] it did not ultimately prevent the creation of the unified council with the participation of both Mizrachi and Aguda. Representatives of both parties, in fact, were active on the important Political Committee, headed by Gedalia Bublick, who was assisted by Zerach Warhaftig and Isaac Lewin.[12]

The Council devoted much of its efforts to the passage of legislation to facilitate the rescue of European Jews. In this respect, it coordinated its activities with the American Jewish Congress, although the Orthodox organization retained its independence throughout its existence. On of the first bills on its agenda was the Barkley Resolution, which called for the punishment of war crimes. The Senate passed the resolution on March 9, 1943, and the House of Representatives followed suit nine days later. Representative Emanuel Celler, one of the leading Jewish congressmen in Washington, was in close contact with *Agudat ha-Rabbanim* throughout, and he guided the rabbis' activities in regard to this legislation.[13]

During this period a delegation was sent to Washington to meet with all seven Jewish members of Congress and urge them to function as a group in order to facilitate the passage of bills that could alleviate the plight of European Jewry. The delegation submitted a detailed "Proposal for Immediate Action" which urged that the U.S. government send food ships to Europe; arrange for the rescue of Jews, especially children, through emigration from Bulgaria, Rumania, and Slovakia; and appeal directly to the German people, by leaflet and/or radio broadcasts, to help stop the murders.[14] Appeals were also made to Jewish leaders to meet with key members of Congress and impress upon them the urgency of the situation and the need for appropriate legislation,[15] and six members of *Agudat ha-Rabbanim* met with Secretary of State Cordell Hull to discuss various rescue proposals (as well as postwar issues).[16]

These activities did not take place in a vacuum, they reflected increased demands by American Jewry for practical measures that would facilitate rescue. One of the important issues the Council had to deal with was to what extent to cooperate with the initiatives of other organizations. For example, shortly after its establishment, the Council urgently appealed to all the major Jewish organizations, with the exception of the American Jewish Committee, to deal with a proposal whereby Jewish organizations in the Free World would be given an opportunity to ransom 70,000 Rumanian Jews.[17] (The offer reached public attention in the wake of a full-page ad headed "At $50 Apiece Guaranteed Human Beings," which was published in *The*

New York Times of February 16, 1943, by the Committee for a Jewish Army of Stateless and Palestinian Jews.[18] No practical results were achieved in this case, however, for a variety of reasons, including the questionable integrity of the Rumanian originators of the proposal, internal power struggles within the Rumanian regime, the Nazis' staunch opposition to the plan, and their temporary success in stopping Jewish emigration.)[19]

In other cases, Orthodox leaders set conditions on their participation with non-Orthodox organizations. A major issue, for example, was whether to participate in the mass "Stop Hitler Now" rally scheduled for Madison Square Garden in New York City on March 1, 1943, under the sponsorship of the American Jewish Congress, the AFL–CIO, the Free World Association, and the Church Peace Union. The unified Orthodox Council decided on February 18 that their organizations would participate only if the demands made at the rally dealt exclusively with rescue and not with political issues. Their fear, which remained a central factor for them throughout 1943, was that political conflicts would seriously reduce the possibilities of launching practical rescue projects. When they were informed that the rally would deal only with rescue issues, the Orthodox agencies joined the sponsors of the events.[20]

Although the Council was a convenient framework for the Orthodox organizations, it was obvious that the plight of European Jewry required action by the entire American Jewish community. Thus when Stephen Wise established the Joint Emergency Committee for European Jewish Affairs on March 15, 1943, both *Agudat ha-Rabbanim* and *Agudat Yisrael* readily supported the initiative. (The Mizrachi participated in the framework of the Emergency Committee for Zionist Affairs, which also joined the newly formed body.)

In February and March, there were more and more reports that the situation of European Jewry was worsening. Wise was working to reconstitute the temporary committee established in the fall of 1942 after the news about the Final Solution had been received. It had consisted of the representatives of the four major defense organizations—American Jewish Committee, American Jewish Congress, B'nai B'rith and the Jewish Labor Committee—as well as the Synagogue Council of America and *Agudat ha-Rabbanim*, and had been disbanded by Wise himself after the meeting of Jewish leaders with President Roosevelt. He now invited the *Agudat Yisrael* and the

American Emergency Committee for Zionist Affairs to join the new committee which would coordinate the rescue activities of American Jewry. Wise (American Jewish Congress), Proskauer (American Jewish Committee), and Goldstein (Synagogue Council) were elected co-chairmen and each organization was accorded three representatives.

Although some Orthodox leaders, like Rosenheim, felt slighted by the fact that none of the religious representatives was appointed as co-chairman, the Orthodox organizations fully cooperated with the Emergency Committee throughout its existence. Their response was a direct result of their sense of urgency and responsibility regarding the rescue issue.[21] Whatever qualms might have existed regarding their cooperation with non-Orthodox groups on other issues,[22] such opposition never prevented cooperation vis-à-vis rescue work. On this issue, leaders like Rabbi Aron Kotler played a dominant role. When he was criticized for working with Stephen Wise, who was a Reform rabbi, the Lakewood *rosh yeshiva* replied that he was willing to "work with the Pope if it would save even the fingernail of one Jewish child."[23]

By participating in the Emergency Committee, the Orthodox organizations contributed their share to the unified community effort to facilitate rescue efforts. Yet on a practical level, their contribution was limited and had relatively little impact on the activities of the Emergency Committee, which registered few concrete achievements during its relatively brief existence. The most active Orthodox member was Isaac Lewin, who served on the Steering Committee and tried his best to get the Emergency Committee to lobby for practical measures which could provide relief for European Jewry living under the Nazi occupation. Among his proposals (very few of which were adopted) were: to approach Myron Taylor, the U.S. envoy to the Vatican, to secure the help of the Holy See;[24] to send a ship with food to help feed Polish Jews, several million of whom he believed were still alive;[25] to drop leaflets in Germany warning that those responsible for the murder of the Jews would be punished;[26] to attempt to have Polish Jews granted the status of civilian internees; to send food parcels to Polish Jews (after word was received that only 1,000 out of 12,000 parcels sent were actually received by Jews living in Poland).[27] Among the other Orthodox leaders who attended meetings of the Emergency Committee were Rabbis Aron Kotler, Avraham Kalmanowitz, Wolf Gold, and Aaron

Burack, as well as Jacob Rosenheim. Their participation had little impact on the organization's activities, however.[28]

Given the relatively minor role played by Orthodox representatives in the Emergency Committee and the failure of that organization to achieve significant concrete results, it is hardly surprising that Orthodox leaders simultaneously initiated some of their own rescue activities. In mid-March Rabbis Rosenberg, Silver, and Levinthal cabled Pope Pius XII to assist Polish Jewry in the wake of appeals for help which they had received from that beleaguered community. According to the information relayed by the rabbis, the Germans had begun to liquidate the Warsaw Ghetto in January and were planning to complete the annihilation of the rest of Polish Jewry in mid-February. (The information, which had been sent from Warsaw via London only reached New York in March.) Rosenberg, Silver, and Levinthal turned to the Pope in their capacity as "religious leaders of American Jewry" and pleaded for his intervention at "this zero hour."[29]

Another initiative by the leaders of *Agudat ha-Rabbanim* related to the Bermuda Conference held in mid-April 1943. Sponsored by the American and British authorities in the wake of growing pressure to assist those being victimized by the Nazis, the conference was ostensibly supposed to approve measures designed to facilitate rescue. With this goal in mind, Rabbi Rosenberg wrote to Congressman Sol Bloom, who was one of the American delegates to the conference, urging him to support the adoption of several practical ideas which the rabbis believed would help rescue Jews. Among the proposals were the shipment of food in neutral ships under the flag of the Red Cross and the exchange of Jews under Nazi occupation for Germans residing in Allied territory. The rabbi noted the recent exchange of Palestinian Jews for Germans as proof that such deals could be made and emphasized the unique opportunity that Bloom had as "the man the Almighty has chosen to bring relief to the indescribable suffering of our brethren in Europe."[30]

The rabbis, in this case, had good reason to believe that their appeal to Bloom would have an impact, since the New York congressman, who chaired the House Foreign Affairs Committee, prided himself on his ties with Orthodox leaders and even claimed to represent Orthodox Jewry.[31] In fact, Bloom, had on several occasions assisted *Agudat ha-Rabbanim* in its efforts to rescue such noted rabbinic luminaries as Rabbi Avraham Duber Kahane Shapiro, the rabbi of Kovno, Lithuania; Rabbi Chaim Ozer Grodzinski of Vilna; and Rabbi Avraham Mordechai Alter, the Gerer Rebbe.[32] Bloom indeed presented several of the rabbis' suggestions at the conference, and even spoke about the possibility of bringing the refugee rabbis and yeshiva students stranded in the Soviet Union to the United States, a project brought to his attention by Rabbi Kalmanowitz. He did not, however, make a concerted effort to have any of these proposals approved by the Conference and, in fact, none was adopted. The Bermuda conference dealt exclusively with those who had already reached neutral territory and totally failed to address the plight of the Jews under Nazi occupation. While this result fully reflected U.S. and British policy,[33] it constituted a highly demoralizing blow to the hopes of those American Jews seeking to assist their beleaguered European brethren.

Besides the failure of the Bermuda Conference, Orthodox leaders faced another serious problem in the spring of 1943. They had hoped to be full partners in the proposed American Jewish Conference, which they envisioned would play a leadership role in rescue efforts of the American Jewish community. As the preparations for the establishment of the conference proceeded, however, it became increasingly clear that the Orthodox organizations were being accorded secondary status.

According to the agreements reached in Pittsburgh, the American Jewish Conference was to consist of 500 delegates, 375 of them to be elected by local communities, and the remaining 125 to be appointed by the various Jewish organizations. Although the specifics regarding the distribution of these seats were not determined, in Pittsburgh it was understood, at least by the Orthodox representatives, that each of the major trends in the community (liberal, Zionist, and Orthodox according to one version; Socialists as well in another) would be granted parity. This, however, did not occur.

On May 15–16, 1943, the executive committee of the American Jewish Conference decided that all the Jewish organizations would be divided into three categories based on the number of branches and their geographic distribution. Those organizations with branches all over the country were categorized as "national" and were allotted three delegates. Those that functioned only in certain parts of the country, or that were nonautonomous affiliates of national organizations, were given two representatives. The groups of rabbis and the other national organizations that did not have local branches were accorded one delegate. On the basis of this system, the executive committee gave *Agudat ha-Rabbanim* and *Agudat Yisrael* only one delegate each, a decision that deeply offended the leaders of these organizations. They protested vehemently and threatened to withdraw from the American Jewish Conference if their representation was not increased. Rosenheim, in a letter to the executive committee, attacked what he considered to be "the unjustifiable discrimination against Orthodox Judaism" and demanded parity with the other major organizations.[34]

In mid-July *Agudat ha-Rabbanim* was granted an additional delegate, as was the Rabbinical Council of America, but *Aguda's* demands were not met. It should be noted that while it may have been convenient for Rosenheim to attribute the decision to limit *Agudat Yisrael* to one delegate to discrimination against Orthodoxy, the facts do not support this accusation. Mizrachi, for example, which had far more branches and members throughout the United States than American *Agudat Yisrael*,[35] was indeed granted three delegates and the same is true for Mizrachi Women and Young Israel. The men's and women's organizations of the Union of Orthodox Jewish Congregations were granted five delegates.

Despite efforts by Orthodox representatives like David Delman of Young Israel to reach a compromise, both *Agudat ha-Rabbanim* and *Agudat Yisrael* withdrew from the American Jewish Conference and did not attend its opening session, which was convened in New York City from August 29 to September 2, 1943. The frustration of Orthodox leaders regarding their inability to make rescue the number one priority, plus the insult of being accorded secondary status, convinced Orthodoxy's most prominent rabbis to opt for a separatist path.[36]

The irony was that the same rabbis who had initially insisted on breaking ranks with the organized community to establish the *Vaad ha-Hatzala* had by this point become convinced of the need for unified action for rescue. If rescue was not going to top the American Jewish Conference's agenda, however, there was no holy obligation for the rabbis to swallow their pride and accept secondary status. Thus, despite being attacked in the Jewish press for their "separatism," Orthodox leaders steadfastly refused to rejoin the American Jewish Conference.[37] They may have based their decision on the continued existence of the Emergency Committee for European

Jewish Affairs, which was supposed to coordinate American Jewry's rescue efforts, but if that is indeed the case, their strategy was to prove erroneous.

Although Orthodox leaders made active efforts during this period to establish a unified American framework for rescue activities, they simultaneously continued their relief activities on behalf of the refugee Torah scholars stranded in the Soviet Union and Shanghai. Throughout the spring, summer and fall of 1943 the rabbis intensified the special relief programs they had initiated on behalf of these groups, sending them hundreds of thousands of dollars worth of aid. They also attempted to arrange the evacuation of these groups to locations they considered safer and more conducive to intensive Torah study. To achieve the latter goal, the *Vaad* worked simultaneously in two directions. It sought to have the scholars in Shanghai included in exchanges of Japanese and Allied nationals, and it tried to influence the Soviet authorities to grant the rabbis and yeshiva students in Central Asia exit permits.

Judging from the efforts invested in each case, it appears that the rabbis were more concerned about the plight of the scholars in Shanghai, probably because they were in Axis territory. Thus even though the physical and economic conditions in Central Asia were probably more dangerous than those in the Chinese port under Japanese occupation, the *Vaad* tried harder to extricate the refugee scholars in Shanghai than they did those in the Soviet Union. Another reason that more intensive efforts were invested regarding Shanghai was the potential for the exchange of the rabbis and yeshiva students through the Japanese–British population exchanges taking place.

The first such exchange took place in October 1942, when six refugee Torah scholars were among the 30 Polish citizens allowed to leave Shanghai. As preparations were under way in the spring of 1943 for a second exchange, the *Vaad ha-Hatzala* tried to ensure that a maximum number of rabbis and yeshiva students would be included. Despite their efforts and the fact that visas to Mexico had been obtained, none of the scholars was among those included in the exchange.[38]

These efforts, which continued throughout the spring, summer, and fall of 1943, were conducted largely via London, since it was the British who decided the number of Polish citizens to be exchanged. The *Vaad ha-Hatzala* worked closely with British Chief Rabbi Joseph

Hertz and Yitzchak (Ignacy) Schwarzbart, who represented the Zionists in the Polish National Council (parliament-in-exile), then in London. Despite the fact that the former had received a warm endorsement of this project by Polish Prime Minister Sikorski, who noted "the importance of saving the lives of those who are the guides and spiritual leaders of Jewry, especially in those tragic moments when millions of their brothers in Poland are being exterminated in the most barbarous way by the Nazis murderers,"[39] their intensive efforts on behalf of the scholars in Shanghai were not crowned with success.[40]

Given this failure, the *Vaad* attempted to enlist the assistance of the American government. In September 1943 Rabbi Yehuda Seltzer, the executive director of the *Agudat ha-Rabbanim*, asked Congressman Sol Bloom to personally present the matter to President Roosevelt or at least arrange a meeting for them with Secretary of State Cordell Hull.[41] Yet despite the fact that the rabbis raised this issue in meetings with Hull, Breckinridge Long, and other top American officials[42] and were also able to enlist the support of Msgr. Amleto Cicognani, the Apostolic Delegate in Washington,[43] no progress was achieved. Not a single rabbi or yeshiva student was among the 80 Polish citizens evacuated from Shanghai and exchanged in Goa in October 1943.[44] In short, neither the Americans nor the British were ready to take any steps to help arrange the evacuation and, in fact, each government, while expressing sympathy with their plight, suggested that the rabbis direct their request to the authorities across the ocean. The Americans sent the *Vaad* to the British and vice versa.[45]

Under these circumstances, the rabbis appealed in mid-November 1943 to the Canadian authorities to arrange the exchange of all the refugee scholars, or at least of those 51 in Shanghai who had been granted visas to Canada in 1941 but had been unable to reach North America when war broke out in the Pacific. Rabbi Kalmanowitz wrote to Victor Podoski, the Polish consul-general in Ottawa, as well as to the local Apostolic Delegate Msgr. Ildelbrando Antoniutti,[46] but in this case as well, the rabbis' efforts were unsuccessful.

In addition to their attempts to arrange this exchange, the *Vaad* also tried to obtain permission from the Soviet authorities for the emigration of the Polish scholars in Central Asia. In this case as well, they turned to both the American and British governments for help, but to no avail. Despite the fact that they had obtained 500 Mexican visas for Polish Torah scholars, as well as promises of intervention on their behalf by the State Department and British Secretary of State Eden, the Soviet authorities refused to allow any of these refugees to leave and they were forced to remain in the Soviet Union for the duration of the war.[47]

While the *Vaad ha-Hatzala* was unsuccessful in its attempts to relocate the refugee rabbis and yeshiva students, they did succeed in helping keep these scholars alive and enabling many of them to continue their religious studies. Most of the assistance provided for those in the Soviet Union was in the form of parcels of food and clothing, which were sent from Iran, Palestine, and the United States.

During 1943 Teheran emerged as the most important center from which relief shipments were sent to the Polish Jewish refugees in the Soviet Union, and the *Vaad* was one of several Jewish organizations, such as the Joint and the Jewish Agency, involved in aid operations from the Iranian capital. In order to facilitate this effort, the *Vaad* sent Rabbi Yitzchak Mayer Levi of Jerusalem to Teheran in May 1943 to personally handle the relief shipments to the rabbis and yeshiva students. Levi was officially the representative of the *Vaad Hatzalat Rabbanim u-Bnei ha-Yeshivot bi-Russya* (The Committee for the Rescue of Rabbis and Yeshiva Students in Russia), which was the name of the committee of rabbis in Palestine who were closely cooperating with the *Vaad ha-Hatzala*. In effect, however, he was directly responsible to New York.[48]

From the very beginning of his mission, Levi's efforts were plagued by two very different types of problems. The first was technical. According to Iranian regulations, initially only one parcel a year could be sent to the Soviet Union, only by residents of Iran who had relatives there. Subsequently, Intourist, the Soviet tourist agency, was granted permission to send 1,000 5-kilogram parcels a month of goods purchased locally. Since the Russians could not fill that quota themselves, they allowed Peltours to send several hundred parcels a month on behalf of the JDC, the Jewish Agency, and other Jewish organizations. But by June 1943 that number had been reduced to less than 300 per month, and there was also an acute shortage of food in Iran.[49]

The other set of problems encountered by Levi was ideological and related to the priorities of the Jewish relief agencies. Since he was the representative of *Vaad ha-Hatzala*, his *raison d'être* was to send as many parcels as possible to rabbis and yeshiva students, but he frequently found himself in conflict with the representatives of the JDC and the Jewish Agency, who regarded themselves as responsible for the welfare of all the Jewish refugees in the Soviet Union. Thus while Levi was more than happy to send several parcels to a refugee rabbi or yeshiva student, the representatives of other Jewish relief agencies objected strenuously to his tactics. For example, Dr. Moshe Yishai of the Jewish Agency claimed that while many individuals whose names were on the lists supplied by the *Vaad* had already received several packages, quite a few other refugees had not received any. He contended, moreover:

> The list of rabbis did not include only rabbis. Rabbis, the sons of rabbis, their relatives, their relatives' relatives, members of religious parties who were never rabbis and acquaintances [were on the *Vaad's* lists]. The list of rabbis did not have the addresses of families, but rather of individuals, and they presented each individual as the head of a family. Thus each was listed separately: the father, his wife, each son and daughter. There were quite a few cases in which the same person was listed at several different addresses. We would find this out from the receipts for the packages and by a comparison of the handwritings. But this was a holy list and no one was allowed to doubt the sanctity of each and every address.[50]

According to Yishai, every time the *Vaad* sent a parcel to a rabbi or student who had already received one, it was denying assistance to a Jewish refugee who had not yet been helped. "The empty stomach," Yishai contended, "is the same, whether it is of a rabbi or of a Jew who was not lucky enough to be included on the list of rabbis." It was for that reason that he ignored instructions from his superiors in Jerusalem to send 350 parcels a month to those on *Vaad ha-Hatzala's* lists and instead agreed only to send 100 parcels in August 1943 and 150 a month starting in September.[51]

The leaders of the *Vaad ha-Hatzala* were incensed by the policy of the Jewish Agency, which they believed should distribute aid to all the Jewish refugees in the Soviet Union, including the refugee Torah scholars. In their opinion, the parcels they sent constituted a special supplement which they hoped, would enable the rabbis and yeshiva students to continue their studies and maintain their unique lifestyle despite the terrible conditions in the Soviet Union.[52] Needless to say, this position was rejected by the other Jewish organizations sending relief to the Jewish refugees in Central Asia.[53]

Despite these problems, the Vaad ha-Hatzala was able to arrange for 1,748 parcels to be sent from Teheran to approximately 900 refugee scholars in the Soviet Union in 1943[54] (with the financial assistance, it should be noted, of the Jewish Agency and the American Jewish Congress), and this program was to be considerably expanded in 1944. According to Rabbi Levi, by the end of the year he had, obtained permission to send 700 parcels a month—400 via the JDC (which had assumed responsibility for the parcels operation in late fall 1943) and the Jewish Agency and an additional 300 via a private company in Teheran.[55] Thus in its projected budget for 1944, the Vaad allocated $210,000 for parcels from Iran, a considerable increase over the sums spent there in 1943.[56]

In addition to the parcels sent from Teheran, Vaad ha-Hatzala was also able to send packages from Palestine and the United States. These operations were initially launched because of the limited number that could be sent from Iran. From both an economic point of view and the amount of time it took to reach the addressees, however, Teheran was by far the best place from which to dispatch relief shipments. Thus in the first half of 1943 a committee of highly distinguished Palestinian rabbis and roshei yeshiva (Rabbis Chizkiyahu Mishkowski of Krinki, Shlomo David Kahana, Eliezer Yehuda Finkel of Mir, and Yechezkel Sarna of Hebron) attempted to send a maximum number of relief parcels to the refugee Torah scholars in the Soviet Union.

Most of the money for this operation was sent from the United States, primarily by the Vaad ha-Hatzala, but funds were raised locally as well, and the cooperation of various local landsmannschaften was also enlisted. In this manner, the rabbis sent at least 821 parcels of food, clothing, and medicine to 753 refugee rabbis and yeshiva students. As more opportunities to send relief from Teheran developed, the relief program from Eretz Yisrael was scaled down; the parcels from there were one-third more expensive than those sent from Iran and took longer to reach their destination.[57] Thus in its proposed budget for 1944 the Vaad indicated that it hoped to send only 200 parcels a month from Palestine, and much larger quantities from Iran and the United States.[58]

During 1943, starting in July, *Vaad ha-Hatzala* also sent several hundred parcels to the Soviet Union from the United States, despite various technical problems which initially plagued this operation.[59] A typical package contained milk powder, egg powder, socks, cocoa, Crisco, thread, needles, Band-Aids, and underwear, all of which were in short supply in Central Asia and could be bartered for foodstuffs and other necessities.

In November 1943 the *Vaad* reached an agreement with the Jewish Council of Russian War Relief, which raised funds in America to assist the civilian population of the Soviet Union. The rabbinic relief agency was granted permission to send 1,200 parcels a month to the refugee scholars in Central Asia. The *Vaad ha-Hatzala* was responsible for the purchase and packaging of the goods, which were to be shipped by Russian War Relief at its expense. This arrangement was an achievement for the *Vaad,* because the Russian relief agency did not usually assume responsibility for sending aid to individuals, but it made an exception in this case. This agreement enabled *Vaad ha-Hatzala* to send far more extensive assistance than it had hereto been able to dispatch, since its share of the expenses was only $10 a parcel—appreciably less than what it had spent in Teheran and Palestine.[60] In fact, the *Vaad* at this point was apparently unable to fill the entire quota by itself, so it agreed to accept 160 names and addresses from the Jewish Labor Committee.[61] In any event, the rabbis hoped to fully exploit this avenue of relief during 1944, planning to send 1,200 parcels a month to the Soviet Union during the year at a projected cost of $144,000.[62]

In summation, during 1943 *Vaad ha-Hatzala* sent 3,101 relief parcels from Iran, Palestine, and the United States to the refugee Torah scholars in the Soviet Union at an expense of $113,771.44, which constituted about thirty-five percent of its overall relief expenditures of $326,814.47 for that year. According to the *Vaad,* the approximately 900 names and addresses in its possession in New York, in addition to other names known to its representatives in Teheran and Palestine, represented families comprising about 4,000 persons who were assisted by this program.

In addition, the rabbinic rescue agency sent this group $48,778 in cash, used primarily to pay customs duties on relief parcels, buy additional supplies, and cover transportation expenses for those seeking to relocate to warmer areas. Thus during 1943 the *Vaad* spent a total of $162,549 on its program to assist the scholars in the

Soviet Union, or approximately fifty percent of its relief budget.[63] By comparison, the JDC and Jewish Agency were able to send 6,827 parcels from Teheran and Palestine, but this total apparently includes at least 2,000 of the packages financed by *Vaad ha-Hatzala*. The JDC allocated approximately $190,000 for this project, but in reality less than half that sum was spent, because of the technical difficulties that plagued the project.[64] This effort, moreover, was from a budgetary point of view, of relatively minor importance for the JDC, which received well over $6 million for its relief activities in 1943.[65]

While the Torah scholars in the Soviet Union received the lion's share of the *Vaad's* relief funds in 1943, the rabbinic rescue organization also raised significant sums on behalf of the rabbis and yeshiva students in Shanghai. Using the transfer scheme via South America originally devised for this purpose in 1942, the *Vaad* succeeded in arranging for $90,709.70 to be given to the yeshiva group during 1943.[66] This sum enabled these scholars to continue their intensive Torah study despite the worsening economic conditions and the forced transfer of all the stateless Jewish refugees to the Hongkew Ghetto in May 1943.[67] This assistance, it should be noted, supplemented the aid provided by the JDC for the needy Jewish refugees in Shanghai. In effect, it meant that each member of the group assisted by the *Vaad ha-Hatzala* received four times as much financial assistance as did the other Polish refugees. (Those helped by the *Vaad* received approximately $20 a month, three-quarters of which was provided by the rabbis, whereas the JDC gave the East European refugees in Shanghai approximately $5 per month.)[68]

In view of the fact that every single refugee in Shanghai who was getting financial assistance from the *Vaad ha-Hatzala* was simultaneously being aided by the JDC, as were at least some of the refugees in the Soviet Union who had received parcels, it is not surprising that the *Vaad's* demands for funds from local federations increasingly angered and frustrated the leaders of the Joint Distribution Committee. This situation was exacerbated during the latter half of 1943 as *Vaad* emissaries increasingly claimed to be using pioneering relief methods and made disparaging references to the JDC's ostensible inability to provide significant assistance to those Jews in need.[69]

The key issues in contention were the relief programs to the Soviet Union and Shanghai. From the JDC's perspective, the most important questions were what methods could legally be used and which organization could best provide the most aid to a maximum number of beleaguered Jews. The JDC was convinced that the *Vaad ha-Hatzala's* efforts were a duplication of their own and that the rabbinic organization's fundraising efforts were draining sorely needed resources from the United Jewish Appeal, which funded the JDC. Moreover, either the *Vaad's* methods were illegal or the achievements they claimed were a figment of the rabbis' imagination. Thus in letters to welfare funds, JDC officials repeatedly stressed that the only general relief programs allowed in the Soviet Union were nonsectarian, that financial remittances to the Soviet Union were not an effective form of aid, and that U.S. agencies were forbidden to communicate with Shanghai. Under these circumstances, either the *Vaad's* claims of being able to provide relief for thousands of Jewish refugees in Central Asia and hundreds in Shanghai were false or the rabbis were in violation of Soviet regulations and/or U.S. laws.[70]

These letters, formulated to discourage contributions to the *Vaad ha-Hatzala*, did not present all the pertinent facts, however. The JDC, initially doubting the *Vaad's* claim of sending aid to Central Asia, soon found itself adopting the same tactic of sending parcels to individuals. Once that was the case, the JDC attempted to convince local federations that their program was by far superior and encompassed those whom the *Vaad* sought to help.[71] While this was true to a certain extent, the JDC was not concerned about the Torah scholars pursuing their studies, which was clearly one of the *Vaad's* major objectives. Another tactic used by the JDC was to quote the relatively large sum allocated for the Soviet Union ($400,000), giving the impression that that much money was being spent, when in effect the amount actually spent was less than half of that because technical problems limited the scope of the project.[72]

In the case of the aid sent by the *Vaad* to Shanghai, the JDC tried to imply that if the rabbis' claims were true, they were in violation of American law. What was rarely if ever explained was that the *Vaad's* methods were only slightly different from those used by the JDC, which promised to repay individuals in dollars after the war for wartime contributions made even in local currency to cover its budget in Shanghai. In this manner, JDC representative Laura Margolis was able to continue to assist the refugees long after Pearl Harbor. The only difference between the methods used by the two relief agencies was that the JDC did not maintain contact with Margolis, who took out loans on her own in return for promises of repayment after the war;[73] the *Vaad ha-Hatzala* was in steady contact with Shanghai via Argentina, so it was able to deposit the sums for the scholars prior to the actual contribution. In addition, the JDC tried to present the funds sent by the *Vaad* to Shanghai as a mere supplement to its own relief program, which encompassed the people being aided by the rabbis,[74] when in effect the opposite was true. The funds sent by the *Vaad ha-Hatzala* during 1943 were three times the aid supplied to these refugees by the JDC.

Perhaps if the JDC had been as convinced that the *Vaad's* program was essential for the survival of Judaism as were the rabbis who headed the Orthodox rescue agency, they would have adopted a more sympathetic approach to its efforts. Under the difficult circumstances of 1943 and with its budget sorely strained, however, the JDC related to the *Vaad ha-Hatzala* primarily as an unwelcome nuisance which was creating more problems than it solved. Unfortunately, the relations between the two organizations were to worsen at the very point when cooperation and unity would be critical.

The failure of the two relief agencies to achieve a degree of meaningful cooperation mirrored the unsuccessful efforts of Orthodox leaders to achieve political unity for the same purpose. Both *Agudat ha-Rabbanim* and *Agudat Yisrael* withdrew from the American Jewish Conference shortly before its official foundation. This step, which was motivated by a combination of ideological and practical reasons, left the rabbinic rescue organization in a very difficult situation vis-à-vis its relations with the rest of the community.

Having excluded themselves from the mainstream, the Orthodox rescue activists now found themselves at a crossroads. They could either continue to chart an independent course, or they could seek to cooperate with other Jewish organizations that were not members of the American Jewish Conference. In the latter case, the options available to the *Vaad ha-Hatzala, Agudat ha-Rabbanim,* and *Agudat Yisrael* were relatively diverse. The rabbis could cooperate with the *shtadlanim* of the American Jewish Committee, whose preferred methods of operation were quiet diplomacy and behind-the-scenes lobbying,[75] or they could join forces with the activist, high-profile Emergency Committee to Save the Jewish People of Europe. The latter group had originally been established (under a different name) as a lobby for the formation of a Jewish army to fight alongside the

Allies, but after news of the Final Solution became public, it had turned its attention exclusively to the rescue issue. In a relatively short time it had captured widespread public attention (and the support of many non-Jews) with a high-profile public relations campaign. It ran numerous full-page ads in *The New York Times*, and it presented a public pageant on the mass murder of European Jewry entitled "We Will Never Die," which was written by Hollywood screenwriter Ben Hecht and staged in several major American cities.[76]

Although it is likely that the anti-Zionist Agudist leader Jacob Rosenheim[77] would have preferred a political alliance with the leaders of the American Jewish Committee, who also opposed the establishment of a Jewish state in Palestine, the activist leaders of the *Agudat ha-Rabbanim* viewed the militant Zionists of the Emergency Committee to Save the Jewish People of Europe as more natural allies, especially in matters of rescue.[78] Under the urgent and difficult circumstances of fall 1943, with the mass murder of European Jewry proceeding apace practically unhindered, it was obvious that the rabbis would opt to join forces with the Emergency Committee. And it was this cooperation that paved the way for the only public demonstration by Jewish leaders in Washington, D.C., calling for increased rescue activity by the U.S. government during the entire period of the Holocaust.

The initiative for the demonstration, which is usually referred to as "the rabbis' march," came from Peter Bergson, the leader of the Emergency Committee, whose workers also handled most of the details. The idea was to bring a group of 250 to 300 rabbis to Washington to meet with President Roosevelt and leading political figures and to march through major streets in the capital to focus public attention on the plight of European Jewry and reinforce the demand for more active rescue measures by the U.S. government.

For the leaders of the *Vaad ha-Hatzala* this was a totally new dimension to their public efforts,[79] but it was precisely the type of activity preferred by the Emergency Committee, whose high-profile tactics had gained widespread community support while also alienating and angering most of the Jewish Establishment.[80] As a result, there was serious opposition to the march by prominent Jewish leaders, such as Stephen Wise, who tried to use their influence to prevent it or at least to minimize its impact. Samuel Rosenman, who was one of President Roosevelt's closest aides, told the

President that the group sponsoring the demonstration was "not representative of the most thoughtful elements in Jewry" and that "the leading Jews of his acquaintance" opposed the march. Rosenman added that he had personally attempted "to keep the horde from storming Washington."[81]

Another such attempt, which ultimately backfired, was made by the Jewish members of Congress. Together with various Zionist leaders, they attempted to dissuade the rabbis from conducting the march. They almost succeeded until Sol Bloom told one of the rabbis that it would be very undignified for a group of such "un-American looking" people to march in Washington. His comment caused a great deal of resentment among the rabbis, and as a result not only was the march conducted as planned but far more rabbis participated than originally were anticipated.[82]

The march took place on Wednesday, October 6, 1943, three days before Yom Kippur during the Ten Days of Penitence, a period marked by intensive retrospection and soul-searching. Approximately 400 rabbis[83] participated in the march, the majority arriving by train at Union Station at 12:35 P.M. from New York, Philadelphia, and Baltimore. There they were joined by some 40 rabbis who had arrived earlier from the south and the west, as well as by five or six local colleagues. Since the Union of Grand Rabbis of the United States and Canada had joined in sponsoring the march, there were Chasidic rabbis among the participants, which would probably not have been the case had the *Agudat ha-Rabbanim* been the sole sponsor.

The group set out from Union Station accompanied by Dr. J. Gordon, national commander of the veterans of the Jewish Legion, and Mr. Lemberger, the organization's national vice-president. Leading the march were the members of the presidium of *Agudat ha-Rabbanim*: Rabbis Bernard Levinthal (at age 77 the doyen of the American Orthodox rabbinate), Yisrael Halevi Rosenberg, and Eliezer Silver. They were followed by Rabbis Wolf Gold and Aaron Burack and the Boyaner Rebbe Rabbi Mordechai Shlomo Friedman. The rabbis recited Psalms as they marched to the Capitol. The five members of the presidium were then joined by Rabbis Karlinsky and Reuven Levovitz, and the delegation of seven rabbis was taken in to meet Vice President Henry Wallace, who received them in the presence of all the Jewish members of Congress. The rabbis gave Wallace a petition addressed to President Roosevelt which described the plight of European Jewry and demanded that the U.S. government take immediate action to rescue these Jews. Among several proposals were the establishment of a special agency for that purpose and the immediate opening of Palestine to Jewish immigration.

Following this meeting, the vice-president, accompanied by Speaker of the House Sam Rayburn, and the majority and minority leaders of both houses, went outside with the delegation, where they rejoined the larger group of rabbis. On the steps of the Capitol, Rabbi Silver read the petition in Hebrew and either Rabbi Gold or Rabbi Burack (depending on the version) read an English translation. Wallace responded by assuring the rabbis that all those present deeply felt the horrible Jewish tragedy and expressed how moved he was by the fact that the rabbis had come to Washington right before the holiest day of the Jewish calendar. At the same time it was important to remember that the tragedy of the Jews was part of a larger problem which would be solved only by an Allied victory.

From the Capitol, the rabbis traveled by car to the Lincoln Memorial, where prayers for the Jewish victims of the war were recited as well as a prayer for the United States and its leaders. At the Memorial, Rabbi Gold outlined the groups' demands in a radio interview.

The rabbis then proceeded on foot from the Lincoln Memorial to the White House, where they hoped to be received by President Roosevelt.[84] The Emergency Committee had been attempting since at least late September[85] to arrange a meeting with the President, but to no avail.[86] Roosevelt had decided that all such meetings would be handled by the Secretary of State and the matter was referred to him.[87] The negative recommendations received from Wise and Rosenman, his closest Jewish friends and aides, no doubt also had an impact,[88] and therefore Roosevelt had arranged to leave the White House shortly before the rabbis arrived. His prior commitment in this case was a trip to Bolling Field to see 40 Yugoslavs join the U.S. Air Force and a dedication of the four bombers they were going to fly. The truth is that Roosevelt had a relatively light schedule that day and could easily have arranged a meeting with the rabbis, but he refused to do so.[89] The President, in fact, subsequently expressed his own considerable displeasure with the rabbis' march, inquiring in a conversation with Zionist leader Nahum Goldmann whether anything could be done to, in Roosevelt's words, "liquidate"(!) the notorious Bergson.[90]

Meanwhile, the rabbis, unaware of the machinations to prevent them from meeting with the President, arrived at the White House, where a delegation consisting of Rabbis Rosenberg, Gold, Friedman, and Karlinsky and escorted by Peter Bergson was received by FDR's secretary, Marvin McIntyre. He informed them that the meeting could not be arranged, apologized for the President's absence, and indicated that he would be glad to convey the rabbis' message. In response, Rabbi Gold, the spokesperson for the group, expressed the rabbis' deep disappointment in unequivocal terms and indicated that in view of the President's absence there was no need for him to read the petition they had prepared.[91]

In the meantime, those rabbis who were not part of the delegation went to the Ohev Shalom synagogue, where some food had been prepared for them. When the delegation arrived there and reported that the President had not received them, the response was extremely bitter. In the words of one of the participants, a prominent rabbi from Brooklyn, FDR's absence was "a slap in the face not only to the delegation but to American Jewry." The rabbis then traveled to Union Station and returned to their respective communities.[92]

The rabbis' march, which was the only demonstration of its kind during World War II by Jewish leaders, received mixed reviews. It was reported by most of the general press but not featured prominently, and it was completely ignored by such major newspapers as the *New York Herald Tribune* and *Los Angeles Times*. In addition, some of the coverage disparagingly compared FDR's snub of the rabbis with the red carpet treatment accorded the same week to Prince Faisal of Saudi Arabia, while other observers wondered whether Roosevelt would have relegated a meeting with several hundred Catholic priests or Protestant ministers to his secretary.[93]

The Jewish press, as might be expected, gave the march far more extensive coverage. The description and analysis of the event was dependent, however, on the political attitude of the various newspapers. Those supportive and sympathetic to the rabbis and the Emergency Committee wrote in glowing terms of a unique and highly significant political achievement, whereas the opponents attacked the march in cynical terms as an irrelevant or even negative event.

One of the most positive descriptions of the march was written by Dr. Samuel Margoshes, the editor of the Yiddish daily *Der Tog*. He wrote in part:

The Pilgrimage of Orthodox Rabbis to Washington... will forever stand out in my memory as the most noble high adventure it has been my privilege to witness during a fairly varied and adventuresome life. To say that it was dignified and impressive is to be guilty of misunderstatement. To characterize it as grand and glorious is, to my way of thinking, to come nearer the truth....

It would seem unbelievable that in a busy city like Washington, accustomed to all kinds of outlandish visitors from all the corners of the earth, people should stop in their tracks to watch and follow a parade of a few hundred individuals singing psalms on their way to the Capitol, but that is precisely what took place. Tens of thousands of bystanders and passersby got to know, possibly for the first time, that millions of Jews were done to death in Nazi-held Europe, and that millions more are in jeopardy, and that the Jews of America profoundly agitated by what is happening to their kind, are appealing to the Government and people of the United States for help in saving their brethren from imminent doom....

What was even more heartening than the amount of attention showered on the Pilgrimage, was the attitude displayed by the populace to the procession of Orthodox Rabbis as it moved through the streets of the capital. As the 500 rabbis, wearing their chassidic garb of long silk and gabardines and round plush hats, moved along Pennsylvania Avenue, they certainly presented a picture which for its exotic quality was unprecedented even in such a cosmopolitan city as Washington. I seriously doubt whether most of the bystanders ever saw anything like it before. Yet they did not gape or guffaw as almost any crowd in a Central or East European land most decidedly would have. They watched in wonderment and in respect. The traffic stopped, and here and there a burgher removed his hat. I myself saw many a soldier snap to salute, as the oldest Rabbis remarkably reminiscent of the patriarchs in Dore's Bible, passed in review. There was something of the quality of a religious procession that characterized the Rabbinical Pilgrimage and compelled the respect of every passerby.[94]

Another journalist who was moved by the spectacle of the rabbis' march was Chaim Lieberman of the *Forwards* who described the event's significance as follows:

Washington has witnessed Jewish delegations, but never has she seen such a delegation and never has she heard the Jewish cry—a cry mixed with prayers. The rabbis brought with them a piece of the synagogue, a piece of Yom Kippur and carried them through the streets of Washington, the capital which has become the capital of the world, saying here is what we bring with us. Of course it would have been preferable if Jews would not have been compelled to go to Washington to arouse it to the Jewish tragedy but unfortunately the politics are so complex and mixed up that our tragedy, the greatest tragedy of the war, has been relegated to the background and Jewish hearts are thus terribly hurt. And if it was therefore necessary to go to Washington in order to dramatize our tragedy, it could not have been done in more effective fashion than was done by the procession of the hundreds of rabbis.

Even more indicative of the support for the march were the positive editorials, particularly in the Yiddish dailies. *Der Tog* editorialized on October 8, 1943, under the heading "The Rabbis' Day in Washington":

> Our capital witnessed an entire people in tears and supplications, an entire people—helpless and defenseless against the greatest evil in human history. If indeed there exist strings of human decency in the world, they were activated in Washington and they played the song of tragedy but also of compassion... the expression of our feelings should at least be commensurate with the pain and suffering of our brothers and sisters in the Nazi hell. It is in this respect that the rabbis' march was one of the most powerful expressions of our anguish which our people have given the world and in that place where there sit those who can be of assistance to us.

The Orthodox *Morgn Dzurnal,* as could be expected, was also extremely supportive and bitterly attacked those Jewish leaders who had influenced Roosevelt not to meet the delegation. "To make Jewish rescue a 'political football' and to bring it up to the President's door is indeed scandalous," the Yiddish daily editorialized. This charge was also given extensive coverage the previous day (October 7) in an interview with Rabbi Yisrael Rosenberg, who attacked "certain elements" in the Jewish community for FDR's decision not to meet the rabbis.

The attitude of these "certain elements" also found expression in the Jewish press. For example, the Tishrei 5704 (fall) issue of the Hebrew journal *Bitzaron* cynically attacked the participants:

> Our great rabbis, *geonim* [geniuses], Chassidic rebbes, and *tzaddikim* [righteous men] of all sorts suddenly left their rabbinical posts, prepared themselves by prettying up their sidelocks and combing their beards and they undertook to storm the gates of Washington. These rabbis may well be great Talmudic scholars, well-versed in all the tractates of the Talmud except one—the tractate of *derech eretz* [proper respect]. They didn't realize that one cannot take Washington by storm. They should have known that there are well-known keys to the White House—keys for outside doors and keys for inner doors leading even to the innermost chambers. But those keys are in the hands of others. There is an ancient rule. "He who toils before the Sabbath has food for the Sabbath." Certainly they know that when Zionism was in great danger who it was that interceded on its behalf to cancel the evil decree. It was not these rabbis who came to storm Washington but rather a well-known rabbi who is always on guard—and it is in his hands and the hands of his associates that the keys to the gates of royalty have been entrusted.[95]

The "well-known rabbi" in question, Rabbi Stephen Wise, also attacked the rabbis' march, particularly its organizers from the Emergency Committee to Save the Jewish People of Europe. In the November 1943 issue of *Opinion* he criticized those involved in the event in harsh terms:

> They who set out to be leaders must bear themselves with a sense of responsibility. There is such a thing as the dignity of a people. It must not be ignored. But the stuntists who arranged the orthodox rabbinical parade are not so much concerned with the results of their pilgrimage as with the stunt impression which it makes.[96]

The leaders of the *Vaad ha-Hatzala* were not influenced by such attacks. The more important question was whether the march had any effect, either on the American government or upon the Jewish community. The truth is that the rabbis' demands, as formulated in the petition submitted to the White House, endorsed approximately the same measures that had already been requested by various American Jewish organizations at the end of 1942: to specifically warn Germany and the satellite countries that crimes against Jews would be punished and help for Jews would be noted; to send food and medicine to Jews in ghettos through the International Red Cross or a neutral commission; to persuade neutral countries to admit Jews escaping Nazi persecution and guarantee their maintenance; to facilitate the entry of refugees to the United States; and to open Palestine to Jewish immigration. The only relatively new proposal was the call for a "special intergovernmental agency to save the remnant of Israel in Europe with powers and means to act at once on a large scale,"[97] a demand which the Emergency Committee had made the focal point of its campaign following its establishment as an organization devoted to the rescue of European Jewry in late July 1943.[98]

The march's significance did not lie, therefore, in the uniqueness of the rabbis' demands, nor was the march alone able to convince the U.S. government to adopt these measures. It was, however, a dramatic event which helped further sensitize the public to the plight of European Jewry and the need for action. At the same time, the march had a highly significant impact on the Orthodox rescue activists, who until then had played a relatively minor role in overall rescue efforts by the American Jewish community. The rabbis' march in Washington projected the *Vaad ha-Hatzala* and its leaders into the larger rescue picture in a meaningful way for the first time, reflecting their growing desire to play a key role in rescuing all Jews and not just rabbis and yeshiva students.

This development became particularly important shortly thereafter, in the wake of the disbanding of the Joint Emergency Committee for European Jewish Affairs in early November 1943. When *Agudat ha-Rabbanim* and *Agudat Yisrael* withdrew from the American Jewish Conference, the Orthodox leaders hoped that rescue activities could still be coordinated by the community through the Joint Emergency Committee. But on September 24, 1943, at the first meeting of that organization held after the establishment of the American Jewish Conference, a motion was made by Henry Montor of the United Palestine Appeal to dissolve the Joint Emergency Committee and transfer all its functions to the new umbrella organization. This proposal, needless to say, was bitterly opposed by the Orthodox organizations which had withdrawn from the American Jewish Conference, since they would be excluded from rescue activities coordinated by the community. Since their position was also supported by the American Jewish Committee and the Jewish Labor Committee,[99] both of which were also wary of giving too much power to the American Jewish Conference, the motion was dropped.

At the next meeting of the Joint Emergency Committee, however, the motion to dissolve the organization and transfer its functions to the newly organized Rescue Committee of the American Jewish Conference was raised again. This time the Zionist organizations (American Jewish Congress and American Emergency Committee for Zionist Affairs) together with the Zionist-dominated B'nai B'rith and the Synagogue Council of America decided to allow Hadassah to join the Joint Emergency Committee, thereby creating the 5–4 majority necessary to pass the resolution over opposition of the American Jewish Committee, Jewish Labor Committee, *Agudat ha-Rabbanim,* and *Agudat Yisrael.*[100] The practical implication of this decision was the dissolution of the only community framework that included almost all the major American Jewish organizations engaged in political action directly linked to rescue attempts. It meant, in practical terms, that there could be no coordination of rescue efforts and that the hopes for unified action by the entire community were no longer realistic.

Under these circumstances, it is not surprising that the *Vaad ha-Hatzala* decided to expand its activities to include rescue projects designed to save all Jews regardless of religiosity or religious affiliation. Excluded from the official American Jewish umbrella organization, which had ostensibly taken upon itself the task of initiating and implementing rescue activities on behalf of the community, the rabbis who headed the *Vaad* realized that the only way they could meaningfully participate in rescue work was to engage in such activities on their own. The need for such activities combined in a practical manner with a new set of circumstances to lead to this decision.

During the final months of 1943 the *Vaad* received via Switzerland increasingly urgent appeals for help from Jews in occupied Europe, especially from the head of the Nitra (Slovakia) Yeshiva Rabbi Shmuel David Ungar and his son-in-law, Rabbi Michael Dov

Ber Weissmandel. They were smuggling Jews from occupied Poland to Hungary, which was not yet under Nazi occupation. The operation required substantial funding (1,000 Swiss francs per person) and the Slovakian rabbis sought the *Vaad's* help through Isaac and Recha Sternbuch, who represented the rabbinic rescue organization in Switzerland.[101] During the latter months of 1943 the *Vaad* sent almost $47,000 to Switzerland for this purpose and in the process assisted in the (temporary) rescue of as many as 1,000 persons.[102]

This project became one of the *Vaad's* most important activities. In addition, earlier attempts to provide Jews in occupied Europe with Latin American passports via Switzerland,[103] operations to rescue noted rabbis such as the Belzer Rebbe and the Rebbe of Wischnitz,[104] and the initial activities of Aguda emissary to Turkey, Yaakov Griffel,[105] all combined to convince the leaders of the *Vaad ha-Hatzala* to expand their mandate. Thus the rabbinic relief organization, which was officially established in November 1939 solely for the purpose of saving rabbis and yeshiva students, became a full-fledged rescue organization which sought to save as many Jews as possible. This change, which was officially made by the *Vaad ha-Hatzala* at its annual conference held January 5–6, 1944,[106] represented the rabbis' realization that their original goal was only one part (albeit a very important one) of the terrible and unprecedented dangers faced by the Jewish people during the war. Their ability to confront this challenge would ultimately determine their place in this tragic chapter of Jewish history.

Notes

1. These efforts had begun shortly after Hitler's rise to power with the establishment in June 1933 of the Joint Consultative Council by the American Jewish Congress, American Jewish Committee, and B'nai B'rith. This body ceased operation in 1936. Another attempt to unite the community was made in 1938, when the General Jewish Council was created by the same organizations plus the Jewish Labor Committee. This organization was also short–lived, and thus when the news regarding the Final Solution reached the United States, American Jewry lacked unified representation. The leading Orthodox organizations (rabbinic associations and political parties) did not participate in the efforts to create a united political framework until the summer of 1942. See Edward David Pinsky, "Cooperation Among American Jewish Organizations In Their Efforts To Rescue European Jewry During the Holocaust, 1939–1945" unpublished dissertation, New York University, 1980; Isaac Neustadt–Noy, "The Unending Task; Efforts to Unite American Jewry From The American Jewish Congress To The American Jewish Conference," unpublished dissertation, Brandeis University, 1976.

2. David Kranzler, *Thy Brothers' Blood*, pp. 91–92; *Churbn un Rettung*, pp. 269–270; *Churbn Airopa*, p. 43.

3. "Joint Emergency Committee on European Jewish Affairs," September 28, 1943, AAJCom, YIVO Archives, RG 347, Box 23, file 4.

4. Pinsky, "Cooperation Among American Jewish Organizations," p. 247.

5. Also in attendance were representatives of Mizrachi, Mizrachi Women, and the Union of Orthodox Jewish Congregations. For a list of the Orthodox delegates see Neustadtz-Noy, "The Unending Task," pp. 425–427.

6. For a presentation of Rosenheim's views on Zionist issues, see his letter to Moshe Blau, May 3, 1943, AAYEY, file 16.

7. Kranzler, "Orthodox Ends, Unorthodox Means," pp. 6–7; Pinsky, "Cooperation Among American Jewish Organizations," pp. 247–260; Isaac Lewin, "Es Iz Nit Genug Zu Zorgen Far di Yidn Far Noch di Milchoma," *Morgn Dzurnal*, February 2, 1943, in *Churbn Airopa*, p. 43.

8. Letter of Gedalia Bublick, Zerach Warhaftig, and Isaac Lewin to Rabbi Joseph Soloveitchik, February 12, 1943, AAH; "Va'ad le–Pikuach Nefashot mei–Agudat Ha–Rabbanim," *Ha–Pardes*, 16, no. 12 (Adar 5703/March 1943), 2; letter of Yisrael Rosenberg and Gedalia Bublick to the presidents of Orthodox Jewish Congregations in the United States, April 15, 1943, AYHR.

9. The Council of Grand Rabbis approached federations for funds, prompting a query by I. B. Seligson of the Council of Jewish Federations and Welfare Funds to Rabbi Friedman as to the necessity for his organization given the existence of the *Vaad ha–Hatzala*. Letter of Seligson to Friedman, February 26, 1943, and the response of Rabbi Yitzchak Twersky to Seligson on March 17, 1943, both ACJFWF, I–69, Box 110.

10. Letter of Rosenheim to Yitzchak Lewin, December 22, 1942, WAYA, file 2.

11. See, for example, the letter of Leon Gellman, president of American Mizrachi, to Rabbi Rosenberg, April 12, 1943, AYHR.

12. Bublick of the Mizrachi was the chairman of the Political Committee, while Warhaftig and Lewin served as its secretaries. See note 8.

13. See the cables of Congressman Emanuel Cellar to Rabbi Kowalski of *Agudat ha–Rabbanim*, March 10, 17, and 18, 1943, AAH.

14. "Vaad le–Pikuach Nefashot mei–Agudat ha–Rabbanim," *Ha–Pardes*, 17, no. 1 (Nissan 5703/April 1943), p. 2; "Fourth Confidential Report to the Chaverim Nichbodim, Agudas Israel World Organization, covering the time from January 1–June 20, 1943," AAYA, file F–3–5–5, pp. 7, 15; letter of Michael Tress to Daniel Ellison, Arthur Klein, Emanuel Celler, and Sol Bloom, March 25, 1943, and to Max Stein, March 26, 1943, both AAYA, file 3–3–1; letter of Daniel Ellison to Michael Tress, March 27, 1943, AAYA, file F–3–15–6.

15. See, for example, the letter of Bublick, Warhaftig, and Lewin to Rabbi Meyer Berlin, February 14, 1943, AAH.

16. "Fourth Confidential Report–Agudas Israel," p. 7.

17. Cable of Rabbi Rosenberg and Bublick to the American Jewish Congress, World Jewish Congress, Jewish Labor Committee, Joint Distribution Committee, B'nai B'rith and the Emergency Committee for Zionist Affairs, February 18, 1943, AAH.

18. Monty Noam Penkower, "In Dramatic Dissent: The Bergson Boys," *American Jewish History*, LXX, no. 3 (March 1981), 287.

19. Henry L. Feingold, *Politics of Rescue: The Roosevelt Administration and the Holocaust 1938–1945* (New Brunswick, NJ: 1970) pp. 181–184.

20. In this respect, the Council was following the policy adopted by the *Agudat ha–Rabbanim*. See for example, the letter of Rabbi Yehuda Seltzer (executive director of *Agudat ha–Rabbanim*) to Rabbi Stephen Wise, January 14, 1943, AAH; "Va'ad le–Pikuach Nefashot mei–Agudat ha–Rabbanim," *Ha–Pardes*, 16, no. 12 (Adar 5703/March 1943), p. 2; Wyman, *Abandonment of the Jews*, pp. 87–89.

21. "Joint Emergency Committee on European Jewish Affairs," September 28, 1943, AAJCom, YIVO Archives, RG 347, Box 23, file 4; "Fourth Confidential Report," Agudas Israel, p. 5; Wyman, *Abandonment of the Jews*, p. 93.

22. See, for example, the letter of Michael Tress to Rabbi Eliezer Silver in which he opposes *Agudat Yisrael* joining the American Jewish Assembly "unless they are willing to recognize the authority and leadership of men who are steeped in the mitzvahs of our Torah." AAYA, file 3–4–8.

23. Amos Bunim, *A Fire in His Soul*, p. 110.

24. "Meeting Of Emergency Committee On European Jewish Affairs," May 24, 1943, AAJCom, YIVO Archives, RG 347, Box 23, file 4.

25. Lewin asked the Joint Emergency Committee to publicize the fact that there were still several million Jews alive in Poland (although it is not clear whether he had any basis other than wishful thinking for this conclusion). "Minutes Of Joint Emergency Committee For European Jewish Affairs," July 15, 1943, AAJCom, YIVO Archives, RG 347, Box 23, file 4.

26. "Joint Emergency Committee For European Jewish Affairs," August 10, 1943, ibid.

27. "Meeting Of The Joint Emergency Committee For European Jewish Affairs," September 24, 1943, ibid.

28. The only practical suggestion by an Orthodox representative (other than Lewin) that was recorded in the minutes was by Rabbi Kalmanowitz, who proposed that a permanent representative of the Joint Emergency Committee be stationed in Washington to lobby in Congress and elsewhere. "Meeting Of The Joint Emergency Committee For European Jewish Affairs," May 24, 1943, ibid. The minutes of all the meetings are in ibid.

29. Cable of Rabbis Rosenberg, Silver, and Levinthal to Pope Pius XII, March 12, 1943, AVH.

30. In the words of Rabbi Rosenberg, "the entire Jewish people all over the world" were now hoping that Bloom could assist European Jewry. Letter of the president of *Agudat ha–Rabbanim* to Bloom, April 14, 1943, AAH.

31. Feingold, *Politics of Rescue*, p. 195.

32. See Bloom's letters to Rabbi Seltzer, June 6 and 13, 1940; to Rabbi Rosenberg, September 4, 1940; and to *Agudat ha–Rabbanim*, October 4, 1939, all AAH.

33. Feingold, *Politics of Rescue*, pp. 190–207; Saul Friedman, *No Haven for the Oppressed; United States Policy Towards Jewish Refugees 1938–1945* (Detroit, 1973), pp. 155–180.

34. "Fourth Confidential Report," Agudas Israel, pp. 7–9; "Minutes of the May 15–16, 1943, meeting of the Executive Committee of the American Jewish Conference," Files of the American Jewish Conference, Zionist Archives, file III/1; cable of Rabbi Eliezer Silver to *Agudat ha–Rabbanim*, May 18, 1943, AAH; cable of

Rabbi Yehuda Seltzer to Henry Monsky, May 19, 1943, AAH; *The American Jewish Conference; Its Organization and Proceedings of the First Session August 29 to September 2, 1943. New York, N.Y.*, ed. Alexander Kohanski (New York, 1944), pp. 44–46.

35. On this issue see, for example, the letter of Leon Gellman to Rabbi Yisrael Rosenberg, April 12, 1943, AYHR.

36. Minutes of the meetings of the executive committee of the American Jewish Conference, July 14–15, 1943 and August 12, 1943, Files of the the American Jewish Conference, Zionist Archives, file III/1; Wyman, *Abandonment of the Jews*, pp. 161–162.

37. "Fourth Confidential Report," Agudas Israel, pp. 8–9; Minutes of "Meeting June 3, 1943" of Agudat Israel, AAYA, file F–3–5/10. Rosenheim attributed this position primarily to the Lithuanian *roshei yeshivot* (who headed the *Vaad ha–Hatzala*), but it is not clear that that was the case. See his letter to Yitzchak Lewin, July 13, 1943, AAYEY, file 16.

38. Cable of Rabbis Rosenberg (*Agudat ha–Rabbanim*), Kotler, and Kalmanowitz (deans of Polish rabbinical colleges) and Silver (*Agudat Yisrael*) as well as Leon Gellman (Mizrachi), David Delman (Young Israel), and Samuel Nirenstein (Union of Orthodox Jewish Congregations), to Minister Joseph Rettinger, May 16, 1943, YVA, M–2, 772; undated cable of Rabbi Rosenberg to Schwarzbart, sometime between May 1 and 15, 1943, AVH.

39. Letter of Sikorski to Rabbi Hertz , May 18, 1943, AVH.

40. Schwarzbart diary, May 5 and 7, 1943, YVA, M–2, 772; cable of Rabbis Rosenberg and Kalmanowitz to Schwarzbart, August 9, 1943, AVH.

41. Letter of Rabbi Seltzer to Sol Bloom, September 17, 1943, AVH.

42. Letter of Rabbi Kalmanowitz to Eldridge Dubrow, November 16, 1943, AVH.

43. See the September 23, 1943, cable of Vatican Secretary of State Maglione to Cicognani in *Le Saint Siege et les Victims De La Guerre*, Vol. IX, January–December 1943, Rome, 1975, p. 488; letter of Myron Taylor's secretary to Rabbi Kalmanowitz, October 4, 1943, AVH; letter of Kalmanowitz to Cicognani, October 7, 1943, AVH.

44. Cable of Rabbis Rosenberg and Kalmanowitz to M. Kwapiszewski, November 1, 1943, AVH.

45. See, for example, the letters of Acting Secretary of State Earl J. Stettinius, Jr., to Myron Taylor, November 2, 1943, and Taylor's letter to Cicognani of November 4, 1943, which was sent to Rabbi Kalmanowitz on November 9, 1943, both AVH; letter of British ambassador to the United States Lord Halifax to Kalmanowitz, November 26, 1943, AVH.

46. Letters of Rabbi Kalmanowitz to Podoski and Antoniutti, both November 22, 1943, AVH.

47. See, for example, the letter of Rabbi Solomon Schonfeld, executive director of the Chief Rabbis' Religious Emergency Council to Rabbis Rosenberg and Kotler, July 21, 1943; cable of the Chief Rabbis' Religious Emergency Council to Rabbis Rosenberg and Kotler, August 25, 1943; cable of Rabbis Rosenberg and Kotler to Rabbi Herzog, September 29, 1943, all AVH.

48. Letter of Rabbis Kahana, Finkel, and Sarna to *Vaad ha–Hatzala*, June 25, 1943, AVH.

49. Charles Passman, "Report On My Visit To Teheran in Connection With Relief To Jewish Refugees in Russia," July 23, 1943, AJDC, file 424.

50. Moshe Yishai, *Tzir be–Lo To'ar* (Tel–Aviv, 1950), pp. 150–151.

51. Ibid.

52. Cable of Rabbis Rosenberg and Kotler to Shilony and Rabbi Levy, October 20, 1943, AVH.

53. Zuroff, "Rabbis' Relief and Rescue", pp. 121–138.

54. "Current Needs and Activities of the Vaad Hahatzala," AVH; letter of Rabbi Levy to Rabbis Rosenberg and Kotler, January 6, 1944, AVH.

55. Letters of Lazer Epstein to *Vaad ha–Hatzala*, December 27 and 29, 1943, AVH; JDC press release, November 8, 1943, AJDC, file 424.

56. "Proposed Budget for 1944," AVH. During 1943 the *Vaad* spent $113,771 for parcels sent to the Soviet Union. "See Statement Of Income And Payments For Year Ending December 31, 1943," AJDC, file 362.

57. Letter of Rabbis Sarna, Finkel, and Kahana to *Vaad ha–Hatzala*, June 25, 1943, AVH.

58. "Proposed Budget for 1944," AVH.

59. "Vaad Hahatzala," Budgeting Bulletin B–49 of the CJFWF, August 24, 1943, p. 2, AVH.

60. "Current Needs and Activities of the Vaad Hahatzala," AVH; Jewish Council for Russian War Relief press release, January 20, 1944, AJDC, file 362.

61. Letters of Lazar Epstein to *Vaad ha–Hatzala*, December 27 and 29, 1943, AVH.

62. "Proposed Budget for 1944," AVH.

63. "Vaad Hahatzala Statement Of Income And Payments For Year Ending December 31, 1943," AVH; Vaad Hahatzala, Budgeting Bulletin B–16 of the CJFWF, June 1944, AJDC, file 362.

64. "Statement on Relief Activities of the JDC for Refugees in the USSR," May 31, 1944, AJDC, file 1056.

65. "Report Of The Secretary To The Executive Committee Meeting Of The Joint Distribution Committee," January 19, 1944, AJDC, file 362.

66. "Vaad Hahatzala Statement Of Income And Payments For Year Ending December 31, 1943," AVH.

67. David Kranzler, *Japanese, Nazis and Jews*, pp. 456 – 485; 489–504.

68. See Laura Margolis, "Report Of Activities In Shanghai, China From December 8, 1941 To September 1943," AJDC, file 463. The calculation is based on the following statistics. The approximately $90,000 raised by the *Vaad* was distributed to 500 persons over a period of twelve months. Assuming that the level of aid provided by the JDC to the Polish refugees in Shanghai from their arrival remained approximately the same, those assisted by the rabbis received four times as much money as their nonobservant counterparts.

69. See, for example, the letters of Sidney Cohen (Boston), David Watchmaker (Boston), and Max Bretton (Kansas City) to the JDC, July 2, 6, and 26 respectively, 1943, AJDC, file 361; letter of Hyman to Rabbi Wohlgelernter, September 16, 1943, ACJFWF, I–69, Box 150; letter of Hyman to Butzel (Detroit), June 11, 1943, AJDC–VH.

70. See, for example, the letters of Buchman to Pearlstein, March 8, 1943, AJDC, file 423; Hyman to Watchmaker, July 9, 1943, AJDC, file 361.

71. See, for example, the letters of Leavitt to Mrs. Stameshkin (St.Paul), May 7, 1943, AJDC, file 361; Buchman to Saloman (Tulsa), May 25, 1943, AJDC, file 423.

72. See, for example, the letter of Leavitt to *Ha–Pardes* magazine, May 26, 1943, AJDC, file 361; "Mr. James N. Rosenberg's Statement To The Emergency Administrative Committee Meeting Held On Tuesday June 8th, 1943," AJDC, file 423; "Statement on Relief Activities of the JDC for Refugees in the USSR," May 31, 1944, AJDC, file 1056.

73. Laura Margolis, "Report Of Activities In Shanghai, China From December 8, 1941, To September 1943," AJDC, file 463.

74. JDC comments regarding CJFWF bulletin on *Vaad ha-Hatzala*, August 11, 1943, ACJFWF, CJFWF reports.

75. For an analysis of the American Jewish Committee's record and methods during the war see Pinsky, "Cooperation Among American Jewish Organizations," pp. 98–114.

76. Originally established by a group of Palestinian Jews affiliated with the Revisionist Irgun Tzvai Leumi underground, and headed by Hillel Kook (known in the United States as Peter Bergson) and local Jews, the group was initially called the "Committee for a Jewish Army of Stateless and Palestinian Jews." See Monty Noam Penkower, "In Dramatic Dissent: The Bergson Boys," *American Jewish History*, LXX, no. 3 (March 1981), 281–309.

77. Rosenheim opposed Zionist efforts to establish an independent Jewish state in Eretz Yisrael so long as its leaders refused to accept *halachah* as their supreme authority. At the same time, he was wary of publicly opposing the establishment of such a state at a time when it might result in the rescue of many Jews. See, for example, his letters to Rabbi Moshe Blau, May 16, 1943, AAYEY, file 16; and to Rabbi Yitzchak Mayer Lewin, December 22, 1942, WAYA, file 2.

78. Thus, for example, Rabbi Eliezer Silver was an honorary officer of the Emergency Committee. M. J. Nurenberger, *The Sacred And The Doomed; The Jewish Establishment vs. The Six Million* (Oakville, NY and London, 1985), p. 197.

79. Letter of Eri Jabotinsky to Dr. Altman, October 12, 1943, Palestine Statehood Collection (records of the Emergency Committee to Save the Jewish People of Europe), Yale University Library (hereafter called AECJPoE), Box 1 Folder 10; *The Sacred and the Doomed*, p. 197; Amos Bunim, *A Fire in His Soul*, p. 127; *Churbn un Rettung*, pp. 283–286.

80. Pinsky, "Cooperation Among American Jewish Organizations," pp. 328–414.

81. William D. Hassett, *Off the Record with FDR 1942–1945* (New Brunswick, NJ: 1958), p. 209.

82. Jabotinsky letter, AECJPoE, Box 1, Folder 10.

83. The estimated number of participants ranged, according to the various press reports, from 300 (JTA) to 500 (*Washington Post, Time, Der Tog, Forwards*), Wyman, *Abandonment of the Jews*, p. 152. The Jabotinsky letter speaks of 400 rabbis and 100 "reporters and friends" and is probably the most accurate source.

84. Jabotinsky letter, AECJPoE, Box 1, Folder 10; *Churbn un Rettung*, pp. 283–284; "Mishlachat Rabbanim be–Vashington," *Ha-Pardes*, 17, no. 8 (Cheshvan 5704/November 1943), p. 2.

85. See cable of Rabbi Levovitz to Marvin McIntyre, October 3, 1943, NA, FW 840.4016/10–543, in which he cites a request for a meeting dated September 29, 1943. According to Wyman, *Abandonment of the Jews*, (p. 152), the Emergency Committee had been trying to arrange the meeting "for weeks."

86. Cable of Edwin Watson to Rabbi Levovitz, October 5, 1943, NA, FW 840.4016/10–543.

87. Letter of Edwin Watson to Cecil Gray, October 5, 1943, ibid.

88. Penkower, "In Dramatic Dissent," p. 294; Kanzler, "Orthodox Ends, Unorthodox Means," p. 9.

89. Wyman, *Abandonment of the Jews*, p. 152.

90. Minutes by Isaiah Berlin, November 11, 1943, Public Record Office, FO 371/35041. Goldmann related the conversation to Isaiah Berlin, who passed on this information to the British Foreign Office via the British Embassy in Washington.

91. *Churbn un Rettung*, p. 284.

92. Jabotinsky letter, AECJPoE, Box 1, Folder 10.

93. *Time* (October 18, 1943, p. 21) compared the rabbis' reception with that of Prince Faisal. For an analysis of the general press see Deborah E. Lipstadt, *Beyond Belief; The American Press and the Coming of the Holocaust 1933–1945* (New York, 1986), p. 225; Wyman, *Abandonment of the Jews*, p. 152.

94. Quoted in *The Answer*, March 12, 1944.

95. The various quotes are reproduced in *Churbn un Rettung*, pp. 286–289.

96. Quoted in David Morrison, *Heroes, Antiheroes And The Holocaust; American Jewry and Historical Choice* (Jerusalem and New London, 1995), p. 218.

97. Letter (petition) of Rabbis Rosenberg, Silver, Levinthal, Bloch, Seltzer, Levovitz, Gold, and Friedman to President Roosevelt, October 6, 1943, NA, 840.48 Refugees/4745. On October 8 the President asked the State Department to reply to the rabbis, and an answer dated October 22, 1943, was sent to Rabbi Rosenberg by Howard K. Travers, Chief of the Visa Division, NA, 840.48 Refugees/4745.

98. Wyman, *Abandonment of the Jews*, pp. 144–146.

99. "Meeting of the Joint Emergency Committee For European Jewish Affairs," September 24, 1943, AAJCom, RG 347, Box 23, file 4.

100. "Meeting of the Joint Emergency Committee For European Jewish Affairs," November 5, 1943, AAJCom, RG 347, Box 23, file 4; "Fifth Confidential Report To The Chaverim Nichbodim, Agudas Israel World Organization, July 1 – December 31, 1943, AAYA, file F 35–19–FF6, pp. 9–10; Edward Pinsky, "American Jewish Unity During the Holocaust—The Joint Emergency Committee," *American Jewish History*, LXXII, no. 4 (June 1983), 493.

101. "Cable from Switzerland arrived through diplomatic channels in Washington," December 20, 1943, AJDC–VH.

102. "Vaad Hahatzala," Budgeting Bulletin B–16 of the CJFWF, June 1944, AJDC, file 362, p. 2.

103. Monty Penkower, *The Jews Were Expendable; Free World Diplomacy and the Holocaust* (Urbana and Chicago, 1983), p. 249; Joseph Friedenson and David Kanzler, *Heroine of Rescue*, p. 101.

104. Isaac Lewin, "Attempts at Rescuing European Jews with the Help of Polish Diplomatic Missions During World War II," *The Polish Review*, Part II, XXIV, no. 1 (1979), 48–49.

105. Griffel arrived in Istanbul in March 1943 as the representative of *Agudat Yisrael* to the local rescue committee. Joseph Friedenson, *Dateline: Istanbul; Dr. Jacob Griffels's Lone Odyssey Through a Sea Of Indifference* (Brooklyn, 1993), pp. 21–59.

106. "Statement on the resolutions adopted by the annual conference of the Vaad Hatzala, January 5th and 6th, 1944," AVH.

Afterword

Two events in January 1944 were to profoundly affect the rescue efforts of American Orthodoxy during the final sixteen months of World War II. The first was the decision by the *Vaad ha-Hatzala* to expand its mandate to save all Jews regardless of religiosity or religious affiliation. The second was the establishment by President Roosevelt on January 22, 1944, of the War Refugee Board, a U.S. agency whose *raison d'être* was the rescue of the Nazis' potential victims.

Both decisions were a natural outgrowth of several developments in the latter half of 1943. As more and more information became available regarding the worsening plight of European Jewry, two processes took place simultaneously which significantly affected the response of the American Jewish community, and the Orthodox rescue activists in particular. The first was the growing realization of the monumental dimensions of the catastrophe which had engulfed most of the Jewish communities in Europe. The second was an intensified search for practical measures to rescue as many Jews as possible, an effort that yielded potentially significant results. The attempts of Jewish leaders living under Nazi occupation or in satellite states to enlist the aid of the Jews in the Free World complemented the latter development.

It was under these circumstances that the *Vaad ha-Hatzala,* which had made several initial attempts to reach and assist Jews in the heart of Nazi Europe, reached a turning point at the end of 1943, when the two processes meshed for the rabbinic rescue organization. On the one hand, the rabbis had to a considerable extent internalized the enormity of the catastrophe. On the other hand, their initial efforts had finally yielded concrete rescue possibilities in occupied Europe which justified a change in the *Vaad's* official policy. This is not to say that the *Vaad ha-Hatzala* abandoned its original ideology. Even this decision to broaden its scope was made in the context of "an uninterrupted flow of appeals from rabbinical authorities abroad for mercy and help for the suffering Jewish masses in Europe." One can safely assume that the tragedy of European Jewry was shocking enough to induce them to make such a decision even without appeals from rabbis, but in the Orthodox community such fateful decisions are always best presented as emanating from or supported by rabbinical jurisdiction.

The decision by President Roosevelt to establish the War Refugee Board perfectly complemented the change in the *Vaad's* policy. The War Refugee Board was, in effect, the governmental rescue agency whose establishment the Emergency Committee to Save the Jewish People of Europe and others had demanded since the summer of 1943. Orthodox rescue activists had strongly supported the campaign to establish such an agency, and this was one of the demands on the petition submitted to President Roosevelt at the rabbis' march. With the establishment of the War Refugee Board, rescue efforts would be conducted by the U.S. government, and by others with its blessing and support, a situation which in theory should have considerably increased their effectiveness. There was an additional important internal benefit for the Jewish community, since there would now ostensibly no longer be any need for Jewish organizations to circumvent U.S. regulations or to quarrel among themselves regarding this issue.

Judging from the *Vaad ha-Hatzala's* proposed budget for 1944, it would appear that, despite the decision to expand its mandate, the leaders of the organization were still intent on devoting most of their resources for the refugee Torah scholars in the Soviet Union and Shanghai. Thus although $500,000, which was an extremely large sum by the *Vaad* ha-Hatzala's standards, was allocated for rescue operations from Switzerland in 1944, the amount set aside for parcels and remittances to the rabbis and yeshiva students in Central Asia ($474,000) and Shanghai ($180,000) was considerably higher. Ultimately the events in Europe dictated a change in the *Vaad's* priorities. As new opportunities for rescue from Nazi-occupied territory developed, the *Vaad ha-Hatzala* increasingly concentrated its efforts on the activities of its Swiss branch, headed by Isaac and Recha Sternbuch. During the first three months of 1944 the rabbis spent approximately $121,000 on rescue operations in Europe while sending $55,047 worth of parcels and cash to the

Soviet Union and arranging for the transfer of $46,500 to Shanghai. As time went by, this trend became much stronger. Although the *Vaad* continued to send aid to these beleaguered refugee Torah scholars throughout the war and persisted in its efforts to bring those in Japanese-occupied Shanghai to a safer location, the agency increasingly devoted its efforts and resources to Nazi-occupied Europe.

Most of the operations funded by the *Vaad ha-Hatzala* were conducted from Slovakia, under the auspices of Rabbi Shmuel David Ungar, the *rosh yeshiva* of the Nitra Yeshiva, and by his son-in-law Rabbi Michael Dov Weissmandel. Their efforts became even more critical in the wake of the Nazi occupation of Hungary on March 19, 1944. Prior to that date Weissmandel had organized the escape of Polish Jews to Hungary, where the situation was far more favorable than in Poland, where the Final Solution was proceeding rapidly. The Nazis' takeover of Hungary not only rendered this escape route obsolete, but endangered the Hungarian Jewish community which now faced the prospect of mass deportation and annihilation.

Rabbi Weissmandel and the leaders of the Orthodox community in Budapest appealed to the *Vaad ha-Hatzala* via Switzerland for enormous sums of money (each requested at least a million dollars) to finance their rescue activities. These efforts, which were coordinated by Orthodox leaders in Slovakia and Hungary, took several forms. One was the smuggling of Jews from Hungary to Slovakia and Rumania, where the situation of the Jews was relatively stable and no deportations seemed imminent. In addition, the transfer of Jews from Poland continued, but to Slovakia, rather than to Hungary.

At the same time, efforts were initiated to bribe the Nazis to discontinue the deportations altogether. This scheme was an outgrowth of similar negotiations conducted by the Slovakian "Working Group," headed by Zionist leader Gisi Fleischmann, of which Rabbi Weissmandel was a prominent member. Weissmandel was convinced that the bribes given to Dieter Wisliceny, Eichmann's representative in Bratislava, had in effect stopped the deportations from Slovakia, and he therefore assumed that the deportations from Hungary and possibly elsewhere could be stopped by the same means. In order to do so, however, he needed the financial support of the *Vaad,* since the Nazis always insisted that the funds come from abroad and sufficient amounts were not readily available to Orthodox circles in Slovakia or Hungary.

The Swiss dimension of this effort was launched in the spring of 1944, but it took some time before the leaders of the *Vaad ha-Hatzala* became fully aware of the pertinent details. (They were totally unaware of the negotiations that had been conducted in Slovakia since 1942.) Although they now had the benefit of War Refuge Board channels of communication (via U.S. diplomatic missions), the project in question was in violation of U.S. regulations, which unequivocally forbade any ransom schemes. Thus Sternbuch, who was in contact with Weissmandel by courier, was forced to communicate with the rabbis in New York via the Polish Legation in Berne. This secret communication channel was developed by Dr. Julius Kuhl, a young Polish Jew who was employed at the embassy, with the blessing of Ambassador Alexander Lados. The channel in fact had been intact since the summer of 1942, when Sternbuch sent the *Vaad* the news regarding the Final Solution in Poland.

During this period the *Vaad ha-Hatzala* was also involved in other rescue projects. One of the most important, from the rabbis' viewpoint, was the effort to save a group of more than 200 Jews who possessed Central and South American passports provided by the rabbinic rescue organization. They had been taken to the Vittel internment camp in France, where they were held for many months pending a decision regarding their papers. Their fate was, in essence, a test case of the *Vaad's* efforts to procure Latin American passports for European Jews and it was therefore of particular concern to the rabbis. Another factor in the *Vaad's* efforts on their behalf was the fact that several in the group were members of Recha Sternbuch's immediate family. When the rabbis ultimately found out that the group had been deported to an unknown destination, they left no stone unturned in their efforts to rescue its members. The *Vaad* worked particularly closely with Juan Cardenas, the Spanish ambassador to the United States, to have Spain, which represented the Latin American countries in Berlin, apply pressure to ensure that the Nazis recognize these documents. Ultimately, however, these efforts were unsuccessful.

The *Vaad* was also particularly anxious to help save the remnants of Lithuanian Jewry. Since early 1944, when the rabbis learned that several thousand Jews were still alive in Lithuania, they attempted various means to establish contact with the community. The efforts continued when the *Vaad* learned that these Jews had been deported to concentration camps in Germany. A very important motivation in this case, was the rabbis' desire to rescue eminent Torah scholars; also the (unfounded) information that Rabbis Avraham Grodzenski of the Slabodka Yeshiva, and Elchanan Wasserman of the Baranowitz Yeshiva, were still alive led to redoubled efforts on their behalf.

Much of this work was done via Sweden, where Rabbi Wilhelm Wolbe, who in 1940–1941 had helped Polish scholars stranded in Lithuania to obtain visas to Curaçao, served as the *Vaad's* representative following the establishment of the War Refugee Board. He was part of the *Vaad's* European network of representatives, which included Yaakov Griffel in Turkey and Renee Reichman in Tangiers. Griffel, with the help of Yoseph Klarman and Ludwig Kastner, played a role in the efforts to assist the Jews of the Balkans and help facilitate their emigration to Palestine. Reichman organized the shipment of thousands of food parcels to Nazi concentration camps, primarily Theresienstadt and Birkenau. Those parcels were sent duty free to individual inmates with the assistance of the Spanish Red Cross. She also attempted (unsuccessfully) to arrange for the evacuation of 500 Jewish children from Hungary to Tangiers.

In the meantime, the *Vaad ha-Hatzala* focused primarily on rescue efforts from Hungary. In mid-July Sternbuch informed New York that 1,000 people had been rescued to Rumania with the *Vaad's* assistance, and he passed on a request (by Weissmandel) in Rabbi Ungar's name to bomb the deportation railway routes between Hungary and Auschwitz. At the same time, efforts continued for the liberation of 1,684 Hungarian Jews who had boarded a train, organized by Hungarian Zionist leader Reszo (Yisrael) Kastner, which was supposed to be sent to freedom. The train, however, had been rerouted by the Nazis to Bergen-Belsen. Kastner headed a group of local Zionists conducting negotiations with the SS (parallel to those being conducted by Orthodox activists) to halt the deportations from Hungary and hoped that the release of this group, which included several prominent rabbis, such as the Satmar Rebbe, Rabbi Yoel Teitelbaum, and communal leaders, would lead to a breakthrough in the negotiations. That, unfortunately, was not the case. The Nazis continued simultaneous negotiations both with the group headed by the JDC's representative in Switzerland, Saly Mayer (with whom Kastner's group was closely linked), and with individuals in the Orthodox community who were in contact with Weissmandel and Sternbuch, but meanwhile the deportations from Hungary continued.

The major problem in this regard was the compensation demand-ed by the Germans in return for the rescue of the Jews. The original offer presented by Eichmann to the Zionists was one million Jews in return for 10,000 trucks to be used only on the Eastern front. It was obvious to Jewish leaders in Europe that such an offer could never be accepted by the Americans and the British, so the question became whether the Nazis would agree to an alternative suggestion, such as food, medicine, or perhaps money. The problem was, however, that the U.S. government refused in principle even to consider the trans-fer of any funds or goods to Nazi Germany in return for the Jews. This stand made it increasingly difficult to continue the negotia-tions, which Saly Mayer had been conducting with the approval of the War Refugee Board. Under these circumstances, any transfer of funds or goods had to be carried out without the knowledge of the Americans. The Orthodox, who certainly did not feel bound by U.S. regulations, indeed made ransom payments to the Nazis during the summer and fall of 1944. However, they did not possess the extremely large sums of money demanded by the Nazis in return for a comprehensive agreement which would have guaranteed the safe-ty of all the Jews still alive in Nazi-occupied territory.

In reality, however, the situation was far more complicated. Without the knowledge of the Americans, both Saly Mayer and Kastner gave the Nazis ransom payments, the former by funding 40 tractors for Sternbuch to turn over to the Nazis in September, the latter in direct cash payments made much earlier in the negotiations. It is not clear, however, what results were thereby achieved. Sternbuch was convinced, for example, that the arrival in Switzerland in August of 320 persons from the train organized by Kastner was a direct result of the deposits he had made on behalf of "friends of the Gestapo in Budapest" in July, but the evidence seems to indicate that this was not the case.

In the meantime, Sternbuch continued to fund the operations headed by Weissmandel to smuggle Jews to relative safety—this time from Poland (10,000 Slovak crowns per person or $93 to $116) and Hungary (6,000 Slovak crowns per person or $56 to $70) to Slovakia—while simultaneously negotiating the larger issue of res-cue with the Gestapo. In addition, he funded maintenance costs for

Jews in hiding in Slovakia (4,000 Slovak crowns or $37 to $47 per person) as well as for those in Slovak labor camps (14,000 Slovak crowns) and also paid to provide Jewish refugees with false papers (3,000 Slovak crowns per person or $28 to $35). Thus by the end of October 1944 the *Vaad ha-Hatzala* had sent Isaac and Recha Sternbuch slightly more than $420,000 in 1944, with the overwhelming majority of those funds being spent to finance rescue activities in, from, or through Hungary, Slovakia, Poland, and Rumania. In comparison, the *Vaad* sent $110,000 to the refugee scholars in Shanghai during this period, and spent about $125,000 on relief parcels and $30,000 on cash remittances to the yeshiva *leit* in the Soviet Union.

These figures mark a significant increase in the *Vaad's* income, which was attained through increased fundraising by both rabbis and lay leaders as well as by numerous volunteers. Motivated by a sense of urgency, which was generated by the desperate appeals from occupied Europe conveyed by Sternbuch, the Orthodox rescue organization considerably intensified its activities during this period. This change was also reflected in more prosaic terms. Various committees were established to deal with specific problems (administration, fundraising, and public relations), and an executive director was hired. In accordance with suggestions by prominent laymen such as Michael Tress and Stephen Klein, the *Vaad's* office was reorganized in a more professional manner. Shortly thereafter, in early 1945, the *Vaad ha-Hatzala* was officially incorporated in the State of New York.

In the meantime the *Vaad's* negotiations with the Nazis continued. In the fall of 1944 the *Vaad* sent Jean-Marie Musy, a prominent right-wing Swiss politician, to Berlin to discuss the possibility of evacuating large numbers of Jews from Germany in return for financial remuneration. The Nazis proposed to allow 300,000 Jews to leave Germany at the rate of 15,000 per month, and they promised to stop the murders in the concentration camps. In return, the Nazis wanted 20 million Swiss francs, to be deposited in installments of one million each month (for twenty months) following the Jews' arrival in a neutral county. Convinced that the only way to achieve concrete results was by bribes, the *Vaad* accepted the proposal in principle, although it was obvious that such a deal would be vetoed by the Americans. They also believed that it would be frowned upon by Saly Mayer and the JDC due to the American refusal to allow

Jewish negotiators to use bribes of any sort. At this point, however, Sternbuch had basically given up hope of working with Mayer (he begged the *Vaad* not to force him to do so), whom he thought had undermined his efforts to bribe the Nazis regarding Hungarian Jewry.

In December, shortly after Musy's return from Berlin with an agreement in principle for an end to the murders, the rest of the "Kastner train" arrived in Switzerland. This development corroborated Sternbuch's conviction that his choice of messenger and methods were the only ones that could yield positive results. The Swiss branch of the *Vaad ha-Hatzala* therefore, decided, to proceed alone, regardless of the consequences. In New York the news from Switzerland was greeted with tremendous enthusiasm, and an emergency campaign was launched to raise the funds to cover the terms of the pending agreement. Among the slogans used was one indicating that a donation of $18 could save a Jewish life in Nazi-occupied Europe.

Despite the enormous increase in the *Vaad's* income during 1944 (over $1,135,000 compared with about $372,000 in 1943) and the impressive success of the emergency campaign launched in December 1944, which netted approximately a quarter of a million dollars, it was obvious that the *Vaad* could not cope alone with the financial obligations inherent in the agreement achieved by Musy. To make matters worse, the *Vaad's* increased general rescue activities and the concommitant expansion of fundraising efforts had led to tension within the American Jewish community and the increased hostility of the JDC. These factors prompted a surprising offer by the rabbis. In early January 1945, they suggested to the JDC that in return for $2 million which would be used exclusively for the rescue of Jews from Nazi-occupied Europe, the *Vaad ha-Hatzala* would restrict its fundraising to a campaign on behalf of rabbis and yeshiva students. For an additional $250,000, the *Vaad* would forgo its fundraising campaign for the rehabilitation of Jewish religious life after the war.

The JDC, needless to say, was not interested in this offer. One can only wonder whether the rabbis actually expected anyone to take it seriously. While they did offer the veteran rescue agency representation on a committee to supervise the expenditure of the funds, the leaders of the *Vaad* were in essence asking the JDC to finance a rescue program that the latter opposed in principle. Within a few weeks, however, the JDC was to make a surprising turnabout of sorts in the wake of a breakthrough in the *Vaad's* negotiations with the Nazis.

Throughout this period, Musy had continued to meet with Nazi leaders and press for the release of the Jews, especially women, children, and men unfit for work. He met with Himmler in Wildbad on January 1, and three weeks later met with Walter Schellenberg. The first concrete indication that the Nazis were serious about the negotiations came the night of February 6–7, 1945, when a transport with 1,210 Jews from Thereseienstadt (among them 663 from Germany, 434 from Holland, and 104 from the Protectorate) crossed the Swiss border at Kreuzlingen. According to Musy, the Nazis were ready to release additional transports each week in return for the deposit of 5 million Swiss francs in a Swiss bank under his name. In addition, Nazi leaders demanded positive reports in the American media. The problem was that the *Vaad*, which had no problem in principle with the terms of the agreement achieved by Musy, did not have the money and was therefore forced to appeal to the JDC for help. The latter was willing to give the rabbis $937,000 to send to Switzerland for this purpose, but the War Refugee Board's representative in Switzerland, Roswell McClelland, who was known for his strict adherence to U.S. regulations, demanded that he be able to control the funds, which he insisted be deposited in a joint account under his name and that of Sternbuch.

With the required funds deposited in Switzerland, Musy returned to Germany. There he learned to his consternation that Saly Mayer, who was simultaneously conducting negotiations with the Nazis, was not insisting on the release of additional Jews from German territory but was content merely to see that they were kept alive. According to Musy's informants, Mayer had in fact hindered the departure of additional transports to Switzerland or other neutral countries. Yet despite these problems, which were in fact not the result of Mayer's negotiations but rather a product of internal dissension among Nazi leaders, Musy continued his mission, focusing on obtaining a promise that, prior to their surrender to the advancing Allied and Soviet armies, the Nazis would not murder the inmates of the concentration camps.

Musy claimed that he had obtained a commitment from the Germans not to harm the camp inmates despite an initial decision to the contrary by Hitler. According to the Swiss politician,

Schellenberg told him that the Nazi dictator was furious when he learned about the release of the transport from Theresienstadt, which was presented in the press as a payoff for the rescue of Nazi officers. In response, Hitler ordered that not a single Jew be allowed to leave Germany and that the camps be evacuated. Musy protested this decision, which was obviously intended to kill off many of the inmates. In return, the Nazis demanded that the camps not be bombed and that the guards not be mistreated immediately, but rather be considered prisoners-of-war. These terms were accepted in principle by American and British representatives in Switzerland and were apparently for the most part observed by the Allied troops.

When Musy and Recha Sternbuch traveled to Germany in late April they heard conflicting reports, not only about whether the Allies had kept their promise, but whether the Nazis had done so. What is clear is that trucks sent by the *Vaad* to concentration camps in March were able to take out two groups totaling 469 Slovak Jews to safety in Switzerland, and that Sternbuch was able to send truckloads of food to the Jews in various concentration camps during the final weeks of the war. The *Vaad* claimed that as a result of Musy's negotiations, many thousands of Jewish concentration camp inmates remained alive, but that claim is extremely difficult to prove conclusively.

The conclusion of the war in Europe on May 8, 1945, officially brought to an end the Nazis' campaign to annihilate European Jewry, but Jewish suffering in the wake of the Holocaust did not end then. Hundreds of thousands of survivors remained in concentration camps, unable to cope with the new reality, incapable of providing for themselves. Thousands emerged from the forests or from other hiding places and were also in need of assistance. Jewish communal and religious life was practically nonexistent in most of Europe. Thus Jewish relief agencies such as the JDC and the *Vaad ha-Hatzala*, which had played such an active role in rescue activities, found themselves facing enormous new challenges in the immediate postwar era.

Under these circumstances, one would assume that the American and European Orthodox rescue activists would prefer to concentrate on future objectives such as the rehabilitation of Orthodox Jewry throughout Europe rather than dwell on the past. This was only partially true, however, for the rabbis and laymen who headed the *Vaad ha-Hatzala*. They were haunted by what they considered to be the

missed rescue opportunities of the war, especially during 1944 and
1945. Emotionally traumatized by the tragic dimensions of the
Holocaust, and especially by the destruction of the Eastern
European world that had spawned them, they sought to identify
those responsible for the failure of world Jewry to save their co-religionists. Shortly after the war the *Vaad* publicly attacked the JDC,
especially its Swiss representative Saly Mayer, blaming them for
interfering with the *Vaad's* attempts to rescue the remnants of
European Jewry. According to the rabbis, Mayer had hindered
Musy's negotiations to arrange the release of additional transports
and had denounced the *Vaad* to the Americans for offering bribes to
the Nazis, thereby hampering the rabbinic relief organization's rescue efforts. Mayer—who preferred to keep Jews alive in the camps
rather than rescue them to safety—had sabotaged the *Vaad's* efforts
to organize an orderly exodus of Jews from Nazi-occupied territory,
and in the rabbis' opinion, was therefore indirectly responsible for
the death of hundreds of thousands.

The rabbis' accusations also related to the JDC in New York,
which they believed not only had totally failed to provide leadership
in rescue work, but had actually interfered with the *Vaad's* efforts.
The rabbis pointed to the JDC's insistence on adhering to U.S. regulations despite the mass murder; it also refused to support the *Vaad's*
rescue initiatives, they charged, which it often regarded as impossible or the product of fantasy, despite the fact that on numerous
occasions these were successful. The JDC, they claimed, had provided relatively minimal financial assistance, and only after a lengthy
delay and under extremely restrictive conditions, for urgent projects
sponsored by the *Vaad ha-Hatzala*. These projects had proven successful and helped rescue many Jews, but they could have rescued
many more with the proper funding.

In the words of the *Vaad*:

> ...the approach of the *Vaad Hatzala* [sic] was motivated by the
> principles of the Torah and by a spirit of complete devotion
> and self-sacrifice on the part of its leaders who themselves per-
> sonally witnessed the scenes in Europe and to whom our great
> tragedy is personal and actual. In fact, the *Vaad Hatzala* [sic]
> stopped at nothing, for everything is fair and legal when it is a
> question of life and death and the rescue of even one life must,
> according to our precept, transcend every law of the Torah....

The *Vaad Hatzala* [sic] by its methods and its undaunted fiery spirit of stopping-at-nothing has blazed a trail for others to follow.... Because of this spirit the *Vaad Hatzala* [sic] was able to accomplish a great deal more with its limited funds than would have been possible otherwise, and was a driving force for other organizations in the field of rescue. This is evidenced by the brilliant page which the *Vaad Hatzala* [sic] has written into the history of our people in its darkest hours. It has actually been proven beyond any doubt, that if the *Vaad Hatzala* [sic] had had more funds during the past years many more of our lost brothers would be alive today.

Yet as serious as this litany of charges was, it was with one exception basically flawed. It was true that the JDC in New York strictly adhered to U.S. regulations, even to the spirit, not to mention the letter, of the law. It was also true that this rigid policy had forced the JDC to adopt different tactics than the *Vaad* did in its negotiations with the Nazis and to limit severely the extent to which it was willing to cooperate with Sternbuch. The other charges, however, were more a product of Musy's wishful thinking than JDC machinations. Saly Mayer, moreover, unbeknownst to Sternbuch and the rabbis in New York, had over the past two years funded numerous rescue initiatives in occupied Europe that were undoubtedly illegal. It was true that upon instructions from New York he had refrained from using false Paraguayan and Dominican Republic passports, and that he had early in the war reluctantly opposed the illegal smuggling of Jews into Switzerland, but Mayer's assistance to illegal rescue activities in France, Slovakia, Rumania, Belgium, Croatia, and Italy helped save the lives of thousands of Jews.

In effect, Musy's efforts fell prey not to Saly Mayer's scheming but to infighting between Himmler and Schellenberg on the one hand and Hitler and Kaltenbrunner on the other. It was very convenient for Musy to take Himmler at face value regarding his willingness to turn over the camps intact, but at this stage of the war even Himmler's word was of limited value. And why should the *Reichsfuhrer* SS's promise to one emissary of the Jews be of any more value than that of his internal rivals in the Nazi hierarchy to a different Jewish representative? In short, the guarantees Musy ostensibly attained for Sternbuch were likely the product of their own delusions, a final form of Nazi torture for Jews so desirous of saving their brethren. Thus in the final throes of the Third Reich, its architects found a way to embitter the lives even of those Jews not physically under their control and set them at each other's throats in the process, a fitting conclusion to their reign of terror against the Jewish people.

There is a strong element of irony in these allegations against the JDC. For while most of the accusations relating to rescue efforts in Switzerland were not accurate, the rabbis could have presented quite a few legitimate complaints against the veteran Jewish relief agency. In fact, from the very beginning of its activities, the *Vaad ha-Hatzala* had opposed the JDC's stance on the rescue of rabbis and yeshiva students and in most cases had been proven right. Several examples come to mind. The Joint tried to discourage the emigration of Polish refugees from Lithuania via the Far East using Curaçao visas, an operation that was actively supported by the *Vaad* and that ultimately resulted in the rescue from death of perhaps 2,000 or more Jews, among them more than 600 rabbis and yeshiva students. The JDC initially attempted to provide relief to the Polish Jewish refugees in the Soviet Union via the nonsectarian channels of the Polish government-in-exile and expressed doubts regarding the validity of the *Vaad's* claim that it had found a means to send aid to the Jewish refugees in Central Asia. Ultimately, the JDC reversed its policy and adopted the relief parcels project as its own, when it realized that in principle the method used by the rabbis was far more effective. To the JDC's credit, despite what turned out to be mistaken decisions regarding specific rescue projects, the veteran relief agency made every effort to provide maximum financial support for as many Jews in distress as possible. And it was this assistance, as we have seen, that made possible some of the *Vaad's* successes in saving refugee Torah scholars.

Any attempt to summarize the activities of the *Vaad ha-Hatzala* must deal with the issue of particularism. To what extent was it justified to break ranks with the entire American Jewish community to save a small, elite of one segment of Jewry? The rabbis who established the *Vaad* were convinced that such a step was not only legitimate but absolutely necessary. It was this staunch belief in the holiness of their sacred mission that motivated them to launch what ultimately became a successful rescue organization, certainly by the standards of American Jewry during the Holocaust.

During World War II the *Vaad ha-Hatzala* rescued approximately 625 Polish rabbis and yeshiva students from Lithuania via the Far East. It helped keep alive hundreds of refugee Torah scholars living under extremely harsh conditions in Central Asia and enabled approximately 500 rabbis and yeshiva students to survive, while continuing their Torah studies, despite the numerous hardships of living under Japanese occupation in Shanghai. To its credit, the leadership of the *Vaad* realized in the wake of the news of the Final Solution that a broader rescue agenda was necessary, and it made a serious attempt to save all Jews regardless of religiosity or affiliation. These efforts led to the release of 1,210 Jews from Theresienstadt, the direct rescue to Switzerland of several hundred Slovak Jews, relief programs to several concentration camps, and negotiations with the Nazis which may have in some way favorably affected the fate of hundreds of thousands of concentration camp inmates.

To this fairly impressive list one must add the efforts to unite American Jewry in order to coordinate rescue activities, and the rabbis' march to Washington, which was the only public protest on behalf of European Jewry by Jewish leaders in the American capital during the Holocaust. The latter is especially noteworthy not only because it marked the rabbis' growing awareness of the need for general rather than particularistic rescue efforts, but because it symbolized more than anything else the effective manner in which the Orthodox rescue activists had learned to use the American political system. For an agency dominated by East European-born and -bred rabbis, most of them not fully fluent in English, this was no small achievement. In fact, it could be said that besides the practical successes in the rescue of Jews achieved by the *Vaad ha-Hatzala*, the organization was an effective tool for the Americanization of the local Orthodox leadership.

The *Vaad's* activities ultimately fostered two seemingly contradictory trends in American Orthodoxy. On the one hand, the European *roshei yeshiva* and rabbis who were brought to the United States encouraged an intensification of religious observance and Torah learning in the traditional East European tradition. Yet on the other hand, the *Vaad's* activities marked the partial "Americanization" of the European-born rabbis and the emergence of an activist laity born in the United States. Both these developments would serve the Orthodox community well in the future and would help strengthen its ranks.

These changes, however, in no way altered the basic Orthodox approach to Jewish life which spawned the *Vaad ha-Hatzala*. It was this ideology that justified the priority given to the rescue of rabbis and yeshiva students and that set the *Vaad* on its initially separatist path. At the same time, it was this way of thinking that motivated and inspired a deep dedication to rescue which ultimately produced significant results—the rescue of a rabbinic elite which succeeded in rebuilding the Torah world after the war, and the rescue of many other Jews as well. And it is this dedication to the saving of Jewish lives that is probably the *Vaad's* most lasting legacy to the Jewish people. Yet while we acknowledge its importance, we should never lose sight of its pitfalls and the heavy price paid by others for its success. It seems likely that as successful as it was in practical terms, had the *Vaad* joined forces with the Joint, the overall results would probably have been more beneficial to the Jewish people than those achieved individually by each organization. And that too is a lesson that should be learned from the history of the Holocaust.

Bibliography

Public Archives and Archival Collections

Agudat ha–Rabbanim (Union of Orthodox Rabbis of the United States and Canada), New York City

Agudat Yisrael be–Eretz Yisrael, Jerusalem

Agudath Israel (Agudat Yisrael) of America, New York City

American Jewish Committee, YIVO Institute, New York City

American Jewish Joint Distribution Committee, New York City

American Zionist Movement, Jewish Agency, New York City

Beit Lochamei ha–Gettaot, Kibbutz Lochamai ha–Gettaot

Canadian Jewish Congress, Montreal

Canadian National Archives, Ottawa

Central Relief Committee, Yeshiva University Archives, New York City

Central Zionist Archives, Jerusalem

Council of Jewish Federations and Welfare Funds, American Jewish Historical Society, Waltham, MA

Emergency Committee to Save the Jewish People of Europe, Yale University Library, New Haven, CT

Franklin D. Roosevelt Library, Hyde Park, NY

Rabbi Yitzhak Halevi Herzog, Heichal Shlomo, Jerusalem

Institute for Holocaust Research, Bar–Ilan University, Ramat–Gan

National Archives of the United States, Washington, DC

Oral History Division, Institute of Contemporary Jewry, Hebrew University of Jerusalem

Public Record Office, London, Great Britain

Rabbinical Council of America, New York City

Rabbi Yisrael Halevi Rosenberg, Jewish Theological Seminary, New York City

Dr. Samuel M. Schmidt, American Jewish Archives, Hebrew Union College, Cincinnati, Ohio

Shanghai office of HICEM, JDC Archives, Jerusalem
Rabbi Eliezer Silver, American University, Washington, DC
Vaad ha–Hatzala (Emergency Committee for War–Torn Yeshivoth),
   Yeshiva University Archives, New York City
Wiener Library, Tel Aviv University
World Agudat Yisrael, Jerusalem
World Jewish Congress, American Jewish Archives, Cincinnati
Yad Vashem, Jerusalem
YIVO (Yiddish Scientific Institute), New York City

Private Papers
Rabbi Meir Ashkenazi, New York City
Rabbi Asher Czeczyk, New York City
Rabbi Yoseph D. Epstein, New York City
Jacob Hellerstein, Jerusalem
Rabbi Aaron Milewsky, Jerusalem
Frank Newman, New York City
Rabbi Eliezer Silver, Harrisburg, PA
Isaac and Recha Sternbuch (HIJEFS), London and Zurich

Manuscripts, Reports, and Dissertations
Bernstein, Herman. "The History of American Jewish Relief." JDC
   library, New York City.
Kubovy, Myriam. "Ultimate Rescue Attempts; Collection of
   Documents From the World Jewish Congress Archives in New
   York." Yad Vashem Library, Jerusalem.
Matzozky, Eliyho. "The Response Of American Jewry And Its
   Representative Organizations Between November 24, 1942 And
   April 19, 1943 To Mass Killings of Jews In Europe." Masters the-
   sis submitted to Yeshiva University, 1979.
Neustadt–Noy, Issac. "The Unending Task; Efforts to Unite
   American Jewry From The American Jewish Congress To The
   American Jewish Conference." Doctoral dissertation submitted to
   Brandeis University, 1976.
Pinsky, Edward David. "Cooperation Among American Jewish
   Organizations and Their Efforts To Rescue European Jewry
   During The Holocaust 1939–1945." Doctoral dissertation submit-
   ted to New York University, 1980.
Porat, Dina. "Rikuz ha–Plitim ha–Yehudim bi–Vilna ba–Shanim
   1939–1941 Ma'matzei ha–Yetzeiya." Master's thesis submitted to
   Tel Aviv University, 1973.

Redlich, Shimon. "The Jews Under Soviet Rule During World War II." Doctoral dissertation submitted to New York University, 1968.

"Report and Financial Statement Agudas Jisroel Immigration Department, May 15 – November 30, 1938."

"Report Of The Activity Of the Committee For Assistance To Refugees. The Jewish Community of Kobe (Ashkenazim) July 1940 – November 1941," Kobe, 1942.

Books

Abella, Irving, and Harold Troper, *None Is Too Many; Canada and the Jews of Europe 1933–1948*. Toronto: Lester and Orpen Dennys, 1982.

Adler, Cyrus, and Aaron M. Margalith, *With Firmness in the Right. American Diplomatic Action Affecting Jews 1840–1945*. New York: The American Jewish Committee, 1946.

Arad, Yitzhak. *Vilna ha–Yehudit be–Ma'avak ve–Kilayon*. Jerusalem and Tel Aviv: Yad Vashem, Universitah Tel–Aviv, Sifriat Poalim, 1976.

Bauer, Yehuda. *American Jewry and the Holocaust; The American Jewish Joint Distribution Committee 1939–1945*. Jerusalem and Detroit: The Institute of Contemporary Jewry, Hebrew University and Wayne State University Press, 1981.

———. *Jews for Sale?; Nazi–Jewish Negotiations 1933–1945*. New Haven and London: Yale University Press, 1994.

———. *My Brother's Keeper; A History of the American Jewish Joint Distribution Committee 1929–1939*. Philadelphia: Jewish Publication Society, 1974.

Benshalom, Benzion. *Bi–Sa'ar be–Yom Sufa*. Tel Aviv: Massada, 1944.

Blet, Pierre, ed. *Le Saint Siege et les Victims de la Guerre*, IX (1–12/1943). Citta del Vaticano: Libreria Editrice Vaticano, 1975.

Bunim, Amos. *A Fire In His Soul; Irving M. Bunim 1901–1980; The Man and His Impact on American Orthodox Jewry*. Jerusalem and New York: Feldheim, 1989.

Churbn un Rettung (Disaster and Salvation, the History of Vaad Hatzala in America). New York: "Vaad Hatzala" Book Committee, 5717/1957.

Dicker, Herman. *Wanderers and Settlers in the Far East*. New York: Twayne Publishers, 1962.

Dobkin, Eliahu. *Ha–Aliya ve–ha–Hatzala be–Shnot ha–Shoa*, Jerusalem: Reuben Mass, 5706/1946.

Edelstein, Yitzhak. *Rabbi Baruch Dov Leibowitz, Chayav u–Peulotav*. Tel Aviv: Netzach, 1957.

Eliav, Mordechai, ed. *Ani Ma'amin*. Jerusalem: Mossad Harav Kook, 5729/1969.

Even–Chen, Yaakov. *Tenua be–Sa'arat Milchama (Derech Vilna le–Yisrael)*. Tel Aviv: Moreshet, 1984.

Feingold, Henry L. *Politics of Rescue; The Roosevelt Administration and the Holocaust 1938–1945*. New Brunswick, NJ: Rutgers University Press, 1970.

Feuchtwanger, O. *Righteous Lives*. London: Lehmann, 1965.

Finger, Seymour Maxwell, ed. *American Jewry During the Holocaust*. n.p., 1984.

Foreign Relations of the United States, 1940, Vol. II, Washington, DC: U.S. Government Printing Office, 1957.

Friedenson, Joseph. *Dateline: Istanbul; Dr. Jacob Griffel's Lone Odyssey Through a Sea of Indifference*. Brooklyn: Mesorah, 1993.

Friedenson, Joseph, and David Kranzler, *Heroine of Rescue; The incredible story of Recha Sternbuch who saved Thousands from the Holocaust*. Brooklyn, NY: Mesorah, 1984.

Friedman, Saul S. *No Haven for the Oppressed; United States Policy Towards Jewish Refugees 1938–1945*. Detroit: Wayne State University Press, 1973.

Garfunkel, Leib. *Kovno ha–Yehudit be–Churbana*. Jerusalem: Yad Vashem, 1959.

Gastwirt, Harold. *Fraud, Corruption and Holiness; The Controversy Over the Supervision of Jewish Dietary Practice in New York City 1881–1940*. Port Washington, NY, and London: Kennikat Press, 1974.

Gilboa, Yehoshua. *Lishmor Lanetzach*. Tel Aviv: Massada, n.d.

Glickman–Porush, Menachem. *Ish ha–Halacha ve–ha–Ma'ase*. Jerusalem: n.p., n.d.

Goldwasser, Kalman. *Phun Der Veisl Bizen Teich Kizel–Su*. Paris: n.p., 1972.

Handlin, Oscar. *A Continuing Task; The American Jewish Joint Distribution Committee 1914–1964*. New York: Random House, 1964.

Hassett, William D. *Off the Record with FDR 1942–1945*. New Brunswick, NJ: Rutgers University Press, 1958.

Helmreich, William. *The World of The Yeshiva; An Intimate Portrait of Orthodox Jewry*. New York and London: The Free Press, 1982.

Herzman, Elchanan. *Mofait ha–Dor; Sefer Ness ha–Hatzala Shel Yeshivat Mir*. Jerusalem: n.p., n.d.

Hollander, Herman. *My Life and What I Did with It*. Jerusalem: Koren, 1979.

Israel, Fred. ed. *The War Diary of Breckinridge Long; Selections from the Years 1939–1944*. Lincoln: University of Nebraska Press, 1966.

Jubilee Book of Esras Torah (1915–1935). New York: Moinester Publishing Co., n.d.

Jung, Leo, ed. *Guardians of Our Heritage*. New York: Bloch, 1958.

———, ed. *Jewish Leaders 1750–1940*. Jerusalem: Boys Town Publishers, 1964.

———, ed. *Men of the Spirit*. New York: Kymson, 1964.

———, ed. *The Path of a Pioneer: The Autobiography of Leo Jung*. London and New York: The Soncino Press, 1980.

Katzburg, Netanel, ed. *Pedut: Hatzala be–Yemei ha–Shoa: Mekorot u–Mechkarim*. Ramat–Gan: Bar–Ilan University Press, 1984.

Klaperman, Gilbert. *The Story of Yeshiva University*. New York and London: Macmillan, 1969.

Kluger–Aliav, Ruth. *The Last Escape*. New York: Doubleday, 1973.

Kohanski, Alexander, ed. *The American Jewish Conference; Its Organization and Proceedings of the First Session August 29 to September 2, 1943. New York, N.Y.* New York: American Jewish Conference, 1944.

Kot, Stanislaw. *Conversations with the Kremlin and Dispatches from Russia*. London: Oxford University Press, 1963.

Kotsuji, Abraham. *From Tokyo to Jerusalem*. New York: Bernard Geis, 1964.

Kranzler, David. *The Japanese, Nazis and Jews; The Jewish Refugee Community of Shanghai*. New York: Ktav, 1975.

———. *Thy Brother's Blood; The Orthodox Jewish Response During the Holocaust*. Brooklyn, NY: Mesorah, 1987.

Kranzler, George. *Williamsburg. A Jewish Community in Transition*. New York: Feldheim, 1961.

Letters and Documents from the Greatest Men of Our Generation to One of the Greatest Rabbis of Our Generation. New York: n.p., n.d.

Levine, Hillel. *In Search of Sugihara: The Elusive Japanese Diplomat Who Risked His Life to Rescue 10,000 Jews from the Holocaust*. New York et al: Free Press, 1996.

Lewin, Yitzchak. *Churbn Airopa*. New York: Research Institute for Post–War Problems of Religious Jewry, 5708/1948.

Lichtiger, Joshua. *The Odyssey of a Jew*. New York: Vantage Press, 1979.

Lipstadt, Deborah H. *Beyond Belief; The American Press and the Coming of the Holocaust 1933–1945*. New York: The Free Press, 1986.

Litvak, Yoseph. *Plitim Yehudim mei–Polin be–Brit ha–Moetzot 1939–1946*. Jerusalem: Ha–Universita ha–Ivrit, Ha–Machon le–Yahadut Zemaneinu, Beit Lochamei ha–Gettaot, Hotza'at ha–Kibbutz ha–Meuchad, 1988.

Lookstein, Haskel. *Were We Our Brothers' Keepers?; The Public Response of American Jews to the Holocaust 1938–1944*. New York and Bridgeport: Hartmore House, 1985.

Medoff, Rafael. *The Deafening Silence; American Jewish Leaders and the Holocaust*. New York: Shapolsky, 1987.

Morrison, David. *Heroes Antiheroes and the Holocaust; American Jewry and Historical Choice*. Jerusalem and New London: Milah Press, 1995.

Morse, Arthur. *While Six Million Died*. New York: Random House, 1968.

Norem, Owen J. C. *Timeless Lithuania*. Chicago: Amerlith Press, 1943.

Nurenberger, M. J. *The Sacred and the Doomed; The Jewish Establishment vs. the Six Million*. Oakville, NY, and London: Mosaic Press, 1985.

Ofer, Dalia. *Derech ba–Yam; Aliya Bet be–Tekufat ha–Shoa*. Jerusalem: Yad Ben–Tzvi, 1988.

Pekier, Alter. *From Kletzk to Siberia; A yeshiva bachur's wandering during the Holocaust*. New York: Mesorah, 1985.

Penkower, Monty Noam. *The Jews Were Expendable; Free World Diplomacy and the Holocaust*. Urbana and Chicago: University of Illinois Press, 1983.

Rakeffet–Rothkoff, Aaron. *The Silver Era in American Jewish Orthodoxy: Eliezer Silver and His Generation*. Jerusalem and New York: Yeshiva University Press and Feldheim, 1981.

Rand, Asher, ed. *Eidut L'Yisrael*. New York: Esras Torah of the Agudas Harabanim, n.d.

———. *Toldot Anshei Shem*. New York: Anshei Committee, 5710/1950.

Raphael, Marc Lee. *A History of The United Jewish Appeal*. Providence: Brown University Studies, Scholars Press, 1982

Rosenblum, Yonasan. *They Called Him Mike: Reb Elimelech Tress–His Era, Hatzala, and the Building of an American Orthodoxy*. Brooklyn: Mesorah Publications, 1995.

Rothenberg, Moshe. *Bikurei Aviv*. St. Louis: n.p., 5702/1942.

Rothkoff, Aaron. *Bernard Revel; Builder of American Jewish Orthodoxy*. Philadelphia: Jewish Publication Society, 1972.

Rozek, Edward J. *Allied Wartime Diplomacy; A Pattern in Poland*. New York: John Wiley, 1958.

Rozen, Leon S. *Cry In The Wilderness; A Short History of a Chaplain. Activities and Struggles in Soviet Russia During World War II*. New York and Tel Aviv: Om Publishing, 1966.

Sabaliunas, Leonas. *Lithuania in Crisis; Nationalism to Communism 1939–1940*. Bloomington and London: Indiana University Press, 1972.

Schachter, Jacob, ed. *Reverence, Righteousness and Rachmanut*. Northvale, NJ, and London: Jason Aronson, 1992.

Sefer ha–yovel Shel Agudas ha–Rabanim ha–Ortodocsim d'Artzot ha–Brit ve– Canada (5662–5687). New York: Arias Press, 5688/1928.

Shalit, Moshe, ed. *Yekapa oyf di Churvos phun Milchomos un Mehumes Pinkas phun Gegent komitet Yekapa in Vilna 1919–1930*. Vilna: Yekapa, 1931.

Shurin, Aaron. *Keshet Giborim*. Jerusalem: Mossad Harav Kook, 1964.

Soltz, Shmuel. *850 Yom Bein Aratzot u–Gevulot*. Givatayim: n.p., 1987.

Stember, Charles Herbert, et al. *Jews in the Mind of America*. New York: Basic Books, 1966.

Sursky, Aaron, ed. *Achiezer: Kovetz Igrot, Pirkei Chayim* B'nei Brak: Netzach Publishers, 5730/1970.

Trunk, Isaiah. *Judenrat; The Jewish Councils in Eastern Europe Under Nazi Occupation*. New York: Macmillan, 1974.

Tushnet, Leonard. *The Pavement of Hell*. New York: St. Martin's Press, 1974.

Urofsky, Melvin I. *A Voice that Spoke for Justice; The Life and Times of Stephen S. Wise*. Albany: State University of New York Press, 1982.

Warhaftig, Zerach. *Palit ve–Sarid be–Yemei ha–Shoa*. Jerusalem: Yad Vashem and Ot ve–Eid, 1984.

Wishnitzer, Mark. *To Dwell in Safety*. Philadelphia: Jewish Publication Society, 1948.

————. *Visas to Freedom; The History of HIAS*. Cleveland and New York: World Publishing Company, 1956.

Wyman, David S. *The Abandonment of the Jews; America and the Holocaust*. New York: Pantheon, 1984.

———. *Paper Walls; America and the Refugee Crisis 1938–1941.* Amherst: University of Massachusetts Press, 1968.

Yishai, Moshe. *Tzir be–Lo To'ar.* Tel Aviv: N. Tversky, 1950.

Zeidl, Hillel. *Adam be–Mivchan.* Tel Aviv: n.p., 1971.

Zeidman, Hillel. *Ishim she–Hikarty.* Jerusalem: Mossad Harav Kook, 1970.

Articles

Adler, Selig. "The United States and the Holocaust," *American Jewish Historical Quarterly,* LXIV (September, 1974), 14–23.

Arad, Yitzhak. "Concentration of Refugees in Vilna on the Eve of the Holocaust," *Yad Vashem Studies,* IX (1973), 201–214.

Barak, Zvi. "Pleetei Polin be–Lita ba–Shanim 1939–1941," *Yahadut Lita.* Tel Aviv: Igud Yotzai Lita be–Yisrael, 5732 (1972), 353–370.

Bauer, Yehuda. "Rescue Operations Through Vilna," *Yad Vashem Studies,* IX (1973), 215–223.

———. "When Did They Know?" *Midstream,* XIV (April 1968), 51–57.

Baumol, Judith Tydor, and Jacob Schachter. "The Ninety–Three Bais Yaakov Girls of Cracow: History or Typology," in Jacob Schacter, ed., *Reverence, Righteousness and Rachmanut.* Northvale: Jason Aronson, 1992, pp. 93–130.

Ben–Mordechai, A. "Metivta Rabata Ohel Torah Shel Baranowitz," in Samuel K. Mirsky, ed., *Mosdot ha–Torah be–Airopa be–Binyanam u–be–Churbanam.* New York: Ogen Publishing, 1956, pp. 329–335.

Bram, Yehoshua. "Misaveev la–Olam le–Eretz Nichsefet," in *Sefer Kehillat Konin.* Tel Aviv: 5728/1968, pp. 725–738.

Davis, Moshe. "Jewish Religious Life and Institutions in America," in Louis Finkelstein, ed., *The Jews, Their History, Culture and Religion.* New York: Harper and Bros., 1949, pp. 354–453.

Edelstein, Yaakov. "Ha–massa u–Matan ha–Rishon Im Shiltonot Brit ha–Moetzot Al Yitzeat Yehudim mei–Russia be–Tkufat ha–Milchama," *Gesher,* 42 (March 1965), 78–82.

Edelstein, Yitzhak. "Be–Yemei Sufa (Yomano shel ha–Rav Yitzhak Edelstein)," *Gal–ed,* 3 (1976), pp. 325–359.

Eliash, Shulamit. "Hatzalat Yeshivot Polin she–Nimletu le–Lita be–Reishit ha–Milchama," *Yalkut Moreshet,* 32 (December, 1981), 127–168.

Epstein, Yoseph D. "Yeshivat Mir," in Samuel K. Mirsky, ed., *Mosdot ha–Torah be–Airopa be–Binyanam u–be–Churbanam.* New York: Ogen Publishing, 1956, pp. 87–132.

Epstein, Zelig. "Yeshivat 'Sha'ar ha–Torah' be–Grodno," in Samuel K. Mirsky, ed., *Mosdot ha–Torah be–Airopa be–Binyanam u–be–Churbanam*. New York: Ogen Publishing, 1956, pp. 291–305.

Gifter, Mordechai. "Yeshiva Telz," in Samuel K. Mirsky, ed., *Mosdot ha–Torah be–Airopa be–Binyanam u–be–Churbanam*. New York: Ogen Publishing, 1956, pp. 169–188.

Goldman, Jacob. "Rabbi Herzog's First Rescue Journey," *Niv Hamidrashia* (Winter 1964), 5–11.

Gottlieb, Moshe. "The Anti–Nazi Movement in the United States: An Ideological and Sociological Appreciation," *Jewish Social Studies*, XXXV (July–October, 1973), 198–227.

————. "The Berlin Riots of 1935 and Their Repercussions in America," *American Jewish Historical Quarterly*, LIX (March 1970), 302–328.

————. "Boycott, Rescue and Ransom: The Threefold Dilemma of American Jewry 1938–1939," *YIVO Annual of Jewish Social Science*, XV (1974), 235–279.

————. "The First of April Boycott and the Reaction of the American Jewish Community," *American Jewish Historical Quarterly*, LVII (June 1968), 329–348.

————. "In the Shadow of War: The American Anti–Nazi Boycott Movement 1939–1941," *American Jewish Historical Quarterly*, LXII (December 1972), 146–161.

Gruenberger, Felix. "The Jewish Refugees in Shanghai," *Jewish Social Studies*, XII (October 1950), 329–348.

Gurock, Jeffrey. "Resisters and Accommodators: Varieties of Orthodox Rabbis in America," *American Jewish Archives*, XXXV (November 1983), 100–187.

Herzman, Chuna. "From Mir to Shanghai," *Jewish Observer*, IX (May 1973), 10–13.

Kagan, Shaul. "Reb Aharon Kotler," *Jewish Observer*, IX (May 1973), 3–13.

Karlinsky, Chaim. "Ha–Gaon Rabbi Eliezer Silver z"l," *Shana Bishana*. Jerusalem: Heichal Shlomo, 5729/1969, pp. 366–371.

Katzburg, Nathaniel. "British Policy on Immigration to Palestine During World War II," in Yisrael Gutman and Efraim Zuroff, eds., *Rescue Attempts During the Holocaust*. Jerusalem:Yad Vashem, 1977, pp. 183–203.

Korzen, Meir. "Problems Arising Out of Research into the History of Jewish Refugees in the USSR during the Second World War," *Yad Vashem Studies*, III (1959), 119–140.

Kranzler, David. "The Japanese Ideology of anti–Semitism and the Holocaust," in Randolph Braham, ed., *Contemporary Views on the Holocaust*. Boston The Hague, Dordrecht, and Lancaster: Kluwer Nijhoff Publishing, 1983, pp. 79–107.

————. "The Jewish Refugee Community of Shanghai 1938–1945," *Wiener Library Bulletin*, XXVI (1972–1973), 28–37.

————. "Orthodox Ends, Unorthodox Means; The Role of the Vaad Hatzalah and Agudath Israel During the Holocaust," *American Jewry During the Holocaust*, 1984, Appendix 4–3, 1–49.

————. "Restrictions Against German–Jewish Refugee Immigration to Shanghai in 1939," *Jewish Social Studies*, XXXVI (January 1974), 40–60.

Kranzler, Gershon. "Setting the Record Straight," *Jewish Observer*, VII (November 1971), 9–14.

Kubovy, Aryeh Leon. "Criminal State vs. Moral Society," *Yad Vashem Bulletin*, 13 (October 1963), 3–11.

Levin, Dov. "Arrests and Deportations of Lithuanian Jews to Remote Areas of the Soviet Union, 1940–1941," *Crossroads*, 11 (1984), 67–107.

————. "Chofesh Dati, Mugbal ve–Al Tnai," *Sinai*, 79 (June–July 1976),164–180.

Lewin, Isaac. "Attempts at Rescuing European Jews with the Help of Polish Diplomatic Missions During World War II," *The Polish Review*, Part I, XXXII, no. 4 (1977), 3–23.

————. "Attempts at Rescuing European Jews with the Help of Polish Diplomatic Missions During World War II," *The Polish Review*, Part II, XXXIV, no.1 (1979), 46–61.

Liebman, Charles S. "Orthodoxy in American Jewish Life," *American Jewish Yearbook*, 66 (1965), 21–97.

Margolis, Laura. "Race Against Time in Shanghai," *Jewish Spectator*, IX (May 1944), 25–29.

Mars, Alvin. "A Note on the Jewish Refugees in Shanghai," *Jewish Social Studies*, XXXI (October 1969), 34–54.

Nekritch, Y. L. "Yeshivot Navaraduk," in Samuel K. Mirsky, ed., *Mosdot ha–Torah be–Airopa be–Binyanam u–be–Churbanam*. New York: Ogen Publishing, 1956, pp. 247–290.

Ophir, Efraim. "Ha–Im Nitan Haya le–Hatzil 70,000 Yehudim mi–Transnistriya?" *Yalkut Moreshet*, no. 33 (June 1982), pp. 103–128.

Oren, Baruch. "Mei–Vilna Derech Yapan El ha–Olam ha–Chofshi," *Moreshet*, II (November 1969), 34–54.

Oshry, Ephraim. "Yeshivat 'Knesset Yisrael' be–Slobodka," in Samuel K. Mirsky, ed., *Mosdot ha–Torah be–Airopa be–Binyanam u–be–Churbanam*. New York: Ogen Publishing, 1956, 133–168.

Paldiel, Mordechai. "Hatzalat Alfei Plitim al–Yedei Me'atim Bodidim," *Yalkut Moreshet*, 40 (December, 1985), 145–160.

Pechenik, Aaron. "Ha–Tenua Bein Shtei Milchamot," in *Chazon Torah ve–Tzion*. Jerusalem: n.p., 5720/1960, pp. 243–245.

Penkower, Monty Noam. "In Dramatic Dissent: The Bergson Boys," *American Jewish History*, LXX. no. 3 (March, 1981), 281–309.

Pinsky, Edward. "American Jewish Unity—The Joint Emergency Committee," *American Jewish History*, LXXII, no. 4 (June 1983), 477–494.

Prager, Moshe. "Plitat Gedolei ha–Torah mi–Toch Lehavot ha–Shoa: Massa ha–Kibushim Shel Nigun ha–Gemara Al Penai Teivel," *Beit Yaakov*, XII, 6–13, 26–31.

———. "Roshei ha–yeshivot she–Nimletu mei–Gai ha–Avadon ve–Lapid ha–Torah be–Yedeihem," *Beit Ya'akov*, XII, 6–11, 22–24.

Rabinowitz, Yisrael. "Yeshivat Lomze," in Samuel K. Mirsky, ed., *Mosdot ha–Torah be–Airopa be–Binyanam u–be–Churbanam*. New York: Ogen Publishing, 1956, pp. 217–227.

Rakeffet–Rothkoff, Aaron. "The East European Immigrant Rabbinate During Its Formative Years," *Gesher*, V (1976), 133–156.

Raphael, Marc Lee. "From Separation to Community: The Origins of the United Jewish Appeal," *Forum*, 37 (Spring 1980), 61–70.

Roseman, Kenneth D. "American Jewish Community Institutions in Their Historical Context," *Jewish Journal of Sociology*, XVI (June 1974), 25–38.

Rothkoff, Aaron. "The 1924 Visit of the Rabbinical Delegation to the United States of America," *Masmid*, 1959, pp. 121–125.

Shapiro, Chaim. "Escape from Europe—A Chronicle of Miracles," *Jewish Observer*, IX (May 1973), 20–24.

———. "Last of a Species," *Jewish Observer*, VIII (March 1972), 13–16.

Szajkowski Zosa. "The Attitude of American Jews to Refugees from Germany in the 1930's," *American Jewish Historical Quarterly*, LXI (December 1971), 101–143.

———. "Budgeting American Overseas Relief (1919–1939)," *American Jewish Historical Quarterly*, LIX (September, 1969), 83–113.

————. "Concord and Discord in American Jewish Overseas Relief 1914–1924," *YIVO Annual of Jewish Social Science*, XIV (1969), 99–158.

————. "Disunity in the Distribution of American Jewish Overseas Relief (1919–1939)," *American Jewish Historical Quarterly*, LVIII (March 1969), 484–503.

————. "Jewish Relief in Eastern Europe 1914–1917," *Leo Baeck Institute Yearbook*, X (1965), 24–56.

————. "A Note on the American–Jewish Struggle Against Nazism and Communism in the 1930's," *American Jewish Historical Quarterly*, LIX (March 1970), 272–289.

————. "Private American Jewish Overseas Relief (1919–1938): Problems and Attempted Solutions," *American Jewish Historical Quarterly*, LVIII (March 1968), 285–350.

————. "Private and Organized American Jewish Overseas Relief (1914–1938)," *American Jewish Historical Quarterly*, LVIII (September 1967), 52–106.

————. "Relief for German Jewry: Problems of American Involvement," *American Jewish Historical Quarterly*, LXII (December 1972), 111–145.

Weisbrod, M. "Bein ha–Meitzarim," in Yom Tov Levinsky, ed., *Sefer Zikaron Lekehillat Lomze*. Tel Aviv: 1952, pp. 83–84.

Wishnitzer, Mark. "Chomer le–Toldot ha–Yeshivot be–Airopa ha–Mizrachit," *Talpiot*, V (Tevet 5712/1952), pp. 603–617.

————. "Die Banayung phun Yeshivas in Mizroch Airopa noch der Ershter Velt Milchome," *YIVO Bleter*, XXXI–XXXII (1948), 9–36.

Zariz, David. "Yeshivat Radin," in Samuel K. Mirsky, ed., *Mosdot ha–Torah be–Airopa be–Binyanam u–be–Churbanam*. New York: Ogen Publishing, (1956), pp. 189–216.

Zeidman, Hillel. "Yeshivat Chachmei Lublin," in Samuel K. Mirsky, ed., *Mosdot ha–Torah be–Airopa be–Binyanam u–be–Chubanam*. New York: Ogen Publishing, (1956), pp. 229–242.

————. "Yeshivat Knesset Beit Yitzhak de–Kammenetz," in Samuel K. Mirsky, ed., *Mosdot ha–Torah be–Airopa be–Binyanam u–be–Churbanam*. New York: Ogen Publishing, 1956, pp. 307–324.

Zuroff, Efraim. "Attempts to Obtain Shanghai Permits in 1941; A Case of Rescue Priority During the Holocaust," *Yad Vashem Studies*, XIII (1979), 321–351.

―――. "Rabbis Relief and Rescue: A Case Study of the Activities of the *Vaad ha–Hatzala* (Rescue Committee) of the American Orthodox Rabbis, 1942–1943," *Simon Wiesenthal Center*, III (1986), 121–138.

―――. "Rescue Priorities and Fundraising as Issues during the Holocaust: A Case Study of the Relations between the Vaad ha–Hatzala and the Joint 1939–1941," *American Jewish Historical Quarterly*, LXVIII (March, 1979), 305–326.

―――. "Rescue Via The Far East: The Attempt To Save Polish Rabbis And Yeshiva Students," *Simon Wiesenthal Center Annual*, I (1984), 153–183.

Interviews and Correspondence

Interview with Rabbi Moshe Cohen, October 10, 1974
Interview with Rabbi Asher Czeczyk, July 5, 1977
Letter of Rabbi Yoseph David Epstein to the author, April 20, 1974
Interview with Rabbi Yoseph David Epstein, November 26, 1984
Interview with Rabbi Zelig Epstein, July 7, 1977
Intervew with Rabbi Zev Gotthold, November 21, 1973
Interview with Rabbi Yizhak Grozalsky, November 14, 1973
Interview with Jacob Hellerstein, November 29, 1973
Interview with Herman Hollander, December 18, 1973
Interview with Dr. Gershon Kranzler, April 29, 1974
Letter of Hermann Landau to the author, December 25, 1973
Interview with Shmaryahu Margalit, October 22, 1973
Interview with Rabbi Aaron Milewsky, September 1, 1975
Interview with Rabbi Yaakov Nayman, July 26, 1977
Letter of Frank Newman to the author, February 5, 1975
Letter of Mayer Pantel, Zvi Milner, and Asher Czeczyk to the author, May 25, 1977
Interview with Rabbi Shimon Romm, July 27, 1977
Letter of Pinchas Schoen to the author, October 1, 1973
Interview with Elijah Stein, April 16, 1974
Interview with Rabbi Meyer Strassfeld, July 1973
Interview with Rabbi Zalman Ury, November 27, 1978
Interview with Rabbi Simcha Wasserman, July 20, 1979
Interview with Rabbi Alex Weisfogel, July 22, 1973
Interview with Tova Wiernik, December 14, 1977

Abbreviations

AAH - Archives of *Agudat ha–Rabbanim*
AAJCom - Archives of the American Jewish Committee
AAM - Archives of Rabbi Aaron Milewsky
AAYA - Archives of Agudath Israel of America
AAYEY - Archives of Merkaz Agudat Yisrael be–Eretz Yisrael
ABLG - Archives of Beit Lohamei ha–Gettaot
ACJC - Archives of the Canadian Jewish Congress
ACJFWF - Archives of the Council of Jewish Federations and Welfare Funds
ACRC - Archives of the Central Relief Committee
AECJPoE - Archives of The Emergency Committee to Save the Jewish People of Europe
AJA - American Jewish Archives
AJDC - Archives of the American Jewish Joint Distribution Committee
AMA - Archives of Rabbi Meir Ashkenazi
ARCA - Archives of Rabbinical Council of America
AVH - Archives of the *Vaad*, Yeshiva University
AWJC - Archives of teh World Jewish Congress
AWL - Archives of the Wiener Library
AYHH - Archives of Rabbi Yitzhak Halevi Herzog
BIA - Archives of the Institute for Holocaust Research, Bar–Ilan University
HICEM - Combined HIAS (Hebrew Sheltering and Immigrant Aid Society), ICA (Jewish Colonization Association), and Emigdirect
CNA - Canadian National Archives
NA - National Archives of the United States of America
SMS–AJA - Papers of Dr. Samuel A. Schmidt, American Jewish Archives
UJRWRA - United Jewish Refugee and War Relief Agency
WAYA - Archives of World Agudat Yisrael
YHRA - Archives of Rabbi Yisrael Halevi Rosenberg
YIVO - YIVO Archives
YVA - Yad Vashem Archives

Indices

Index of Persons

Index of Places

Index of Organizations

Index of Titles

Appeal by the *Agudat ha-Rabbanim* to President Roosevelt to help obtain permission for 500 rabbis and yeshiva students to leave the Soviet Union for Mexico, May 11, 1943 (*Vaad ha-Hatzala* Archives, Yeshiva University)

Cable of *Vaad ha-Hatzala* to Rabbi Yitzchak Levi in Teheran with list of 200 refugee Torah scholars to whom parcels should be sent, June 20, 1943 (*Vaad ha-Hatzala* Archives, Yeshiva University)

Council of Jewish Federations and Welfare Funds report on the *Vaad ha-Hatzala*, August 24, 1943 (*Vaad ha-Hatzala* Archives, Yeshiva University)

Letter of Rabbis Rosenberg and Silver to Joseph Hyman of the JDC, June 9, 1942. Note Henrietta Buchman's comments in the margin. (JDC Archives, New York)

Shanghai Permit obtained for Hirsz Levinsohn, May 13, 1941 (Courtesy of Rabbi Asher Czeczyk)

List of yeshiva *leit* who left Shanghai on September 29, 1941 aboard President Pierce bound for Canada (Archives of HICEM, JDC Archives, Israel)

Letter of Rabbi Aron Kotler to Rabbi Ashkenazi regarding the distribution of the Shanghai permits, March 25, 1941 (Papers of Rabbi Yoseph David Epstein)

Cable of Rabbi Kotler then in Kobe, Japan to Rabbi Ashkenazi and Frank Newman in Shanghai regarding the Shanghai permits, March 12, 1941 (YIVO Archives)

Letter of Rabbi Chaim Ozer Grodzinski to Dr. Cyrus Adler of the JDC appealing for aid for the refugee Torah scholars in Vilna, December 31, 1939 (JDC Archives, New York)

Letter of Rabbi Eliezer Finkel, Mir rosh yeshiva to Moshe Shapiro of the Jewish Agency asking for aliyah certificates for his students, January 28, 1940 (Yad Vashem Archives)

Letter of Rabbi Aron Kotler, Kletzk rosh yeshiva to the leaders of the Jewish Agency asking for aliyah certificates for his students, March 11, 1940 (Yad Vashem Archives)

List of Kletzk yeshiva students for whom aliyah certificates were requested, March 11, 1940 (Yad Vashem Archives)

Invitation to Rabbi Eliezer Silver to attend a conference of American Jewish organizations convened to deal with the plight of the refugee yeshiva students in Lithuania, August 1, 1940 (Papers of Rabbi Eliezer Silver, American University)

Appeal by Rabbis Bloch (Telz) and Shulman (Slabodka) to Frank Newman and Zerach Warhaftig in Japan to save their students, January 28, 1941 (YIVO Archives)

Cable of *Vaad ha-Hatzala* to Frank Newman regarding the purchase of ship tickets from the NYK shipping company, February 1, 1941 (YIVO Archives)

Rabbi Avraham Kalmanowitz (Orthodox Jewish Archives, Agudath Israel of America)

Rabbi Aaron Kotler (Orthodox Jewish Archives, Agudath Israel of America)

Rabbi Eliezer Silver (Orthodox Jewish Archives, Agudath Israel of America)

Rabbi Chaim Ozer Grodzinski (Orthodox Jewish Archives, Agudath Israel of America)

Mike Tress (Orthodox Jewish Archives, Agudath Israel of America)

Vaad ha-Hatzala March in Washington, October 6, 1943 Front row from right: Rabbi Bernard Levnthal, Rabbi Yisrael Halevi Rosenberg, Rabbi Eliezer Silver (Orthodox Jewish Archives, Agudath Israel of America)

Zerach Warhaftig (Courtesy of Dr. Warhaftig, Jerusalem)

Dr. Samuel Schmidt (Courtesy of Blessing Schmidt Sivitz, Cincinnati)

Rabbi Aaron Milewsky (Courtesy of Aliza Milewsky Sofer, Jerusalem)

Frank Newman (second from right) meeting with Japanese Captain Koreshiga Inuzuka (first from left) (Courtesy of Florence Newman, New York)

Dutch honorary consul in Kaunas Jan Zwartendijk (Simon Wiesenthal Center Archives)

Japanese transit visa issued in Kaunas by Sempo Sugihara (Simon Wiesenthal Center Archives)

Japanese consul in Kaunas Sempo Sugihara (Simon Wiesenthal Center Archives)

Refugees on line to obtain transit visas at the Japanese consulate in Kaunas, Summer 1940 (Simon Wiesenthal Center Archives)

Henrietta Buchman of the JDC and Gerhardt Riegner of the WJC (American Jewish Joint Distribution Committee Archives, Jerusalem)

Laura Margolis, JDC emissary to Shanghai (American Jewish Joint Distribution Committee Archives, Jerusalem)

Moses Beckelman, JDC emissary to Vilna (American Jewish Joint Distribution Committee Archives, Jerusalem)

Saul Hayes, Director of the United Jewish Refugee and War Relief Agency, Canada (American Jewish Joint Distribution Committee Archives, Jerusalem)

Joseph Hyman, JDC, New York (American Jewish Joint Distribution Committee Archives, Jerusalem)

Moses Leavitt, JDC, New York (standing) (American Jewish Joint Distribution Committee Archives, Jerusalem)